AF606057

THE *DECAMERON* NINTH DAY IN PERSPECTIVE

The *Decameron* Ninth Day in Perspective

EDITED BY SUSANNA BARSELLA
AND SIMONE MARCHESI

UNIVERSITY OF TORONTO PRESS
Toronto Buffalo London

Toronto Buffalo London
utorontopress.com

ISBN 978-1-4875-4049-4 (cloth)
ISBN 978-1-4875-4051-7 (EPUB)
ISBN 978-1-4875-4050-0 (PDF)

Library and Archives Canada Cataloguing in Publication

Title: The Decameron ninth day in perspective / edited by Susanna Barsella and Simone Marchesi.
Names: Barsella, Susanna, editor. | Marchesi, Simone, editor.
Series: Toronto Italian studies.
Description: Series statement: Toronto Italian studies | Includes bibliographical references and index.
Identifiers: Canadiana (print) 2021036016X | Canadiana (ebook) 20210360186 | ISBN 9781487540494 (cloth) | ISBN 9781487540517 (EPUB) | ISBN 9781487540500 (PDF)
Subjects: LCSH: Boccaccio, Giovanni, 1313–1375. Decamerone.
Classification: LCC PQ4287 .D423 2022 | DDC 853/.1–dc23

We wish to acknowledge the land on which the University of Toronto Press operates. This land is the traditional territory of the Wendat, the Anishnaabeg, the Haudenosaunee, the Métis, and the Mississaugas of the Credit First Nation.

The publication of this volume was made possible by the generous support of the American Boccaccio Association, Fordham University, and the Alfred Foulet Fund at Princeton University.

University of Toronto Press acknowledges the financial support of the Government of Canada, the Canada Council for the Arts, and the Ontario Arts Council, an agency of the Government of Ontario, for its publishing activities.

Funded by the Government of Canada
Financé par le gouvernement du Canada

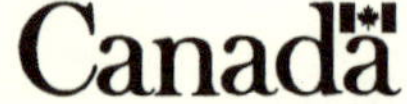

Contents

Introduction

The Ninth Day of the *Decameron* occupies a notable position in the textual organization of the work, and yet it continues to be understudied.[1] The situation is perhaps paradoxical: while several different proposals to partition the *Decameron* and thus conceptualize its structural machinery have assigned a significant role to the ninth slot in the work, the variety of themes treated in the stories and their diverse strands of narrative inspiration have undermined these attempts at categorization. The essays collected here represent an attempt to compensate for this adverse effect and produce a cohesive and complete account of the workings of the day, one that exploits both the strategic advantage connected to its position in the work, its *rendita di posizione*, and the relations that each story (or group of stories) establishes with other portions of the text. Through the internal dialogue they institute with one another, as well as their constant cross-referencing to other textual portions of the *Decameron*, these essays provide a reticular image of the day and illustrate its unique role within the complex organization of the book.

When compared to other books in the *Lectura Boccaccii* series, this volume includes a singularity; namely, an essay penned by the volume's editors that is designed to outline the special nature of Day Nine by focusing on the *cornice*. The working relationship established among the members of the *brigata* reaches a new stage at this juncture of the framing narrative, one worth exploring in detail. While this day has

1 See Surdich, "La 'varietà delle cose,'" a particularly relevant essay for the attention it devotes to structural interconnections between Days One and Nine (229–32) as well as to the preparatory role that Day Nine plays vis-à-vis the last day of the *Decameron* (259–64). To Surdich's useful review of preceding contributions should now be added Gittes, "'Dal giogo alleviati.'"

often been seen as apparently marking a simple return to the initial narrative freedom granted by Pampinea, its frame contains much more. Emilia's rule comes, in fact, to redefine the initial constitutive charter of the group's communal life, triggering a radical recodification of the *brigata*'s social setting. As it emerges from our review of the framing narrative, Emilia's exploration of the limits of the law triggers a shift in the dynamic interplay among the narrators. It does so perhaps in a less marked way than will be the case with the heated narrative contests of Day Ten, but just as essentially. What is more, and as will be the case in the following *giornata*, the change in interpersonal relations among narrators extends from the framing narrative, in which they intervene both personally and within their institutional roles, to the individual narrative acts for which they each take responsibility. The intranarrative ramification of Emilia's rule recommended that they be brought into focus, and our essay thus be of service to the following contributions that treat the individual *novelle*.

A further element that emerges from the interplay between the framing essay and the individual contributions characterizing this volume is the holistic approach to the day's work in relation to the various layers of interconnected narrative which organize the *Decameron*. Both our introduction and the *lectura* essays strive to capture the dynamic formation of new power relations in the interplay among the social subjects that act in the stories as well as among individual narrators. From our collective and multifocal reading, Day Nine emerges as interested in pursuing the definition of a new social equilibrium, not only for the *brigata* itself but also for the society outside the limits of the book that the narrators embody and model. This equilibrium takes the form of a new social contract, one in which all parties are represented in a balanced system. The new compact affects not only the institutions of marriage (and the day has significant examples of unbalanced marital relations) but also, more generally, the interaction between different social figures (artists and merchants as well as members of the urban elites and the servile class). What appears as a necessary reassessment of the social dynamics in extratextual reality is mirrored in the ambivalent persona of the day's queen, Emilia. While she is, in the field of gender relations, advocating for woman's subjection to man in marriage, one may argue that she is also, in her apparently contradictory role as female ruler of the day, extending to her subjects the restorative freedom from the yoke of narrative homogeneity.

Like the stories told in each day of the *Decameron*, the essays collected in this volume dialogue with one another on several levels. Taken together, they also approach the Ninth Day of storytelling in a holistic fashion. In practice, they explore three main areas of the text. First, all essays devote attention to the intratextual sequencing of the tales within Day Nine and to the connections they establish with stories told in other *giornate*. Secondly, taking various approaches and directions in their investigations, but with remarkable coherence, all essays highlight the intertextual connections existing between the tales and specific external sources and analogues. Finally, all also coherently explore the dialogue that the individual stories establish with wider discourses, both social and literary, dominating the culture in which and for which the *Decameron* has been written.

In general, the reflection on novel modes of expressing a new perception of reality is a central theme of the *Decameron* and one that seems particularly relevant to the sequence of stories in Day Nine. The topics chosen by the narrators of this day often recall those they had chosen as queens or kings during their own days of sovereignty. These thematic occurrences link the *novelle* of this "liminal" day in order to build a network of internal narrative echoes, reuniting the various threads Boccaccio disseminates in the previous seven days. Even from a different thematic perspective, these readings often discover important points of contact, such as in IX.1 (David Lummus), which notes the general feeling of weariness among the day's storytellers, and which connects queen Emilia to the first narrator. This observation leads us to consider the relation between *novelle* (IX.1 and IX.9), for example, as well as the link between Emilia's introduction to Day Nine and that of the frame.

Beyond a general consonance of themes and questions broached across different narratives, some interconnections between stories are signalled by the narrators themselves. One may point to the onomastic imbrication between IX.5 and IX.6, which is based on the recurrence of the name Niccolosa, or the sequencing of IX.3 and IX.5, with both stories celebrating Calandrino's exploits and treating the figure of the artist as an innovative interpreter of reality who questions its relationship with appearances, as both Anichini (IX.3) and Ciccuto (IX.5) show. Similarly, the trope of the impossible pregnancy, with metaphorical implications spanning the semantic field of production from the religious to the artistic to the economical, links *novelle* IX.3 and IX.10. As these contributions suggest, what makes this day notably "repetitive" is not at all a "crisis of creativity" but rather its internally dialogic dynamics, in which narrators respond to one another, as if in preparation for the game of one-upping which will mark the next and final segment of the narrative.

Also noted in the various essays are continuities not explicitly signalled in the frame or in the prologues to the individual stories, but nevertheless essential for the plot of the meta-*novella* and the dynamics of interpretation which it presents (and mimics for the readers). One may point to the triptych of IX.7–IX.9–IX.10, with the first two stories revolving around the violent retribution economies which the patriarchy establishes for women's agency and societal role (as explored by Grace Delmolino and Albert Russell Ascoli, respectively), and the latter two being devoted to a contrastive (and satirical) depiction of women as animals, in the language of both metaphor and magic (as both Ascoli and Max Matukhin point out).

Day Nine's tales present a very high degree of intratextuality with other days; for example, Lummus shows how the opening tale IX.1 has textual ties with I.1 and even II.4. A central theme of the *Decameron* – the metaliterary reflection on authorship – finds exceptional relevance in IX.4 (Patrizio Ceccagnoli), where Boccaccio stages a dialogue between two Ceccos, the author and his fictional double, by exploiting Boccaccio's recurrent rhetorical strategy of metaphoric literalization as in VI.1 or III.5. *Novella* IX.2, analysed by Maria Pia Ellero, provides a prime example: it is the literal realization *in factis* of a similar situation which Dioneo presented *in verbis* in I.4 and found as well in other *novelle* with parodic religious themes, such as VII.6 or III.1.[2]

The stories of Day Nine also align with their predecessors in the *Decameron* when they rely on the rich mental library of readers to produce meaning (to *make* sense in an active way). Essays in this volume which point to these connections range from Simona Lorenzini's attention to Chaucer's redeployment of the plot of IX.6 in his *Reeve's Tale* to Johnny L. Bertolio's evocation of a Dantean background for IX.8, an underlying allusion which is based on a set of characters (Ciacco and Filippo Argenti) who have been featured in the first circles of *Inferno*. Along the same lines, Lummus signals the relevant presence of Cavalcanti in the parody of the "mortal" effects of unrequited love in IX.1, and Ceccagnoli that of Cecco Angiolieri's lyrical corpus for IX.4. In the same vein, Lummus and Ellero indicate the importance of models taken from French and Occitan traditions such as the Oitanic *fabliaux* (*Dit de la Nonnete*, Jean de Condé) for IX.2 or the *fins* and *fols amor* for IX.1. One may view the constant attention which Matukhin pays to texts (specific *fabliaux*), models (Apuleius's *Golden Ass*), and wide cultural discourses (the treatment of sexuality within grammatical categories)

2 On this issue, the work of Pier Massimo Forni remains a crucial reference point for several essays. See his *Adventures in Speech*.

in his reading of IX.10 as a comic meditation on the natural-unnatural divide in matters of both sexuality and culture.

Finally, the tales of Day Nine are of the same cloth as their predecessors in the *Decameron*, in the ways in which they dialogue with wider cultural discourses and their historical and geographical contexts. Lummus stresses the importance of Pistoia not only as a place connected to the stilnovistic poetic tradition through Cino da Pistoia but also as the birthplace of political conflict between white and black Guelphs, which constitutes the backdrop of Florence's peak poetic season. The Tuscan landscape of Calandrino's *novelle* is another element leading these narratives out of the city of Florence and into the countryside, while the tale of the two Ceccos brings us to the tradition of comic poetry and indirectly to Dante's *tenzoni* with the Aretine author. Bertolio's inter-code reading of the pun at the centre of Ciacco's trick on Biondello brings into play the Bible as a macro-code that acts as decryptor for expressions of a baffling idiolect around which the tale actually revolves: the *arrubinare* of the wine resonates with the biblical *grapes of wrath*. Similarly, Ascoli's crucial reading of Emilia as a Queen Solomon (both in her role as a somewhat paradoxical ruler of the day and as the narrator of the specific and highly contested Solomonic ninth *novella*) is based on the intersection of a wide array of traditions that have at their centre the figure of the biblical king: from the treatment which the wise ruler receives in Dante to the way his figure is handled in the popular Solomon and Marcolf stories.

The essays of this volume do not just form a collection of readings retracing the allusions and evidencing the network of interrelations among individual *novelle*, days as well as the overarching structure and poetics of the *Decameron*. Each of them also presents original contributions to a new understanding of an all too often understudied day. The polyphonic and yet organized quality of the narrative interactions between the stories told in Day Nine, we hope, will transpire from the individual critical readings that make up the body of the volume. It is now time to turn to their individual contributions and critical interconnectedness.

In reading the opening story for the day, David Lummus starts by isolating Filomena's attention to the "physicality" of storytelling, a feature embedded in the metaphor of yoking she uses in her preamble. It is a choice of language that relocates the *brigata*'s narrative act from the field of pastimes into that of work. The incipitary move will have repercussions throughout the day, running as a *fil rouge* through several of the themes mobilized in the various stories. Lummus's reading then proceeds to explore two interconnected themes in Filomena's tale, in which a resourceful lady rids herself of two unwanted suitors, tricking them into metaphorically and quite literally courting death – by impersonating a dead outlaw and stealing his corpse, respectively. The first theme is the transposition of the traditional lyrical love-death connection from the realm of cultural tropes to the narrative mechanics of the plot. This shift is not just parodically comic; it also brings to the fore the irreducible presence in the world of desiring bodies and measures their impact on literary antecedents, such as Cavalcanti's negative phenomenology of love or Dante's treatment of Francesca's pursuit of an irrational and deadly passion. The second interpretive thread Lummus isolates concerns the geopolitical circumstances of the story, which is significantly staged in the recognizably factional society of the Guelph city of Pistoia. In this light, the essay reads the political-familial connections between the family of the protagonist (Madonna Francesca de' Lazzari), the two Florentine White Guelph exiles (her suitors), and the mysterious Scannadio (in whose figure Lummus detects traces of a specific Pistoiese starring in Dante's *Inferno*: Vanni Fucci). Mobilizing their knowledge of the literary intertexts that structure the plot and their awareness of historical circumstances connoting the story's personnel, the tale asks its audience to coordinate both dimensions, appreciating how Boccaccio transfers his criticism of uncontrolled desire from the philosophical and moral to a political level. Boccaccio's use of geographical and historical references appears, thus, not aesthetic or allusive, but rather structural: a way of casting light on his historical "realism" as a crucial, functional element in the narrative workings of the story and its meaning.

By reconstructing and emphasizing the vast network of subliminal echoes and connections with other *novelle* in the *Decameron*, Maria Pia Ellero reads Elissa's story as a return to the narrator's favourite theme: the power that a *leggiadro motto* possesses to structure social interactions to the advantage of its users. The case in point is the clever riposte a young and courtly nun devises during her hasty trial, after she is caught having sex with a lover in her cell. Isabetta's *motto* allows her to escape punishment by pointing out that her abbess has just indulged in the same activity, as her wearing a man's breeches instead of her wimple amply proves. In the quick retort she produces, the story also showcases the power of a carefully crafted response to rend the veil of appearances and bring into sharp, critical light the truth of the power dynamics that underlie them. The story's message emerges from the coming together of several strains equally investigated in the reading: a traditional *fabliau* plot (that found in the *Dit de la Nonnete* and in the *Roman de Renart*), gnomic and skoptic classical treatments of an ethical theme (the critique of those who attack a vice while being guilty of the same), and philosophical considerations about the role of witticism as a cultural form of necessary respite from work (the Aristotelian and Thomistic coordinated definition of the social use of *lusus*). Intimately related to the Aristotelian concept of *lusus*, Boccaccio's comic has an implicit ethical and political connotation, as directed to and functional for enhancing social eutrapelia. Ellero's exploration of the comic as one of the tools Boccaccio presses into the service of his criticism of current cultural paradigms also potentially has, however, a dark side. By placing on trial the comic and elegiac versions of typical *fol'amor* characters (the abbess and Isabetta, respectively), Elissa's narrative also tries and tests a literary tradition whose alleged and partial realism is at odds with the need to give order to reality. Ellero's focus on the disruptive consequences of apparent virtue and real lack of moral coherence referred to the internal dimension of the conventual life may lead one to wonder whether her considerations may apply to the external social dimension of having an entire community be only apparently virtuous but essentially corrupt. The abbess's and Isabetta's lack of virtue essentially produces and condones chaos in what should be an ordered community. It also contains, in embryo, the same destabilizing potential associated with a lack of virtue in institutions – be they religious or secular – to prevent the formation and preservation of a well-ordered society.

Revolving around the iconic juxtaposition of Calandrino's imaginary fertile womb and the literally well-fed, swollen bellies of his tricksters, Federica Anichini's reading of Filostrato's third instalment in Calandrino's cycle emphasizes the illusionistic quality of the prank that Bruno, Buffalmacco, and Nello play on their gullible fellow painter, which is of one cloth with the imaginary narrative space in which *Decameron* readers are attracted by Boccaccio's art of storytelling. Just as painters endow appearances with the force of truth, a *fatto*, Anichini insists, so too does the text in which storytellers operate. Thus, in her reading, the tale becomes an opportunity to investigate not only the continuous reversal of traditional, medieval gender expectations, which is so prominent in this particular story, or the potentially antisocial quality of the vice that the *beffa* targets in Calandrino, namely his lack of liberality, but also the more profound power of verbal fiction to serve the critical exploration of the factual world outside the text. Anichini subverts the traditional framing of Calandrino as the embodiment of an a-critical reading of reality's images and makes him the symbol of the dangers intrinsic to a literal interpretation of fictive realities. Thus, the play between emptiness and fullness, simultaneously physical and imaginary, defines Calandrino as a figure at the centre of gender dynamics, inappropriately occupying the female space of verbal invention and reproduction.

Patrizio Ceccagnoli's intertextual analysis of Neifile's story recounting the trick that Cecco di Fortarrigo plays on his travel mate Cecco Angiolieri by stealing his identity and his possessions, after having gambled away his own, concentrates on the potential metaliterary significance of Boccaccio's onomastic dyadic choice for the *novella*'s protagonists. The mixing and mistaking of the protagonists' identities become Ceccagnoli's key to a reading of the plot through the many lexical and thematic connections it exhibits with poems from Angiolieri's corpus. The two characters named Cecco move within the confines of the story, Ceccagnoli argues, just as two other Ceccos – the author and his autobiofictional persona – emerge from a critical reading of Angiolieri's poetry. Instead of considering this *novella* as a biographical reference to Angiolieri, or simply a comic parody of his poetry, Ceccagnoli shows how its very structure suggests not a mimetic staging of the Sienese poet's provocative poetry but rather a subversion of it. In the story, Cecco di Fortarrigo becomes the agent of a quasi-Dantean contrapasso, a morally inferior and yet eerily successful doppelganger of Cecco Angiolieri, who in the end is made to suffer at the hands of a character who has all the features of his own literary persona. Cecco's existential journey toward emancipation turns out to be also a poetic one, and both prove similarly a failure. Boccaccio's double play with Cecco and his fictional persona may point to a rejection of Angiolieri's brand of comic as unfit to provide the cultural foundation for rebuilding an ethically sound new political body.

Marcello Ciccuto's essay goes back to the play of appearance and reality, by framing the final chapter in Calandrino's cycle, his misadventures in courting the young Niccolosa, within the *Decameron*'s wider reflection on the artistic revolution of the fourteenth century. By presenting the new generation of painters as emancipated subverters of those unchecked and unchallenged notions of imitation to which Calandrino is said to adhere, Ciccuto maintains that Boccaccio equates their narrative superiority to their ability to use art for testing and crossing the boundaries of representation. Since images are deceiving and no longer linearly connected to their referents, any mimetic approach to reality also ceases to grant access to its inner truth. Calandrino's gullibility thus becomes the foil for his companions' creativity and emerges as an emblem of the epistemological crisis of mimesis as a privileged mode of artistic expression. The painters in Fiammetta's tale are not simply the master artificers, in the pranks they organize for Calandrino, of a new kind of illusion. They are also the best-suited mediators of the new epistemological approach characterizing the *Decameron*. Articulated in the clashing of the phantasies of erotic prowess Calandrino cannot uphold and the reality of a beating by his wife he cannot escape, their lesson ultimately consists in an invitation to move beyond sterile imitation of models in art to testing the boundless force of human imagination.

Simona Lorenzini's new approach to the comedy of errors connected to the adventurous bed-trading triggered by Niccolosa and Pinuccio's night of furtive love-making in her father's inn takes into account the multiple dimensions of Boccaccio's narrative strategy. She considers how the *ars combinatoria* is here deployed at a structural level, and projects it onto the rhetorical ability of the central character in the tale, the innkeeper's wife, to defuse a potentially dangerous crisis in the household. The wise manipulator of both verbal signs (her words carefully craft a different story and a different reality that soothes her husband) and practical circumstances (the darkness of the room in which the sexual transgressions take place, the established effects of wine on people), Niccolosa's mother wields for Lorenzini the therapeutic power of imagination to bring peace to a troubled social setting, intervening with words into the masculine realm of deeds. Again, the theme of imagination and its power emerges as one of the threads Boccaccio weaves into the fabric of this meta-day in which he reflects on the art, purpose, and limits of literature in re-establishing a desired order in the presence of chaos.

In her reading of the tale of Talano d'Imolese's predictive dream punishing the *ritrosia* of Margherita, his wife, Grace Delmolino offers a stimulating reverse perspective on a story traditionally interpreted from the male point of view of the "prophetic" husband. Her reframing proves the viability of a non-misogynist reading of Pampinea's tale, one in which the female protagonist's agency in the face of the violent suppression of her will is central to the plot. The essay pays crucial attention to the normative and moralizing rhetorical mechanisms that guide the *brigata*'s reaction to the story, as a confirmation of the power intrinsic to patriarchal order to mete out exemplary punishment on any woman's effort toward self-determination. Connecting the story to some heroines from the *De mulieribus claris*, Delmolino shows the coexistence of an apparently contradictory binary disposition in Boccaccio, whose texts at once praise women's firmness of will as constancy and blame their steadfastness as unsettling stubbornness. In her analysis, the term *ritrosia* is thus both the ideological linchpin and the destabilizing weakest link in the essentialist misogynistic rhetoric that the narrator adopts and at once exposes in her telling of the story. This rhetoric, which equates a subject's exercise of her own will to a trigger for physical violence, may be transposed into the order of the ferine (in the present story) as well as into those of the supernatural (in the visions of V.8) or the metaphysical (in Emilia's prologue to IX.9). The combined effort of Pampinea and Emilia as narrators and rulers over days of free and freed storytelling, respectively, brings this core notion under coordinated, though ambiguous, attack. The lesson emerging from the story once again works on both the individual ethical level and on the collective political one: men's violence in suppressing women's will is as socially disruptive as women's determination never to yield.

Johnny Bertolio reads Lauretta's short tale about the strike-and-counterstrike pranks that Biondello and Ciacco play on each other in this strictly Florentine *novella* by focusing on the combinatorial effects and the symmetrical construction that characterize it. His analysis hinges on the reverberations of a biblical metaphor, the wine of wrath, which is deployed in the mysterious language undergirding the *beffa.* The allusion to wine as "ruby-like" in the story's plot is for Bertolio the entry point for reading an episode of violence and social dissension in the body politic of Dante's Florence. The hell-like *città partita,* split by factions which the *novella* evokes by mobilizing some prominent members in Dante's infernal nomenclature, is not a neutral backdrop for the tale. Lauretta not only introduces Ciacco and Biondello as two classical hangers-on to the dinner parties in the powerful houses of Vieri de' Cerchi and Corso Donati, the emblematic heads of the White and Black Guelph parties in Florence, but also evokes the no less Dantean Filippo Argenti as the instrument of one's contrapasso-like revenge on the other. The result is a multi-layered tale that barely hides beneath its lighthearted surface the diagnosis of a deeper civic moral and bodily disorder than the venial and comic faults of the protagonists may suggest.

After carefully evaluating a wide range of what he labels "recuperative" readings of Emilia's *novella,* Ascoli stakes one essential claim; namely, that Emilia is intended as a divisive character at no fewer than three levels: in the tales she tells throughout the *Decameron,* in the way she frames and narrates the present story, and in her demeanour as ruler of the day. The divisiveness Emilia embodies is articulated first in her choice to narrate the violent outcome of Melisso's and Giosefo's consultations with King Solomon on how to deal with a contrary wife and garner friendship, respectively. The enigmatic and equally contradictory Solomonic judgment pronounced in the story (love those you want to be loved by, and beat your wife) is mirrored in Emilia's own contradictions. Associated on the one side with the theme of authority, exercised over a community of free men and women, and on the other with the theme of violence, designed to obtain submission of those who want to exercise their own will, Emilia's story works as a general memento not to transgress what she calls the order of nature (the misogynist aspect) and the nature of the law (the political question). Interpretation is the second level at which Ascoli detects the tale's complexities and ambiguities. In presenting her tale as impossibly allegorical, Ascoli argues, Emilia showcases on the hermeneutic level the same authoritarian stance she endorses both as a woman narrator who demonstrates a violent antipathy to the female sex and as a day's queen who is at once authoritarian and libertarian in her ruling. She embodies, thus, an interpretive and political contradiction, being at once a figure of power and providing with her misogyny the grounds to question her very authority. She is, in sum, central to Boccaccio's reflection on governance and wisdom. In stressing the complex and contradictory character of Emilia, which calls into question the nexus of women's "education" and male "authority," Ascoli's reading also interrogates from a distance the other famous case in which the same violent logic of mad brutishness finds an equally successful and equally troublesome application; namely, *Decameron* X.10.

Max Matukhin's careful intertextual study of the apparently linear and often dismissed parodic final tale of the day mobilizes classical (Apuleius), patristic (Augustine), scholastic (Alan de Lille), and romance (*fabliaux*) antecedents. These sources reveal Boccaccio's particular attention to the link between language and sexuality and show the tale's potential to speak several discursive truths at once. With respect to his models, Boccaccio uses his narrative techniques of demotion, reversal, and parody to produce a narrative connected on the one hand with the overarching theme of initiation and transformation through metamorphosis (which was at the core of Apuleius's narrative), and on the other with theological concerns about sacramental rituals. Boccaccio uses this technique to dramatize the unproductive character of the sexual act "deviated" from reproduction and animated, as in this case, by a "mercantile" desire for material goods. Under Matukhin's lens, Donno Gianni's magical metamorphic equine incantation – the unachieved turning of Gemmata, the wife of his *compare* Pietro, into a mare – becomes an opportunity not only to explore the porous boundaries between high and low culture but also, and perhaps more essentially, to test the no less fraught divide between culture and nature, as it was articulated in the medieval discourse around sodomy. A tale in which a priest has sexual intercourse with a married woman, in an animal-like and allusive position, implicates social, positional, and topographical breaches in sexual normativity, on which Dioneo's story sheds a quite literal light.

As we hope has emerged from these introductory pages, this volume sees its reading of Day Nine as an analysis of individual elements – the ten stories as well as the various proceedings which take place in the frame – not as a gathering of independent entities, but in a holistic vein. We have attempted, both in the individual essays and in the introductory contribution we co-signed, to unearth the possible threads connecting the *cornice* of the day to the broader economy of the macro-tale, its *novelle* to the themes and logical nodes that tie together the *Decameron* as a whole. Boccaccio's text is a network of subordinated and coordinated verbal objects, which encourages us to distinguish different narratives planes while discouraging us from considering each as separate or independent from those that surround it. The *Decameron* thus appears not simply as a container for narratives but as a carefully constructed literary invention that entrusts its pedagogical message to the interplay of all its parts. Finally, we have attempted to illustrate the special relationship between Days One and Nine, particularly in the ways they tackle the interconnected questions of freedom and order. Through the dialogue established between these two days, their queens, and their respective rulership, we have endeavoured to provide a glimpse into one of Boccaccio's educational goals: namely, that the construction of a well-regulated text and the building of a well-regulated community are interrelated practices – be it the *brigata* in their days in the countryside, or the future city reborn after the plague, both must be organized, given form, and provided with the necessary means to be maintained.

THE *DECAMERON* NINTH DAY IN PERSPECTIVE

Introduction to Day Nine: Emilia's Rule of Freedom

SUSANNA BARSELLA AND SIMONE MARCHESI

Finisce l'Ottava giornata del Decameron: Incomincia la Nona, nella quale, sotto il reggimento d'Emilia, si ragiona ciascuno secondo che gli piace e di quello che più gli agrada.

[Here ends the Eighth Day of the *Decameron*. Here begins the Ninth Day, wherein, under the rule of Emilia, it is left to all the members of the company to speak on whatever subject they choose.]

The positional relevance of Day Nine within the narrative organism of the *Decameron* has been acknowledged in the past, especially in structural hypotheses on the macro-narrative which privilege a cyclical unfolding of the work. The ninth slot in the ten-day system is significant for both numerological and structural reasons. Whether we consider the *Decameron* as reproducing an itinerary toward the attainment of virtue or following other possible interpretive schematics, Day Nine remains a liminal moment of pause before the inception of the final stories dedicated to the highest civic virtues of liberality and magnificence.[1] Among several proposed methods of organizing the dynamics of the work is the option to view the *Decameron* as two

1 For different approaches to the general structure of the *Decameron*, see Mazzotta, *The World at Play*; Forni, *Adventures in Speech*; Migiel, *The Ethical Dimension of the Decameron*; Hollander and Cahill, "Day Ten of the Decameron"; and Mariani Zini, "Du plaisir d'être indifférent." Particularly meaningful may be the existence of the so-called *Frammento magliabechiano*, which encompasses Days One to Nine. On the Dantean structural resonances of the *Decameron*, in addition to the numerological ones, see Cappelletti, "Una proposta per la struttura del *Decameron*" and "La brigata in Purgatorio." See also Branca, "Coerenza ideale e funzione unitaria dell'Introduzione"; Barolini, "The Wheel of the Decameron."

quite distinct and massively uneven blocks: nine days dedicated to exploring the interplay of passions and their consequences in everyday circumstances, and one culminating segment, in which narrators compete in detailing climactic and often extreme examples of heroic liberality and magnificence. In this light, the journey into the complexity of human affections and the contradictions which they produce, an overarching theme at the core of the first nine days of storytelling, would be followed quite contrastively by the divergent exploration of the phenomenology of excess. The work would therefore be composed of two connected parts, separated by a sort of *caesura*, a discontinuity signalled abruptly by the final tale of Day Nine. Contrary to common interpretations, however, we argue that Day Nine is not a mere repetition or a debasement of Day One, but rather, in continuity with the opening day's theme, Emilia's rulership creates a new meaning for the term "freedom," thus making a contribution to the core mechanisms of the *Decameron*.

In this arrangement of the *Decameron*'s subject matter and narrative practices, Days One and Nine would be symmetrical endpoints of the main block, which would start and finish with two similar loci of ethical bathos. At one end stands Cepparello, a character who presents a perverse version of the sacrament of confession and sheds a preemptively sobering light on the acts of narration to follow; at the other end, as Cepparello's counterpart, is Donno Gianni, the shaman-priest who, in his parodic ritual enchantment of the mare, agrees to perform a supreme act of deception, calling into question the highest ritual of ontological transformation, the eucharistic transubstantiation.[2]

Symmetry, however, does not signify identity. Having reached Day Nine, the *Decameron* does not return to its point of origin. Days One and Nine interact dialectically, both in terms of their storytelling theme, which is only apparently the same, and the quite different profiles of their ruling queens: Pampinea and Emilia, respectively. In other words, through their collective itinerary exploring the flaws and virtues of humankind in social interrelations, the first nine days do not describe a parabolic or circular trajectory, but rather a non-linear progression ending at a point that represents an achieved development in terms of intellectual and moral awareness. With this industrious passing of time, the members of the *brigata* undergo a transformation that is embodied in their changed practice of freedom.

2 Cottino-Jones, *Order from Chaos*; Marino, *The Decameron "Cornice"*; Smarr, "Symmetry and Balance in the *Decameron*"; Hollander, "The Struggle for Control."

As we are about to see, the kinds of freedom in storytelling which Pampinea and Emilia grant to the *brigata*, and the overall interventions of each narrator throughout the proceedings of the storytellers, are in a chiaroscuro relation. As we examine Emilia's words introducing the open theme of the day on which she rules, we can appreciate that, rather than the product of an allegedly unavoidable narrative weariness or the dénouement at the end of a parable begun in Day One, these stories mark a moment of respite, setting the stage for the radical change in narrative strategies that will be triggered under Panfilo's governance in Day Ten. The narrators, who have been asked to treat specific themes in the central days (Two to Eight) and will be compelled to return to that modus in the concluding day (Ten), are now given a moment of pause in their work. The two free days, which seemingly bookend the fixed-theme days of narration, represent two stages in the unfolding of the narrative structure, as well as two stages in (and possibly two different kinds of) narrative freedom. As such, they do not mark the circular path of a macro-cycle concluding with Day Nine; rather, they trace the spiralling movement of the narrative as a whole.

Emilia and Pampinea: A Study in Contrast

A syncrisis of the two rulers of Days One and Nine produces interesting results that shed light on the progression in the *Decameron*. From the start of the frame narrative, Pampinea emerges as a leading character who takes charge of several founding acts for the community of storytellers. First, she is responsible for proposing to the women assembled in Santa Maria Novella that they form a *brigata*. Her invitation is foundational as much as it proves irresistible to the other members of the group:

> Io giudicherei ottimamente fatto che noi, sí come noi siamo, sí come molti innanzi a noi hanno fatto e fanno, di questa terra uscissimo, e fuggendo come la morte i disonesti essempli degli altri onestamente a' nostri luoghi in contado, de' quali a ciascuna di noi è gran copia, ce ne andassimo a stare, e quivi quella festa, quella allegrezza, quello piacere che noi potessimo, senza trapassare in alcuno atto il segno della ragione, prendessimo. (I.Intro.65)

> [I would think it an excellent idea … for us all to get away from this city, just as many others have done before us, and as indeed they are doing still. We could go and stay together on one of our various country estates, shunning at all costs the lewd practices of our fellow citizens and feasting

and merrymaking as best we may without in any way overstepping the bounds of what is reasonable.][3]

As we shall see in more detail below, once the group moves to the first villa, Pampinea continues in her leading role, authoritatively endorsing Dioneo's festive attitude and devising a structure of communal living which she believes will support their endeavour (95–6). Her proposal, which she advances as the initiator of the associated life of the group, entails that every day the *brigata* have a central figure of authority, a *principale*, whom everyone else should honour and obey. Adhering to her proposal, the group proceeds to acclaim her queen of Day One. At that point she also takes charge of the governance of their associated life, thus offering a model to the monarchs of the following days (99–101), who are no longer elected but each designated by the exiting monarch. Finally, one should remember, it is she who offers storytelling as the defining leisure activity for the community, thus allowing the *Decameron* to become what it is: a framed collection of stories (110–12). From all these preliminary interactions, to which we shall return in due course, Pampinea emerges as a "law-giver" for the company.

This brief digression into a survey of Pampinea's inaugural role is not gratuitous. When we bring into focus Pampinea's foundational acts, we also acquire a vantage point from which to evaluate the differences between her governance and Emilia's queenly role in Day Nine.[4] From this perspective, the relation between these two days, which take freedom as their governing concept, extends from their founding charters to the pointed interventions of their respective rulers. Pampinea and Emilia articulate two different notions of freedom in their speeches, thus suggesting that what differentiates their rulership is not simply a narrative matter but also a juridical one. In the interplay of their days, a clear message is also articulated: namely that, in the absence of a

3 The Italian text is from Giovanni Boccaccio, *Decameron*, edited by Branca (1992). The numbers in parenthesis indicate the paragraphs. The English translation is by McWilliam (1995).

4 Emilia is introduced in the frame of the *Decameron* as the "fourth" woman, after Pampinea, Filomena, and Fiammetta (I.51). She narrates the following *novelle*: I.6 (a *motto*, which condemns the hypocrisy of a member of the clergy); II.6 (the vicissitudes of Fortune in the life of Madama Beritola and her children); III.7 (once again on Fortune and against religious hypocrisy); IV.7 (the tragic and accidental death of Simona and Pasquino); V.2 Gostanza and Martuccio (the vicissitudes of Fortune in a story of love and geopolitics); VI.8 Fresco and his vain niece (a *motto*); VII.1 (on Fortune); VIII.4 (the vices of a religious man, the *Proposto di Fiesole* – pitted against a woman's resourcefulness); IX.9 Solomon (Justice); X.5 Madonna Dianora.

governing order, of an overarching structure which allots power to different subjects, there is no room for the full exercise of freedom.

While both characters assume a technically political role, their functions are not completely juxtaposed, just as their positions on individual points of merit are not fully aligned. Unlike Pampinea, who acts on the institutional policies of the community built in the *cornice*, Emilia appears to be interested in codifying the moral code that should orient the behaviour of the community itself. In a complementary relation to Pampinea, in fact, Emilia-the-queen approaches the work of forming the community from a perspective of social interrelations and production. Put differently, of the three sets of rules – religious, legal, and moral – which provide the scaffolding for any community and which need to be reconstituted within the broader society after the plague, each queen embodies one aspect. Correspondingly, each ruler also provides a singular, diverging and yet balanced, insight into the connected sphere of freedom. While freedom in narrative was a key element in the *brigata*'s formation and a specific quality of their associated life as established by Pampinea, the concept of freedom in Day Nine is of a different ilk. Conceived not as the opposite but rather as the desired and necessary product of the law, freedom is Emilia's crucial concern as ruler, but, as is the case with all societal rules and codes, which do not simply establish the limits of safe behaviour within a community but also define the scope and limits of the freedom which the law precipitates, the command to practise freedom which she extends to the narrators triggers their exploration of such ethical boundaries.[5]

But there is more. When Emilia's choice is evaluated in structural terms, her relation to Pampinea as the founder of the narrators' social body is complicated by the early and yet essential intervention of Filomena. Students of the *Decameron* tend to associate the First Day with an open-ended theme, and, by retrogressively attributing to Pampinea the control over the narrative subject which each king or queen will subsequently exercise in the following days, they may be tempted to say that the first queen "chooses" an open theme for the day. This habit in fact

5 As is the case with other members of the *brigata*, Emilia too has an intertextual past in Boccaccio's corpus of writings. In the *Teseida*, Emilia is one of the Amazons. It may be interesting to note that in the *Teseida* Boccaccio re-proposes the origin myth of the Amazons in terms of freedom from the masculine yoke, mobilizing the same terms that Emilia as narrator in the *Decameron* will impose upon her subjects. See especially the keywords *signoria*, *soggiogate*, *signoreggiate*, and *libere* in *Teseida* I.6–7. For a thorough evaluation of Emilia's prehistory, see the essay by Albert R. Ascoli in this volume, note 4.

misrepresents the carefully organized dynamics of the text. Pampinea had established that every ruler of each day should exercise discretionary power regarding the place and modality of living (the *luogo* and *modo* of their lives away from the plague-ridden city), but she said nothing of the themes that narrators should treat in their work. Boccaccio's text is precise on this point:

> Dico che a ciascuno per un giorno s'attribuisca e il peso e l'onore; e chi il primo di noi esser debba nella elezion di noi tutti sia: di quelli che seguiranno, come l'ora del vespro s'avicinerà, quegli o quella che a colui o a colei piacerà che quel giorno avrà avuta la signoria; e questo cotale, secondo il suo arbitrio, del tempo che la sua signoria dee bastare, del luogo e del modo nel quale a vivere abbiamo ordini e disponga. (I.Intro.96)
>
> [I propose that the burden and the honor should be assigned to each of us in turn for a single day. It will be for all of us to decide who is to be our first ruler, after which it will be up to each ruler, when the hour of vespers approaches, to elect his or her successor from among the ladies and gentlemen present. The person chosen to govern will be at liberty to make whatever arrangements he likes for the period covered by his rule, and to prescribe the place and the manner in which we are to live.]

While she had established the mechanisms and goals of their associated living, Pampinea had also given free rein to her subjects in terms of choosing a topic for their acts of narration. As Filomena interprets it at the end of Day One, however, the ruler's organizational discretion included the choice of topic for the storytelling, and she immediately proceeds to establish the single-day single-topic correspondence that will hold for the following seven days and will not yield until Emilia's ruling day (I.Concl.10). It is only at this point, with the passing of the crown at the end of Day Eight, that the day's theme, which had been limited to a single subject until that point, becomes open again. Emilia's oppositional response (today, exceptionally, narration is free-themed) targets Filomena's restrictive interpretation (each day should be devoted to one topic) of Pampinea's framework (narration is the crucial activity of the community). Notably, Emilia's intervention leaves intact the force of both Pampinea's and Filomena's ruling acts. In particular, the effect of her choice is double: on the one hand, it reinforces the general framing, by showing that each law should foresee and control its own exception; on the other hand, it forces the dialectic between order and freedom to emerge in a fully new light. It is, thus, in terms of the dialectic of freedom and order that the absence of an explicit theme in Day Nine should be viewed, not as a return to an allegedly initial or original freedom.

The relationship of continuity and complementarity between freedom and order can also be observed in the apparent contrast between nature and artifice which Day Nine stages in the spaces framing the narration. The oak grove which the *brigata* visits in the morning, and the flowery meadows of Neifile's concluding ballad, are spaces set in a contrastive and yet productive relationship with the garden in which the narration actually takes place. The activities that will unfold under Emilia's rule begin, in fact, with a morning outing into a new space, a *boschetto* near the villa in which the *brigata* is staying:

> La luce, il cui splendore la notte fugge, aveva già l'ottavo cielo d'azzurrino in color cilestro mutato tutto, e cominciavansi i fioretti per li prati a levar suso, quando Emilia levatasi fece le sue compagne e i giovani parimente chiamare; li quali venuti e appresso alli lenti passi della reina avviatisi, infino a un boschetto non guari al palagio lontano se n'andarono, e per quello entrati, videro gli animali, sí come cavriuoli, cervi e altri, quasi sicuri da' cacciatori per la soprastante pistolenzia, non altramenti aspettargli che se senza tema o dimestichi fossero divenuti. E ora a questo e ora a quell'altro appressandosi, quasi giugnere gli dovessero, faccendogli correre e saltare, per alcuno spazio sollazzo presero: ma già inalzando il sole, parve a tutti di ritornare. Essi eran tutti di frondi di quercia inghirlandati, con le mani piene o d'erbe odorifere o di fiori; e chi scontrati gli avesse, niuna altra cosa avrebbe potuto dire se non: "O costor non saranno dalla morte vinti o ella gli ucciderà lieti." (IX.Intro.2–5)

> [The light whose radiance dispels the shades of night had already softened into pale celestial hues the deep azure of the eighth heaven, and the flowerets in the meadows had begun to raise their drooping heads, when Emilia arose and caused the other young ladies to be called, and likewise the three young men. Answering her summons, they set off at a leisurely pace behind the queen, and made their way to a little wood, not very far from the palace. On entering the wood, they observed a number of roebucks, stags, and other wild creatures, which, as though sensing they were safe from the hunter on account of the plague, stood their ground as if they had been rendered tame and fearless. However, by approaching these creatures one after another as though intending to touch them, they caused them to run away and leap in the air; and in this way they amused themselves for some little time until, the sun being now in the ascendant,

> they thought it expedient to retrace their steps. They were all wreathed in fronds of oak, and their hands were full of fragrant herbs or flowers, so that if anyone had encountered them, he would only have been able to say: "Either these people will not be vanquished by death, or they will welcome it with joy."]

The specific place of this setting within the topographical architecture of the *Decameron* is significant. The *Decameron* begins in a sacred urban space, the church of Santa Maria Novella; it then moves into the garden of the first villa; a second garden is then chosen as the setting for the daily work of narration, starting from Day Three, and will remain so until the end of the work, with the exception of the one-day parenthesis in the Valle delle Donne for Day Seven; finally, a shorter parenthesis away from the second narrative garden marks the beginning of Day Nine, with the *boschetto* populated with peacefully roaming and quasi-domesticated animals that approach the *brigata* with confidence. There, all members of the group receive a crown of oak leaves and collect herbs and flowers so that, when they make their way back to the palace to start the second half of their day, they appear for a fleeting moment immune to death and utterly happy.[6] Their *lietezza* is a product of the freedom they enjoy in the uncultivated space of the grove, and it may be said to derive from the temporary experience of natural freedom. But just as this foray into nature is designed to bring them back into the space of the garden, a space created by work, so too the freedom of the narrators is correlated with a sense of order.

The opening note finds a clear echo at the closing of the day. The real (that is, narratively actual) space of the *cornice* corresponds to the metaphorical space Neifile evokes in the concluding *ballata* of Day Nine. The imaginary pleasant meadow of Neifile's song is similarly permeated by the joyful presence of natural elements, which spontaneously arise from it and are just as freely experienced and enjoyed:

> Io vo pe' verdi prati riguardando
> i bianchi fiori e' gialli e i vermigli
> le rose in su le spine e' bianchi gigli,
> e tutti quanti gli vo' somigliando
> al viso di colui che me amando

6 Note the remarkable density of the term *lieto* in the paragraphs describing the outing into the oak wood and the return to the villa garden (three times in three sentences). On the force of the term, see Veglia, "*La vita lieta*", emphasizing the Epicurean ascendancy of the idea of pleasure in Boccaccio.

ha presa e terrà sempre, come quella
ch'altro non ha in disio che' suoi piaceri. (IX.Concl.9)

[I see in green fields as I go
Yellow and red and white flowers blow,
Briar-roses and fair lilies grow.

And in all these his face I see
Who has so taken hold of me
His wish is mine eternally.]

Notably, the roses and lilies that usually appear in garden settings are here associated with the natural space of the meadow. In such a pairing, the revaluation of nature, spontaneity, and freedom which marks the day again evidences its connection with a similarly strong subordination to the principles of work, organization, and order. Panfilo, who will bring to a close both the Ninth Day and the narrative cycle of the *Decameron*, will retrospectively confirm (and prospectively counterbalance) the *libitum* status of the narrative which Emilia has instituted and allow its force to flow back into the orderly pointedness of narrative. The new theme Panfilo proposes will not only be singular (as opposed to the many explored in Day Nine) but also ethically and aesthetically higher:

Innamorate donne, la discrezion d' Emilia, nostra reina stata questo giorno, per dare alcun riposo alle vostre forze arbitrio vi diè di ragionare quel che piú vi piacesse; per che, già riposati essendo, giudico che sia da ritornare alla legge usata, e per ciò voglio che domane ciascuna di voi pensi di ragionare sopra questo, cioè: di chi liberalmente ovvero magnificamente alcuna cosa operasse intorno a' fatti d'amore o d'altra cosa. (IX. Concl.4)

[Enamoured ladies, he said, our queen of today, Emilia, prudently left you at liberty to speak on whatever subject you chose, so that you may rest your faculties. But now that you are refreshed, I consider that we should revert to our customary rule, and I therefore want you all to think of something to say, tomorrow, on the subject of those who have performed liberal or munificent deeds, whether in the cause of love or otherwise.]

Arbitrium and law are contrasted, just as rest (and pleasure) are set in opposition to the new imperative of (ethical) work – "valorosamente adoperare." Panfilo articulates in terms of the brevity of life and long-lasting effect of fame the opportunity and necessity for the *brigata* to move away from its restful ease and freedom and return to its initial narrative variety:

> Queste cose e dicendo e udendo senza dubbio gli animi vostri ben disposti a valorosamente adoperare accenderà: ché la vita nostra, che altro che brieve esser non puote nel mortal corpo, si perpetuerà nella laudevole fama; il che ciascuno che al ventre solamente, a guisa che le bestie fanno, non serve, dee non solamente desiderare ma con ogni studio cercare e operare. (IX.Concl.5)

> [The telling and the hearing of such things will assuredly fill you with a burning desire, well disposed as you already are in spirit, to comport yourselves valorously. And thus our lives, which cannot be other than brief in these our mortal bodies, will be preserved by the fame of our achievements – a goal that every man who does not simply attend to his belly, like an animal, should not only desire but most zealously pursue and strive to attain.]

Again, terms pointing to the active side of life resurface with allusion to the sphere of work and labour and its dialectical relation with the parallel opposition between freedom and order. These elements will be the focus of the next section.

Freedom and Order

As we mentioned at the beginning, a quality often imputed to the *novelle* collected in Day Nine is the relative lack of coherence in the storytelling. This feature is, however, neither unique to the day nor unexpected. Variety, rather, is a programmatic trait of the day's narrative work. The value of this liminality has much to do both with the specific slant which Emilia imposes upon the day's work – the absence of any constrictive direction for individual narrations – and with one of the most pervasive and deepest concerns defining the *Decameron* as a whole; namely, the radical codependency of order and freedom. The formula that perhaps best encapsulates the cohesive relation of these two principles ricochets across the two days of narrative freedom. Pampinea in Day One and Emilia in Day Nine, as queens of these apparently twin days, *impose* freedom on their subjects. Pampinea's words "*voglio* che libero sia a ciascuno di quella materia ragionare che piú gli sarà a grado" (I.Intro.114) resurface once again in Emilia's formula "*voglio* che ciascun secondo che gli piace ragioni" (VIII.Concl.5). The potential internal contradiction embedded in these formulations should give us pause. With an apparent oxymoron, both queens *command* that the *brigata* exercise *freedom*, thus establishing, in their respective days, that neither order nor freedom may exist in isolation.

The queens' dispositions reveal their shared preoccupation not only to associate freedom with pleasure ("secondo che gli piace" and "che piú gli sarà a grado") but also, and perhaps more importantly, to frame such freedom of choice within the parameters of their ruling. However paradoxical it may seem that they "impose" freedom, such configuration of power is aesthetically and ethically crucial to the meaning of the *Decameron* as a text that includes among its goals the provision of a template for a well-regulated community. For the *Decameron*, and perhaps for Boccaccio as the ultimate organizer of the work, order is the necessary condition for freedom, but from Day Nine we also learn that freedom is necessary to maintain order. In the apparent randomness of Day Nine, in sum, there is nothing gratuitous.

The interconnectedness between rulers is clear, but clear as well are the distinctions which the text carefully constructs. The order which Pampinea and Emilia establish and promote, respectively, has two different shades, as does the freedom they advocate and extend to their subjects. In the case of Pampinea, as we have seen, order is that of the lawmaker, and her dispositions acquire an institutional character from the start. In Emilia's case, order arises from and consists in the network of social relations that form the very fabric of the city. It also takes shape through family and economic relations. Her insistence on the theme of labour in the preamble to her day, when she metaphorically frames the "work" of narration as the labour of farm animals, suggests as much. Accordingly, for Pampinea, freedom lies *within* the clear and stable set of parameters that regulate political life; for Emilia, it is freedom *with respect to* the strictures of the practical organization of social life.

The distinction is, again, crucial, and it may be best explored according to the characters who advocate for each part of this distinction. Let us begin with Pampinea. As we have seen, she is the originator of the *brigata*'s formation. She also is the first proponent of storytelling as its main activity, and the proponent of the *modo* and *loco* for the company's existence. This *modo* consists of practical determinations, the smaller tasks of governance connected to organizing the company's daily routines, and at the same time comprises the principle for the orderly setup of society: the necessity of a leader, who receives honour and obedience, and whose only concern should be steering the life of the community toward happiness. Her founding charter is detailed and specific:

> Ma per ciò che le cose che sono senza modo non possono lungamente durare, io, che cominciatrice fui de' ragionamenti da' quali questa cosí bella compagnia è stata fatta, pensando al continuar della nostra letizia, estimo che di necessità sia convenire esser tra noi alcuno principale, il quale noi e onoriamo e ubidiamo come maggiore, nel quale ogni pensiero stea di doverci a lietamente vivere disporre. E acciò che ciascun pruovi il peso della sollecitudine insieme col piacere della maggioranza e, per conseguente da una parte e d'altra tratti, non possa chi nol pruova invidia avere alcuna, dico che a ciascuno per un giorno s'attribuisca e il peso e l'onore; e chi il primo di noi esser debba nella elezion di noi tutti sia: di quelli che seguiranno, come l'ora del vespro s'avicinerà, quegli o quella che a colui o a colei piacerà che quel giorno avrà avuta la signoria; e questo cotale, secondo il suo arbitrio, del tempo che la sua signoria dee bastare, del luogo e del modo nel quale a vivere abbiamo ordini e disponga. (I.Intro.95–6)
>
> [And since it was I who led the discussions from which this fair company has come into being, I have given some thought to the continuance of our happiness, and consider it necessary for us to choose a leader, drawn from our own ranks, whom we would honor and obey as our superior, and whose sole concerns will be that of devising the means whereby we may pass our time agreeably. But so that none of us will complain that he or she has had no opportunity to experience the burden of responsibility and the pleasure of command associated with sovereign power, I propose that the burden and the honor should be assigned to each of us in turn for a single day. It will be for all of us to decide who is to be our first ruler, after which it will be up to each ruler, when the hour of vespers approaches, to elect his or her successor from among the ladies and gentlemen present. The person chosen to govern will be at liberty to make whatever arrangements he likes for the period covered by his rule, and to prescribe the place and the manner in which we are to live.]

The autocratic role which Pampinea takes, and to which the whole community reacts positively, accepting it in full, is functional to the establishment of order.[7] It is particularly noteworthy that, as hinted

---

7 Pampinea's role mirrors that of the author himself in giving order to the text he composes and whose words seems to echo in those Pampinea pronounces in Santa Maria Novella encouraging her companions to seek refuge outside Florence. The

above, even Dioneo agrees with the plan which Pampinea devises, reacting only to Filomena's autocratic inflection thereof. In this way, his exceptionalism is folded back into the fabric of the community. Even his strategic divergency entails no threat to the orderly unfolding of the storytellers' work, but is necessary to the well-being, the re-creation of the group.[8]

There are several elements worthy of note in the passage quoted above. First is the idea that a *modo* is essential to achieve and maintain a happy life ("continuare nostra letizia"), a modality of associated living on which to run the community. This preoccupation is already articulated by Filomena in Santa Maria Novella and taken up again once the group has moved to the first villa. Second, Pampinea deems it necessary that the community agree to elect one among them to a position of primacy; that is, to give one member a temporary preeminence. Such distinction among peers aims at guaranteeing the orderly progression of the community's life. Variety, incidentally the same principle organizing the narrating activity in both Days One and Nine, ensures fairness in the allotment of discretionary power to an individual. Third, one should remark that the two main characteristics of the *principale* are that they should be honoured and obeyed not in themselves, but for the role they play in service to the community – that is, insofar (and as long) as they devote their full attention to directing the *brigata*'s activities toward living happily. The individual kings and queens of each day are, in sum, the guarantors and facilitators of their collective happiness. The system of alternation that is enforced starting from Day One dispels any trace of individual self-affirmation from the primacy of the role as *principale* which each narrator and member of the *brigata* will play. Once framed as a service to the community, a community that adopts a government of laws, even Dioneo's quite personal and potentially diverging approach to life outside the city is brought back into the fold.[9]

metapolitical reflection that is entrusted to the narrative strategies of each narrator potentially has a metapoetic dimension. See Barsella, "Travestimento autorale."

8 In Dioneo's own words: "Donne, il vostro senno più che il nostro avvedimento ci ha qui guidati" (I.Intro.96).

9 On Dioneo's privilege, one should also note that it is constantly formulated in terms of grace, not of freedom: "ma di spezial grazia vi cheggio un dono" and "questa grazia voglia," a phrasing confirmed by Filomena (I.Concl.12–13). The freedom Dioneo seeks consists in his not being "costretto da questa legge." Correspondingly, the point of the concession of such freedom is that it shall relieve the *brigata* of any potential tiredness: "dovere la brigata, se stanca fosse del ragionare, rallegrare" (14).

The balanced quality of the power entrusted to each day's monarch immediately emerges in the narrative. As soon as Pampinea is elected by the other members of the *brigata* as the first queen, she concerns herself with both aspects of her mandate. Startlingly, she imposes silence on her peers, but her imposition is devised to create the material conditions for the coexistence of the *brigata*'s members:

> Pampinea, fatta reina, comandò che ogn'uom tacesse, avendo già fatti i famigliari de' tre giovani e le loro fanti, ch'eran quatro, davanti chiamarsi; e tacendo ciascun, disse: "Acciò che io prima essemplo dea a tutti voi, per lo quale di bene in meglio procedendo la nostra compagnia con ordine e con piacere e senza alcuna vergogna viva e duri quanto a grado ne fia, io primieramente constituisco Parmeno, famigliare di Dioneo, mio siniscalco, e a lui la cura e la sollecitudine di tutta la nostra famiglia commetto e ciò che al servigio della sala appartiene. Sirisco, famigliar di Panfilo, voglio che di noi sia spenditore e tesoriere e di Parmeno seguiti i comandamenti. Tindaro al servigio di Filostrato e degli altri due attenda nelle camere loro, qualora gli altri, intorno alli loro ufici impediti, attender non vi potessero. Misia, mia fante, e Licisca, di Filomena, nella cucina saranno continue e quelle vivande diligentemente apparecchieranno che per Parmeno loro saranno imposte. Chimera, di Lauretta, e Stratilia, di Fiammetta, al governo delle camere delle donne intente vogliamo che stieno e alla nettezza de' luoghi dove staremo. E ciascun generalmente, per quanto egli avrà cara la nostra grazia, vogliamo e comandiamo che si guardi, dove che egli vada, onde che egli torni, che che egli oda o vegga, niuna novella altra che lieta ci rechi di fuori." (I.Intro.98–101)
>
> [Upon her election as their queen, Pampinea summoned the servants of the three young men to appear before her together with their own maidservants, who were four in number. And having called upon everyone to be silent, she said: "So that I may begin by setting you all a good example, though which, proceeding from good to better, our company will be enabled to live an ordered and agreeable existence for as long as we choose to remain together, I first of all appoint Dioneo's manservant, Parmeno, as my steward, and to him I commit the management and care of our household, together with all that appertains to the service of the hall. I desire that Panfilo's servant, Sirisco, should act as our buyer and treasurer, and carry out the instructions of Parmeno. As well as attending to the needs of Filostrato, Tindaro will look after the other two gentlemen in their rooms whenever their own manservants are prevented by their offices from performing such duties. My own maidservant, Misia, will be employed full-time in the kitchen along with Filomena's maidservant, Licisca, and

they will prepare with diligence whatever dishes are prescribed by Parmeno. Chimera and Stratilia, the servants of Lauretta and Fiammetta, are required to act as chambermaids to all the ladies, as well as seeing that the places we frequent are neatly and tidily maintained. And unless they wish to incur our royal displeasure, we desire and command that each and every one of the servants should take good care, no matter what they should hear or observe in their comings and goings, to bring us no tidings of the world outside these walls unless they are tidings of happiness.]

The keen attention she pays to the necessity of devising a way of life that guarantees the duration of the social compact is worthy of note. While her mandate is temporary, she makes sure to project the effects of her dispositions beyond her personal time in power. This attention to the future entails two aspects: first, Pampinea presents the constitution she devises for the *brigata* as a model for its future rulers ("constituisco … essemplo"); secondly, her ruling model is devised to provide a way of life that extends for the whole span of time in which the community desires to stay together ("duri quanto a grado ne fia").[10] For Pampinea, in other words, the practical work of ruling over the community is functional to the establishment of a durable and balanced system of life, in which *ordine* and *piacere* are coordinated principles. This is an order meant to guarantee not simply the preservation of a status quo, but also the progress of the associated life of the company for as long as it will decide to stay together – "di bene in meglio procedendo." The paradigmatic quality of her ruling is, in sum, asserted from the start.

The second decree which Pampinea issues as soon as she has ascended to power is in line with the same principles that have become apparent in her taking control of the governance of communal life. In proposing narration as the main activity of the group, she is again concerned with the communal well-being of the *brigata*. Formulated now as a modest proposal, rather than an arbitrary imposition, Pampinea's invitation to consider storytelling as a socializing pastime is equally foundational. Unlike the zero-sum games of chance or skill in which one party wins only when the opponent is defeated, storytelling, she convincingly notes, is an individual activity that offers communal pleasure.

Ma se in questo il mio parer si seguisse, non giucando, nel quale l'animo dell'una delle parti convien che si turbi senza troppo piacere dell'altra o di

10 For the political dimension of the *brigata*'s organization, in particular the equilibrium between "Pampinea's egalitarian and hierarchical impulses," see Sherberg, *The Governance of Friendship*, 32–41 (36).

> chi sta a vedere, ma novellando (il che può porgere, dicendo uno, a tutta la compagnia che ascolta diletto) questa calda parte del giorno trapasseremo. Voi non avrete compiuta ciascuno di dire una sua novelletta, che il sole fia declinato e il caldo mancato, e potremo dove piú a grado vi fia andare prendendo diletto: e per ciò, quando questo che io dico vi piaccia, ché disposta sono in ciò di seguire il piacer vostro, faccianlo; e dove non vi piacesse, ciascuno infino all'ora del vespro quello faccia che piú gli piace. (I.Intro.111–12)

> [But if you were to follow my advice, this hotter part of the day would be spent, not in playing games (which inevitably bring anxiety to one of the players, without offering very much pleasure either to his opponent or to the spectators), but in telling stories – an activity that may afford some amusement both to the narrator and to the company at large. By the time each one of you has narrated a little tale of his own or her own, the sun will be setting, the heat will have abated, and we shall be able to go and amuse ourselves wherever you choose. Let us, then, if the idea appeals to you, carry this proposal of mine into effect. But I am willing to follow your own wishes in this matter, and if you disagree with my suggestion, let us all go and occupy our time in whatever way we please until the hour of the vespers.]

The coordination of individual pleasures and collective action is the key concept she articulates in these lines. In an exceptionally dense configuration, the term *piacere* appears four times in the short span of one sentence. Pampinea's decree is presented, at least in this inaugural moment, as fully dependent on the free agreement of the other members. In order for her decision to become the internal law of the community, in fact, she stipulates that this should be a pleasure-driven decision of the company ("quando … vi piaccia"). Furthermore, that her invitation is not an imposition is guaranteed by the clause she immediately appends; namely, that she is ready to conform to their desire in this decree (again, "il piacer vostro"). Also, and just as importantly, in case such a pleasure-subordinated agreement is not reached ("dove non vi piacesse"), she concludes that each should follow his or her individual desires in their activities ("ciascuno … quello faccia che piú gli piace"). *Piacere*, in sum, features as *both the goal* of all collective activities which the first queen recommends *and the principle* to which the individual decision to accede to her plan should conform. In this double role, pleasure reveals itself as an integral part of the order Pampinea has instituted. When pleasure is aimed at achieving and ensuring the collective good, as it is in the serious play of storytelling on which the *brigata* agrees, it enters the same general dynamic interaction of *utile* and *diletto* that is at the core of the *Decameron* as a literary project.[11]

Pampinea's original freedom soon receives, however, a qualification that does not necessarily reflect her original intent: the narrative directionality that Filomena imposes is a possible but not necessary implication of Pampinea's ruling. At the end of the proceedings of the First Day, Filomena marks the boundaries of narrative for the following day by stating:

> È il vero che quello che Pampinea non poté fare, per lo esser tardi eletta al reggimento, io il voglio cominciare a fare: cioè a ristrignere dentro a alcun termine quello di che dobbiamo novellare e davanti mostrarlovi, acciò che ciascuno abbia spazio di poter pensare a alcuna bella novella sopra la data proposta contare. (I.Concl.10)
>
> [I do however wish to initiate a practice which Pampinea, because she was elected late as our queen, was unable to introduce: namely, to restrict the matter of our storytelling within some fixed limit which will be defined for you in advance, so that each of us will have time to prepare a good story on the subject prescribed.]

What we read here is not simply a first intimation of the link that binds Pampinea and Filomena, who will often revisit each other's words.[12] Filomena's move has two notable consequences. First, the new queen connects her choice of determining in advance the topic for the next day of narration with her predecessor's (authorial) architectural intentions, thus insinuating a perhaps unwarranted full continuity. While not explicitly contradicted anywhere in the text, such connection is perhaps formulated in stronger and more radical terms than those which the text actually supports. Nowhere in the *Decameron* prose is it stated that Pampinea would have liked her subjects to keep to a specific topic for the day, had they been afforded sufficient time to prepare. Second,

---

11 See Hollander's reasoning in "Utilità."

12 This exchange will happen more than once. In Pampinea's metanarrative interventions as well as in the stories she tells, one may perceive a distinct attention to the women's question, starting from the long prologue to *Decameron* I.10.3–8 (Mastro Alberto), where she attacks the vain and insipid women of her age, who are, she claims, no longer able to practise the socially valued art of *motteggiare*. Notably, after her story, which relates an example of precisely that feminine shortcoming, she passes the crown to Filomena, who, at the start of Day Six, will cite almost verbatim Pampinea's prologue to introduce the tale of an able *motteggiatrice*, Madonna Oretta, thus retrospectively endorsing her authoritative status and views.

and more importantly, Filomena's restrictive move is perfectly in character with her attentive delimitation of the scope of Pampinea's general initiative already at its point of origin in Santa Maria Novella. After all, Filomena was the one member of the assembling *brigata* who had articulated – and eventually imposed, with Elissa's help – the necessity of having men join the core company of the seven women on their retreat from Florence (I.Intro.74–5).[13]

That there may be something of an "institutional" overreach entailed in Filomena's move, when she attempts to amend Pampinea's constitution, is perhaps impossible to prove. Arguing the point would mean working from an actual silence in the text. There is one element, however, a slight but significant corrugation in the narrative which may indicate that Filomena's limitation follows only temporally (and thus not logically) Pampinea's first ruling act. It is quite remarkable that Dioneo reacts only to Filomena's specific restriction when asking for his narrative privilege: namely, to be kept free from the narrative yoke imposed on every other narrator in the *brigata*. In other words, *il privilegio di Dioneo* enters the mechanisms of the work not as an intrinsic requirement of his identity as a character, but as a conjunctural and political act, a balancing reaction to a specific and just as conjunctural choice on the part of Filomena. If we look more closely at the way in which the mechanisms of the *brigata* activities coalesce, we see that the ruling agenda for the communal life of the *brigata* is first devised by Pampinea (who sets narrative as the core of the day's work), then defined by Filomena (who establishes that, for each day, there will be a chosen topic – with the sole exception of Dioneo's free telling), and finally, as we are about to see, refined by Emilia (who introduces the exception to the one-topic-per-day habit, imposing a new kind of freedom).

Let us return to Emilia's own rulership. In choosing narrative freedom for her subjects, Emilia does two things at once. First, she fully exploits the power Pampinea has given the queens and kings of the days and uses it to return to the open-ended narration of Day One, undoing Filomena's restrictive move. Second, she establishes a new order, insofar as she introduces a relationship between Filomena's

13 The preoccupation with the hierarchy of gender as necessary to the social and political order of the *brigata* seems to be shared not only by Emilia but also by Filomena and Neifile, who corrected Pampinea's initial program of forming an exclusively female community, and eventually also by Fiammetta in her prologue to *novella* VII.5, where she too insists on deploying legal lexicon to frame gender and power dynamics in the institute of marriage. See Barolini, "A Philosophy of Consolation," 96. On the philosophical genealogy of the argument espoused here by Emilia, see also Sherberg, *The Governance of Friendship*, 100–6.

and Pampinea's "ordering" of things. Under Emilia's aegis, freedom is neither an absolute given (an initial state of narrative indeterminacy, as it was under Pampinea) nor an exception to a strict monothematic rule (as was the necessarily transgressive status of Dioneo, triggered by Filomena's restriction), but the result of the dialectical interplay between the two demands: the need to restore their energies in view of the challenges of the most engaged day, on the side of order, and the pleasure of unrestricted creativity, on the side of freedom. Freedom in Day Nine is, thus, presented as a function of the order that has been established at the convergence of Pampinea's and Filomena's successive acts as rulers.

With her meditated and mediated choice of a free topic for the day's narration, Emilia offers herself as a counter figure, or a mirror image, of both the first and primary ruler of the *brigata*, Pampinea, who had put no narrative restriction in place, and the second ruler, Filomena, who had made the restrictive principle of monothematic narrative the distinctive trait of her rulership – while following in all other aspects the model established by her predecessor. In choosing freedom as the specific narrative theme of her day, moreover, Emilia achieves an architectural institutionalization of Dioneo's personal exception. In her ruling over Day Nine, she shows that this kind of freedom can and should be folded back productively into the orderly setup of the narrative life and work of the society she momentarily controls.

Emilia's apparent return to the initial openness of theme has perhaps distracted from the legislative quality of her intervention, which perfects the law by including the exception to the norm. It is certainly possible that free-topic narration was only a contingent aspect of the *brigata*'s cohabitation contract (as Filomena claims), but it is also possible that this aspect was a structural one (the silence of the text on this point allows, at the very least, for the consideration of this option). When she declares her day to be one of temporary freedom in narrative choice, Emilia stretches Filomena's rule of focalized narration to include and reabsorb the free theme within a focalized perspective. In doing so, she ensures the strengthening of the community for which Pampinea had provided a constitutional law and, at the same time, protects it from any potentially restrictive implementation based on an overly rigid interpretation of its principles.

Emilia's Analogical Thinking: Work and Leisure

Emilia's executive act at the start of her queenship deserves a closer examination for the figurative language that she uses. As was the case for Pampinea's constitutive statement, pleasure is also a keyword in

Emilia's inaugural speech, but the valence of the term here is quite different from Pampinea's use of it in constituting the narrators' society. The triangulation established through the characters of Pampinea, Filomena, and Emilia brings to the fore the political aspect of the dialectical relationship between order and freedom which the *Decameron* explores at this juncture. Pampinea's constitution, Filomena's governance, and Emilia's refinement of the relationship between the two all work together to allow freedom to serve the rule of order, and thus ensure the continuation and health of the community. The same dialectic, which constitutes the core of civic life, is embedded in Emilia's metaphor of the oxen. Central is the social and economic aspect of the interrelation between freedom and order, one which she articulates in terms of the necessary and productive alternance between labour and leisure. Her speech pivots around these notions, which transpire from the analogical rhetoric she adopts:

> Dilettose donne, assai manifestamente veggiamo che, poi che i buoi alcuna parte del giorno hanno faticato sotto il giogo ristretti, quegli esser dal giogo alleviati e disciolti, e liberamente dove lor piú piace, per li boschi lasciati sono andare alla pastura … per le quali cose io estimo, avendo riguardo quanti giorni sotto certa legge ristretti ragionato abbiamo, che, sí come a bisognosi, di vagare alquanto e vagando riprender forze a rientrar sotto il giogo non solamente sia utile ma oportuno. (VIII.Concl.3–5)

> [Delectable ladies, we may readily observe that when oxen have labored in chains beneath the yoke for a certain portion of the day, their yoke is removed and they are put out to grass, being allowed to roam freely through the woods wherever they please … And therefore, having regard to the number of days during which our deliberations have been confined within a predetermined scheme, I consider that it would be both appropriate and useful for us to wander at large for a while, and in so doing recover the strength for returning once again beneath the yoke.]

While articulating her argument by way of a georgic analogy, Emilia never loses sight of the legal terminology that endows her thought with a collectivity-binding force. We know that Emilia indicates a specific reason for her choice. She embeds her idea of freedom in the metaphor she adopts to phrase (and frame) the narrative activities of Day Nine. For the first time she associates narration with the idea of labour. The *brigata*, we learn from her choice of language, has been restrained under the arbitrary rule of queens and kings, who have set the limits (and delimited the field) of their narration. She now feels the necessity to give free rein to her temporary subjects, in order for them to have their strengths restored. In this way, they will be ready to face the toils that will come, she anticipates, with the imposition of a new topic in Panfilo's day. The freedom Emilia imposes, i.e., the temporary respite from the labour of channelled storytelling, is connected to the orderly proceeding of the *brigata*'s life in two ways. It is freedom *with respect to* the social and economic mechanisms of associated life, but it is also instrumental to the achievement of a balanced condition in that dimension of life. In Emilia's speech, the leisure of freedom is ordained as necessary to the resumption of fruitful labour with the return of a single narrative theme in Day Ten.

In Emilia's words, one should note, this movement into freedom is both "utile" and "oportuno": not only is it useful, but also right and timely, taking place at the appropriate juncture in the company's activities. It is not coincidental that Emilia also sang a *ballata* in which the themes of activity and labour inflected the paradigm of contemplative life which she apparently constructed in her song. Accompanied by Dioneo at the end of Day One, under queen Pampinea, Emilia begins her performance by highlighting contemplative themes:

> Io son sì vaga della mia bellezza,
> che d'altro amor già mai
> non curerò né credo aver vaghezza.
> Io veggio in quella, ogn'or che io mi specchio,
> quel ben che fa contento lo 'ntelletto:
> né accidente nuovo o pensier vecchio
> mi può privar di sì caro diletto. (I.Concl.18–22)
>
> [In mine own beauty take I such delight
> That to no other love could I
> My fond affections plight
> Since in my looking-glass each hour I spy
> Beauty enough to satisfy the mind,
> Why seek out past delights, or new ones try
> When all content within my glass I find?]

The first impression gathered from the ballad suggests a possible association between Emilia and a Rachel-like figure of contemplation: she sings of a young woman who finds intellectual fulfilment every time she perceives and considers the beauty of her own image in the mirror. The lexicon she uses specifically alludes to contemplation: *gustando, appago, contento, diletto* are terms that tend to appear within contexts emphasizing the fulfilment associated with leading a "contemplative" life. Yet, through her potential relationship with another locus in Boccaccio's works, the *Comedía delle ninfe fiorentine,* Emilia also emerges as a figure connected to the active life, on par with all the young narrators, protagonists of the moral macro-tale of the *Decameron.* Both Emilia's diction and the image of the mirror, her pseudo-iconographic attribute of choice, provide connotations that allow for a less obvious reading of the image her ballad constructs. In Emilia's voice echoes the voice of Lia from the *Comedía,* in the ballad where she defines her identity not only as the watery daughter of Cefiso and Liriopè but also as a nymph who contemplates her own features in the mirror of her fatherly waves *only* in order to move her hands and adorn her image:

> [Cefiso] me ingenerò, lo qual tante fiate
> quant'io veggo onde, tante son costretta
> del mio padre onorar la deitate;
> avvegna che ciò far molto diletta
> a me per ciò che'n esse riguardando,
> mi rendon la mia forma leggiadretta.
> La qual come sia bella in me pensando,
> di verdi erbette, di rami e di fiori
> adorno lei d'ogni labe purgando. (*Comedia delle ninfe fiorentine* IV.10–18)

> [Cefiso] generated me; his divinity I am compelled to honor every time I look at the river waves. And I am delighted to do so, for in them I find mirrored my own fair image. Thinking how beautiful it is, I clean her of any impurity by adorning her with green shoots, twigs, and flowers.]

As Emilia will do in her turn, Lia here mobilizes the symbol of the mirror and the activity of self-contemplation, but she frames self-adornment as an active process of making. In so doing, Boccaccio's Lia is following in the footsteps of her Dantean namesake, the Lia appearing in *Purgatorio* 27 as the central figure in the protagonist's third and final dream, which he receives at the very threshold of Eden. Dante's Lia, too, uses her mirror as an instrument in an active process of adornment, as the interplay between lines 103 and 108 in her self-presentation establishes with some force:

> Sappia qualunque il mio nome dimanda
> ch'i' mi son Lia, e vo movendo intorno
> le belle mani a farmi una ghirlanda.
> Per piacermi a lo specchio, qui m'addorno;

ma mia suora Rachel mai non si smaga
dal suo miraglio, e siede tutto giorno.
Ell'è d'i' suoi belli occhi veder vaga
com'io de l'addornarmi con le mani;
lei lo vedere, e me l'ovrare appaga. (*Purg.* 27:100–8)

[Let anyone who asks for my name know that I am Lia, and I am moving my beautiful hands to make me a wreath. To like myself in the mirror, I adorn myself here; but my sister Rachel never takes her gaze from her mirror, and she sits all day. She is so eager to see her beautiful eyes as I am to embellish myself with my hands; seeing is what contents her, making contents me.]

The point which Dante's canto makes is perhaps a surprising one, but it is made with definitional clarity: while retaining her traditional connection to the active life, Lia is also associated with the mirror of contemplation, the same that is traditionally the exclusive purview of her sister Rachel. Lia's contemplation is presented, in other words, as one facet of her activity. Just as it appears in Dante's exemplar and in Boccaccio's own early poetry, the relation between Lia and Rachel, between contemplative and active life, is not one of mutual exclusivity but of harmonious coordination. This is true as well in Emilia's reign. Emilia's ballad frames her character in precisely the same balanced system of ethical determinants.[14]

Another element in Emilia's speech is worth bringing to the fore. Having established the principle that leisure, too, may serve to enforce order within work and freedom, she continues in the same metaphorical vein, stressing the idea of necessity. Several keywords, all pointing to determining factors, dot this new facet of her argument:

E per ciò quello che domane, seguendo il vostro dilettevole ragionar, sia da dire non intendo di ristrignervi sotto alcuna spezialità, ma voglio che ciascun secondo che gli piace ragioni, fermamente tenendo che la varietà delle cose che si diranno non meno graziosa ne fia che l'avere pur d'una parlato, e così avendo fatto, chi appresso di me nel reame verrà, sí come piú forti, con maggior sicurtà ne potrà nelle usate leggi ristrignere. (VIII.Concl.5)

14 This section of our argument has been developed in close dialogue with Ascoli's essay in this volume (cf. note 64, to which we refer readers for additional considerations).

> [Accordingly, when we resume our storytelling on the morrow, I do not propose to confine you to any particular topic; on the contrary, I desire that each of us should speak on whatever subject he or she may choose, it being my firm conviction that we shall find it no less rewarding to hear a variety of themes discussed than if we had restricted ourselves to one alone. Moreover, by doing as I have suggested, we shall all recruit our strength, and thus my successor will feel more justified in forcing us to observe our customary rule.]

In her words, Emilia makes clear that she will not restrict anyone within special limits ("spezialità"). The formula is not simply a polite litotes, based on a double negative; rather, it responds quite systemically and adds a new dimension to what Pampinea had previously established. While Pampinea had invited each narrator to follow their pleasure in telling stories, thus formulating her mandate in a positive way, Emilia technically insists on her choice not to limit their pleasure, and in this sense her determination is not a return to Pampinea's rule, but rather a reaction to that of Filomena.

Emilia thus serves the purpose of preparing the narrators for their final task: their return to the strictures of the *usate leggi*, the common law that has framed their activities thus far. While the last queen facilitates this move, she is not, one should note, strictly subservient to Panfilo.[15] Emilia presents her work as preparation for the narrative impulse to follow, incidentally given by the last male member of the *brigata*. Her work as handmaiden is in line with what she says, as a storyteller in her own queenship day, about the subordination of one sex to the other:

> E chi ha bisogno d'essere aiutato e governato, ogni ragion vuol lui dovere essere obidiente e subgetto e reverente all'aiutatori e al governator suo: e cui abbiam noi governatori e aiutatori se non gli uomini? Dunque agli uomini dobbiamo, sommamente onorandogli, soggiacere; e qual da questo si parte, estimo che degnissima sia non solamente di riprension grave ma d'aspro gastigamento. (IX.9.5)

15 Panfilo's own position is certainly one of relevance: as the last king he has the privilege of establishing the concluding (if not the dominant) note of the work. However, he is also the only king who is neither elected nor chosen. He is simply the last one remaining in the rotation, which means that no one has called upon him before, and it is his duty of bringing the experience to a conclusion which makes that condition a privilege – a privilege balanced by his forgoing the ability to choose a successor in turn.

> [And it stands to reason that those who need to be aided and governed must be submissive, obedient, and deferential to their benefactors and governors. But who are the governors and benefactors of us women, if they are not our menfolk? Hence we should always submit to men's will, and do them all possible honor, and any woman who behaves differently is worthy, in my opinion, not only of severe censure, but of harsh punishment.]

For Emilia, this cooperative subordination is part of the natural order. In this sense, she is also in line with Filomena and Elissa in their initial resistance to Pampinea's idea of constituting an all-female society. In Day One, as a latter-day Ippolita, Pampinea did not seem interested in establishing an inter-gender community and was thus not invested in foreseeing any inter-gender relational structure. For Emilia, as for Filomena and Elissa, instead, this relation is not only necessary but also framed in hierarchical terms.[16] For them, women are created weak in body and spirit, and naturally subject to the rule of men:

> Amabili donne, se con sana mente sarà riguardato l'ordine delle cose, assai leggermente si conoscerà tutta la universal moltitudine delle femine dalla natura e da' costumi e dalle leggi essere agli uomini sottomessa e secondo la discrezione di quegli convenirsi reggere e governare, e però, a ciascuna, che quiete, consolazione e riposo vuole con quegli uomini avere a' quali s'appartiene, dee essere umile, paziente e ubidiente oltre all'essere onesta, il che è sommo e spezial tesoro di ciascuna savia. E quando a questo le leggi, le quali il ben comune riguardano in tutte le cose, non ci ammaestrassono, e l'usanza o costume che vogliam dire, le cui forze son grandissime e reverende, la natura assai apertamente cel mostra, la quale ci ha fatte ne' corpi dilicate e morbide, negli animi timide e paurose, nelle menti benigne e pietose, e hacci date le corporali forze leggieri, le voci piacevoli e i movimenti de' membri soavi: cose tutte testificanti noi avere dell'altrui governo bisogno. (IX.9.3–4)

> [Lovable ladies, if the order of things is impartially considered, it will quickly be apparent that the vast majority of women are through nature and customs, as well as in law, subservient to men, by whose opinions their conduct and actions are bound to be governed. It therefore behooves any woman who seeks a calm, contented and untroubled life with her

16 For these issues, see Barolini, "Sociology of the *Brigata*" and "'Le parole son femmine.'"

> menfolk, to be humble, patient, and obedient, besides being virtuous, a quality that every judicious woman considers her special and most valued possession. Even if these lessons were not taught to us by the law, which in all things is directed to the common good, and by usage (or custom as we have called it), nature proves it to us very plainly, for she has made us soft and fragile of body, timid and fearful of heart, compassionate and benign of disposition, and has furnished us with meagre physical strength, pleasing voices, and gently moving limbs. All of which shows that we need to be governed by others.]

Emilia, who narrates *novelle* with strong female characters such as Madama Beritola, Simona, and Madonna Dianora, is nonetheless convinced that in the "order of things" women are naturally subordinate to men, and their virtues should be humility, patience, and obedience as well as honesty. This is not only evident – she argues – from laws, customs, and traditions (which had a strong power of coercion), but it is written in the very code of nature. Rebellion against natural law deserves punishment similar to what is meted out in her narration of *novella* IX.9 according to Solomon's judgment. Yet Emilia governs, organizes, and defines freedom in her day in a more philosophically sophisticated way than the rhetorically wise Pampinea.

The order of nature entails a partial divergence for Emilia and Pampinea. While Pampinea invokes natural order as the principle that establishes self-preservation as a general rule of human behaviour, for Emilia the same notion guarantees the social status quo when it comes to the "natural" subaltern status of women to men. The discrepancy is quite remarkable: Pampinea never endorsed the principle of subjugation spelled out in Santa Maria Novella – she accepts the company of men but does not in any way acknowledge their superiority. Emilia, on the other hand, insinuates in her narrative that when this order is contravened, the immune system of the threatened social organism reacts, and bad things happen to women.

The divergence of Pampinea and Emilia on this point will also emerge in the interplay between their respective stories, those of Talano d'Imolese (IX.7) and Solomon (IX.9), as the readings of these two *novelle* included in this volume will show. Two elements are crucial to their dialogue, both articulated on the level of the diction they adopt. First, the tricolon with which Emilia responds to Pampinea's profile of the shrew – on the one hand, the woman is "sopra ogni altra bizzarra, spiacevole e ritrosa"; on the other hand, according to Emilia, each woman "dee essere umile, paziente e ubidiente – oltre all'essere onesta" and all should be "piacevoli, benivole, pieghevoli." The opposition surrounding the behaviour of Talano's wife is also marked: for Pampinea, her mistake was her inability to have faith in the truth-telling power of the dream (she treated it as a projection of the husband's desires); for Emilia, instead, the problem is her unruliness, for which she is punished. Hence, Emilia's story will insist on the necessary qualities which women should possess in order to conform to their natural subordination to men. While Emilia views the punishment in terms of the natural order, in Talano's story there is no mention of any breach of that principle.

The second element of divergence is their sense of the role that *il diritto* should play in society. For Emilia, the law follows, logically and chronologically, nature and custom: "come la natura, l'usanza e le leggi vogliono." In this sense, and in accordance with medieval conceptions of the law, both *legge* and *usanza* are rooted in nature.[17] On the contrary, for Pampinea what matters is the projective force of law, which should not only ratify what exists but also produce the framework for new species of socio-economic relations and interpersonal dynamics relevant to the functioning and well-being of the community.

17 For the concepts of tradition, custom, law, and natural law in the Middle Ages, see Maglio, *La coscienza giuridica medievale*.

Love and Death in Pistoia: *Decameron* IX.1 between Poetry and History

DAVID LUMMUS

Introduction

At first glance, the first tale of the Ninth Day of the *Decameron*, told by Filomena, seems unexceptional. It is yet another farcical take on the lofty notions of love poetry that pits naïve male lovers against a conniving female intellect. It is realistic in its setting and principal characters, but not so much that it becomes a chronicle of quotidian or historical events. The way in which the plot literalizes the metaphorical language of the love lyric is familiar. It is repetitive and repeatable and it has garnered very little critical or creative attention over the centuries since its composition.[1]

Filomena seems to enact an awareness of the difficulty of continuing to tell stories after eight days. Her preamble opens by speaking of storytelling in terms of sport and competition:

> Madonna, assai m'aggrada, poi che vi piace, che per questo campo aperto e libero, nel quale la vostra magnificenza n'ha messi, del novellare, d'esser

---

1 I should like to thank Nicola Esposito and Sabrina Ferri for their feedback on a draft of this *lectura*, as well as colleagues at Dartmouth, Notre Dame, and the Opera del Vocabolario Italiano for their helpful comments when I presented this as a work in progress.

Surprisingly few critics have given this tale attention, while those who have paid it regard tend to dedicate very little space to it in broader thematic readings. Baratto (*Realtà e stile* [1984], 101–9 and 115–18) is struck by its realism and sees it as a parable, grouping it together with several other realistic tales that seem to have no identifiable source and are set in the recent Tuscan past. Bàrberi Squarotti ("*Decameron*," esp. 46–8) shows how it engages with the tradition of the *servizio d'amore*. Gittes ("'Dal giogo alleviati,'" 389–91) sees in its parody of courtly love commonplaces a reflection on gaining one's freedom. On the reception of this tale in fifteenth- and sixteenth-century Germany, see Cammarota, "La storia di Donna Francesca."

> colei che corra il primo aringo, il quale se ben farò, non dubito che quegli che appresso verranno non facciano bene e meglio. (IX.1.2)
>
> [Since it is your wish, my lady, that I should be the first to sally forth into this broad and spacious arena to which we have been brought by your bounteous decree, I shall do so with the greatest of pleasure. And if I should acquit myself favorably therein, I daresay those who follow me will do as well as I, and even better.][2]

She draws an analogy to a contest of racing or jousting ("aringo"), perhaps forecasting the more competitive spirit that will gradually overtake the storytellers during Day Nine and dominate the frame of Day Ten.[3] The mention of physicality may also denote that the fulfilment of pleasure in the act of storytelling requires the expenditure of effort, or work, and that it is not just play. She nevertheless allows for the tale's shortcoming – its main theme is well-trodden territory.

> Molte volte s'è, o vezzose donne, ne' nostri ragionamenti mostrato quante e quali sieno le forze d'amore; né però credo che pienamente se ne sia detto, né sarebbe ancora, se di qui ad uno anno d'altro che di ciò non parlassimo. (IX.1.3)
>
> [In the course of our conversations, dear ladies, we have repeatedly seen how great and mighty are the forces of Love. Yet I do not think we have fully exhausted the subject, nor would we do so if we were to talk of nothing else for a whole year.]

Her excuse for the repetition is that there is an almost infinite wealth of material about love. In what seems an effort to account for the thematic repetition, she combines it with the popular theme of womanly intelligence: "non solamente la potenzia d'amore comprenderete, ma il senno da una valorosa donna usato a torsi da dosso due che contro al suo piacere l'amavan, cognoscerete" [you will not only comprehend the power of Love, but learn of the ingenious means employed by a

---

2 All quotations from the *Decameron* are from Branca's 1967 edition for *Tutte le opere*. English translations are from McWilliam's 1995 Penguin translation. Unless otherwise noted, all other translations are my own.

3 A similar turn of phrase is also used by Elissa at the beginning of II.8. For an example of how the members of the *brigata* are responding to each other in Day Nine, see Fiammetta's reaction to Lauretta's tale at the beginning of IX.5. On the competitive tone of Day Ten, see Hollander and Cahill, "Day Ten of the *Decameron*."

worthy lady to rid herself of two unwanted admirers (IX.1.4)]. In fact, despite Filomena's efforts to make it stand apart from the rest, the tale will feel immediately familiar to readers after the stories of deceit and trickery of Days Seven and Eight and the tales of love and desire that populate the *Decameron* as a whole.[4]

The story tells of how Francesca de' Lazzari, a beautiful widow in Pistoia, devises an intelligent way to get rid of the two men who are courting her, Alessandro Chiarmontesi and Rinuccio Palermini, Florentine exiles living in Pistoia.[5] Her plan is to promise her love to each separately if each completes what she thinks to be an impossible task. She has her maid tell Alessandro to go by night to the grave of the recently buried Scannadio, a seemingly invented character who happens to be the most evil man in the world, and to pretend to be the corpse, so that when her family goes to retrieve it, they will bring him to her. Rinuccio must go later on the same night to bring the corpse to her, so that her family can take it. Each man believes that he will end up alone with her to take his pleasure. Although they are both plagued by doubts and fears along the way, the two lovers independently complete their tasks, neither knowing the other is involved, only to be interrupted on her doorstep by the city's night watch, which frightens them away before either has a chance to realize it is a trick. The next morning the city is abuzz with rumours about Scannadio's empty tomb, and Francesca has a good excuse to deny her suitors access.

Playing on the link to the biblical Lazarus in Francesca's family name,[6] the story's parody of resurrection explores in humorous terms how love has the power to drive men to madness and thence to the grave. The adventures of the two Florentines end rather well, given the circumstances. They are not harmed or killed while completing their tasks, but neither are their wishes granted. The lady ends up free of her

4 Many of the themes that this story repeats derive from I.1, where Ciappelletto is called the most evil man in the world in almost exactly the same terms as Scannadio, and II.5, where Andreuccio's fear upon entrapment in the tomb is described in very similar terms to that of Alessandro. Further similarities are noticeable with I.10, where Maestro Alberto teaches a woman a lesson about love, II.1, where Martellino pretends to be cured of his paralysis when placed on top of Saint Arrigo's body in Treviso, and VI.9, where Guido Cavalcanti is cornered in a graveyard, just to mention a few specific examples. Verbiage from this last tale is employed here in Filomena's preamble, in which tombs are referenced as "le case de' morti" [the houses of the dead (IX.1.4)].

5 Only one other story takes place in Pistoia: III.5. Another Palermini (Aldobrandino) is protagonist of III.7, in which he is also framed for murder (and later exculpated).

6 See Gittes, "'Dal giogo alleviati,'" 390–1.

annoying suitors and the men end up no worse than they had started. The simplicity of the story's comic plot is betrayed by its complex interplay with the motif of love and death inherited from the lyric tradition. As in other *novelle* that deal with the nature of love, Boccaccio lowers the reflections of lyric poetry about a stable metaphysical reality, testing and revising their applicability to a constantly changing historical world populated by desiring bodies.[7] More than just a comic parody of the motifs of the love lyric tradition, this story develops these themes in space and time in order to propose a new ethics of desire that is both based on and different from that of the previous generation's poets.

Furthermore, the minor details that the narrator provides about the identity of the characters and the setting of the events ask readers to reconcile the tale's reflection on love and death with the geopolitical reality that underlies the narrative. The two main Florentine characters belong to White Guelph families, some of whom had been Ghibelline, while Francesca de' Lazzari was a member of a long-standing Guelph family that belonged to the Black faction. Pistoia itself was one of the most factious cities of late medieval Italy and was the point of origin of the divisions between White and Black Guelphs linked to the exile of Dante, Petrarch's father, and many others in 1302.[8] In *Inferno* 24 and 25, Dante immortalized the thief and Black Guelph Vanni Fucci de' Lazzari and inveighed against Pistoia:

> Ahi Pistoia, Pistoia, ché non stanzi
> d'incenerarti sì che più non duri,
> poi che 'n mal fare il seme tuo avanzi? (25.10–12)
>
> [Ah, Pistoia, Pistoia, why do you not decree your incineration, so that you may not endure, since you surpass your sowers in doing ill?][9]

7 For the theoretical premises of this kind of reading, see Forni, *Adventures in Speech*, esp. 43–88 on the "Poetics of Realization." See also Mazzotta, *The World at Play*, 70. As examples of this approach, which sees a kind of critique in the literalization of poetic metaphor, see Forni, "Boccaccio tra Dante e Cino," and Barsella, "Boccaccio e Cino da Pistoia." On Boccaccio's poetics of the body across his works, see Kriesel, *Boccaccio's Corpus*. See also Lummus, "The *Decameron* and Boccaccio's Poetics," where Boccaccio's discussion of poetics in the *Genealogie Deorum Gentilium* is posited as the theoretical foundation of his humble poetics in the *Decameron*. As an example of how Boccaccio uses the concretization of poetic metaphor in his narratives to link poetic reflection to lived experience, see Lummus, "Boccaccio's Three Venuses," 77–80.

8 See Guido Pampaloni in *Enciclopedia Dantesca*, s.v. "Bianchi e Neri."

9 All quotations and translations from Dante's *Comedy* are from the edition and translation by Durling.

Even Petrarch, in his eulogy of friend and fellow poet Cino dei Sinibaldi, couldn't resist a jab at the divisive city: "Pianga Pistoia, e i citadin perversi / che perduto ànno sí dolce vicino" [Let Pistoia weep and her wicked citizens, who have lost so sweet a neighbor (*Lyric Poems* 92.12–13)].[10] As one of two *novelle* set in Pistoia, Filomena's humorous rendering of the effects of mad love should also be viewed in its engagement with the complex geopolitical relationship between Florence and Pistoia during the late thirteenth and early fourteenth centuries. The historical and geographical details embedded in Boccaccio's fiction act as identifying markers that allow the reader to link the world of history with the reflections of lyric poetry.

In what follows, I will first offer a close textual reading of the tale that shows how it takes the language of love and death, connected with the theme of *fol'amors*, or mad love, from the Provençal lyric tradition, and sets it in an embodied and historical narrative time-space. As I will show, Filomena's tale engages with the negative love experience exemplified in the lyrics of Guido Cavalcanti and in the fifth canto of Dante's *Inferno*. The main female character of the story is a rewriting of Francesca da Rimini from the *Inferno*, with whom she shares a name. Then I will trace the historical origins of the tale's setting and characters, outlining how the story links the motif of love and death with the geopolitical realities that form its backdrop. These two connected readings show how much Boccaccio relied upon readers' knowledge of both the literary intertexts and the historical subtexts at work in the story. In the search for meaning in the *Decameron*'s stories, readers must trace the way fiction brings poetry to bear on history. This seemingly unexceptional story's parody of love poetry concretizes the language of love in order to critique the form of mad desire that leads both lovers and cities to ruin.[11]

Boccaccio between Cavalcanti and Dante: The Poetic Intertext

Filomena signals in her preamble that her story will deal with a concrete, material manifestation of love's power, not merely its effects on

10 All quotations and translations from Petrarch's *Canzoniere* are from the edition and translation by Durling (*Petrarch's Lyric Poems*).

11 It is important to note that in the troubadour tradition *fol'amors* essentially denotes a misdirected desire aimed at physical consummation. For a poet like Cavalcanti, however, the concept develops into a psychological and indeed metaphysical illness akin to madness.

the state of mind of the lover. In its exploration of the power of love, the story will show how love brings lovers to death's door: "[amore] non solamente a vari dubbi di dover morire gli amanti conduce ma quegli ancora ad entrare nelle case de' morti per morti tira" [Love not only leads lovers into divers situations fraught with mortal peril, but will even induce them to enter the houses of the dead in the guise of corpses (IX.1.4)]. Although there is no sign that Filomena intends this description to be humorous, with it she reduces the terms of her engagement with the philosophical question of love's influence on the male lover's psyche to a materialization that places men's bodies in different kinds of physical movement. Her story will show that love causes men – literally – to enter into tombs as if they were dead. It is important to keep in mind, however, that at the beginning of the following story, "non amor ma pazzia era stata tenuta da tutti l'ardita presunzione degli amanti" [one and all described not as love but as folly the daring presumption of the lovers (IX.2.2)]. That is, the story recounts the effects of a specific kind of affection, known as *fol'amors*, or mad love – the same kind of desire that led Dante's Francesca da Rimini and Paolo Malatesta "ad una morte" [to one death (*Inferno* 5.106)].

It is not necessary to seek out a specific poetic origin for the subject of Filomena's tale. The combined themes of madness and death have long been commonplace in love poetry, especially the Tuscan love lyric of the late thirteenth and early fourteenth centuries. In the lyrics of Guido Cavalcanti, however, the experience of the lover is more macabre and self-destructive than in the work of any of Boccaccio's precursors. They will therefore serve as exemplary for the current inquiry. A line from Cavalcanti's "Donna me prega" best expresses the idea that forms the lyric basis of Filomena's story:

> Di sua potenza segue spesso morte,
> se forte – la vertù fosse impedita,
> la quale aita – la contraria via. (35–7)[12]
>
> [Death is often the result of [Love's] power,
> if the ability should be blocked,
> which aids the way against [Love].]

12 All quotations from the lyrics of Guido Cavalcanti are from the *Antologia della poesia italiana*, edited by Segre and Ossola. When citing lyric poetry, references are to verse numbers, unless the entire poem is cited, in which case page numbers are provided.

Filomena's narrative playfully echoes at several points such a link between love and death.[13]

In IX.1, Rinuccio and Alessandro are tricked into thinking that the "servigio" [service (IX.1.7)] requested by Francesca will allow them to fulfil their desire for her. The basic pretence of the story's action derives from the commonplace of the lover's service to the god of love by serving his beloved, or *servizio d'amore*. Already a topos of Roman elegy (as *servitium amoris*) and the lyrics of the troubadours (as *dompneis*), the lover's service to his lady was codified in Andreas Capellanus's *De amore* and was often a stimulus to narrative action in romances such as Chrétien de Troyes's *Lancelot ou le Chevalier de la charrette*. In the tradition of courtly love, this service would lead to a refinement of the lover's character and possibly to the fulfilment of the lover's desire. The relationship established between lover and beloved was ideally reciprocal, even if the lover was often left without physical fulfilment.

One well-known example of how *servizio d'amore* could turn against the lover and lead to death is expressed in Cavalcanti's sonnet "Li mie' foll' occhi" – one of several poems whose circumstances could be at the basis of IX.1.[14] Here Cavalcanti employs this topos together with that of *follia*, or madness, linking his experience of desire with death:

Li mie' foll' occhi, che prima guardaro
vostra figura piena di valore,
fuôr quei che di voi, donna, m'acusaro
nel fero loco ove ten corte Amore,
e mantinente avanti lui mostraro
ch' io era fatto vostro servidore:
per che sospiri e dolor mi pigliaro,

13 It is important to note that Boccaccio's engagement with Cavalcanti goes beyond creative allusion. It is well known that he copied "Donna me prega" in the Chigi codex (MS Chigi L V 176) and included the glosses by Dino del Garbo. On Cavalcanti, the del Garbo commentary, and the Chigi's significance for understanding aspects of the *Decameron*, see Eisner, *Boccaccio and the Invention of Italian Literature*, 95–112.

14 Many of Cavalcanti's lyrics on the negative effect of love on cognition could be at the basis of this story's engagement with the motif of love and death, just as several of Cino da Pistoia's poems would work as well, such as "Degno son io ch'io mora" or "La dolce vista e 'l bel guardo soave." The philosophical manifesto on the topic would necessarily be, however, Cavalcanti's "Donna me prega." Except for a few references to this complicated *canzone*, I have chosen shorter, more manageable poems to address the topic in relation to Boccaccio's *novella*. On the representation of this kind of love in relation to Cavalcanti's influence on Dante, see Barolini, "Dante and Cavalcanti."

vedendo che temenza avea lo core.
Menârmi tosto, sanza riposanza,
in una parte là'v' i' trovai gente
che ciascun si doleva d'Amor forte,
Quando mi vider, tutti con pietanza
dissermi: "Fatto se' di tal servente,
che mai non déi sperare altro che morte." (400–1)

[My mad eyes, which first looked upon
your form, full of worth,
were what accused me of being yours, lady,
in the savage place where Love holds court,
and in that moment before Him they made clear
that I had been made your servant:
for which sighs and sadness took hold of me,
seeing that fear held my heart.
They led me quickly and without repose,
to a place where I found people
who all suffered greatly with Love.
When they saw me, together they said to me
with pity: "You have been made servant to such a one,
that you mustn't hope for anything except death."]

This poem provides the skeleton of a story about a man who is found to be engaged in hopeless servitude to his beloved. The lyric subject is filled with fear as he is led without rest from the harshness of love's court to an isolated place where nothing is left but suffering and death.

There are several intersections between the premises of the sonnet and those of the *novella*. Cavalcanti's philosophical lyric elevates the notion of *servizio d'amore* and the metaphors of madness and love unto death so that they are no longer located within a verisimilar socio-historical reality, such as a court.[15] They have become a part of a figurative language used to describe human emotion and cognition. Boccaccio, however, brings these notions back down to earth by giving names, histories, and personalities to the human actors within concrete situations of desire.

15 In the Old French and Provençal tradition, the court of Love was already a psychological allegory rather than a realistic setting. In the Italian tradition, however, Love's court continues its separation from physical reality on its way to becoming fully metaphysical.

The beloved of the lyric subject in the sonnet, as is common in the *stilnovo* tradition, is reduced to the minimum level of embodiment by the male gaze. His eyes look onto her "figura," or form, and ascribe value to it. Unlike the *stilnovo* beloved, Francesca has a name and a lineage. She is also a "bellissima vedova" [very beautiful widow (IX.1.5)], which puts her in the same category of Boccaccian heroines as Ghismonda in *Decameron* IV.1. Her social status implies not only a certain youth but also a sophisticated knowledge of the world of love. Like the beloved in the sonnet, however, whose form is "full of worth," Francesca is also a noble lady, described similarly as "una valorosa donna" [a worthy lady (IX.1.4)]. The narrative moves away from the lyric's abstraction of feminine value in order to restore nobility of spirit and social standing to the woman qua woman.

Furthermore, the task that Francesca sets for her two lovers comically literalizes the end that the lyric subject imagines for himself in the sonnet as a result of his slavery to his beloved. He must hope for death, while the two lovers must physically mime a proximity to death as an act of servitude to Francesca. The lyric subject's fear is also mimicked by the two men, who are both almost overcome by their imaginations as they approach the tomb of Scannadio. Alessandro conjures up several possibilities by which he might end up truly dead and not just dressed as a dead man, such that "fu tutto che tornato a casa" [he was on the point of turning around and going back home (IX.1.24)]. Similarly, Rinuccio "in molti e varii pensieri entrò delle cose possibili a intervenirgli" [was assailed by a multitude of thoughts on the various things that might happen to him] and was "tutto che rattenuto" [all but deterred from going on (IX.1.27)]. In both cases, their love for Francesca and their fear of losing her good graces keep them from abandoning their tasks.

Another element of the story evokes a common motif in the negative experience of love, according to which the lover experiences spiritual frustration. In Cavalcanti's lyrics, this experience is described as *sbigottimento*, or a sense of dejection. In another of his sonnets, Cavalcanti writes:

> L'anima mia vilment'è sbigotita
> de la battaglia ch' e[l]l' ave dal core:
> che·ss'ella sente pur un poco Amore
> più presso a lui che non sòle, ella more.
> Sta come quella che non à valore,
> ch'è per temenza da lo cor partita;
> e chi vedesse com' ell' è fuggita
> diria per certo: "Questi non ha vita." (1–8)

[My soul is vilely dejected
by the assault it has had from the heart:
such that if the soul feels Love just a little
closer to the heart than usual, the soul will die.
It is like a soul without worth
that has left the heart out of fear;
and whoever should see how it fled
would say for sure: "This man has no life."]

Here, as in the earlier poem, Cavalcanti links the experience of love to fear and lifelessness of the soul, which has been engaged in a struggle for control over the heart. Whereas for Cavalcanti's lyric subject a battle takes place physiologically and psychologically within the human body and mind, in the narrative economy of the story both Alessandro and Rinuccio become dejected in a more mundane way. Upon being discovered, Rinuccio is "dolente e bestemmiando la sua sventura" [heartbroken ... and cursed his evil luck], just as Alessandro is "dolente di tale sciagura" [bitterly disappointed that things should have turned out so disastrously (IX.1.34)]. Alessandro experiences a bodily version of this dejection when Rinuccio drops his body in the street, a scene that is variously described from the narrator's perspective as "lasciatosi cadere Alessandro" [let Alessandro fall (IX.1.31)], from Francesca's perspective as "veder gittar giuso Alessandro" [seeing Alessandro being thrown down (IX.1.32)], and from Rinuccio's perspective as "dove Alessandro aveva gittato" [where he had thrown Alessandro (IX.1.34)]. The lyric subject's spiritual struggle and anguish are acted out in a theatrical farce that is presented to the reader from different perspectives, as Alessandro loses control not of his heart, but of his body.

This story also describes the negative experience of desire in terms that echo Dante's famous encounter with Francesca da Rimini in *Inferno* 5, which itself is linked to the Cavalcantian representation of love, as Teodolinda Barolini has shown.[16] Before his body is dropped to the ground, Alessandro experiences the assault of love, which Cavalcanti had described so sublimely, as a series of bumps and bangs on his body. In the internal monologue in which his fears manifest themselves in the story, Alessandro expresses his concern that Francesca's relatives "mi cacciasser gli occhi o mi traessero i denti o mozzassermi le mani o facessermi alcuno altro così fatto giuoco" [[might] gouge my eyes out, or wrench out my teeth, or cut off my hands, or do me some other piece

16 See Barolini, "Dante and Cavalcanti."

of mischief (IX.1.22)]. In place of these fantasies of physical torment, which are reminiscent of a kind of Giottesque Hell, Alessandro's body is carelessly battered here and there as Rinuccio carries him down the street:

> e così andando e non riguardandolo altramenti, spesse volte il percoteva ora in un canto e ora in un altro d'alcune panche che allato alla via erano; e la notte era sí buia e sí oscura che egli non poteva discernere ove s'andava. (IX.1.29)
>
> [It was such a dark night that he couldn't really see where he was going, and being none too particular about his burden, he frequently banged Alessandro's body on one side and the other of certain benches that were set along the side of the street.]

The language of this description can be connected to Dante's description of the punishment of the lustful:

> Io venni in loco d'ogne luce muto,
> che mugghia come fa mar per tempesta,
> se da contrari venti è combattuto.
> La bufera infernal, che mai non resta,
> mena li spirti con la sua rapina;
> voltando e percotendo li molesta.
> Quando giungon davanti a la ruina,
> quivi le strida, il compianto, il lamento;
> bestemmian quivi la virtù divina.
> Intesi ch'a così fatto tormento
> enno dannati i peccator carnali,
> che la ragion sommettono al talento.
> E come li stornei ne portan l'ali
> nel freddo tempo, a schiera larga e piena,
> così quel fiato li spiriti mali
> di qua, di là, di giù, di sù li mena;
> nulla speranza li conforta mai,
> non che di posa, ma di minor pena. (*Inferno* 5.28–45)
>
> [I came to a place where all light is silent, that groans like the sea in a storm, when it is lashed by conflicting winds. The infernal whirlwind, which never rests, drives the spirits before its violence; turning and striking, it tortures them. When they come before the landslide, there the shrieks, the wailing, the lamenting; there they curse God's power. I understood that

to this torment were damned the carnal sinners, who subject their reason to their lust. And as their wings carry off the starlings in the cold season, in large full flocks, so does that breath carry the evil spirits here, there, down, up; no hope ever comforts them, not of lessened suffering, much less of rest.]

First, the verb used to describe how Rinuccio inadvertently swings Alessandro's body against the benches along the street – *percuotere*, to beat or strike – is the same that is used in line 33 to describe how the souls of the lustful are beaten by the infernal wind. Soon after, at line 43, Dante specifies that the wind drives the damned lovers hither and thither, which may be at the basis of the ridiculous description of Rinuccio banging Alessandro's body on this side and that side of the street, because he simply cannot see where he is going. Finally, the darkness of the setting of the street scene evokes the absolute darkness of line 28, which Barolini has argued is directly related to Cavalcanti's lines in "Donna me prega" about the formation of love from darkness and its location in darkness.[17]

The movement of the story's plot from a place of love to a place of suffering also seems evocative of Dante's Cavalcantian punishment of the lustful. To return to the first example that I chose above, in "Li mie' foll'occhi" Cavalcanti describes the subject's movement from the "savage place" of Love's court to "a place where I found people / who all suffered greatly with Love." In a darker vein than Thibaut of Champagne's description of a lover's prison in "Ausi conme unicorne sui,"[18] such a prison is at the basis of the circle of the lustful in Dante's *Inferno*, where the pilgrim descends to hear the "dolenti note" [grief-stricken notes (5.25)] of the souls who inhabit the "doloroso ospizio" [dolorous hospice (5.16)]. In Filomena's story, the movement from the abode of love to the darker environment of the tomb, where Rinuccio

17 See ibid., 41, where Barolini points to the following lines from "Donna me prega": "sì formato, come / diaffan da lume, d' una scuritate" [thus formed, as transparency by light, by a darkness (16–17; 406)] and "assiso 'n mezzo scuro, luc' e' rade" [it takes its place in a dark medium, and excludes the light (68; 409)].

18 "Dame, quant je devant vous fui, / Et je vous vi premierement, / Mes cuers aloit si tressaillant / Qu'il vous remest, quant je m'en mui. / Lors fu menez sans raençon / En la douce chartre en prison / Dont li piler sont de talent / Et li huis sont de biau veior / Et li anel de bon espoir" [Lady, when I was in your presence, / And I saw you for the first time, / My heart trembled such / That it remained yours, after I had gone away. / Then it was led without ransom / Into the sweet jail, imprisoned / Whose pillars are of desire / And whose doors are of beauty / And whose chains are of good hope (Thibaut de Champagne, *Les chansons*, "Ausi conme" 10–19; 113)].

and Alessandro will suffer fear and doubt, is linked explicitly to a voyage to Hell in their responses to Francesca's maid: "risposto fu da ognuno che non che in una sepoltura ma in Inferno andrebber, quando le piacesse" [in each case receiving the same answer, namely that they would venture into Hell itself, let alone a tomb, if she wanted them to do so (IX.1.18)]. So far as the story of the two men is concerned, the story demonstrates in a comic vein the power of love to bring men to death's door, making them act out the mad lover's courtship of death.[19] Its narrative arc follows a broadly Cavalcantian experience of love that also comically echoes Dante's punishment of the lustful in *Inferno* 5.

If the tale of the two men's misadventures is linked to a primarily Cavalcantian intertext and is meant to demonstrate the power of love to lead men to the grave, the story of Francesca de' Lazzari can be understood by way of the Dantean intertext as a reappraisal of the character traits of Francesca da Rimini as Boccaccio understood them. One of the purposes of Filomena's story, after all, is to demonstrate a woman's *senno*, or intelligence, in the context of the negative power of love. Dante's Francesca, like all carnal sinners, ended up in hell because she made reason subject to desire. Dante's definition of lust, as Barolini has convincingly argued,[20] is itself linked to Cavalcanti's negative vision of love in "Donna me prega," where he writes that love

for di salute giudicar mantene,
ché la'ntenzione per ragione vale:
discerne male in cui è vizio amico. (32–4)

[keeps our judgment away from well-being,
because desire stands in place of reason:
whoever has this vice discerns poorly.]

From this perspective, then, in contrast to Francesca da Rimini, Francesca de' Lazzari is an example of how a woman's intelligence can maintain the upper hand in its confrontation with desire.

---

19 It is worth mentioning that what happens to the two characters will later form the basis of idiomatic terms for the fawning lover: Alessandro is the *cascamorto* (lit. fall-over-dead), whereas Rinuccio is the *beccamorto* (lit. gravedigger). It is possible that these two expressions were already a part of the spoken idiom, even if no written evidence is available to prove it.

20 See Barolini, "Dante and Cavalcanti," 38. It is probable that Dante's definition of lust, along with that of Cavalcanti, was related to earlier sources as well, such as Brunetto Latini's *Tresor*. On the parallels with Latini's chapter on chastity in the *Tresor* (II.20.6), see Mazzoni, "Il canto V dell'*Inferno*," 108–9.

The story of Dante's Francesca is emblematic of how natural erotic desire combined with the fantasy of romance all but forces youth to death, causing the breakup of a dynastic marriage.[21] Her monologue in the poem is a tour de force in self-exculpation in the name of the power of love. Following the courtly commonplace that "Amor ch'a nullo amato amar perdona" [Love, which pardons no one loved from loving in return (*Inferno* 5.103)], she claims to have had no choice but to reciprocate her brother-in-law Paolo's love. In his *Esposizioni sopra la Comedia di Dante*, Boccaccio attempts to attenuate her guilt by setting the moment of her falling in love with Paolo before her wedding with Gianciotto and by giving her the same "altiero animo" [proudness of heart (esp. litt. V.148)] that is used to characterize Ghismonda ("animo altiero") in *Decameron* IV.1.30. Boccaccio tells the story of how she was tricked by her father into thinking that she would marry Paolo instead of his brother Gianciotto, so that when she realized she had been tricked, she became furious and did not abandon her illicit love. When Gianciotto is informed of their affair and interrupts them *in flagrante delicto*, he aims to kill only his brother, but is forced to murder Francesca as well when she places herself between them.[22]

The Francesca of Filomena's tale is a kind of alter ego to Dante's Francesca. In an alternate reality, what would Francesca of Rimini have learned from her experience of love's power had she outlived Gianciotto to become a widow? Most of all, Francesca de' Lazzari feels no obligation to reciprocate the love of the men by whom she is courted. She violates the courtly dictum that Dante's Francesca uses as her excuse, thus avoiding the moral conundrum in which Francesca da Rimini found herself trapped. Like most of the widows in the *Decameron*, Francesca de' Lazzari has gained a kind of knowledge provided by experience of the world – both amorous and otherwise. If, in Boccaccio's version of the story in the *Esposizioni*, Dante's Francesca was able to be tricked because of the power of love over her mind, which made desire stronger than reason, then Filomena's Francesca is able to see things more clearly. Although she may have been unwise enough to accommodate her male suitors at the beginning,[23] she quickly grows weary of their advances and devises a ruse to trick them. Evoking the

---

21 On Dante's representation of Francesca da Rimini and on the additions to her story in the commentary tradition, see Barolini, "Dante and Francesca da Rimini."

22 See Boccaccio, *Esposizioni*, 317 (esp. litt. V.154–5; 316–17). See Barolini, "Dante and Francesca da Rimini," 16–17.

23 "E essendo questa gentil donna … assai sovente stimolata da 'mbasciate e da prieghi di ciascun di costoro, e avendo ella a esse men saviamente più volte gli orecchi porti" [The gentlewoman ... was subjected to a steady stream of messages and

ethos of the women of Days Seven and Eight, the *Decameronian* alter ego of Francesca da Rimini thus becomes the trickster herself, whose *senno* not only keeps her from falling into love's prison but also sends her suitors through a virtual representation of the punishment that they would find there.

Thus, this tale would seem to be both playing irreverently with Cavalcantian notions about love's negative power and upturning the most famous example of its consequences provided by Dante's Francesca, who never ceases to blame Love for her death and damnation. Her alter ego, as the heroine of this story, places reason above desire and makes the men undergo the power of love to turn reason into madness and to mime with their bodies the lovers' *danse macabre*. Boccaccio follows Dante in ascribing agency in the love relationship to the beloved, but he goes even further by making her more capable than the male lover of using her intelligence against the influence of desire. Francesca de' Lazzari ultimately maintains the agency and responsibility that Francesca da Rimini surrendered to Love. There is, however, a subtle ambiguity in IX.1 about the true agent responsible for the fate of the men. As Rinuccio approaches Francesca's door with Alessandro's body in tow, the city's night guards suddenly appear as if out of nowhere:

> E essendo già Rinuccio a piè dell'uscio della gentil donna, la quale alle finestre con la sua fante stava per sentire se Rinuccio Alessandro recasse, già da sé armata in modo da mandargli ammendun via, avvenne che la famiglia della signoria, in quella contrada ripostasi e chetamente standosi aspettando di dover pigliare uno sbandito, sentendo lo scalpiccio che Rinuccio co' piè faceva, subitamente tratto fuori un lume per veder che si fare e dove andarsi, e mossi i pavesi e le lance, gridò: "Chi è la?" (IX.1.30)
>
> [The gentlewoman, being eager to see whether Rinuccio would fetch Alessandro, was standing with her maidservant at the window, forearmed with a suitable pretext for sending them both packing. But just as Rinuccio came up to her front door, he was challenged by the officers of the watch, who happened to be lying in ambush for an outlaw in that very part of the city. On hearing the sound of Rinuccio's laboured tread, they promptly produced a lantern to see what was afoot, and seizing their shields and their lances, they called out: "Who goes there?"]

---

entreaties from the two men, to which on occasion she had been incautious enough to lend a ready ear (IX.1.6)].

If taken as an intervention of fortune, we might understand that, in the world of the *Decameron*, however well-armed Francesca might have been with her intelligence, human ability requires an element of chance (or an intervention of some kind, as it may be) to succeed.[24] Indeed, she ends up "molto lieta e lodando Idio che dallo'mpaccio di costoro tolta l'avea" [delighted ... and giving thanks to God for ridding her from their tiresome attentions (IX.1.33)], in opposition to the sadness of the carnal sinners, who curse God's power (*Inferno* 5.36, cited above). From the political perspective, however, we might also understand this fortuitous event to signal the necessity of the extra-individual power of the city-state for a communal life without violence. Intelligence only has the ability to keep one safe if the state does its part to police the sometimes mad desires of its inhabitants.

Like Dante's representation of Francesca da Rimini, Boccaccio's tale gives history and personality to the woman as object of male desire, which is generally represented in the lyric tradition as an all but disembodied, quasi-supernatural force. The tale's realism may contribute to its humour, inasmuch as the historical setting makes possible the debasement and embodiment in space and time of the philosophical notions of the lyric tradition. Yet, if we are to take seriously the realism of the *Decameron* as we do that of Dante's *Comedy*, an effort must be made to situate the literary-philosophical meaning of stories like this within the socio-political context that was chosen as their setting.[25]

The Politics of Desire between Florence and Pistoia: The Historical Subtext

As I have argued elsewhere, the poetics of the *Decameron* allow for the production of a diversity of interrelated meanings in various interpretative contexts that depend on the reader's abilities.[26] If, with no regard to the tale's historical and geographical setting, we are able to read this tale's engagement with poetic notions of the negative effects of love and to understand its parody of Cavalcantian pathos and its representation

24 The fortuitous death of Scannadio at the beginning of the story is the event that led Francesca to the *pensiero*, or thought/plan, that sets the plot of the story in motion. Her intelligence (*senno*) lies in the way she is able to prepare for and react to the opportunities and challenges presented by fortune.

25 See Olson, *Courtesy Lost*, for just such an endeavour.

26 See Lummus, "The *Decameron* and Boccaccio's Poetics." See Marchesi, *Stratigrafie*, for a theoretical discussion and practical demonstration of a layered approach to reading the *Decameron*.

of an alternative version of Francesca da Rimini, this does not mean that the historical realism of the tale is entirely accidental to the substance of the story. Critics have long noted the verisimilitude of the tale's characters and locations, but have deemed it unnecessary to examine them in depth or in relation to the story's narrative or meaning.[27] I will approach the question of this relationship by examining the historical subtext of this story in the biographies of its characters and the geopolitics of the Florence and Pistoia at the turn of the thirteenth century. My goal in this section is not to provide a full reading of the tale as a historical allegory but merely to suggest how certain signs within the tale itself suggest that it could be read as such.

Filomena's tale provides readers with a minimum amount of detail to make it historically possible. We know that it takes place in Pistoia, between the home of a certain Francesca de' Lazzari and the Church of the Friars Minor.[28] The main characters belong to noble families of Pistoia (the Lazzari) and Florence (the Chiarmontesi and Palermini) that historically existed, but there is no historical record of the individuals in question (Francesca, Alessandro, and Rinuccio). The place of the narrative action within historical time is also set very generally in the recent past – "fu già" [there was once (IX.1.5)].

It is clear, however, that Alessandro and Rinuccio were living in exile from Florence in Pistoia, a detail that provides readers with the opportunity to locate the narrative in a more precise historical moment. The Chiarmontesi and Palermini families are named in Giovanni Villani's *Nuova Cronica* in sections that list the noble families around the

27 See, e.g., Manni, *Istoria*, 522–3, whose vague, eighteenth-century notions of the tale's historical realism have been repeated into the twenty-first century.

28 The story refers both to the church (*chiesa*) and to the place (*luogo*) of the Franciscans in Pistoia (IX.1.9–10). It does not refer to the church of San Francesco specifically, which is how Branca glosses both instances in the text. On the history and construction of the Church of San Francesco, see Andreini, Cerrato, and Feola, "Dalla chiesa alto-medievale" and "I cicli costruttivi." The Franciscans had been located in Pistoia since 1249, in the small church of Santa Maria al Prato, which was given to them and later destroyed in order to build the Church of San Francesco in its place. The foundation ceremony took place in 1289, but regular construction did not begin until 1314. The church was not completed until 1333, when it was given a roof (Andreini et al., "I cicli costruttivi," 54). Boccaccio is careful not to refer to this specific building, which did not exist at the time of the story, but which did exist when he wrote it. Instead, he refers to the location of the Franciscans' church more generally. The line drawing that appears above the story in BNF MS Ital. 482, fol. 176r seems to represent the Church of San Francesco. See Piras, *La Toscana di Boccaccio*, 47.

time of Holy Roman Emperor Conrad II (c. 990–1039).[29] Later on in the same text, both families come up again in a list of Guelphs and Ghibellines around the year 1250, where they are noted as belonging to the Guelph faction.[30] Still later chronologically, the Chiarmontesi are mentioned again in the *Cronaca Fiorentina* of Marchionne di Coppo Stefani at a key moment of political upheaval. Between 15 June and 15 August 1301, Geri di ser Durante Chiarmontesi sat on the College of Priors and deliberated in favour of the provisions taken against Corso Donati and his Black Guelph faction.[31] As soon as Donati returned to Florence in November 1301, Geri Chiarmontesi and his brothers were captured and held for ransom. Eventually freed, they were exiled along with the rest of the White Guelphs in April 1302.[32] The Palermini family, whose masculine line came to an end in 1312, is nearly impossible to trace in this period, but they are mentioned as business associates of the Scali family, which belonged to the White Guelph faction.[33] It is probable that at least some members of the Palermini clan also found themselves going against the tide as the Black faction took control of Florence.

Although there is no historical documentation that shows where the Chiarmontesi went in their exile, Pistoia was an option.[34] The Black Guelphs had been exiled from Pistoia in May 1301 with the help of Florentine White Guelphs Cantino Cavalcanti, appointed as Capitano del Popolo there, and Andrea Gherardini, who served as Podestà. Pistoia had been directly controlled by the ruling factions of Florence and Lucca since 1296, but had been caught in Florence's sphere of influence since much earlier in the same century.[35] It was this interest in the

---

29 The Palermini are mentioned together with the Scali family as living in the area around the Duomo (Villani, *Nuova Cronica*, I.5.10). The Chiarmontesi are listed as living in the area of Porta San Piero (ibid., I.5.11).

30 The Chiarmontesi are noted as Guelphs (ibid., VI.39.15; 1:270), whereas the Palermini are noted as Ghibellines who later became Guelphs (ibid., VI.39.30; 1:270).

31 See Stefani, *Cronaca Fiorentina*, 86 (rubrica 229) and Arnaldo D'Addario in *Enciclopedia Dantesca*, s.v. "Chiaramontesi." Although the Chiarmontesi are not named by Dante, they are mentioned implicitly by Cacciaguida as "quei ch'arrossan per lo staio" [those who blush for the bushel] (*Paradiso* 16.105).

32 See Davidsohn, *Storia di Firenze*, 4:249–50; D'Addario in *Enciclopedia Dantesca*, s.v. "Chiaramontesi."

33 See Peruzzi, *Storia del commercio*, 161. On the association of the Scali with the White faction, see Davidsohn, *Storia di Firenze*, 4:303.

34 See Villani, *Nuova Cronica*, IX.49.160: "e chi n'andò a Pisa, e chi ad Arezzo e Pistoia, accompagnandosi co' Ghibellini e nimici de' Fiorentini" [and some went to Pisa, some to Arezzo and Pistoia, associating with Ghibellines and enemies of the Florentines].

35 See Francesconi, "Firenze e Pistoia."

affairs of Pistoia that brought Pistoian factionalism to Florence. Just a month after the exile of the Whites from Florence, Lucca and Florence tried briefly to take the strategic city by siege in May 1302, but gave up after three weeks and began to take control of the city's castles and territories in the countryside beyond its walls.[36] Pistoia would remain independent of and at war with the Black factions of Lucca and Florence until the city ceded control after a devastating eleven-month siege on 11 April 1306. This is all to say that the most probable historical moment for the setting of this tale is the period between the two sieges, June 1302 to May 1305, when exiled Florentine White Guelphs could presumably have found refuge in a Pistoia controlled by the Whites, which was operating independently of Florentine oversight.

The Lazzari family, to which Francesca belongs, was oriented on the opposite side of the factional spectrum to her Florentine suitors. It was a noble, Black Guelph family, which was second only to the Cancellieri in its influence in the city.[37] Its most well-known member was the illegitimate son of Guelfuccio dei Lazzari, Vanni Fucci, the murderer and thief punished for *sacrilegium,* or theft from a church, in *Inferno* 24 and whose obscene gesture of pride and disdain toward God opens *Inferno* 25. Fucci had already presumably died sometime between 1295 and 1300,[38] but his prophecy at the end of *Inferno* 24 about the eventual victory of the Blacks over the Whites in Florence and Pistoia hangs over the plot of the narrative. The story, then, pits the intelligence of a Black Guelph Pistoian woman against the mad desire of two exiled White Guelph Florentine men at the beginning of the events announced in the prophecy of Vanni Fucci, who shared with her a family name: "Pistoia in pria d'i Neri si dimagra; / poi Fiorenza rinova gente e modi" [Pistoia first thins itself of Blacks; then Florence makes new its laws and people (*Inferno* 24.143–4)].[39]

Besides the anonymous maid, the only other character in the story is the dead body of Scannadio, whose hyperbolic malevolence seems to make him a creation of the imagination. In fact, his name seems purposefully invented to frighten the two lovers, inasmuch as it means literally "he who slits God's throat." Tobias Gittes has noted that this

36 See Francesconi, "11 aprile 1306."

37 See Renato Piattoli in *Enciclopedia Dantesca,* s.v. "Lazzari."

38 See Emilio Bigi in *Enciclopedia Dantesca,* s.v. "Vanni Fucci."

39 Fucci not only prophesies the expulsion of the Blacks from Pistoia and that of the Whites from Florence, but in the lines that follow also – according to some commentators – to the taking of Pistoia in 1306 by the Blacks, led by Moroello Malaspina.

name "suggests that [Scannadio] is ... a fourteenth-century scion of Otus, Capaneus, Lucifer and the various other would-be slayers of God" ("'Dal giogo alleviati,'" 391). With Gittes's observation in mind, it is difficult not to associate this supervillain with Dante's Vanni Fucci, whom the poet himself compares to Capaneus:

> Per tutt' i cerchi de lo'nferno scuri
> non vidi spirto in Dio tanto superbo,
> non quel che cadde a Tebe giù da' muri. (*Inferno* 25.13–15)

> [Through all the dark circles of Hell I saw no spirit so proud against God, not him who fell from the wall at Thebes.]

The identification of Scannadio with Vanni Fucci rings even truer if we consider the description of Scannadio in the story: "quantunque stati fossero i suoi passati gentili uomini era reputato il piggiore uomo che, non che in Pistoia, ma in tutto il mondo fosse; e oltre a questo vivendo era sí contraffatto e di sí divisato viso, che chi conosciuto non l'avesse, vedendol da prima, n'avrebbe avuto paura" [a man who, despite the nobility of his lineage, was reputed to be the greatest rogue who had ever lived, not only in Pistoia but in the whole world. Moreover, he was so deformed of body and his features were so hideously distorted that any stranger, on seeing him for the first time, would have been terrified out of his wits (IX.1.8)].[40] This description seems fitting for a character who, in Dante's poem, describes himself as a "bestia" [beast] and a "mulo" [mule], saying that "vita bestial mi piacque e non umana" [bestial life pleased me, not human] and calling Pistoia a "degna tana" [worthy lair (*Inferno* 24.124–6)]. Early commentators identified Vanni Fucci as far more evil than his punishment as a thief implied, noting that he was also a murderer and a blasphemer, whose gesture at the end of the first tercet of *Inferno* 25 demonstrated his desire to do violence against God:

> Al fine de le sue parole il ladro
> le mani alzò con amendue le fiche,
> gridando: "Togli Dio, ch'a te le squadro!" (*Inferno* 25.1–3)

> [At the end of his words the thief raised his hands with both the figs, crying: "Take them, God, I'm aiming them at you!"]

40 Although Dante does not describe Fucci as deformed in the *Inferno*, the deformation of Scannadio may be aimed at evoking Fucci's moral turpitude or perhaps his violent punishment by snakes. See *Inferno* 25.4–24.

Benvenuto da Imola expresses it most clearly in his gloss on this tercet:

> Sed quare autor fingit istum furem fecisse talem actum turpem? Certe ut melius ostendat naturam istius hominis diabolici qui, ultra hoc quod fuerat violentus latro et fraudulentus fur, erat superbissimus, iracundissimus, [et] blasphemus. (*Comentum* 2:226)
>
> [But why does the author imagine that this thief made such an ugly gesture? Surely so as better to reveal the nature of this diabolical man who, besides the fact that he had been a violent bandit and fraudulent thief, was extremely proud, excessively wrathful, and blasphemous.]

It is reasonable to suspect that Vanni Fucci would be the referent of a character called the worst man to have lived in Pistoia and perhaps in all the world. While Boccaccio would not normally hesitate to name historical characters in the *Decameron* – even those from the *Inferno*, such as in *Decameron* IX.8 – the constraints of historical verisimilitude here prevent the naming of Vanni Fucci, who would have already been dead for some time by 1302.

Fictional invention is used to evoke the memory of the "diabolical man" in the fantastical form of Scannadio, whom the Florentine men are charged with resurrecting from the grave, a perversion of the stories of Lazarus or Christ. Filomena's story, with such a charged geopolitical setting, gives readers the opportunity to link the question of the widow's intelligence and the men's mad love with the political backdrop against which it is set. Read in terms of the love story, the two men are enacting the proximity to death caused by their mad, irrational love. Seen from the perspective of politics, however, Alessandro's imitation of Scannadio's corpse and Rinuccio's faux resurrection of it may signal the imminent demise of the Florentine White Guelph faction to which these men belong. The memory of Fucci's prophecy and mad bestiality is evoked in the background of the story as the result of a politicized insane desire.[41]

In addition to the historical setting and political affiliations of the characters, there are other details that further suggest a possible political

41 Fucci's character in the *Inferno* is glossed in the *Ottimo Commento* as being ruled by "matta bestialitade" [mad bestiality (1:421)]. It is possible that Dante's representation of the heretics in *Inferno* 10 is also evoked by this story, inasmuch as Cavalcante de' Cavalcanti and Farinata degli Uberti, a Guelph and a Ghibelline respectively – both involved in political factionalism – enact a dead body rising from the tomb as their punishment for denying the immortality of the soul.

interpretation of the story. For example, the terms used to denote the lovers' insistent approaches to Francesca have double meanings, allowing them to apply to both amorous and political situations. The first, *messo*, means both an amorous message and a political messenger,[42] while the second, *ambasciata*, denotes both an official political announcement (as well as the diplomatic delegation that bears it) and a request for love.[43] Furthermore, as Alessandro is approaching the tomb and imagining what might go wrong, he worries that Francesca's relatives have discovered his love for her and are using this escapade as an excuse to kill him:

> O che so io se i parenti di costei, forse avvedutisi che io l'amo, credendo essi quel che non è, le fanno far questo per uccidermi in quello avello? Il che se avvenisse, io m'avrei il danno, né mai cosa del mondo se ne saprebbe che lor nocesse. O che so io se forse alcun mio nemico questo m'ha procacciato, il quale ella forse amando, di questo il vuol servire? … io debbo credere che [i suoi parenti] il corpo di Scannadio non vogliono per doverlosi tenere in braccio o metterlo in braccio a lei, anzi si dee credere che essi ne voglian far qualche strazio, sí come di colui che forse già d'alcuna cosa gli diserví. (IX.1.20–1)

> [For all I know, her kinsfolk may have discovered that I'm in love with her. Perhaps they think I've seduced her, and have forced her into this so that they can murder me inside the tomb. If that's the case, I shan't stand a dog's chance, nobody will be any the wiser, and they'll escape scot free. Or possibly, for all I know, it's a trap prepared for me by some enemy of mine, who persuaded her to do him this favour because she's in love with him … It's hardly likely [her kinsfolk] would want Scannadio's body in order to embrace it or put it to bed with the lady. On the contrary, one can only conclude that they want to wreak vengeance upon it in return for some wrong he has done them.]

Rinuccio, too, worries that he risks being caught by the watch and "esser come malioso condennato al fuoco, o … venire in odio de' suoi parenti" [being condemned to the stake as a sorcerer, or incurring the hatred of Scannadio's kinsfolk]. Read with the awareness of the historical setting, the spectre of familial and factional violence seems to lie behind the paranoid fantasies of the lovers. That they are able to overcome their

42 See *Vocabolario degli Accademici della Crusca*, s.v. "messo."

43 See *TLIO*, s.v. "ambasciata."

fears and complete the insane task points to the irrational impetus of their desire on both individual and social planes.

If, as argued above, the character of Francesca de' Lazzari is constructed in specular opposition to that of Francesca da Rimini, it is worth remembering the dynastic and political import of that story, especially for an interpreter like Boccaccio. Francesca da Rimini's marriage to Gianciotto was organized by her father to serve the dynastic function of bringing together the two most powerful families of Romagna and to end their feud. Love intervenes in this political story and transforms it into a tragedy, as Francesca da Rimini finds herself to be a victim of Love's power, which took hold thanks to her father's trickery. As Francesca da Rimini's alter ego, Francesca de' Lazzari refuses the reciprocity of love, which was the cause of the other's downfall, and becomes more circumspect and cunning. She does not allow herself to be manipulated by the will of men. This is especially interesting if we consider her actions in terms of Vanni Fucci's prophecy in *Inferno* 24, since the Black Guelphs – like Scannadio's corpse – would return to the streets of Pistoia and the Whites would be eliminated. Within the world of the historical fiction, Francesca's acquiescence to one or both of the White Guelph Florentine lovers would have been disastrous.[44]

Conclusion

Boccaccio's attention to historical verisimilitude in this tale, as in others, allows readers to apply the critique of these two men's uncontained desire and his praise of their lady's circumspection to a socio-political reality. His stories do not merely engage with the lyric tradition or with Dante's *Comedy* in order to debase or critique them. Rather, narrative fiction acts as a middle ground between poetry and history, through which readers may apply the erudite reflections of poetry to the fluxes of history and test the ethereal ideas expressed in poetry by embodying them in a historically verisimilar world. As was true in the analysis of the tale's intertextual relationship with lyric poetry, there is no absolute correspondence between fiction and history. Enough details are provided, however, to cause reflection in the interrogating reader.

From within the narrative frame of the *Decameron*, this tale may not be anything more than a parody. Only as read and appropriated by readers beyond the frame can it become an engagement with the

44 On a similar play on *fol'amors* and dynastic impasse that Boccaccio inherits from Dante, see Marchesi, "Intenzionalità tragica e intendimento comico in *Decameron*, V 8."

philosophical notions about desire of the poets of the previous generation or a historical allegory that takes aim at the insane motivations behind the political feuds that plagued Florence and Pistoia. This is not to say that it does not invite other, more sublime readings, if one is so induced, as Petrarch was by the story of Gualtieri and Griselda (X.10). After all, the story ends with a parody of Christ's empty tomb (IX.1.35).[45] But at the very least, this tale's representation of feminine intelligence and masculine desire asks its readers to rethink individual and collective agency and responsibility.

45 See Gittes, "'Dal giogo alleviati,'" 390.

The Priest's Breeches: Unveiling Reality in *Decameron* IX.2

MARIA PIA ELLERO

Introduction

After the conclusion of Filomena's long *novella* about the cleverness of Madonna Francesca and the folly of her suitors, Elissa enjoys the thematic freedom granted by the queen by returning to a favoured topic of hers. As the queen of the Sixth Day, Elissa herself had assigned this theme to her companions, inviting them to speak of those who "by means of a *leggiadro motto* gave a fitting riposte to a provocation or else avoided ruin, peril or humiliation with their wit or a quick response" (VI. Rubric).[1] In the introduction to *Decameron* IX.2, there is a direct reference to the tale of the Sixth Day, although here it is a young woman's astute speech that frees her from impending danger:

> Carissime donne, *saviamente* si seppe madonna Francesca, come detto è, *liberar* dalla *noia* sua; ma una giovane monaca, aiutandola la fortuna, sé da un soprastante *pericolo leggiadramente parlando diliberò*. (IX.2.3)

> [Dearest ladies, the manner in which Madonna Francesca released herself from her affliction was indeed very subtle; but I should now like to tell you of a young nun who, with the assistance of Fortune, freed herself by means of a timely remark.]

1 All quotations of the *Decameron* are from the edition by Quondam, Fiorilla, and Alfano (2013). Translations are from McWilliam (1995). Hereafter all italics are mine. During the Ninth Day, all of the narrators tend to recount stories that evoke either the principal theme or an important element of the day when they reigned. See Tateo, *Boccaccio*, 120.

And it will be a "pronto … avvedimento" [quick thinking/realization] that prompts the *motto* which will allow her to direct "onestamente villania" at her antagonist. With this *novella*, Elissa is not merely making one of those invisible connections that integrate this thematically free day into the overall structure of the collection. Rather, she also wishes to take up the invitation of the previous narrator, Filomena, who encouraged her companions to imitate and outdo her in a game of virtuous emulation. At the stylistic level, the emulative relationship between the two stories is signalled by the placement of an adversative conjunction in a syntactically foregrounded position ("*ma* una giovane monaca …") when the theme of IX.2 is introduced, and by the ascending relation between "noia"/"pericolo" [trouble/danger], which present the story of young Isabetta both as a variation on the preceding *novella* and as a semantic intensification thereof. In fact, alongside the analogies that relate the two stories, Elissa takes care to underscore the main difference that distinguishes them. If the act of freeing oneself from trouble or danger by employing one's own wit or "leggiadramente parlando" [speaking aptly] places both *novelle* in the thematic register of *ingegno*, the decisive intervention of Fortune distinguishes the story of the young nun from that of Francesca de' Lazzari, since Isabetta's wit would not have manifested itself without a chance discovery.

The young nun's antagonist appears on the story's stage as soon as the links with the preceding *novella* have been established:

> E come voi sapete, assai sono li quali, essendo *stoltissimi*, maestri degli altri si fanno e gastigatori, li quali, sì come voi potrete comprendere per la mia novella, *la fortuna* alcuna volta e meritamente *vitupera*: e ciò addivenne *alla badessa* sotto la cui obedienzia era la monaca della quale debbo dire. (IX.2.4)
>
> [As you all know, a great many people are foolish enough to instruct and condemn their fellow creatures, but from time to time, as you will observe from this story of mine, Fortune deservedly puts them to shame. And that is what happened to the Abbess who was the superior of the nun whose deeds I am now about to relate.]

Alongside the character of the antagonist, the narrator also introduces one of the guiding themes of the story: the foolish hypocrisy of those who wish to punish others for vices they share. Both the introduction of the abbess and the emphasis on her hypocrisy are related to the logic of the *motto*, which, according to classical sources, usually targets physical or moral flaws. The idea that a good *Witz* requires a flaw deserving of censure is commonplace in the whole classical tradition, beginning with Aristotle. As Cicero writes in *De oratore*,[2] a well-shaped *motto* rebukes physical ugliness or moral vice, as long as its target does not inspire compassion or utter hatred: "materies omnis ridiculorum est in iis vitiis, quae sunt in vita hominum neque carorum neque calamitosorum neque eorum qui ob facinus ad supplicium rapiendi videntur" [what is laughable is always based on the vices that affect the life of individuals, except those who are either held dear or are commiserated [with] or who seem worthy of being dragged to the gallows for their crimes (*De oratore* II.59)]. Thus, neither the pitiful nor those destined for the gallows, but rather lesser rascals practising minor vices, especially if they are vexing or aggressive, since *Witze* uttered in response to a provocation or a personal attack are much more effective than unprovoked witticisms and more readily receive the approval of others. Furthermore, the quick-wittedness entailed by the *motto* is more apparent if, being "tentato," as Elissa would say, one must instantly improvise a retort:

> Omnino probabiliora sunt, quae lacessiti dicimus, quam quae priores; nam et ingenii celeritas maior est quae apparet in respondendo ... Videmur enim quieturi fuisse, nisi essemus lacessiti. (Cicero, *De oratore* II.56)
>
> [Surely more liable to be approved are those that we utter only because provoked than those we initiate ourselves: for indeed our quickness of mind is more evident when we return a barb ... We give the impression that we were going to remain calm, had we not been provoked.]

In IX.2.2, the foolishness of the abbess is contrasted both with the wit implicit in the riposte of the young nun and with the expedient devised by Francesca to "torsi di dosso coloro li quali amar non voleva." The contrastive symmetry that relates Isabetta to her antagonist is further emphasized by the double play of Fortune, which aids Isabetta and "meritamente vitupera" [deservedly vilifies] the abbess. In fact, it

2 Which Boccaccio might have known through the intermediary of Quintilian, *Institutio oratoria*: "Habet enim, ut Cicero dicit, sedem in deformitate aliqua et turpitudine; quae cum in aliis demonstrantur, urbanitas, cum in ipsos dicentis reccidunt, stultitia vocatur" [As Cicero states, it consists in some deformity and ugliness. When it is exhibited in others, it is called urbanity; if it rebounds onto the speaker, it is called stupidity (VI.3.8, p. 734)]. A fragmentary codex of the *Institutio oratoria* was in Boccaccio's possession during the years when he was writing the *Decameron*. See Coulter, "Boccaccio's Knowledge of Quintilian."

is Fortune which, along with the witty *motto*, will reverse the initial relation of antagonism between the two characters into a relation of analogy,[3] demonstrating that the abbess is neither wiser nor more virtuous than the nun. The plot of the *novella* is briefly summarized in the rubric:[4]

> Levasi una badessa in fretta e al buio per trovare una sua monaca, a lei accusata, col suo amante nel letto; ed essendo con lei un prete, credendosi il saltero de' veli aver posto in capo, le brache del prete vi si pose; le quali vedendo l'accusata e fattalane accorgere, fu diliberata, ed ebbe agio di starsi col suo amante.
>
> [An abbess rises hurriedly from her bed in the dark when it is reported to her that one of her nuns is abed with a lover. But being with a priest at the time, the Abbess claps his breeches on her head, mistaking them for her veil. On pointing this out to the Abbess, the accused nun is set at liberty, and thenceforth she is able to forgather with her lover at her leisure.]

The theme of the foolish "gastigatori" [chastisers] envisaged by Elissa as the *novella*'s interpretative key can already be found in both versions of Boccaccio's source. The *fablel* of the priest's breeches circulated in two nearly contemporary Old French redactions, both slightly anterior to the *Decameron*: the *Dit de la Nonnete*, written by the minstrel Jean de Condé, and a shorter version included in the *Roman de Renart*.[5] The *Dit* ends with the moral that

> On se doit mout bien aviser
> S'il a sour lui que deviser,
> Ains que sour autrui on mesdie. ("Le Dit de la Nonnete," 269)
>
> [One should be careful not to be liable to criticism before criticizing others.]

Similarly, the *fablel* inserted in the *Roman de Renart* ends with the proverbial epiphonema: "Ja nulz ne *chastïés* / Du vice dont estes liez" [refrain

3 The double relationship of analogy and antagonism between the two characters is described in Alfano, "Scheda introduttiva a *Decameron*, IX.2," 1364.

4 On rubrics, see Milanese, "Affinità e contraddizioni tra rubriche e novelle del *Decameron*," and D'Andrea, "Le rubriche del *Decameron*." On rubricating as a critical act, see Clarke, "The Poetics of the Paratext," 82–3.

5 In both of its redactions: the first datable to the years between 1319 and 1322, the second to the years between 1328 and 1342.

from chastising others for the vices that affect you].[6] But it is worth noting right away that Boccaccio relates this propensity for punishing in others one's own vice to the broader theme of fools who venture to play the role of "maestri," inflecting in an anti-hierarchical sense the more generic moral of the two *fabliaux*.

Rather than rewriting a specific source, Boccaccio's *novella* reworks a traditional narrative matter. Indeed, Elissa's tale shows a convergence of both versions of the priest's breeches story: a highly simplified form of the *fabula* like that of the *Roman de Renart*, developed with some of the secondary themes already employed by Jean de Condé, such as the brief initial description of the convent setting, the inexorability of love, the psychological motivation for certain actions, and even the minuscule detail of the "usulieri," the laces made to attach breeches to one's stockings, which instead are hanging from the abbess's forehead.[7]

Setting the Stage

The story is set in Lombardy, in a convent "famosissimo … di santità e di religione" [widely renowned for its sanctity and religious fervor]. The same phrase is used, almost unaltered, to describe several other monasteries in the *Decameron*, such as that of I.4 ("un monistero già di santità e di monaci più copioso che oggi non è" [a monastery that once had a greater supply of monks and saintliness than it has nowadays]), and it reoccurs in a nearly identical description of the convent in which Masetto proves his mettle: "In queste nostre contrade fu e è ancora un munistero di donne *assai famoso di santità*" (III.1.6) [In this rural region of ours, there was and still is a nunnery, greatly renowned for its holiness]. In all three cases, the subsequent narration will undertake to show that the public reputation of these holy places hardly matches up with the private behaviour of their inhabitants, thereby making of these monasteries an ideal metaphor for the dialectic between reality and appearance, as well as between nature and culture (*natura* and *nutritura*).[8]

6 *Le Roman de Renart le Contrefait*, p. 65, vv. 28817–18. See also the maxim that concludes the work immediately preceding our *flablel* (vv. 28773–4): "Qui *chastie* aultrui du sien vice, / Il se tient pour *fol et pour nieche*" [whoever chastises another for the vice he is himself affected by is held to be deranged], where one finds the theme of foolishness; italics mine.

7 See Rossi, "In luogo di sollazzo," 18–22. As I go along I will only add a few observations to Rossi's excellent analysis of the interplay between *Decameron* IX.2 and the two versions of the *fablel*.

8 A thoughtful analysis on the nature/education pair in the *Decameron* is to be found in Neuschäfer, *Boccaccio und der Beginn der Novelle*, 61–4. On the appearance/reality

A similar description of the convent as promiscuous and permissive is also displayed in the *Dit*, albeit in an entirely different key. Jean de Condé is not interested in the opposition between reality and appearance; he says from the beginning that his monastery "iert legiers con vens, / Car amours reparoit en l'iestre / Qui legieres les faisoit iestre" [it was light like the wind, since love found refuge there, which made it light indeed ("Le Dit de la Nonnete," 264)]. For his readers, then, the discovery of the abbess's sin will hardly be surprising. Boccaccio, on the other hand, describes the convent paradoxically with respect to the events he is about to recount; a retrospective rereading therefore reveals the guiding theme of the *novella*: the disjunction between reality (being "stoltissimi") and appearance (seeming "maestri ... e gastigatori").

Within the enclosed space of this Lombard monastery, the dynamic elements arriving from without are rare and marginal: a young man, with whom a novice falls in love through the grille of the parlour, and a priest, who furtively enters the convent locked in a chest. Although the action unfolds in the cloistered space of the abbey and over the course of a single night, the *novella* is narratively more intricate than other *motto*-stories – usually characterized by few events and little action – divided as it is into three brief scenes, with various changes in setting.[9]

The first scene takes place in the parlour and serves as the backstory to the narration: Isabetta's love for a young man she sees through the grille as he accompanies a relative of hers. The sequence of the "first sight" and enamourment is described according to the conventions of courtly love:

> Sapere adunque dovete in Lombardia essere un famosissimo monistero di santità e di religione, nel quale, tra l'altre donne monache che v'erano, v'era una giovane *di sangue nobile* e di meravigliosa bellezza dotata, la quale, Isabetta chiamata, essendo un dì a un suo parente alla grata venuta, d'un bel giovane che con lui era s'innamorò; e esso, *lei veggendo bellissima*, già *il suo desiderio avendo con gli occhi concetto*, similmente di lei s'accese: e

dialectic and its cultural implications, see Barsella, "The Tale of Tedaldo degli Elisei (III.7)"; Kircher, "Boccaccio and the Appearance of Reality"; and Marcello Ciccuto's reading of *Decameron* IX.5 in this volume.

9 See Picone, "Leggiadri motti e pronte risposte," 163–4. For this reason, Segre ("La beffa e il comico nella novellistica del Due e Trecento," 89) interprets *Decameron* IX.2 as a "novella a intrigo," whereas Baratto (*Realtà e stile* [1996], 248) sees it as a "mimo d'ambiente," "una forma germinale di commedia, nella quale il personaggio è colto con rapida immediatezza nei gesti e nelle battute essenziali." The tripartition of the plot matches the syntactic articulation in three clauses of the rubric.

non senza gran pena di ciascuno questo amore un gran tempo senza frutto sostennero. (IX.2.5)

[You are to know, then, that in Lombardy there was once a convent, widely renowned for its sanctity and religious fervour, which housed a certain number of nuns, one of them being a girl of gentle birth, endowed with wondrous beauty, whose name was Isabetta. One day, having come to the grating to converse with a kinsman of hers, she fell in love with a handsome young man who was with him; and the young man, observing that she was very beautiful, and divining her feelings through the language of the eyes, fell no less passionately in love with her. For some little time, to the no small torment of each, their love remained unfulfilled.]

As the conventions of *fin'amor* imply, the young lady is of noble blood, and her beauty, passing through her lover's eyes, becomes the object of desire. In the *fablel* of the *Roman de Renart* we also find an allusion to the courtly register, but the anonymous author inflects it ironically by referring it to the antagonist: the foolish abbess, "sote," "qui par amour amoit."[10] In Boccaccio's version, the reference to the code of courtly love does not have a paradoxical function and therefore disjoins the *novella* both thematically and stylistically from the *fabliau*. This allusion to a high literary code on the one hand shows Boccaccio's predilection for combining different styles, genres, and cultural traditions; on the other, it connotes Isabetta's love and solicits the reader's sympathy for the character's behaviour, setting it apart from that of her antagonist.[11]

The second scene is framed by the nocturnal and private setting of the nuns' cells. Envying Isabetta's amorous fortune, the other nuns plot against the lovers, watching in order to see them caught red-handed by the abbess Usimbalda, "buona e santa donna secondo la oppinion

---

10 *Le Roman de Renart*, p. 65, vv. 28775–6: "Une abesse jadis estoit / Sote qui par amour amoit" [There once was an abbess who loved in her foolish heart].

11 By tracing Isabetta's love back to courtly conventions, Boccaccio not only contaminates the high matter of the lyrical tradition with the comic material of his story, but also, as Rossi observes ("In luogo di sollazzo," 20–1), breaks down the horizon of expectations implicit in the *livre de chevet* of the courtly codex – the treatise of Andreas Cappellanus, where the love of nuns is considered a pestilence of the soul, deserving divine punishment (*De amore* I.20). Indeed, in the *Decameron*, the love affairs of the clergy are never given a courtly patina, but are rather attributed by the narrators to "concupiscenza carnale" (I.4.5) or "feminili appetiti" (III.1.2). The infraction of codes both internal and external to the text enacted by IX.2 embodies the impossibility of reducing the infinite variety of human behaviour to excessively rigid, predefined categories.

delle donne monache e di chiunque la conoscea" [whose goodness and piety were a byword among all the nuns and everyone else who knew her (IX.2.7)]. Their joint action is recounted in a stylistic register that presupposes ironic distance:[12]

> così taciutesi, tra sé *le vigilie e le guardie segretamente partirono* per incoglier costei ... quando a lor parve tempo, essendo già buona pezza di notte, *in due si divisero*, e *una parte se ne mise a guardia* dell'uscio della cella dell'Isabetta e *un'altra n'andò correndo* alla camera della badessa. (IX.2.7–8)

> [So they kept it to themselves, and secretly took it in turns to keep her under close and constant watch in order to take her *in flagrante* ... After biding their time until well into the night, the nuns formed themselves into two separate groups, the first mounting guard at the entrance to Isabetta's cell whilst the second hurried off to the chamber of the Abbess.]

The coordinated efforts of the nuns are described as those of a small army: the sentinel shifts, the secrecy of the operations, the regiment divided in two – all to carefully guard the door of the guilty nun and immediately run to denounce her. This linguistic register of grand military manoeuvres is at odds with the enclosed environment, the petty interests, the gossip, and the minor envies that make up the subject matter of the narration, in accordance with a technique of antiphrastic irony which contrasts high *verba* with low *res.*

At the centre of this episode sits the fortuitous event that sets the stage for the witty *motto* and will create the conditions for the resolution of the *peripeteia*:

> Era quella notte la badessa accompagnata d'un prete il quale ella spesse volte in una cassa si faceva venire. La quale, udendo questo, temendo non forse le monache per *troppa fretta* o troppo volonterose tanto l'uscio sospignessero, che egli s'aprisse, *spacciatamente si levò* suso e come il meglio seppe si vestì al buio; e credendosi torre certi veli piegati, li quali in capo portano e chiamangli il saltero, *le venner tolte* le brache del prete; *e tanta fu la fretta*, che senza avvedersene in luogo del saltero *le si gittò* in capo e *uscì* fuori e prestamente l'uscio si *riserrò* dietro dicendo: "Dove è questa maladetta da Dio?" (IX.2.9)

12 According to Baratto, in IX.2 the choral dimension of monastery life, pungently depicted in the *novella*, dictates the logic of the narrative. The rhythm is based on the actions of the nuns, who move as a collectivity, a "piccola folla femminile" existing within a repressive environment (*Realtà e stile* [1996], 249).

> [The Abbess was keeping company that night with a priest, whom she frequently smuggled into her room in a chest, and on hearing this clamour, fearing lest the nuns, in their undue haste and excess of zeal, should burst open the door of her chamber, she leapt out of bed as quick as lightning and dressed as best she could in the dark. Thinking, however, that she had taken up the folded veils which nuns wear on their heads and refer to as psalters, she happened to seize hold of the priest's breeches. And she was in such a tearing hurry, that without noticing her mistake, she clapped these onto her head instead of her psalter and sallied forth, deftly locking the door behind her and exclaiming: "Where is this damnable sinner?"]

In contrast with the lyric and courtly modalities that feature Isabetta's love, Usimbalda's affair is played out in a comic register: a priest sneaks into the abbey at night, concealed in a chest; in the dark his breeches are mistaken for a head-covering, and the abbess puts them on for a solemn assembly. The caricature-like traits of the abbess's erotic adventure emphasize the estrangement effect enacted by this part of the text. Unexpectedly and without pausing on this new information, the reader learns that not only is the abbess indulging in the same sin as Isabetta but this also occurs regularly: "Era quella notte la badessa accompagnata d'un prete il quale ella *spesse volte* in una cassa *si faceva venire.*" In a sort of vertiginous anti-climax, we also learn that the two sins are not to be considered equivalent, since one is described with the full dignity of courtly love, whereas the other results in a ridiculous story of chests and breeches. The surprising and estranging effect springs from a sequencing of information that first aligns the reader's viewpoint with the limited-to-appearances notions of those who believe Usimbalda is "buona e santa" [good and holy], and only later, in parallel with the plot's unfolding, lets the reader learn what the omniscient narrator, aware of the abbess's sin, already knows.

The agitation of the abbess, caused by her fear that the nuns might force the door and burst in, is introduced to explain the confusion of the breeches and the veil. In other words, it rationalizes the irrational and fortuitous event that will be decisive for the outcome of the plot. In a narrative pared down to essentials, at almost every single syntactic clause, Elissa emphasizes the quickness of each gesture, and hence the hurry that causes Usimbalda's mistake: "temendo non forse ... per *troppa fretta* ... *spacciatamente* si levò ... e *tanta fu la fretta,* che senza avvedersene ... le si gittò in capo ... e *prestamente* l'uscio ... riserrò." At the syntactic level, the rapidity of the action is conveyed through the use of parataxis and parallelisms, of preterites that seal every phrase and hasten it toward its conclusion, and of the polysyndeton introducing every main clause: "*si levò* suso *e* come il meglio seppe *si vestì* al buio; *e* credendosi torre certi veli piegati … le *venner* tolte le brache del prete; *e* tanta fu la fretta, che senza avvedersene in luogo del saltero le si *gittò* in capo *e uscì* fuori *e prestamente* l'uscio si *riserrò* dietro." The swiftness of the syntax, whose clauses become progressively shorter, leads in a crescendo toward the final *ralenti* – almost a narrative pause that ends the scene with an insertion of direct discourse: "Dove è questa maladétta da Dìo?" The diegetic delay created through this interpolation is made even more solemn by the phrase's hendecasyllabic metre and its alliteration, which also underline the climax of the story, the critical moment that precedes the capture of Isabetta. The rapid scene changes, with the transition from Isabetta's cell to Usimbalda's and then back to Isabetta's, correspond to the alacrity of the storytelling.

The third and last scene takes place in the chapter, where Isabetta is taken to be publicly punished. The alternating focus of the narrative, which at times adopts Isabetta's perspective and at others Usimbalda's, mirrors the antagonistic relation between the two characters, which comes to the fore especially in this culminating scene. In this setting, Isabetta will utter the witty riposte that will reverse the two characters' antagonism into an analogy,[13] publicly revealing that the abbess is guilty of the same sin for which she intends to censure the nun. This reversal is the prelude to the explicit proclamation of that natural law to which everyone in the *Decameron* is subject: "impossibile essere il potersi dagli stimoli della carne difendere" [it is impossible to defend oneself against the goadings of the flesh (IX.2.18)]. But the inherent analogy, concealed by the hypocrisy of appearances and the uncertainty of opinions, has been prepared throughout the *novella*,[14] beginning with the syntactic parallelism of the rubric's opening, it too based on an alternation of the two characters: "Levasi *una badessa* in fretta e al buio *per trovare una sua monaca* … *col suo amante* nel letto; ed *essendo con lei un prete*" (IX.2.1).

13 The development of the narrative sequence from sentence 13 to sentence 18 is the following: "(13) La badessa, postasi a sedere in capitolo … (14) La giovane, vergognosa e timida … (16) La badessa, che non la 'ntendeva … (17) Allora la giovane un'altra volta disse … (18) Di che la badessa avvedutasi …".

14 Like Isabetta and her lover, who are discovered by the nuns "*senza avvedersene* e egli o ella" (IX.2.7), the abbess also puts on the priest's breeches "senza avvedersene" (IX.2.10). Analogously, if the nuns wait to catch Isabetta in the act, "acciò che la negazione non avesse luogo," so the abbess, caught with the priest's breeches for a headdress, understands that her mistake "[non] avea ricoperta" (IX.2.18). If, lastly, the abbess fears that the pressing nuns might open her door, thus catching her red-handed, Isabetta's door is violently opened and the young woman is well and truly caught *in flagrante delicto* (IX.2.9 and 11).

The narrative development of the *novella,* which is directed toward the *motto,* is paired with a corresponding rhetorical development centred on the blindness/sight opposition, which amplifies the comic of the final scene.[15] The resolution of the plot takes on the form of a true recognition, almost an *anagnorisis* in the classical sense of the term, which unveils not only the unsubstantial quality of Usimbalda's authority but also the fallibility of opinions and appearances. This unexpected realization is described as a transition from a condition of physical and cognitive blindness to a state of unimpeded and unvarnished vision: "Venne alla giovane alzato il viso e *veduto* ciò che la badessa aveva in capo e gli usulieri che di qua e di là pendevano: di che ella, *avvisando* ciò che era, tutta rassicurata disse ..." [she happened to raise her eyes and perceive what the Abbess had on her head, with the laces dangling down on either side. Realizing what the Abbess had been up to, she took heart and said ... (IX.2.14–15)]. Similarly, "la badessa, *avvedutasi* del suo medesimo fallo e *vedendo* che da tutte *veduto* era" [whereupon the Abbess, recognizing that she was equally culpable and that there was no way of concealing the fact from all the nuns (IX.2.18)]. The repetition of the verb *vedere* – or rather, of its etymological root – verges on the obsessive, while in the preceding scenes, the inability to see or realize something is related to all of the protagonists of the *novella*:[16] Isabetta and her lover (IX.2.7), the abbess (IX.2.9–10), and the small group of nuns (IX.2.11).

As in other *novelle* of the *Decameron,* darkness both plays a narrative role and has a symbolic significance.[17] In this sense it is the objective correlative of Fortune, as well as of the cognitive blindness of the characters, who either do not see, or do not realize what they are seeing. Similarly, Usimbalda's literal mis-taking one thing for another stands as a metonym for the more general cognitive error of mistaking opinions for facts or sanctimonious appearances for actual sanctity. In

15 In "La beffa e il comico nella novellistica del Due e Trecento" (93), Segre observed that the comic effect arises from the interaction of the stories' narrative plot ("la trama narrativa") and their discursive fabric ("una trama discorsiva").

16 The salience of the semantic register of sight has been noted by Peirone, "Per aver festa," 153.

17 One may consider the story of Andreuccio or else IX.6, where the actions of fortune are intertwined with an epistemological disorientation produced by the nighttime setting, and especially those of Catella and Ricciardo Minutolo (III.6) and of Sismonda and Arriguccio (VII.8), where darkness constitutes the narrative equivalent of another type of disorientation, that provoked by anger. On this last theme, see Pascale, "La 'camera oscura molto.'" On the role of darkness in the narrative economy of IX.2, see also Peirone, "Per aver festa," 153.

Decameron IX.2, the blindness/sight opposition may be interpreted as a kind of narrative reification of the appearance/reality interplay that Elissa views as the interpretive key for her story. However, the transition from blindness to sight is not the product of industriousness or intelligence, but rather a fortuitous occurrence: in a world where appearances blind, access to reality becomes an adventitious and unforeseeable event, which nothing can guarantee or even promise.

The conclusion excuses the two nuns' clamorous infraction of the vow of chastity in accordance with the laws of nature and integrates it into the rhythm of an almost banal normality: "e liberata la giovane [la badessa] col suo prete si tornò a dormire, e l'Isabetta col suo amante" [Isabetta was then freed, and she and the Abbess returned to their beds, the latter with the priest and the former with her lover (IX.2.18)]. The night of confusion therefore ends in a draw, in a re-establishment of the *status quo*, which constitutes the happy ending of the story. The dynamic nature of the plot is contrasted by the circularity of the *fabula*, already anticipated in the rubric: "Levasi una badessa … per trovare una sua monaca, a lei *accusata, col suo amante* nel letto" / "le quali vedendo *l'accusata* e fattalane accorgere, fu diliberata, ed ebbe agio di starsi *col suo amante*." The non-progressive quality of the *fabula* is underlined by the epistrophic repetition which conveys the ultimate return to the story's starting point.

Connections

During Emilia's reign, the establishment of links between *novelle* turns into an almost systematic practice, becoming one of the salient features of the day.[18] The narrators tend to compensate for the thematic freedom granted by the queen by explicitly recalling earlier stories and characters. As a general rule, each of the ten *novelle* creates a web of often unmarked pathways that connects it to other tales, highlighting the compact nature of the macrotext and rendering the architecture of the day cohesive. We have already seen that *Decameron* IX.2 is an extra-numerary *"motto" novella*; the story is reminiscent of *Decameron* VI.7, in which Madonna Filippa, having been discovered with her lover, escapes impending peril thanks to her ability to "ben parlare … dove la necessità il richiede" [speak well … when necessity demands it (VI.7.3)], i.e., during the public trial where she stands accused.[19] But

18 See Surdich, "La 'varietà delle cose,'" 242.
19 The analogy has been noted by Bruni, *Boccaccio*, 265–6.

one may also recall the stories of Masetto and (especially) of the abbot and the young monk in I.4, which develops (albeit from a male point of view) the same theme as IX.2, though without the same courtly *décor* or references to the ineluctable nature of erotic desire. The ending is also somewhat different, since in I.4 the infraction of the rule does not become a collective norm but rather a search for bilateral complicity between superior and subordinate.[20]

As we have said, more visible and solid ties connect Elissa's *novella* to the preceding one. A marginal theme of IX.1 may be taken up again and developed further in IX.2, or vice versa, what was central in the former may be confined to the margins in the latter. An example is offered by the handling of the theme of Fortune, which also plays a role in the *novella* of Madonna Francesca, but here Fortune is no more than an unforeseen move in a zero-sum game that would have yielded the same results without the interference of aleatory circumstances. In fact, it is precisely chance that thwarts the two suitors' plans, and yet its role is significantly diminished vis-à-vis the outcome envisaged by their lady, who, as Filomena notes, was "già da sé armata in modo da mandargli ammendun via" [forearmed with a suitable pretext for sending them both packing (IX.1.30)], whatever the success of their adventure.

The theme of "love's powers" also occurs in both *novelle*, but in the first it is presented as the interpretive key to the story (IX.1.4), whereas in the second it is merely a component of the plot, since in this case the maxim that sanctions the impossibility of countering "gli stimoli della carne" is reported as a part of Usimbalda's speech, but not directly spoken by the narrator. In the two *novelle*, the theme of love's powers is intertwined with that of wit or *ingegno*, a connection already highlighted during the Third Day and which is affirmed ever more explicitly in the seventh,

20 See *Decameron* I.4.22: "L'abate … si vergognò di fare al monaco quello che egli, sì come lui, aveva meritato. E perdonatogli e impostogli di ciò che veduto aveva silenzio, onestamente misero la giovanetta di fuori e poi più volte si dee credere ve la facesser tornare" [The Abbott … was loath to inflict upon the monk a punishment of which he himself was no less deserving. So he pardoned the monk and swore him to secrecy concerning what he had seen, then they slipped the girl out unobtrusively, and we can only assume that they afterwards brought her back at regular intervals]; and IX.2.18: "e per ciò chetamente, come infino a quel dì fatto s'era, disse che ciascuna si desse buon tempo quando potesse" [she told them that provided the thing was discreetly arranged, as it had been in the past, they were all at liberty to enjoy theselves whenever they pleased]. On the endings of these two *novelle*, see Baratto, *Realtà e stile* [1996], 249.

the day of erotic *beffe*.[21] It is a theme that Boccaccio generally develops in an anti-Guittonian and anti-Cavalcantian vein,[22] showing that desire does not deprive lovers of their wits but rather renders astute even the most simpleminded. However, in the first two tales of the Ninth Day, the love/*ingegno* nexus may have opposing outcomes.[23] In the second *novella*, love does not deprive Isabetta of her wit, but at the same time it is not love that inspires the "pronto avvedimento" that saves her, as is the case for Ghita, the "semplicetta" of VII.4. In the first tale, on the contrary, the theme of love's powers is interpreted as folly ("[Francesca] aspettò di vedere se sì fossero pazzi che essi il facessero" [her mistress … waited to see whether they were mad enough to carry out her request (IX.1.18)]): if, in the story of Alessandro and Rinuccio, "ogni cosa diviene agli amanti possibile," it is only because love has deprived them of all discretion and of any ability to understand what sort of behaviour is appropriate in the given circumstances. Therefore, their undertaking is not a true act of courage or magnanimity, but an "ardita presunzione" of which Francesca herself is the first to disapprove.

A similar explanation applies to the moral pronounced by Usimbalda, who finds herself compelled to "mutare sermone" in the midst of her speech. The notion that the concupiscent appetite, as a natural stimulus, tends to prevail over cultural assumptions is a fact that, by the Ninth Day, Boccaccio has confirmed on several occasions, with varying degrees of forcefulness but without hesitation. However, in *Decameron* IX.2, the reference to erotic appetite as a law of nature resurfaces, surprisingly, in a degraded and estranged context[24] – in the purely instrumental speech of the abbess, and as a functional component of a plot aimed at showing the hypocrisy of fools who presume to teach others.

---

21 Cf. *Decameron* VII.4.3: "O Amore, chenti e quali sono le tue forze, chenti i consigli e chenti gli avvedimenti!" [O Love, how maniflod and mighty are your powers!]; *Decameron* VII.6.3: "Molti sono li quali, semplicemente parlando, dicono che Amore trae altrui del senno e quasi chi ama fa divenire smemorato" [Many are those who naïvely maintain that Love impairs the intellect and that anyone falling in love is more or less turned into a fool].

22 See Cavalcanti, *Rime* 27.32–3: "for di salute giudicar mantene, / che la 'ntenzione per ragione vale"; compare further with Dino del Garbo, *Scriptum super cantilena Guidonis de Cavalcantibus ("Donna me prega")*, 88, in Fenzi, *La canzone d'amore di Guido Cavalcanti e i suoi antichi commenti*, 124: "in ipso [sc. in love] nulla est sapientia neque discretio. imo potius quasi ultimo illo qui amat, cum bene est in fervore ipsius, devenit in fatuitatem et insipientiam."

23 On this topic, see David Lummus's reading of IX.1 in this volume.

24 See Chiecchi, "Sentenze e proverbi nel *Decameron*," 154. Indeed, Usimbalda's maxim prepares for the story's sudden reversal.

Alongside the thematic variations of *Decameron* IX.1 and 2, we may list several structural variations. If IX.2 is a comic *novella* by definition, there is also a comic side to IX.1, when the *beffa* against the two lovers is set into motion and, of course, in the conclusion. The temporality of the two stories is also identical: the action of both takes place over the course of a single night. The structural variations therefore consist in the different interrelation between the temporality of the story and the temporality of the narration, as well as in the differing developments of the comic.[25] In IX.2, the pace of the narration is brisk, as a *motto* novella demands. The plot and the characters themselves fully coincide with their actions and gestures. There is no narrative lingering on the characters' psychology, their characterization (with the exception of Isabetta), or indeed their words: there are only four utterances conveyed via direct discourse. Although the comic effect relies not so much on the *motto* as on the confusion of the veil with the breeches, the narrator does not detail this event. Elissa's report is limited to a brief and succinct mention of the mistake, fully describing only the ridiculous detail of the "usulieri che di qua e di là pendevano" (IX.2.14),[26] as this feature is central to the *Witz* which concludes the story.

In IX.1, narrative time is more extended, as is required for a *novella a intrigo*,[27] with a lengthy preamble introducing the night of *servitium amoris*, detailed presentations of the characters (including the minor ones), and direct reporting of their discourses. The comic effect of the *novella* relies entirely on the situation, whose humorous quality is enhanced by a full-scale description of its particulars: Alessandro being grabbed by the feet and unceremoniously banged against the benches along the road before being left in the street so that Rinuccio can better escape; the fake corpse rising and fleeing, still in its shroud; Rinuccio, who, having escaped from peril, returns cursing to search for the body.

---

25 Segre's general observations are particularly illuminating on this point: while the *motto* is sudden and trenchant, and thus needs to emerge from a barebones and uncomic narrative, the architecture of the *beffa* includes intermediate steps, which may be underscored, or even triggered, by explicitly comic moments ("La beffa e il comico nella novellistica del Due e Trecento," 88).

26 This detail is already present in the *Dit* (267): "Vit les lanieres qui pendoient / devant se[n] front et baulioient" [Saw the strings dangling up and down in front of her forehead].

27 The term is originally Segre's ("La beffa e il comico nella novellistica del Due e Trecento," 88), who lists *beffe* stories among the "novelle a intrigo."

Ethic and Aesthetic of the *Witz*

The sequence of the two stories can be seen as a first instance of the principle of variety that grounds Emilia's choice of a free theme for the day:

> Dilettose donne, assai manifestamente veggiamo che, poi che *i buoi* alcuna parte del giorno hanno faticato sotto il giogo ristretti, quegli esser dal giogo alleviati e disciolti, e liberamente dove lor più piace, per li boschi lasciati sono andare alla pastura: e veggiamo ancora non esser men belli, ma molto più *i giardini* di varie piante fronzuti che i boschi ne' quali solamente querce veggiamo; per le quali cose io estimo, avendo riguardo quanti giorni sotto certa legge ristretti ragionato abbiamo, che sì come a bisognosi, di vagare alquanto e vagando *riprender forze* a rientrar sotto il giogo non solamente sia utile ma oportuno. (VIII.Concl.4)
>
> [Delectable ladies, we may readily observe that when oxen have laboured in chains beneath the yoke for a certain portion of the day, their yoke is removed and they are put out to grass, being allowed to roam freely through the woods wherever they please. Similarly, we may perceive that gardens stocked with numerous different trees are much more beautiful than forests consisting solely of oaks. And therefore, having regard to the number of days during which our deliberations have been confined within a predetermined scheme, I consider that it would be both appropriate and useful for us to wander at large for a while, and in so doing recover strength for returning once again beneath the yoke.]

By resorting to a double simile (narrators as oxen freed from the yoke; narration as a garden), Emilia refers the principle of variety both to the narrators, who will better prepare for the next day's labour if they are allowed to change their routine, and to the narration, which will be more pleasing if varied. Therefore, variety has both an ethical significance – concerning the narrators' lives at the *cornice* level – and an aesthetic-rhetorical significance, referring to the framed narration. The idea that leisure is a necessary interlude from labour and a preparation for it is traditional.[28] We may trace it back to the paragraphs of the *Ethics* devoted to play (*eutrapelia*), where Aristotle and his commentator, Thomas Aquinas, explain that *ludus* is necessary for work itself,

28 On this topic, see Barsella and Marchesi's Introduction in this volume.

and suggest a resemblance between rest from activities of the mind and rest from physical activity (implied in the oxen simile in VIII.Concl.).[29] Both Aristotle and Aquinas stress the links between play, comicality, and speech, which results in the development of a theory of ethical entertainment *and* of ludic discourse. What makes a good entertaining speech is the same principle that rules ethical behaviour, that is, measure:

> Existente autem *requie* in vita *et in hac conversatione cum ludo*, videtur et hic esse *collocutio* quaedam *consona et qualia oportet dicere* et ut, similiter autem et *audire*. (1128 a 1)
>
> [Since life also includes leisure and in that is included pleasant social interaction, it is apparent that there is some form of proper conversation and specific things to be said and ways of saying them, and similarly to be heard.][30]

Play is a form of experience *and* a form of communication. It is not gratuitous, then, that the narration of the Ninth Day prevalently relies on the two principal comic genres in the *Decameron*: the *motto* and the *beffa*. In this sense, the first two *novelle* of the day can be seen as a prolongation of those that could be called the *giornate* of *eutrapelia*: *in verbis* (the Sixth Day) or *in factis* (the Seventh and Eighth Days).[31]

Pampinea, Filomena, and Lauretta – the theorizers of the witty *motto* – are particularly attentive to the "ethics" of the ludic narrative and highlight its double nature, moral and rhetorical. Making an eloquent *motto* is both a mode of behaviour and a form of discourse, a particular type of *ornatus* whose aesthetic success requires a careful application of the

---

29 See Aristotle, *Ethicorum libri*, in *S. Thomae de Aquino Sententia libri Ethicorum*, 256; italics mine: "*sicut* enim homo indiget a *corporalibus laboribus* interdum desistendo quiescere, *ita* etiam indiget ut *ab intentione animi* qua rebus seriis homo intendit interdum anima hominis requiescat, quod quidem fit per ludum" [Just as humans need to rest at times, stopping in their bodily toils, so too they need to have their soul rest from the effort of mentally attending to serious endeavors. And this is realized through play].

30 Aristotle, *Ethicorum libri*, 255; italics mine. Ever since his Neapolitan years, Boccaccio had owned a copy of the *Ethicorum libri*, which is now in the Biblioteca Ambrosiana and in whose margins he copied out Aquinas's commentary in his own hand. For a description of the codex, see Cesari, "L'*Etica* di Aristotele del codice Ambrosiano A 204 inf."; Barsella, "I 'marginalia' di Boccaccio all'Etica Nicomachea di Aristotele"; and Cursi, "Giovanni Boccaccio – Autografi," 52–3.

31 On the ludic quality of the *Decameron* as a whole, see Mazzotta, *The World at Play*.

principle of *aptum*. Indeed, if "è da guardare e come e quando e con cui e similmente dove si motteggia" [one ... has to be careful about how, when, on whom, and likewise where one exercises one's wit (VI.3.4)], this is not only to adapt words to things and to the circumstances of speech, but also to ensure that the *motto* does not become a *villania*, so that it may limit itself to biting "come la pecora morde" (VI.3.3) without offending the interlocutor.[32] In the realization of the *motto*, rhetorical *aptum* therefore reproduces the ethical model from which it is derived, corresponding to the Aristotelian criterion of measure.

Contrary to what Usimbalda believes, Isabetta knows how to speak aptly, how to choose the right time and place for her *motto*. Indeed, she speaks when constrained by the necessity of the moment, in the midst of a public trial and against direct accusations whose outcome could be tragic. What's more, she knows how to say "onestamente villania," stigmatizing the abbess's vice without attacking it directly: "Madonna, se Dio v'aiuti, annodatevi la cuffia e poscia mi dite ciò che voi volete"[33] [By the grace of God, Mother Abbess, tie up your bonnet, and then you may say whatever you like to me (IX.2.15)]. Isabetta's *motto* is not a direct aggression; if taken literally, it sounds like an innocent and perhaps slightly foolish observation, apparently lacking any relevance. Are the "usulieri" not indeed hanging down from Usimbalda's "headdress"? Are they not actually made to be tied? The comic and aggressive quality of the riposte is dissimulated,[34] as Cicero's *De oratore* prescribes: "Salsa sunt etiam, quae habent suspicionem ridiculi absconditam" (II.69). The comic effect is due to the disjunction between the uttered *verba* and the *res* that they imply (sexual sin, inadequacy as an abbess, hypocrisy, etc.). And if the abbess does not immediately understand the *motto*'s meaning, it is not because she is one of the (few) "non intendenti" characters of the *Decameron*, but because of the very nature of the *motto*, whose humour lies not *in verbis* but *in re*.[35] Usimbalda therefore cannot understand it until she has touched this *res* with her own hands: "molte

32 As Aristotle explains, the forms of ludic speech are primarily aggressive, hence moderation is of especial importance in the witticism.

33 Similarly, in VI.9.12 Cavalcanti's *motto* grants Betto and his brigade a comparable conditional liberty: "Signori, voi *mi potete dire* a casa vostra *ciò che vi piace*."

34 From a rhetorical point of view, Isabetta's witty reply is comparable to dissimulative irony, on whose relevance in the *Decameron*, see Delcorno, "Ironia/Parodia," 169. As Tateo remarks (*Boccaccio*, 155), a rhetoric of dissimulation is implicit in the anti-hierarchical nature that the witticism assumes in the tale.

35 Cicero, *De oratore* II.59: "Duo sunt enim genera facetiarum, quorum alterum re tractatur alterum dicto" [For there are two kinds of jokes, one of which is concerned with things, the other with words].

delle monache levarono il viso al capo della badessa e, ella similmente *ponendovisi le mani, s'accorsero* perché Isabetta così diceva" [Several of the nuns looked up at the Abbess, and the Abbess likewise raised her hands to the sides of her head, so that they all saw what Isabetta was driving at (IX.2.17)]. Isabetta's *Witz* is an exemplary instance of courteous eloquence; it merely brings to full light the intrinsic comicality of the circumstances, but with perfect understatement.[36]

What Are We Laughing About?

Aside from some significant thematic differences, the main dissimilarity between IX.2 and its male counterpart, I.4, rests on the realization of the *motto*. The comicality of IX.2 relies primarily on "things," on the breeches that perch on the head of Usimbalda while she solemnly sits in the chapter. The comicality of I.4, instead, is not *in rebus* but *in verbis*, consisting in the word-play of the novice rather than in the narrative situation. The young monk has invited a young woman to his cell, and, jesting with her "men cautamente" than he should, is heard by the abbot. Unlike Isabetta, the monk realizes that he has been found out. He therefore pretends to leave to fetch some wood so that the abbot may fall into the same sin. When his superior then wishes to punish him, the novice says:

> voi ancora non m'avavate monstrato che' monaci si debban far *dalle femine priemere come da' digiuni e dalle vigilie*; ma ora che mostrato me l'avete, vi prometto ... di mai più in ciò non peccare, anzi farò sempre come io a voi ho veduto fare. (I.4.21)
>
> [you had failed until just now to show me that monks have women to support, as well as fasts and vigils. But now that you have pointed this out, I promise that ... I will never again commit the same error. On the contrary, I shall always follow your good example.]

---

36 Also in the two *fabliaux* the comic effect of the *motto* rests *in re* rather than *in verbis*, but the rhetorical technique is very different. The quip "gardés bien qu'a l'oeul vous pent" [beware of what dangles in front of your eye] is not based on a seemingly irrelevant observation, but on a literal rendering of the expression "pendre a l'oeul," which means "to run a risk or be in danger." (And cf. *Le Roman de Renart*, v. 28806; "Que savés vous que il vous pent / Bielle dame, devant vos ieuls" [what do you know, fair lady, of what is right in front of your eyes?], in the version of the *Dit*, 268). On the technique of the *motto* in the *Decameron*, see Cuomo, "Sillogizzare motteggiando e motteggiare sillogizzando"; Mineo, "La sesta giornata del 'Decameron.'"

The *motto* has a conclusive function in both *novelle*, but in I.4 its humoristic effect is prepared by the narrator's description of the sexual intercourse between the abbot and the young woman, which aims at rendering humorous a situation that is not comic *per se*:

> La giovane … assai agevolmente si piegò a' piaceri dell'abate: il quale … in su il letticello del monaco salitosene, *avendo forse riguardo al grave peso della sua dignità* e alla tenera età della giovane, temendo forse di non offenderla *per troppa gravezza*, non sopra il petto di lei salì ma lei sopra il suo petto si pose, e per lungo spazio con lei si trastullò. (I.4.18)[37]
>
> [The girl … fell in very readily with the Abbott's wishes. He … lowered himself onto the monk's little bed. But out of regard, perhaps, for the weight of his reverend person and the tender age of the girl, and not wishing to do her any injury, he settled down beneath her instead of lying on top, and in this way he sported with her at considerable length.]

By contrast, Isabetta's *motto* does not require any rhetorical preparation, since it simply makes visible a comicality that is already inherent in the situation. Whereas in I.4 the narrator's rhetoric of metaphorical and literal pressure is crucial for triggering the comical effect, Elissa's rhetoric in IX.2 is not related to the comical side of the story, but rather to its thematically more serious aspect: the hypocrisy of figures of authority and of fools who presume to act as "maestri."

Rupturing the dynamic of looking but not seeing, the *motto* unmasks the hypocrisy of Usimbalda's reprimands and literally makes visible what appearances conceal,[38] revealing her inadequacy

37 Both the novice's quip and Dioneo's narration are based on a rhetorical technique that exploits the polysemy of a single semantic register: that of the pressure exerted by weight. Since Dioneo converts the metaphoric weightiness of the abbot's status into the literal weight of his body, the novice can then compare the physical "pressing" of a woman's body to the spiritual pressure of fasting, thereby converting his erotic adventure into a meritorious act, a "particular" of Saint Benedict's rule he has just learned from the abbot. See Rossi, "Ironia e parodia nel 'Decameron,'" 367. On the differences between the *motti* of I.4 and IX.2, see further Surdich, "La 'varietà delle cose,'" 241–2.

38 From its first appearance in the *Decameron*, the *motto* is related to the disjunction between interiority and exteriority, being and appearance: "oggi poche o niuna donna rimasa ci sia la quale o ne 'ntenda alcun leggiadro [motto] o a quello, se pur lo 'ntendesse, sappia rispondere … Perciò che quella vertù che già fu nell'anime delle passate hanno le moderne rivolta in ornamenti del corpo" [nowadays … few or none of the women who are left can recognize a shaft of wit when they hear one, or reply to it even if they recognize it. For this special skill, which once resided in a

qua abbess.[39] If the narration does not need to prepare or linger on the comic, it is because the image of the breeches-turned-headdress speaks for itself and does not need to be emphasized (by the narrator), but only brought to the attention of the spectators' gaze (by the character's *Witz*). The sudden epiphany of "things" reveals the vanity of speech and the exteriority of behaviours: the solemnity of the public hearing, the fame of Usimbalda and her monastery.[40] Laughter is prompted by the unveiling of reality, finally freed from the intolerably cumbersome incrustation of falsities. Its intrinsic comic nature sweeps away the abbess's pretence to moralization and the authority of unjustified hierarchies. As in other humoristic tales in the *Decameron*, the comic in IX.2 produces two contrasting effects: a destructive and inherently negative one and a reconstructive, positive one, which, as E. Fenzi writes, "we could distill into the formula 'accepting the real.'"[41]

If the destructive issue of the priest's breeches tale is clearly aimed at questioning the legitimacy of authority not grounded on ethical prominence, in what does its *pars costruens* consist? The *novella* does, of course, conclude with a collective recognition of a particular state of affairs, with a triumph of the principle of reality that contrasts natural laws with an ideal behaviour that is publicly declared impracticable. Nevertheless, in the context of IX.2, this blunt triumph of the natural law of appetite is problematic and contradictory – one must not forget that this law is affirmed in the context of Usimbalda's opportunistic speech. Hence, comic pleasure does not so much spring from "nature" prevailing over *ingegno* or ethical choice as much as from the sporadic and fortuitous disclosure of what has been hidden behind the veil of

---

woman's very soul, has been replaced in our modern women by the adornment of the body (I.10.5)].

39 On this notion, see Savelli, "Riso." On the comic in the *Decameron*, see Neumeister, "Die Praxis des Lachens im Decameron"; Fenzi, "Ridere e lietamente morire"; Ciccuto and Furlan, "Dossier" (also for the earlier bibliography on the subject); Bausi, "Le *forme del comico* nel *Decameron*." On the anti-hierarchical nature of the *motto*, see Chiappelli, "L'episodio di Travale," 23.

40 When it reappears in the auto-apologetic context of the Author's Conclusion (7), the figurative image of walking about with breeches on one's head also alludes to a disjunction between words and things, speech and behaviour.

41 I quote from Fenzi, "Ridere e lietamente morire," which has significantly influenced this section of the essay. Here is the full citation, paraphrased above: "la miracolosa vitalità del comico di Boccaccio sta … nell'equilibrio perfetto tra l'istanza dissolutoria e dunque propriamente negativa del comico … e un'istanza che, nella negazione, appare propriamente ricostruttiva e positiva, che potremmo riassumere nella formula 'accettazione del reale' e che è essenzialmente affidata al riso" (141).

appearances. Instead of the oppositions between *natura/nutritura* and reality/ideal at stake in other *novelle* of the *Decameron*, where the comic is entrusted unambiguously to the triumph of sexual desire, Elissa's rhetorical strategy enhances the reality/appearance binary, as befits a narration focused on the hypocrisy of fools who presume to be teachers, where the comic effect lies in the dissolution of their authority.

The story's conclusion retrospectively lends a new meaning to the rhetorical strategy deployed in the *novella*: the insistence on the semantic field of vision/realization, the modalities of comic narration, the ironic register, and the sudden inversion of the *fabula*. The pleasure of laughter issues not only from the sexual topic but also from the passage from blindness to sight, from the unexpected satisfaction of a natural quest for knowledge. And it is also the somewhat bitter intellectual pleasure of a usually "impossible" epiphany, subtracted from the cognitive capacities of man and entrusted to the caprice of Fortune.

Empty Womb and Full Bellies in *Decameron* IX.3

FEDERICA ANICHINI

The third tale of Day Nine is included in the "ciclo di Calandrino," a cluster of four novellas (VIII.3, VIII.6, IX.3, and IX.5) built around the Florentine character. Like a mask of the *Commedia dell'Arte*, Calandrino acts throughout the four stories in a consistent and predictable manner. A man made "di grossa pasta,"[1] he is the epitome of foolishness – by the third novella that features him, inasmuch as Calandrino has steadily demonstrated his limited mental abilities, the *Decameron*'s audience has become thoroughly familiar with the uncompromising credulousness that makes him the privileged target for a *beffa*. Filostrato, the narrator of IX.3, treats Calandrino's profile as common knowledge, since certainly "di sopra," before, the listeners have already heard about him: "Mostrato è di sopra assai chiaro chi Calandrin fosse e gli altri de' quali in questa novella ragionar debbo; e perciò senza più dirne, dico che …"[2] [We have already heard a good deal about Calandrino and his companions … I shall now proceed to recount … (IX.3.4)]. Fulfilling the audience's expectations, the story that Filostrato is about to tell

1 In VIII.3 Calandrino is caught helplessly trying to remember the name that he just heard – heliotrope, the miraculous stone that could make him invisible: "A Calandrino, che era di grossa pasta, era già il nome uscito di mente" [Calandrino, being rather dense, had already forgotten its name (VIII.3.31)]. All quotations from the *Decameron* are drawn from Branca's edition in *Tutte le opere di Giovanni Boccaccio*, vol. 4 (1976). All translations are from McWilliam (1995).

2 In VIII.6, another narrator, Filomena, omits to introduce Calandrino, similarly concerned with the pace of the narration: "Chi Calandrino, Bruno e Buffalmacco fossero non bisogna che io vi mostri, ché assai l'avete di sopra udito; e perciò più avanti faccendomi dico che Calandrino aveva un suo poderetto …" [It is unnecessary for me to explain to you who Calandrino, Bruno and Buffalmacco were, for you have heard enough on that score in the earlier tale. So I shall omit the preliminaries and tell you that Calandrino had a little farm not far from Florence … (VIII.6.4)].

depends on Calandrino's belief in what he is told, no matter how far-fetched the implications are. Making full use of Calandrino's nature, Bruno, Buffalmacco, and Nello, the chief pranksters in IX.3,[3] design a *beffa* aimed at making him believe he is pregnant.

The Prank: Avarice on Trial

Filostrato begins the novella by describing Calandrino engaged in negotiations with a few Florentine brokers after having received an inheritance from his aunt. The sum is small, but large enough in Calandrino's mind to purchase an estate. Bruno and Buffalmacco learn of Calandrino's fortune and try to convince him to enjoy the money in their company instead. Once they fail to prevail upon him, and acting on the advice of their friend Nello, Bruno and Buffalmacco design a trick that will chastise Calandrino's avarice and allow them to finally have a meal at his expense. First they make Calandrino believe that he looks so gravely ill as to seem half-dead – "tu par mezzo morto" (IX.3.797) – then they instruct a doctor, Maestro Simone, also a returning character (he is the victim of one of Bruno and Buffalmacco's pranks in VIII.9) to inform Calandrino that his disease is decisively a pregnancy. Calandrino does not hesitate to trust such a diagnosis and responds as his general attitude no less than his cultural context dictates. In tune with his unworldliness and with the misogynistic commonplaces of medieval culture, he immediately lashes out at the most preposterous culprit in his imaginary predicament: his wife Tessa. Supportively introduced in VIII.3 by Boccaccio as a "bella e valente donna" [a handsome-looking gentlewoman (VIII.3.51)], Monna Tessa never fails to uncover the tricks played on her husband, while Calandrino regularly blames (or beats) her every time reality proves her right.[4] In IX.3 Calandrino holds her accountable for his pregnancy because of her sexual appetite and position of choice: "Oimè! Tessa, questo m'hai fatto tu, che non vuogli stare altro che di sopra: io il ti diceva bene!" [Ah, Tessa, this is your doing! You will insist on lying on top. I told you all along what would happen (IX.3.21)]. Given his anatomical deficiencies, Calandrino looks at his pregnancy as life-threatening: "Come partorirò io questo figliuolo? onde uscirà egli? Ben veggo che io son

3 Bruno and Buffalmacco appear in VIII.3, VIII.6, VIII.9, and IX.5; Nello in IX.5.

4 In VIII.3 Calandrino claims that Tessa invalidated the heliotrope's virtue and therefore made him visible again. In his fury, he associates his wife *tout court* with the devil: "questo diavolo di questa femina maladetta" [this blasted devil of a woman (VIII.3.61)].

morto per la rabbia di questa mia moglie, che tanto la faccia Idio trista quanto io voglio esser lieto" [What am I to do? How am I to produce this infant? Where will it come out? This woman's going to be the death of me now ... may God make her as miserable as I desire to be happy (IX.3.23)]. Terrified at the upcoming event, Calandrino places his trust in Maestro Simone, offering him the entire sum of his inheritance to pay for the suggested cure, a potion made with three fat capons. The capons turn, in fact, into a rich broth destined for the table of the tricksters, who feast on it after having served the allegedly pregnant man an alcoholic medicinal concoction. As promised by Maestro Simone, this "chiarea"[5] promptly restores Calandrino's health, and marks the success of the *beffa* – it makes Calandrino "spregno" and grateful, the pranksters well fed and satisfied, and Tessa yet again annoyed with her easily deluded husband:

> Calandrino lieto, levatosi, s'andò a fare i fatti suoi ... E Bruno e Buffalmacco e Nello rimaser contenti d'aver con ingegni saputa schernire l'avarizia di Calandrino, quantunque monna Tessa, avvedendosene, molto col marito ne brontolasse." (IX.3.33)

> So Calandrino got up and went happily about his business ... Bruno, Buffalmacco and Nello were delighted with themselves for getting round Calandrino's avarice so cleverly, but they had not deceived monna Tessa, who muttered and moaned to her husband about it for a long time afterwards.

The concluding lines of the novella remind readers of the moral repercussions of the prank, namely Calandrino's avarice. Bruno, Buffalmacco, and Nello plan a *beffa* literally "alle spese di Calandrino" [at Calandrino's expense (IX.3.6)] – they plot against Calandrino's ungenerosity and measure their success by the fact that Calandrino's money ultimately did not buy his curative potion, the "chiarea," but rather the three capons that went to fill their stomachs. From this perspective, Calandrino's imaginary disease, his pregnancy, stands as the indirect remedy to Calandrino's lack of liberality. This character's flaw surfaces

5 "Chiarea" is a term for a medicinal beverage. In the Lessicografia of the Accademica della Crusca (1st edition, 1612, www.lessicografia.it) its ingredients are listed as cinnamon, cloves, black pepper, long pepper, wine, and apples ("togli cennamo dramme una, garofani grani venti, pepe nero grani venti, pepe lungo dramme una e mezzo, vin buono uno mezzo quarto, mele once quattro").

as a trigger to the plot also in VIII.6 and is a relevant element in other Calandrino stories.[6]

In another novella from the same day, VIII.3, Calandrino seems for once to obey the rules of empathy and generosity, when he sets forth frantically looking for his friends "li quali spezialissimamente amava" in order to share the search for the heliotrope and his prospect of wealth with them.[7] This occurrence is, however, an isolated example. Calandrino's moral compass has no foundation, and in the same novella his fantasy of becoming invisible also prompts his plan to steal money from the counters of the money-changers, unnoticed:

> Noi la troverem per certo [the heliotrope] per ciò che io la conosco; e trovata che noi l'avremo, che avrem noi a fare altro se non mettercela nella scarsella e andare alle tavole de' cambiatori, le quali sapete che stanno sempre cariche di grossi e di fiorini, e torcene quanti noi ne vorremmo? (VIII.3.29)

---

6 In VIII.6, Calandrino's refusal to share a pig with Bruno and Buffalmacco launches the story, which concludes with the tricksters blackmailing Calandrino and demanding two capons: "'Noi sì siamo usi delle tue beffe e conoscianle; tu non ce ne potresti far più! e per ciò, a dirti il vero, noi ci abbiamo durata fatica in far l'arte, per che noi intendiamo che tu ci doni due paia di capponi, se non che noi diremo a monna Tessa ogni cosa.' Calandrino, vedendo che creduto non gli era, parendogli avere assai dolore, non volendo anche il riscaldamento della moglie, diede a costoro due paia di capponi. Li quali, avendo essi salato il porco, portatisene a Firenze, lasciaron Calandrino col danno e con le beffe" ["You can't fool us anymore: we've cottoned on to these tricks of yours. As a matter of fact, that's why we took so much trouble with the spell we cast on the sweets; and unless you give us two brace of capons for our pains, we intend to tell Monna Tessa the whole story." Seeing that they refused to believe him and thinking that he had enough trouble on his hands without letting himself in for a diatribe from his wife, Calandrino gave them two brace of capons. And after they had salted the pig, they carried their spoils back to Florence with them, leaving Calandrino to scratch his head and rue his losses (VIII.6.55–6)].

7 "Calandrino, avendo tutte queste cose seco notate, fatto sembianti d'avere altro a fare, si partì da Maso e seco propose di volere cercare di questa pietra; ma diliberò di non volerlo fare senza saputa di Bruno e di Buffalmacco; li quali spezialissimamente amava. Diessi adunque a cercar di costoro, acciò che senza indugio, e prima che alcuno altro, n'andassero a cercare, e tutto il rimanente di quella mattina consumò in cercargli" [Having made a mental note of all that he had heard, Calandrino pretended that he had other things to attend to and took his leave of Maso, determined to go and look for one of these stones; but he decided that before doing so, he would have to inform Bruno and Buffalmacco, who were his bosom friends. He therefore went to look for them, so that they could all set forth at once in search of the stone before anyone else should come to hear about it, and he spent the whole rest of the morning trying to trace them (VIII.3.25)].

[We will find it without a doubt, because I know what it looks like; and once we've found it, all we have to do is to put it in our purses and go to the money-changers, whose counters, as you know, are always loaded with groats and florins, and help ourselves to as much as we want.]

Despite the solid evidence of Calandrino's unethical mindset, such mindset is in IX.3 only a tangential target for the pranksters. Bruno, Buffalmacco, and Nello have ultimately no interest in converting their "sozio" to liberality. On one hand, they obviously enjoy the fact that Calandrino does not even suspect he has been gulled into spending his money on them as opposed to on himself; on the other, their primary aim is, in fact, to survive. Bruno, Buffalmacco, and Nello are driven by the urge to fulfil a basic human necessity, their need for food: "diliberar tutti e tre di dover trovar modo da ugnersi il grifo alle spese di Calandrino" [the three of them decided they must find some way of stuffing themselves at Calandrino's expense (IX.3.6)]. Given the fact that Calandrino becomes generous despite, and unbeknownst to, himself, the act of liberality that the three fellows force upon him as a result of a *beffa* can hardly be taken as moral progress.

In his *Proemio*, Boccaccio indicates moral teaching as a programmatic component of his work. In it he famously declares that the "sollazzevoli cose" he is about to present to his female audience come with "utile consiglio," "utile," that is, to discern good and evil:

Delle quali [novelle] le già dette donne, che queste leggeranno, parimente diletto delle sollazzevoli cose in quelle mostrate e utile consiglio potranno pigliare, in quanto potranno cognoscere quello che sia da fuggire e che sia similmente da seguitare. (5)

[In reading them [the tales], the aforesaid ladies will be able to derive, not only pleasure from the entertaining matters therein set forth, but also some useful advice. For they will learn to recognize what should be avoided and likewise what should be pursued.]

In the case of IX.3, the obvious moral issue at stake is Calandrino's avarice. Yet, the "utile" is illustrated by a further thread of the novella, spun by Calandrino's nonpareil ability to believe that any word uttered at him creates, and therefore corresponds to, a real circumstance. This specific aspect of Calandrino's foolishness is not necessarily a weakness. Through the character of the fool, actually, the novella imparts a teaching that concerns language as a tool of creation and, ultimately, the value of poetic imagination.

The Moral of Fictions and Depictions

The fact that in IX.3 the four main male characters, pranksters and victim alike, share the same trade – they are all painters – can hardly be overlooked. As it has been suggested, by choosing one of the most common Florentine trades Boccaccio carries out a geographical and temporal strategy – he brings back the readers' focus to the plague-ridden city and heralds the return of the ten narrators to Florence.[8] While possibly pointing at a place and time of resolution of the *Decameron*'s plot, these "dipintori" embody a theme of great import for Boccaccio. The presence of Giotto among the characters of the *Decameron*, as well as the high praise the artist is given there, is a sound indication of the interest Boccaccio developed in the fine arts, and especially in the achievements of the artists among his contemporaries. In VI.5 Boccaccio introduces Giotto as "una delle luci della fiorentina gloria" [a shining monument to the glory of Florence (VI.5.6)], acknowledging his pivotal role in building the reputation of Florence as capital of the arts. Boccaccio focuses on what he considers Giotto's main accomplishment, namely the realism of his painted works.[9] Giotto's gift for infusing life into his figures – a talent that is celebrated also by Vasari in his gallery of artists' lives[10] – and the innovative "narrative" painting he created

8 "Although suggestive recent studies have postulated distinct groupings for the tales based on Boccaccio's inclusion of other Trecento artists, Calandrino's exploits with his fellow painters Bruno and Buffalmacco and with other Florentine wits such as Maso del Saggio, and with the Bologna-trained doctor Maestro Simone, may also suggest a cluster of Florentine types (artisans, wags, frauds clever, pompous, or failed) whose concatenated adventures herald the return of the *brigata* itself to the complex social order of the city after the recreative excursus of storytelling" (Martinez, "Calandrino and the Powers of the Stone," 1–2).

9 "E l'altro, il cui nome fu Giotto, ebbe uno ingegno di tanta eccellenzia, che niuna cosa dà la natura, madre di tutte le cose e operatrice col continuo girar de' cieli, che egli con lo stile e con la penna o col pennello non dipignesse sì simile a quella, che non simile, anzi più tosto dessa paresse, in tanto che molte volte nelle cose da lui fatte si truova che il visivo senso degli uomini vi prese errore, quello credendo esser vero che era dipinto" [The second, whose name was Giotto, was a man of such outstanding genius that there was nothing in the whole of creation that he could not depict with his stylus, pen, or brush. And so faithful did he remain to Nature (who is the mother and the motive force of all created things, via the constant rotation of the heavens), that whatever he depicted had the appearance, not of a reproduction, but of the thing itself, so that one very often finds, with the works of Giotto, that people's eyes are deceived and they mistake the picture for the real thing (VI.5.5)].

10 "Et insieme a Fiorenza inviatisi, non solo in poco tempo pareggiò il fanciullo la maniera di Cimabue, ma ancora divenne tanto imitatore della natura, che ne' tempi suoi sbandì affatto quella greca goffa maniera, e risucitò la moderna e buona arte

stood as a relevant model for the *Decameron*'s author.[11] Beyond providing an opportunity for acknowledging a great master, figurative art is a consistent point of reference for the author of the *Decameron*. The four fellows of Days Eight and Nine have quite rudimentary painting skills – at least for Calandrino, who points out in VIII.3 that they spend their days besmearing the walls "like snails do."[12] Still, their trade is deployed in the narrative strategy of the novellas, specifically as a key factor for the effectiveness of the *beffa*. Because Nello, Bruno, and Buffalmacco are painters, they can convincingly manufacture the essential backdrop for a prank, i.e., a persuasive imitation of reality[13] – especially, as in IX.3, if their fiction is supported by artfully chosen words. When they call attention to the appearances they have just fabricated, the three painters repeatedly refer to Calandrino's pregnancy as factual reality even before the examination of the doctor, who, instructed by them, will shortly thereafter scientifically and officially diagnose Calandrino's condition:

> Calandrino allora disse: – Deh! Sì, compagno mio, vavvi e sappimi ridire come il *fatto* sta, ché io mi sento non so che dentro. – Bruno, andatosene al Maestro Simone, vi fu prima che la fanticella che il segno portava, ed ebbe informato maestro Simon del *fatto* … – Calandrino, io non voglio che tu ti

della pittura, et introdusse il ritrar di naturale le persone vive, che molte centinaia d'anni non s'era usato" [Having moved to Florence, the young boy did not only in a short time reach Cimabue in his style, but he also became such a deep imitator of nature that he totally banished the clumsy Greek style in his time and resurrected in its stead the good and modern art of paining. Also, he introduced the portrayal of people from life, something that had not been done for hundred of years] (Vasari, *Le Vite*, 118)].

11 Marcello Ciccuto confirms Vasari's point, specifying that it was Giotto's openness toward naturalism and narrative painting that, by emerging powerfully from the core of Giotto's own poetry, convinced Boccaccio to take the painter as cipher ("la figura araldica") for some essential aspects of his own poetics (Ciccuto, "Un'antica canzone di Giotto," 412).

12 Calandrino's debasing description is partially explained by the fact that the prospect of becoming invisible, and rich, is at that moment eclipsing what he does for a living: "Niuno ci vedrà; e così potremo arricchire subitamente, senza avere tutto dì a schiccherare le mura a modo che fa la lumaca" [No one will see us; and so we'll be able to get rich quick, without being forced to daub walls all the time like a lot of snails (VIII.3.29)].

13 "The power to create and dissolve appearances has been noted by a number of the novella's readers as peculiarly appropriate to a group of painters; and though Bruno and Buffalmacco do no painting in VIII.3, it is clear that their skill in feigning appearances is clearly marked in the text" (Martinez, "Calandrino and the Powers of the Stone," 10).

sgomenti, ché, lodato sia Iddio, noi ci siamo sì tosto accorti del *fatto*, che con poca fatica e in pochi dì ti diliberrerò; ma conviensi un poco spendere. (IX.3.18, 26, emphases added)

[– Ah, yes, there's a good fellow! – said Calandrino – go to him and find out for me how matters stand. Goodness knows what's going on inside my poor stomach. I feel awful. Bruno therefore set off for the doctor's, arriving there ahead of the girl carrying the specimen, and explained to Master Simone what they were up to … – Now there is no cause for alarm, Calandrino. By the grace of God we've diagnosed the trouble early enough for me to cure you quite easily in a matter of a few days. But it's going to be cost you a pretty penny.]

The presence of Calandrino brings about a clash of imagination and truthfulness in another novella of his cycle. In the introduction to IX.5, Fiammetta, the narrator, almost anticipating a suspect excess of fantasy in the Calandrino tale she is about to tell, draws the readers' attention to the "truth of the fact" on which the tale is based. She further elaborates by explaining that true content is essential to the entertainment of the audience.[14] If the narrator were not to abide by the truth, Fiammetta reasons with her fellow narrators, the audience's pleasure would be diminished:

Per la qualcosa, posto che assai volte de' fatti di Calandrino detto si sia tra noi, riguardando, sì come poco avanti disse Filostrato, che essi son tutti piacevoli, ardirò, oltre alle dette, dirvene una novella: la quale, se io dalla verità del fatto mi fossi scostare voluta o volessi, avrei ben saputo e saprei sotto altri nomi comporla e raccontarla; ma per ciò che il partirsi dalla verità delle cose state nel novellare è gran diminuire di diletto negl'intendenti, in propria forma, dalla ragion di sopra detta aiutata, la vi dirò. (IX.5.5)

[Hence, albeit we have referred many times to the doings of Calandrino, they are invariably so amusing, as Filostrato pointed out a little earlier[,] that I shall venture to add a further tale to those we have already heard about him. I could easily have told it in some other way, using fictitious names, had I wished to do so; but since by departing from the truth of what actually happened, the storyteller greatly diminishes the pleasure of

14 Truth and pleasure are combined in *De arte poetica* – a text familiar to Boccaccio – in which Horace states that what the artist creates should be realistic, if the aim is to please the audience: "ficta voluptatis causa sint proxima veris" [things that are feigned for pleasure's sake should have a near resemblance to the truth (I.338)].

the listeners, I shall turn for support to my opening remarks, and tell it in its proper form.]

Fiammetta's argument, that the "diletto" of the listeners is a function of the "verità del fatto," is a rare instance in which Boccaccio brings to the fore the issue of realism, and deals with it in direct terms. Realism in the *Decameron* is a complex notion that can be only partially addressed in terms of a representation of historical reality, an approach usually identified as a mark of the emerging mercantile culture.[15] While the *Decameron*'s tales resonate with historical references, which have the immediate goal of captivating the audience,[16] those references operate in the text as mere allusions. Rather than functioning as components attesting the documentary value of the *Decameron*, they serve as centres of gravity for meaningful contents.[17] Historical truth is not necessarily, or always, the measure for the *Decameron*'s realism, if one considers that Boccaccio employs the historical and the supernatural as materials equally valid for the general objective of delivering exemplary stories.[18]

15 "Although with different nuances of definition, realism remains by and large the trait that scholarship associates with the *Decameron* as testifying emblematically to the mercantile culture and 'bourgeois' mentality permeating Boccaccio's world. The verisimilar representation of historical reality, in other words, tends to be associated with the character of 'modernity' in Boccaccio's masterpiece" (Barsella, "The Merchant and the Sacred," 12).

16 As Pier Massimo Forni noted, narrator and audience share a solid reference system for perceiving and evaluating the world around them, so much so that when reality enters the narrative (in the form of historical determination for characters or events) it does so already as incorporated (or incorporable) into that horizon. Any aspect that appears in the text "con la punta del nuovo" is always already accepted within a rhetoric of reality "categorizzante e generalizzante" that leaves readers the sole task of assenting to the event and its established categorization (Forni, "Retorica del reale," 187).

17 As Vittore Branca noted, the *Decameron*'s historical figures have an eminently evocative function. Boccaccio resorted to historical references – in the form of the evocation of well-known names, places, deeds – to give concrete evidence and narrative imaginative range ("visualizzare in grandiosi cicli di affreschi") to the ethical truths of his time ("queste verità prammatiche nella visione medievale della vita") (Branca, *Boccaccio medievale* [1990], 169–70).

18 Barsella suggests defining the *Decameron*'s realism as "effectual," i.e., what is represented is true inasmuch as it imparts moral teachings to the readers, therefore effecting a real change in their minds. She connects this potential attributed to literature to the declining ability of reality to contain decipherable signs, a consequence of the inefficacy of religion in communicating with the newly emerged mercantile culture: "It seems that a fruitful approach for investigating the *Decameron*'s dialectics between truth and appearance is that of thinking of realism in terms of an internal coherence of the fictional illusion created by the literary artifice,

In IX.5 in particular, Fiammetta points at a "verità del fatto" that is validated not by its adherence to the real world lying outside the text but by the structural coherence within the text, as dictated by the *Decameron*'s intrinsic logic. The "diletto negl'intendenti" that Fiammetta indicates as the product of the "verità del fatto" consists in the satisfying and entertaining realization on the part of the audience that a pattern of internal correspondences exists. In other words, in Fiammetta's introduction the "verità del fatto" corresponds to one of the products of Boccaccio's invention, interwoven with the historical components included in the stories.[19]

The four novellas starring Calandrino are a good example of the layered notion of realism at the core of the *Decameron*'s composition. On one hand, Boccaccio alludes to a piece of historical evidence: the Florentine chronicles testify that Calandrino was the nickname of Giovannozzo (Nozzo) di Perino, a painter renowned for his poor skills among his contemporaries and most likely turned into the character of the credulous man by the oral popular tradition.[20] On the other, Boccaccio manipulates these historical details, i.e., he arranges the Calandrino

---

in terms of the effect of reality it produces, and in terms of its effects on the extra-textual reality (i.e., the educational goal of the ludic narrative). Given these premises, we may think of Boccaccio's 'effectual realism' as a conscious rhetorical strategy that always – and particularly in the space of the sacred – sets at play history and literary discourse, a strategy that relies on what Roland Barthes has defined as referential illusion or 'effect of reality,' and which coincides with the rhetorical figure of 'oggettività'" (Barsella, "The Merchant and the Sacred," 16).

19 The point is made most forcefully by Pier Massimo Forni, who insists on the ability of the "intendenti" to see in Fiammetta's axiom much more than a simple homage to the conventions of truth and verisimilitude: stating, as she does, that departing from narrative truth diminishes the narrative pleasure involves the rhetorical and structural artificiality of the story and of the whole book in the truth-making process. What Forni calls a "squisito paradosso, squisitamente boccacciano," he also sees as the paradox controlling the relation between "verità fattuale" and "verità inerente al libro," from the interplay of which emerges the ultimate truth of the text: "Questa è verità testuale, una verità di gran valore per l'artista, una verità in un certo senso più vera del vero. Questa è verità in abito retorico" (Forni, *Parole come fatti*, 25–6).

20 In his article "Un tassello per Calandrino pittore," Marco Santagata collects the sparse documents available to support the existence of the painter Giovannozzo (Nozzo) di Perino, known solely by his nickname, Calandrino, and made into a literary character by Sacchetti and Boccaccio: "L'ipotesi più plausibile è che le dicerie sulla grullaggine e la semplicità di Calandrino si siano diffuse in anni lontani e che poi siano entrate nel bagaglio della cultura popolare sotto forma di motti di spirito, raccontini beffardi, esempi topici" [The most plausible hypothesis is that the gossip about Calandrino's gullibility and simplemindedness began circulating in early years and have then entered popular culture, crystallized in jokes, short ridiculing stories, examples of foolish behaviour (1036)].

tales into a sequence generating an internal pattern that the listeners are called on to recognize, and enjoy, as the *Decameron*'s textual truth. This pattern functions as a tool essential for a body of work that strives to be comprehensive. The Calandrino cycle, which hinges on the fool's capacity to believe that reality can hold any possibility and is organized into a sequence that elicits the readers' participation and acknowledgment, fulfils Boccaccio's ambition to give his readers the impression of being immersed into the totality of the real world. In the Calandrino cycle, the combination of characters and events replicate in a microcosm the infinite possible combinations that make the fabric of the human macrocosm.[21]

The Reality of Facts and the Illusion of Reality

In IX.3, the distinctive Decameronian interplay of factual reality and invention is embodied and staged by the characters, and specifically by their defining features: the full bellies of the pranksters, and the imaginary womb of Calandrino. Bruno, Buffalmacco, and Nello fabricate Calandrino's fake pregnancy in order to fill their stomachs. A bodily need, food consumption, engenders their real bellies, that become literally full, while being juxtaposed to the belly of Calandrino, that becomes full for a leap of the fool's imagination. The plot of the novella pivots on these two complementary images.

Calandrino's fictional womb is a locus bearing multiple meanings. First and foremost, the imaginary predicament of the character causes a shift in his male identity. Surprisingly, gender balance is traditionally not affected within the tradition of the trope of the pregnant man. In one of its first occurrences, Greek mythology, it originates as a symbol of paternity. One of its first manifestations from the Greek archaic period consists of the births of Athena and Dionysus from, respectively, the head and the thigh of their father Zeus. Pregnant men stand also as symbols of authorship, when they are employed to illustrate the process of thinking, of nurturing one's mind with fertile ideas.[22]

---

21 "Non essendo infatti possibile predicare letteralmente tutta la realtà, lo scrittore deve accontentarsi di dare il senso della totalità, ciò che si può fare congegnando – con ricorso tanto alle singole novelle quanto alle singole giornate – strutture di corrispondenza oppositivo-complementari" [Since it is impossible to treat literally all reality, the writer opts for producing a sense of totality. This can be done by organizing a system of oppositive or complementary correspondences across individual stories and individual days of narration (Forni, "Realtà/verità," 249)].

22 "In fact, myths of male pregnancy are often invoked in classical Greek authors as a way to talk about patrilineal descent and citizenship more generally, and the

In medieval and early modern literature, the image of the pregnant man by and large challenges the conventional gender division only to actually reaffirm it. In her study, Olga V. Trokhimenko explores the treatment of this motif, supporting the claim with significant examples. Among them are Marie de France's *Del vilein e de l'escarbot* (A Peasant and a Beetle), the Old French romance *Aucassine and Nicolette*, the German tale *The Monk's Predicament*, the *Golden Legend*, and *Decameron* IX.3. In these stories, the image of the male pregnancy seems at first to affect the gender domains. These tales touch on the subversive potential of such an image, but, Trokhimenko argues, fail to fully undermine gender categories. Rather, they end up reinforcing gender categories through their characterizations. Trokhimenko bases her argument on the fact that the male character is usually attributed features that are punitively diminishing: the character has made a move into the female sphere, he has trespassed an established norm and entered a doomed territory.[23] In the stories selected in Trokhimenko's study, the pregnant men are fools, and the circumstances of their pregnancy ridiculous: in *Del vilein e de l'escarbot* the character is impregnated by a beetle who enters his anus, while in the *Golden Legend* the Emperor Nero is described as pregnant with a frog. Additionally, in the finale, the pregnant men are almost invariably beaten or scorned as a punishment "for their conscious overstepping the established boundaries of gender-appropriate behavior" Trokhimenko, "Believing That Which Cannot Be," 122). Trokhimenko includes *Decameron* IX.3 among the examples supporting her claim. Yet, the tale of Calandrino fits in with them only partially. In the final scene of IX.5, the last novella of the cycle, Calandrino is indeed beaten. Unlike the examples mentioned above, however, the scene does not bespeak a punishment directed at a case of gender expropriation and inflicted for the purpose of reaffirming the correct gender order. The fact that Calandrino is beaten by his wife Tessa, a female character, suggests that the Decameronian fool's behaviour illustrates a significant alteration of

---

metaphor of pregnancy was often deployed as a way of claiming metaphorical paternity ... as when rival poets claim artistic 'paternity' of the same written work" (Letao, *The Pregnant Man*, 7).

23 "Medieval stories such as Marie de France's *Del vilein e de l'escarbot* (A Peasant and a Beetle), the Old French romance *Aucassin and Nicolette*, Giovanni Boccaccio's *Decameron* (IX.3), or tales about the infamous emperor Nero present their 'pregnant' male protagonist as sexually inexperienced, gullible, or plainly idiotic, in order to convey and reinforce a uniform message: 'You can't change who you are.' They define what a man is by drawing a clear line between maleness and femaleness, as well as between masculinity and femininity" (Trokhimenko, "Believing That Which Cannot Be," 121–2).

the conventional gender-based division of roles. The same alteration comes into play in IX.3 as well. In the novella the gender domains have unstable boundaries, as made clear by Calandrino's pregnancy and by additional aspects in the behaviour of the characters.

Calandrino: Gender at Play

Gender exchange is a process at play throughout the whole *Decameron*. Teodolinda Barolini encapsulates this dialectics in the Italian proverb "Le parole sono femmine e i fatti sono maschi." The *motto* synthesizes the main argumentation of the *Proemio*, in which we read that Boccaccio dedicates the *Decameron*, and therefore his words, to a female audience, on the grounds that men can be distracted by their activities, that is by the facts of their lives. Yet, the gender-based distribution of *parole* and *fatti* in the *Decameron* is only apparent. Exactly as it happens in the proverb – as Barolini argues, a division of spheres is announced only to be grammatically blurred ("since *fatti* are masculine, but the word 'fatti' is a *parola*, and thus feminine")[24] – the female characters of the *Decameron* are anything but excluded from the realm of facts and action. In the Calandrino tales, and especially in IX.3, Monna Tessa is a manifest example of a female character who takes action, and, in doing so, successfully trespasses on the male sphere.

Tessa prepares her incursion into the realm of *fatti* by Calandrino's sickbed. When her husband publicly, and absurdly, blames her sexual position of choice for his pregnancy, Monna Tessa responds at first by showing the modest demeanour imposed by her gender: "La donna, che assai onesta persona era, udendo così dire al marito, tutta di

24 Barolini argues that in the *Decameron*, as a result of the fact that the boundaries between maleness and femaleness are permeable, some female characters are invested with independence and freedom in their actions: "'Le parole son femmine e i fatti sono maschi' succinctly captures Boccaccio's sexual poetics by suggesting both a mutual exclusion between the sexes and their proper spheres, and an inevitable contamination between these same spheres, since *fatti* are masculine, but the word 'fatti' is a *parola*, and thus feminine. In other words, the boundary that the proverb at first glance so emphatically delineates, between women and words, on one hand, and men and deeds, on the other, is much less rigid than it first appears ... Dioneo's argument thus hinges on the notion that there is no limit to what the ladies can say – to the *parole* they can use – as long as they do not translate words into deeds, as long as they do not cross the bridge that separates the world of women from the world of men ... And yet the *Decameron* does nothing if not effect the translation from words into deeds, from the sequestered world of women to the engaged world of men, and Dioneo is the chief investigator of this process" (Barolini, "'Le parole son femmine,'" *Studi sul Boccaccio*, 175–6, 178).

vergogna arrossò" [When she heard him say this, Calandrino's wife, who was a very demure sort of person, turned crimson with embarrassment (IX.3.22)]. Yet, Boccaccio makes Monna Tessa's strongly gendered response more layered, by adding that she leaves the room "without words" ("senza risponder parola s'uscì della camera" [she left the room without uttering a word (ibid.)]). Stripped of her words, the tool that is left to women once they have been excluded from the male domain of deeds, Tessa temporarily exits the stage of IX.3 only to reappear, at the end of the novella, to demonstrate her judgment. In the final sequence, the association between facts and the male protagonist is apparently restated and emphasized. Upon the conclusive medical examination, Calandrino is told that he can go about his business, and he complies:

> – Calandrino, tu se' guerito senza fallo; e però sicuramente oggimai va a fare ogni tuo *fatto*, né per questo star più in casa. – Calandrino lieto levatosi s'andò a fare i *fatti* suoi. (IX.3.32, emphasis added)
>
> [– You are cured[,] Calandrino, without a shadow of a doubt; so there's no need for you to stay home any longer. It's quite safe now for you to get up and do whatever you have to do.]

Although the term "facts" seems to gravitate to the male character, the novella ends with a decisive shift in the conventional division of "male" facts and "female" words. The readers are made well aware that Monna Tessa, hopelessly berating her foolish and fooled husband, is the only character, other than the tricksters, who can understand that her husband has been once again the victim of a *beffa*. In other words, she is the female character who possesses the "male" feature of being able to navigate and properly read the world of the *fatti*. As mentioned before, this is not the only novella concerned with the masculinization of Monna Tessa. Her incursions in the male space build up, preparing the *Decameron*'s audience, by the end of the Calandrino cycle, to watch her act like a man.[25] In IX.3 specifically, Boccaccio associates Monna Tessa with the

25 In IX.5, Monna Tessa physically assaults Calandrino and insults his appalling stupidity, after she catches him cheating on her during the staged seduction of Niccolosa: "Monna Tessa corse con l'unghie nel viso a Calandrino, che ancora levato non era, e tutto gliele graffiò e presolo per li capelli, e in qua e in là tirandolo cominciò a dire: – Sozzo can vituperato, dunque mi fai tu questo? Vecchio impazzato, che maladetto sia il bene che io t'ho voluto: dunque non ti pare aver tanto a fare a casa tua, che ti vai innamorando per l'altrui? Ecco bello innamorato! Or non ti conosci tu, tristo? Non ti conosci tu, dolente? che premendoti tutto, non uscirebbe tanto sugo che bastasse ad una salsa. Alla fé di Dio, egli non era ora la

male domain not only by making this character well acquainted with the world of facts but also by having her perform the dominant role in her household. Two details at the centre of Calandrino's reprimand consolidate Tessa's male-coded behaviour and contribute to her identification as the head of the house:[26] her pursuit of pleasure and her sex position of choice. The objects of Calandrino's accusation are key in expanding the meaning of the marital scene in the novella.

The connection between sexual positions and gender codes was rooted in the dominant contemporaneous theological discourse concerned with sex and conception. A major issue at stake was that, while sex was obviously necessary for reproduction, it had to be kept distinct from pleasure in order not to become sinful. In the thirteenth century, the treatments of the question indicate that the only sexual position the church considered permissible was what is nowadays referred to as the "missionary position."[27] Because it was also regarded as the most

---

Tessa quella che t'impregnava, che Dio la faccia trista chiunque ella è, che ella dee ben sicuramente esser cattiva cosa a aver vaghezza di cosí bella gioia come tu se" [You filthy, despicable dog, so you'd do this to me, would you? A curse on all the love I ever bore to you, demented old fool that you are. Don't you think you have enough to do, keeping the home fires burning, without going off to stoke up other people? A fine lover you would make for anyone! Don't you know yourself, villain? Don't you realize, scoundrel, that if they were to squeeze you from head to toe, there wouldn't be enough juice to make a sauce? God's faith, it wasn't your wife who was getting you with child this time. May the Lord make her suffer, whoever she is, for she must surely be a depraved little hussy to take a fancy to a precious jewel like you (IX.5.63–4)].

26 Martinez reaches similar conclusion in his reading of this character: "The pig that Calandrino dresses and then loses to Bruno and Buffalmacco is in fact Tessa's, as the property derives from her dowry (VIII.6.4: 'in dote avea avuto dalla moglie'); and the secrets of the marriage bed revealed in IX.3.21 show that Tessa is a 'woman on top,' with the elevation of her sexual posture confirming that she is the real head of the household with the power of chasing Calandrino out of the house (VIII.6.7)" (Martinez, "Calandrino and the Powers of the Stone," 20). Calandrino finds himself in a submissive sexual position not just in relation to his wife. In IX.5 it is again a woman, Niccolosa, who sits atop him: "donde Calandrino la toccò con la scritta. E come tocca l'ebbe, senza dir nulla volse i passi verso la casa della paglia, dove la Niccolosa gli andò dietro; e, come dentro fu, chiuso l'uscio abbracciò Calandrino, e in su la paglia che era ivi in terra il gittò, e saligli addosso a cavalcione, tenendogli le mani in su gli omeri" [Calandrino therefore touched her with the scroll, and immediately directed his steps towards the barn without saying a word. She followed him in, closed the door behind her, and threw her arms about his neck; then she pushed him over on to some straw that was lying on the floor and promptly sat astride his prostrate form, forcing his hands back against his shoulders (IX.5.57)].

27 "There was a shift in the treatment of this admonition toward the end of the twelfth century. In addition to seeing Jerome's admonitions against excessive or too ardent

favourable for conception, it was the one of choice for a married couple[28] and the one that could arguably be defined as "natural," from the standpoint that nature had given men the commanding lead, consequently making any other position a treacherous reversal of the order.[29] By describing Tessa through Calandrino's words caught in a "perverse" position – a perversity that could justly call for a biblical punishment[30] – Boccaccio tells the readers not only that in Tessa the search for pleasure prevails over the choice for procreation, but also that she claims the male role in her intercourse with her husband. Tessa and Calandrino comply with the rules of marital sex, only with switched roles. Thus, Calandrino accuses Tessa of having impregnated him on the grounds that she opted, out of her perverted inclination, for the sex position traditionally thought to improve a man's ability to impregnate his wife.

The Unimaginative Creativity of Calandrino

The fake belly of Calandrino in IX.3 functions at first as a mark of this character's debasement, a sign that he is subject both to the pranksters, who have successfully fooled him, and to his wife, who can read facts

love as a caution against too frequent intercourse, writers at the end of the century also interpreted his words as a prohibition of 'unnatural' marital intercourse, by which they meant among other things the use of unusual coital positions. They assumed that the proper position for marital sex ought to be the one in which the man lay atop his wife. Deviations from this posture were perversions, motivated by a quest for unusual pleasures (*extraordinaria voluptas*). Sexual experimentation was thus equated with attempts to surpass the order that nature had dictated for marital relations" (Brundage, *Law, Sex, and Christian Society in Medieval Europe*, 367).

28 "Albert [Albert the Great in the *Commentaria* on the *Sentences* of Peter Lombard] taught that no type of 'natural' coitus was mortally sinful in marriage, but that variations from the 'natural' position were venially sinful if they were adopted in order to increase sexual pleasure. The 'missionary' position, he taught, was dictated by human anatomy as the 'natural' position for intercourse; it was also the optimal position for conception" (Brundage, "Let Me Count the Ways," 86).

29 "Intercourse in any position where the woman lay or sat atop the man seemed to canonists 'unnatural,' since they believed that such a posture reversed the proper order of relationship between the sexes by making the female superior to the male" (Brundage, "Sex and Canon Law," 40).

30 "A few late medieval theologians adopted a moderate view of sexual transgressions within marriage. Others saw the matter quite differently; and a few of the major moral writers of the Reformation period considered non-standard coital positions a heinous kind of 'unnatural' sex. After all, one of them remarked, it was the practice of having sexual intercourse with the woman on top that cause God to send the Biblical flood (*Romans* 1:26–7) – a drastic cure for this perversion (Lindner 1929:162)" (Brundage, "Let Me Count the Ways," 87).

that Calandrino's dense mind cannot read. The fool's pseudopregnancy, however, bears further meaning. When connected to the theme of food consumption, the fool's belly becomes a tool of empowerment. Against the backdrop of the *beffa*, Calandrino's ability to believe that his belly has turned into a womb makes this character into an agent of poetic imagination and creativity. The *Decameron*'s readers are introduced to the association between Calandrino and food in one novella from the previous day. The appointed trickster of VIII.3, Maso del Saggio, lures Calandrino into the prank he is about to carry out by describing the land where stones of virtue, such as the heliotrope, can be found. The land that Maso reports about is called Bengodi, a version of the "paese di Cuccagna." In Bengodi, food is the sole element of the landscape, and food production the sole activity of its inhabitants, the Baschi. Sitting atop a mountain of Parmesan cheese, the Baschi ceaselessly make "maccheroni e ravioli" that they cook "in brodo di capponi" (VIII.3.9) and then throw at the passersby.[31] One detail of the representation of Bengodi that Maso is depicting in Calandrino's mind resonates with IX.3 – the capons. Capons make several appearances in the *Decameron*.[32] Since they are a rich and expensive food, they are employed as a medium of exchange, in IX.3, but also, for example, in VIII.6 (in which the joke involves a stolen pig, and the two capons that Calandrino hands over to Bruno and Buffalmacco in order to escape Tessa's beating).[33] While listening to Maso in VIII.3, engrossed in the description of Bengodi, Calandrino has not missed the detail that the capons have somehow disappeared, and he inquires about them:

---

31 "Maso rispose che le più [le pietre] si trovavano in Berlinzone, terra de' baschi, in una contrada che si chiamava Bengodi, nella quale si legano le vigne con le salsicce, e avevasi un'oca a denaio e un papero giunta; e eravi una montagna tutta di formaggio parmigiano grattugiato, sopra la quale stavan genti che niuna altra cosa facevan che far maccheroni e raviuoli, e cuocergli in brodo di capponi e poi gli gittavan quindi giù, e chi più ne pigliava più se n'aveva; e ivi presso correva un fiumicel di vernaccia, della migliore che mai si bevve, senza avervi entro gocciola d'acqua" [Maso replied that they [the stones] were chiefly to be found in Nomansland, the territory of the Basque, in a region called Cornucopia, where the vines are tied up with sausages, and you could buy a goose for a penny, with a gosling thrown in for good measure. And in those parts there was a mountain made entirely of grated Parmesan cheese, on whose slopes there were people who spent their whole time making macaroni and ravioli, which they cooked in chicken broth and then cast it to the four winds, and the faster you could pick it up, the more you got of it. And not far away, there was a stream of Vernaccia wine, the finest that was ever drunk, without a single drop of water in it (VIII.3.9)].

32 "Capponi" appear in VII.1, VIII.3, VIII.6, VIII.7, and VIII.9.

33 See note 6.

"– O, – disse Calandrino – cotesto è buon paese; ma dimmi, che si fa de' capponi che cuocon coloro?" [– That's a marvelous place, by the sound of it – said Calandrino – but tell me, what do they do with all the chickens they cook? (VIII.3.10)]. As a reply, he hears that all the capons are to be found in the stomachs of the fictional Baschi "– Mangiansegli i Baschi tutti." (ibid.). Capons fall outside of Calandrino's sight in the novella of the heliotrope as well as in IX.3, where they disappear from the curative "chiarea" in order to make a meal for the tricksters. In both novellas, VIII.3 and IX.3, Boccaccio presents the readers with a group of characters, the Baschi in one case, Bruno, Buffalmacco, and Nello in the other, who make their own bellies full (of capons, in both cases) while leaving Calandrino empty. In both novellas, that is, Calandrino points out an absence, of which the missing birds are the first evidence. The void that Calandrino anticipates is further exemplified in the text: in VIII.3, by Calandrino's attempted invisibility, and, in IX.3, by his imagined pregnancy. In IX.3, the empty space outlined by the non-existent womb becomes the grounds for Calandrino's verbal imagination. Calandrino the fool has no difficulty in believing in his own pregnancy, that is, in filling that empty space. The contrast between the literally full bellies of the *beffatori* and the imaginarily full belly of Calandrino is not only essential to spin the narrative in the novella IX.3 but also represents the dynamic between actuality and invention that composes the fabric of the *Decameron*. The Decameronian fool occupies a distinct position in the text because of his trust in words, without regard to their incongruence with reality. As a result of his peculiar relationship with verbal communication, Calandrino is an outsider, especially when one considers the world of merchants that makes the background of his stories.

A detail in IX.3 explicitly tells readers that Calandrino obviously lacks the gainful logic that governs the world of trade in the *Decameron*. When he meets with the Florentine brokers trying to purchase an estate with a ridiculously small sum of money, he is described as a prospective dealer, someone who "teneva mercato." Since his bargaining tools are quite poor, though, he lets the deals fall through as soon as a price is brought up: "e con quanti sensali aveva in Firenze, come se da spendere avesse avuti diecemilia fiorin d'oro, teneva mercato, il quale sempre si guastava quando al prezzo del poder domandato si perveniva" [he approached every broker in Florence and entered into negotiations, all of which were abruptly broken off as soon as the price of the property was mentioned (IX.3.4)]. Despite his subordination to the merchants when he tries to engage in their economic exchanges, Calandrino still reclaims a position of authority when observed from a different perspective. Next to his failing skills in a market is Calandrino's potential to believe in the abilities of language.[34] In IX.3 he never doubts that the words he hears from the tricksters correspond to existing circumstances, and stubbornly avoids any countercheck, not hesitating to punish Monna Tessa when she measures those words against reality, detecting the prank. Notwithstanding that the events associated with Calandrino do not match any rational expectation, they abide by the principle of the Decameronian "verità del fatto," which weaves together historical truth and invention, for the sake of the readers' pleasure. As Fiammetta reminds us in her introduction to IX.5 quoted above, the "fatti di Calandrino" ensure the audience's pleasure because they are both amusing, "piacevoli," and true. They are, that is, the product of Calandrino's unbridled fantasy organized into, and legitimized by, the structure of the text. From this perspective, the Decameronian fool's role is not diminished by the irrationality of his behaviour. Albeit short-lived, as the clash with reality is inevitable, Calandrino's fantasies are a celebration of the potential of his imagination, and the control that, through his imagination, he temporarily enjoys over reality.[35]

In IX.3 Calandrino's exceptional trust in words allows him to stand at the threshold of reality and imagination, weaving both components, without distinction, as his stories unfold. Calandrino's attitude toward language is an additional element that, together with his invented pregnancy, affects the gender dynamics of the characters. Calandrino is rooted, to a fault, into the verbal realm. Therefore, on the premises of the distinction established by the *Decameron*'s author between male facts and female words, he belongs to the female realm. In IX.3 he becomes certain of his predicament because he heard the tricksters say so:

---

34 "We have seen how, as in the tales featuring Ciappelletto and Frate Cipolla, Calandrino's delusional belief in the magic heliotrope stone in tales [is] closely associated with the power of language and rhetoric to enchant, mystify, delude, and illude, for both good and ill" (Martinez, "Calandrino and the Powers of the Stone," 27).

35 "The merchants are the true tricksters who manipulate events and are in full possession of rationality … Yet, by the *beffa* the world of rationality and self-possession, ostensibly celebrated in the *Decameron*, is subjected to a fierce critique and Boccaccio has a way of insinuating that the fool, dispossessed of value, is always somehow right … By the quest of the heliotrope, he [Calandrino] seeks an absolute autonomy and pursues his own fantasy to become transcendent and invisible, and gain the invulnerable standpoint from which he can govern and control the world. His steady reappearance as a fool in the *Decameron*, however, shows that he is doomed to be visible and that his desire is shattered … Calandrino's foolishness is banal and his banality is profoundly disturbing. For in the measure in which he is a fool, he asserts the value of the imagination and at the same time sanctions its inevitable failure to create vital resemblance" (Mazzotta, *The World at Play*, 192–3).

"Calandrino, udendo ciascun di costoro così dire, per certissimo ebbe seco medesimo d'esser malato" [When he heard both of them saying the same thing, Calandrino was quite certain he was ill (IX.3.14)]. In his mindset, words, once they are uttered, generate unquestioned reality, including words conveying the unlikely circumstance of a male pregnancy. Given Calandrino's tendency to believe in the generative power of language, it's not surprising to find the theme of gestation elsewhere associated with this character – as has been convincingly remarked, the description of Calandrino loading himself with stones on the banks of the Mugnone in VIII.3 also prefigures the image of a pregnant woman.[36] In IX.3, the *beffa*, and the fake pregnancy it fabricates, become instrumental in showing Calandrino's actual ability to gestate when placed within the verbal sphere. In fact, Calandrino verbally creates his own pregnancy even before he is "diagnosed" by Maestro Simone: "Deh! sì, compagno mio, vavvi, e sappimi ridire come il fatto sta, ché io *mi sento non so che dentro*" [Go to him and find out for me how [the] matter stands. Goodness knows what's going on inside my poor stomach (IX.3.18, emphasis added)].[37] This instance, in which the story springs from the verbal act of one of the characters, exemplifies a distinct narrative device at play in the *Decameron*: following the encounter between the author and the world, while the writing imitates reality, textual

36 Simone Marchesi, in his study of the allusive strategies of the *Decameron*, investigates the themes of hermeneutics and procreation within the "ciclo di Calandrino." With regard to procreation, Marchesi reads the scene in which Calandrino gathers the stones on the banks of the Mugnone in VIII.3 as the anticipation of the character's eventual and phantasmatic being with child. Marchesi insists on keywords such as "seno" (appearing in paragraphs 52 and 60) and "scinto" (54) as well as on potential allusions to classical and biblical antecedents connecting stones and the idea of pregnancy (*Stratigrafie Decameroniane*, 107). In a more recent note, Marchesi establishes and documents a further connection between VIII.3 and IX.3 grounded in the causal relation between God's punishment by the flood (a theme evoked in VIII.3 by the reference to the image of Deucalion and Pyrrha casting stones that become human beings who repopulate the earth after the flood) and perverse sexuality (exemplified by Tessa's sexual position in IX.3, a position that a full range of texts connect with sodomy) ("Sex, Floods, and a Learned Gloss").

37 From this perspective, Calandrino's pregnancy stands as an example of "metafora realizzata," the expression Forni employs to indicate those instances in the *Decameron* that are generated by the material actualization of phraseological units. The first case Forni examines is IX.2, which turns the metaphor of figuratively "going around with one's breeches on one's head" into the case of a character who really (i.e., concretely) wears someone else's breeches on her head, thus becoming a flesh-and-bone metaphor. As Forni notes: "Questa è retorica che diventa narrativa: la metafora è letteralizzata mentre viene riimpiegata in forma narrativa" (Forni, *Parole come fatti*, 62–3).

reality can stem from words.[38] The imaginary pregnancy of Calandrino is a condition connected with his distinct trust in language and his fertile imagination. This is true not only because Calandrino's tool of choice is the conventionally female one, words, but also because novella IX.3 established the pregnancy of this character as a metaphor for the fool's power to make the language fecund. Calandrino's fictitious pregnancy in IX.3 is the metaphor that stands for what is also his asset; namely, his ability to make space between the layers of historical truth, in order for textual invention to operate. The empty spaces by which he stands are gaps opened in the flux of events and opened to the author's work of creation.

38 Again, the most apt formulation is in Forni: "Le novelle del *Decameron* sono indubitabilmente realistiche … Cionondimeno, ci si sente obbligati a rendere giustizia al lavoro del Boccaccio mostrando non solo come le parole imitino la realtà extratestuale, ma anche come la realtà testuale imiti le parole" [It is certainly true that the *Decameron* novellas are realistic … yet, we should also give Boccaccio's work its due, pointing to how his words imitate extratextual reality, but also how textual reality imitates words (ibid., 65).

The Tale of the Two Ceccos: *Decameron* IX.4

PATRIZIO CECCAGNOLI

The fourth tale of the *Decameron*'s Ninth Day presents a case of litigious and literary homonymy. The name of the two protagonists of the story is Cecco, and they are both historical figures. Over the centuries, the historical identity of the two Ceccos has played an important role in the reception of the tale, but, at first glance, it does not seem to affect the internal narrative dynamics of this story. Paired by the same name and the same Tuscan hometown, united by their shared hatred for their respective fathers, the two Ceccos agree to leave Siena together, despite their fundamental dissimilarities, after Cecco Angiolieri is presented with the opportunity to improve his living conditions by joining the household of a powerful cardinal in the Marches of Ancora. The tale becomes the story of an interrupted journey as Cecco Angiolieri falls victim to a trick conceived by his travelling companion. Cecco Fortarrigo, a well-known drunkard and gambler, does not act out of character when, at the first opportunity, he loses all his possessions at the gambling table and therefore also the money belonging to Angiolieri, who meanwhile is sleeping. Upon awakening, after having discovered that he has been robbed and after a failed and confused attempt to attribute the responsibility to Fortarrigo, Cecco Angiolieri leaves his companion behind and tries to continue the journey on the back of his steed. And here, on the road, just outside Buonconvento, the perverse genius of Fortarrigo inspires him to stage a deception with which he nullifies the good intentions of Cecco Angiolieri. Left in his shirt sleeves, Fortarrigo chases Angiolieri by pretending to be the injured party, victim of a theft, in front of a group of peasants who, indifferent to the remonstrance of the other Cecco, block Angiolieri and pull him from his horse, thus allowing Fortarrigo to appropriate Angiolieri's palfrey and clothes. Left with nothing but the shirt on his back, Cecco Angiolieri can only wait for his father's help and future revenge.

As a consequence of the fact that the two homonymous characters are both historical figures, this tale has been problematically read as a source of biographical information, especially about the life of Cecco Angiolieri, the famously infamous champion of Italian medieval comic poetry and the victimized deuteragonist of the story.[1] Cecco Angiolieri was a widely read poet in medieval Italy, as evidenced by his prominent place in the manuscript tradition.[2] In choosing him as a main character, Boccaccio mobilizes the figure of a literary predecessor for literary purposes.

Claudio Giunta has recently questioned and denied the scholarly commonplace that sees Angiolieri's poetic corpus as occupying a parodic stance with respect to the Italian tradition of courtly love.[3] Giunta's caveat against an excessive and indiscriminate recourse to intertextuality is itself a reaction to Mario Marti's metaliterary interpretation of the so-called *poesia comico-realistica*, in which Cecco plays a pivotal role (*Cultura e stile*). Marti's goal was, in turn, to reverse the biographical reading typical of the positivistic approach taken by Cecco's earliest modern critics, starting with Alessandro D'Ancona in Italy and even earlier abroad with Dante Gabriel Rossetti's English translations.[4]

In the *Decameron*, the intradiegetic Angiolieri is never explicitly depicted as a writer; yet, in naming one of his characters after the Sienese poet, Boccaccio seems intentionally to build a link between Cecco's sonnets and his own tale. To explore the nature of this connection is the principal goal of the present *lectura*, which will read the

1 The tale does not stand autonomously in the reception of readers and critics: Luigi Russo, for instance, isolates what he calls a "heteronomous meaning" (*Letture critiche*, 276); Vittore Branca introduces the tale by specifying that the facts of the plot have been too easily read as historical (1054n1). Hereafter, all references to Branca's critical apparatus are signalled in text by his name only. All quotations from the *Decameron* are from Branca's 1980 edition. The English text is from McWilliam's 1972 translation, except when otherwise indicated. English translations of secondary literature originally in Italian are mine.

2 For Cecco Angiolieri's manuscript tradition, see the Note to the Text in Lanza's edition of the *Rime* (lxi–lxii) and Alfie, *Comedy*, 9. All quotations of Cecco Angiolieri's poems are from Lanza. The English versions are by Scott and Mortimer (*Sonnets*).

3 See Giunta, *Versi per un destinatario*, especially chapter 3 (267–354), for a new and yet controversial reading of the *poesia comico-realistica*. For an early reception of Giunta's study, see Marrani, "La poesia comica," 101–2n2 and 111, and Bettarini Bruni, "Cecco Angiolieri," 80.

4 For D'Ancona's interpretation, see *Cecco Angiolieri*, 163–275. As Anthony Mortimer points out, the Pre-Raphaelite painter Dante Gabriel Rossetti was the first to give credit to Angiolieri's sonnets, including them in his groundbreaking anthology *The Early Italian Poets* in 1861, and more than a decade before Cecco's rediscovery started with D'Ancona's seminal study, which appeared first in "Nuova Antologia" in 1874 ("Extra Material," 276).

protagonists' homonymy as a case of parodic intertextuality. Seen in this light, the story corroborates Fabian Alfie's conclusion that "Boccaccio is representing Angiolieri's poetic corpus through narrative" ("Poetics Enacted," 191) and, more generally, Marco Berisso's belief that parody is the preferred literary strategy among Italian medieval poets writing in comic style (*Poesia comica*, 26; 38).

In "Ironizzazione letteraria come rinnovamento di tradizioni," Vittore Branca emphasized the author's ability to appropriate and parody the literary conventions of his day as an innovative feature of Boccaccio's *Decameron*:

> Il procedimento Nuovo e inatteso è quello che punta risolutivamente a prendere le distanze dalle tradizioni letterarie più divulgate rovesciandole dall'interno, o meglio ironizzandole sottilmente e risolutamente. È una controletteratura per rinnovare la letteratura, è una forzatura di codici linguistici e strutturali per rinnovare dall'interno temi e intrecci ormai topici e stanchi. (*Boccaccio medievale* [1996], 337)

> [The new and unexpected device is one that decisively aims to distance itself from the most popular literary traditions by turning them upside down from within, or rather, by subtly and decisively making them the object of irony. It is a counter-literature meant to renew literature. It is a stretching of linguistic and structural codes with the goal of renewing from within themes and plots that had become typical and tired.]

It is certainly true, as Branca proceeds to argue, that "there is hardly a tradition, living in the autumn of our Middle Ages ... that does not become the target of Boccaccio's irony in his masterpiece" (ibid., 343). The relationship between the *Decameron* and the *poesia comico-realistica* has, however, been largely understudied. Although Branca himself establishes a genealogy between Cecco's poetry and Boccaccio's lyrical production (ibid., 266), the *Decameron* tale in which Cecco features as co-protagonist has not typically been received as an authorial commentary on his contemporary literary world. By focusing on the intricate intertextuality connecting the tale and Cecco's sonnets, my essay will read the action in this *beffa* as a quasi-Dantean *contrapasso*, in which the Sienese poet becomes the victim of a friend who has all the features of his literary alter-ego.[5] As I shall argue, this enactment of Cecco's

5 The only critic who openly interprets the tale as a case of intertextual dialogue with Cecco Angiolieri's sonnets is an American scholar of medieval comic poetry, Fabian Alfie. See his articles "Poetics Enacted"; "Yes ... but Was It Funny?"; "Cecco vs. Cecco"; and his book *Comedy and Culture* (90).

poetics is conceived through a reversal of roles and the employment of a doppelgänger. The staging of Cecco's literary identity, thus, makes his poetry a subject of irony and parody. Boccaccio's ultimate goal is not a mimetic representation of literary poetics through the fictional *mise en scène* of their aesthetics, as Alfie argues ("Poetics Enacted," 188–9), but rather the inclusion and subversion of Angiolieri's sonnets.

The tale of the two Ceccos is the story of a failed journey started on a palfrey and ended on a nag. In a way, it is the metaliterary ride that covers the distance between the courtly world ("pallafreno," palfrey) and comic, picaresque literature ("ronzino," nag).[6] Situated in between two stories of the so-called Calandrino cycle, the longest and, arguably, the most comic series of the whole book, this tale "of no great length" unfolds in a picaresque setting – the road, the tavern, fields populated by gullible but solicitous farmers – and yet fails to reach high comic effect, at least judging from the lukewarm response of the band of storytellers:

> Finita la non lunga novella di Neifile, senza troppo o riderne o parlarne passatasene la brigata, la reina, verso la Fiammetta rivolta, che elle seguitasse le commandò. (IX.5.2)

> [Neifile's story was of no great length, and when it drew to a close it was passed off by the company without much laughter or comment. The queen now turned to Fiammetta, ordering her to follow.]

In his commentary, Vittore Branca too notices the exceptionality of this response, almost unique for the indifferent, if not dismissive, disposition of the company of narrators toward the tale that has just been told by Neifile.[7] What Branca does not emphasize, however, is that the story is not in fact particularly short. The fourth tale with its 1405 words, in fact, is not even the shortest of Day Nine, being actually longer than four other stories: the seventh (767 words), the second (1025 words), the eighth (1244), and the tenth (1260).[8] It is not, then, the length of the tale that restrains the *brigata* from the usual reaction typically consisting of laugher, embarrassment, and brief discussion. The story of the two

6 For the transition from courtly to picaresque tone in this tale, see Getto, *Vita di forme* (1972), 188.

7 See Branca, 1061n3: "riflesso critico negativo quasi unico nel D." [a negative critical response almost unique in the D.].

8 These data can be found in Alberto Asor Rosa's general study in collaboration with Lanfranco Fabiani, *Decameron" di Giovanni Boccaccio*, table I, p. 514.

Ceccos remains enigmatic, possibly also emblematic, for the storytellers' reticence to reveal what they themselves made of it.

By highlighting the narrators' "negative evaluation," in a brief but insightful essay entirely devoted to this tale, Fabio Coccetti reads a "discordant voice" in Neifile's story ("Decameron IX.4," 6). That the victim of the prank, Angiolieri, is morally superior to his alter ego, Fortarrigo, is another mark of the exceptionality of this tale, and the response of the *brigata* sanctions this anomaly, a deviation from the general rule: up to this point, in every *beffa*, the superiority of the trickster has consistently been established by the outcome of the prank. In this example of malice, however, as the trick trespasses spitefully into a mere hoax, Angiolieri is pitied by Boccaccio rather than mocked (Russo, *Letture critiche*, 278).

Drawing on Coccetti's study, Luigi Surdich also remarks the unusual condition of the victim in IX.4 ("La 'varietà delle cose,'" 240). Unlike, for instance, Calandrino, the character of Cecco Angiolieri is not intellectually inferior to his homonymous trickster, nor does he lack the proper awareness to understand what happens to him. The story also represents an exception to the usual corrective device consisting of a "counter-trick" ("una controbeffa"), whose function is to balance an irregular, inappropriate trick, as we see for instance in the tale of the scholar in Day Eight, the longest of the *Decameron* (Coccetti, "Decameron IX.4," 306; Surdich, "La 'varietà delle cose,'" 257). Cecco Angiolieri's defeat seems to infringe upon the authorial attempt to recreate a perfect order, in which, at the end of every tale, positive characters are those who marshal the resourcefulness of rhetoric and prudence to prevail against their foes, in a system that rewards skill and ingenuity.

In this specific case, though, Boccaccio's immediate introduction of Cecco Angiolieri as "bello e costumato uomo" [handsome and courteous (IX.4.6)] is perhaps disorienting for modern readers of the Sienese poet, given the self-debasing portrait associated to his lyric persona. Running counter to Angiolieri's self-portrayal as a scoundrel or, at least, as an immoralist drinker and gambler, somebody who even celebrates the death of his own father, Boccaccio surprisingly conceives a tale in which a character called Cecco Angiolieri is the innocent victim of another Cecco, who more closely resembles the literary Angiolieri, the bohemian *poète maudit* rediscovered by D'Ancona's essay. It is the other Cecco then, il Fortarrigo, who is represented with the goliardic and comic credentials more likely to be expected of his victim, on account of the "legend of Angiolieri's life, based on an autobiographical reading of his sonnets" (Branca, 1055).

In Boccaccio's tale, Angiolieri shows a problematic impotence before Fortarrigo, falling short in his attempt to advance his social condition.

Although he leaves Siena with the goal of improving his lot by working for a new papal ambassador in the Marches of Ancona, Fortarrigo's cunning upsets his best-laid plans, returning him to a state of dependence on his father. The circular trajectory of the story does not derive from the last paragraph of the *novella*, with its brief mention of a future revenge, but rather from the failure of Angiolieri's emancipatory journey. In the open ending of the tale, the handsome and courteous Cecco must wait in shame in Corsignano-Pienza to be restored to his previous status, only thanks to his father's intervention after having been robbed of his own identity, clothes, and palfrey by the other Cecco, the manipulating gambler.[9]

As Coccetti rightly argues, *Decameron* IX.4, a tale described as "not long," is actually not short, but rather not long enough. The audience of storytellers is surprised by Neifile, whose choice of simply hinting at a future revenge seems to exclude the expected counter-trick necessary to re-establish the major principle of every trickster narrative in the *Decameron*, i.e., the moral and intellectual inferiority of the victim of the prank. If we accept Coccetti's interpretation, the apathetic response of her peers stems from Neifile's unexpected narrative cut, one that triggers her audience's sanction (IX.4.305).

Carlo Muscetta, who reads the whole of Day Nine as a "festive farewell to the comic world," explains this difficulty in responding to the story as an excess of sympathy toward the character of Cecco Angiolieri ("Giovanni Boccaccio e i novellieri," 460). The *brigata*, he argues, is taken by a sense of melancholy due to a sympathetic feeling toward Cecco's misfortunes and most specifically his failed attempt to escape an anonymous existence of financial dependence on his father, even though he has come of age (IX.4.5). Muscetta points out the serious tone of the tale that he too ascribes to a group of "novelle di beffa" [trickster narratives], which are predominant on a day devoted, like this one, to an open topic.[10] At the end, Muscetta praises Boccaccio's realism in

9 The attribution of Angiolieri's literary persona to the character of Fortarrigo leads David Lummus to argue that, in the following tale (IX.5), the storyteller Fiammetta, in her opening remarks, is criticizing Neifile for her lack of verisimilitude (78). Although it is questionable to speak of a full inversion of "the historical attributes of [the tale's] characters" ("The *Decameron* and Boccaccio's Poetics," 78), Lummus's observation rightly points out the tension between the fictitious and the verisimilar as it applies to our tale.

10 For Muscetta, six tales from Day Nine belong to this group (1, 3, 4, 5, 8, 10). Giuseppe Petronio excludes from the series the first tale, and lists only five (3, 4, 5, 8, 10). See Boccaccio, *Decameron*, 737. Giancarlo Alfano counts only five of them, as he ascribes the last tale (10) to a different group centred on a sexual topic

depicting the bohemian life typical of Cecco Angiolieri's sonnets and wishes for the poetry of the historical Cecco the more nuanced palette displayed in Boccaccio's colourful portrait of the character-poet. Indeed, Muscetta appears convinced that Boccaccio depicts Cecco Angiolieri with "fond congeniality" ("simpatia affettuosa," ibid.) and that the tale works to redeem the poet's compromised reputation after the violent dispute with Dante.[11] Unlike Muscetta, however, I do not believe that IX.4 is meant to be simply a homage that Boccaccio pays to Cecco Angiolieri, "the other non-conformist writer mentioned in the *Decameron*" (ibid.), the first one being Guido Cavalcanti in VI.9.[12] While it remains a tribute to the role Cecco Angiolieri played in Boccaccio's apprenticeship as a comic writer in vernacular Italian, *Decameron* IX.4 seems to override Cecco's model, thereby providing a playful, metaliterary farewell to his comic mode.

This is also the opinion of Giancarlo Alfano, who underlines the importance of the cold response of the storytellers to this tale, which he calls a "plebeian and fraudulent prank" ("beffa plebea e truffaldina"), with the obvious goal of linking it to the goliardic tradition of poetry championed by Cecco Angiolieri. The little success obtained by Neifile's tale among the other nine members of the *brigata* (see IX.5.2) could be due, according to Alfano, to the excess of aggressiveness displayed in the dispute between the two Ceccos ("Scheda introduttiva," 1360). For Alfano, the final allusion to a future vendetta decrees the "irremediableness" of Fortarrigo's conduct within a story "fully

(2, 6, 10). For Alfano, IX.4 pairs with IX.8, since both tales focus on "aggressiveness and interpersonal rivalry." See Boccaccio, *Decameron*, 1359, Alfano, "Scheda introduttiva."

11 The three sonnets written by Cecco for Dante have often been read as a sign of a literary opposition that justifies an interpretation of Cecco's poetry in metaliterary terms; that is, as a poetry written against the poetics of the *stilnovo* embodied by Dante. See Giunta, *Versi per un destinatario*, 271. Luigi Surdich uses the term "cryptodantism" to emphasize the hidden presence of Dante's influence with respect to this tale and the eighth one, featuring Ciacco and Filippo Argenti ("La 'varietà delle cose,'" 239). On the long shadow of Dante, see Picone, "Il principio del novellare," 67–8, where Dante is defined as the "tutelary deity" of the whole *Decameron*. Alfie argues that the choice of Neifile as a storyteller could be a sign of a Dantesque correction of the tale. Neifile is a name often associated with Dante's work, as a literary clue toward la Pargoletta (Muscetta, "Giovanni Boccaccio e i novellieri," 377) or *La Vita nova*, i.e., Beatrice (Alfie, "Poetics Enacted," 180).

12 Cavalcanti and Angiolieri are the only two writers to feature in the *Decameron*'s tales. Nevertheless, Boccaccio explicitly refers to the literary triad made up of Dante Alighieri, Guido Cavalcanti, and Cino da Pistoia in his Introduction to Day Four, IX.4.33.

devoid of positive values" (ibid., 1369). The almost disdainful distance of the *brigata* formalizes the condemnation of Cecco Angiolieri's comic world: that paroxysmal and "paradoxical glorification of irregularity ... and of a world of rascals, which is the opposite of the well-ordered and regulated system aimed at by the ten young people of the *Decameron*" (ibid.).

Yet Cecco's brand of comic poetry is not embodied by Angiolieri but rather by Fortarrigo. As Luigi Russo points out, the triumphant protagonist of the story is the "other" Cecco, "[the] mischievous hero of cynical trickery, seen as a new Cepparello from Prato, liar, boldfaced, thief, and dark impostor" (*Letture critiche*, 276).

The rubric unequivocally states the centrality within the plot of this lesser-known Cecco:

> Cecco di messer Fortarrigo giuoca a Bonconvento ogni sua cosa e i denari di Cecco di messere Angiolieri; e in camiscia correndogli dietro e dicendo che rubato l'avea, il fa pigliare a' villani; e i panni di lui si veste e monta sopra il pallafreno, e lui, venendosene, lascia in camiscia. (IX.4.1)
>
> [Cecco Fortarrigo gambles away everything he possesses at Buonconvento, together with the money of Cecco Angiulieri. He then pursues Cecco Angiulieri in his shirt claiming that he has been robbed, causes him to be seized by peasants, dons his clothes, mounts his palfrey, and rides away leaving Angiulieri standing there in his shirt.]

Grammatically, Cecco di messer Fortarrigo, whose prominence in the story is enhanced by the position in the *incipit* of the rubric, remains the only subject. However, the interchangeability of the two main characters is embedded in the paratext and is developed in a symmetry conveyed through the position of their names in the first sentence and the repetition of the word "camiscia" [shirt] in the second part of the rubric (second and third sentences). In other words, although at the beginning of the trip out of Siena the two riders share only a name, by the end they also share clothes and horses, while the emphasis on the term "camiscia" highlights the mirroring relationship between the two characters' parallel states of undress. By exchanging these belongings – isolated as clear indicators of their respective socio-economic statuses – the characters' identities themselves become ostensibly interchangeable. The rubric displays a rigorous symmetrical structure. The first sentence establishes the protagonists' homonymy with a formal circularity (first name at the beginning of the sentence and second name at its end). The second sentence, which describes the final *beffa*, begins with a reference to the shirt, which is also the last word of the third, concluding sentence of the rubric.

Extending its centrality beyond the paratext, the word "camiscia," which occurs six times in the tale, is a crucial signifier of the exchange of status and identity at play in the *novella*. In no other *Decameron* tale is this word used with such great frequency. For Fortarrigo first and Angiolieri later, being left wearing only a shirt is a clear sign of destitution. Fortarrigo loses all his possessions at the gambling table, an accident leaving him quite literally with only the shirt on his back. Likewise, Angiolieri remains in his shirtsleeves when Fortarrigo deceitfully robs him. For the latter, this semiotics of dress indicates the bottom of his depravity; for the former, it represents a final humiliation that returns him to his initial situation of dependence on his father. In this state of dispossession and impotence, the character Angiolieri goes back to the condition of poverty often thematized in the sonnets of the historical Cecco.[13] As Alfie remarks, "Boccaccio is clearly mirroring Angiolieri's theme of his own poverty" ("Poetics Enacted," 188).

In their analysis of the last tale of the *Decameron*, Ann Rosalind Jones and Peter Stallybrass point out that in Renaissance England, "translation," as a technical term, designated an act of reclothing; to translate a garment was to repurpose its materials for new clothes (*Renaissance Clothing*, 220). In this sense, one can say that Boccaccio is "translating" Cecco when he uses Angiolieri's poetic body to craft a new garment for his own tale. Boccaccio's telling of an episode supposedly

13 See, for instance, in Lanza's edition, sonnet LVIII, "Qual è senza danari 'nnamorato" [A man who has no cash and falls in love (sonnet LXXXVIII in Mortimer's translation)]; sonnet LXIII, "Or odite, signor', s'i' ho ragione" [Now listen, sir, if my opinion's right (LXIX)]; sonnet LXIV, "Se l'omo avesse 'n sé conoscimento" [A man who truly knows what's for the best (LXVIII)]; sonnet LXV, "La povertà m'ha sì disamorato" [Now poverty has cooled my love at last (LXXII)]; sonnet LXXXVI, "In questo mondo chi non ha moneta" [In this world anyone devoid of pelf (LXVI)]; sonnet LXXXVII, "Così è l'uomo che non ha denari" [The man who has no more the means to pay (LXVII)]; sonnet LXXXVIII, "Un danaio, non che far cottardita" [If only I had one last coin to spare (LXX)]; sonnet LXXXIX, "Di tutte cose mi sento fornito" [At least what I possess is comprehensive (LXXI)]; sonnet XC, "Quando non ho denar', ogn'om mi schiva" [When I've no money left men turn away (LXXVI)]; sonnet XCI, "A chi nol sa non lasci Dio provare" [To one that does not know let God not tell (LXXIV)]; sonnet XCII, "In una ch'e' danar' mi dànno mono" [As my supply of cash keeps getting shorter (LXXV)]; sonnet XCIII, "I' son sì magro che quasi traluco" [So lean that I'm transparent, that's my style (LXXIII)]; sonnet XCV, "La Stremità mi richèr per figliuolo" [I was brought forth by Misery distressed (LXXX)]; sonnet CI, "Ogne mie 'ntendimento mi ricide" [See, all my plans and resolutions fail (LXXVII)].

from the life of Cecco Angiolieri ends with an exchange of clothes that represents a translation or, in other words, a transformation of the two main characters into one another. Only when the character of Cecco Angiolieri is robbed, undressed, and divested of his belongings by the other Cecco is he returned to his more "authentic" literary persona, and the material of the historical Angiolieri can be fully integrated into the *Decameron*.

Following on Jones and Stallybrass's discussion of the tale of Griselda and her "camiscia" (X.10), the trope of stripping as a means of manifesting dependence on a patriarchal figure – the husband for Griselda and the father for Cecco – can easily be extended to other stories of the *Decameron* in which the same word "camiscia" occurs, indicating a status of semi-nudity and consequent exposure to precariousness and danger.[14] The first time this term appears is in the conclusion of the opening tale of the Second Day, in which the protagonist Martellino is found fearful in front of a judge wearing only his shirt (II.1.31). In the following tale, Rinaldo, like Cecco Angiolieri, is robbed and left barefoot and wearing only his shirt, quivering in the cold weather (II.2.15). In the same Day Two, the ninth story also uses the act of undressing and redressing as a clear vehicle of change. Here, the translation of the clothes of Bernabò's wife, Zinevra, is instrumental in her metamorphosis into a man: "e fattosi della sua camiscia un paio di pannilini e i capelli tondutisi e trasformatasi tutta in forma di un marinaro, verso il mare se ne venne" [She also converted her shift [camiscia] into a pair of knee-length breeches, cut her hair, and, having transformed her appearance completely so that she now looked like a sailor, she made her way down to the coast (II.9.42)]. While the emphasis on the two Ceccos' shirts and the exchange of their clothes clearly works as a material signifier of their transformation, however, it also enacts the conflict between them as two opposing selves.

The story of the two Ceccos is introduced by the narrator Neifile as an example of "malizia" [malice, cunning], pitting one Cecco against the other:

> La qual cosa una a sé contraria nella mente m'ha recata: cioè come la malizia d'uno il senno soperchiasse d'un altro con grave danno e scorno dello soperchiato. (IX.4.4)

14 For more on the role of clothing in the *Decameron*, see Getto, *Vita di forme* (1972), 228, and, more specifically, Weaver, "Dietro il vestito."

> [But the story of Calandrino brings to mind a tale of a totally different sort, wherein one man's cunning defeats the wisdom of another, to the latter's extreme distress and embarrassment.]

According to Dante's definition in *Inferno* 11.79–80, deriving from Aristotle's *Nicomachean Ethics*, *malizia* is one of "tre disposizion che'l ciel non vole" [three dispositions / that strike at Heaven's will].[15] Surely, Boccaccio was also familiar with the use of the term in the comic episode of the grafters in *Inferno* 22, and an equally satirical use also pertains to the portrait of the first main character of the *Decameron*, Cepparello (I.1). In the first tale of the book, this evil disposition is attributed to a man who, exactly like Cecco di Fortarrigo in IX.4, is a gambler, a tavern-goer, a heavy drinker, and, most importantly, an unreliable but very persuasive liar. Drawing on Giovanni Getto's reading of Cepparello's tale in *Vita di forme e forme di vita nel Decameron*, Franco Fido also emphasizes the pivotal role of reversal in the construction of three successive "portraits" of the notorious character ("The Tale of Ser Ciappelletto," 60–1). Cepparello's transformation from sinner to saint, his distortion of the sacrament of confession, and the resulting parody of hagiographical texts mirror the two Ceccos' final reversal of fortune, the exchange of their identities, and the parodying of the Italian burlesque tradition.

If, as has been noted in previous scholarship, Cecco di Fortarrigo bears a striking resemblance to Cepparello,[16] Cecco Angiolieri, introduced as "handsome and courteous" ("bello e costumato," IX.4.6), is presented in similar terms to the three male storytellers in the Introduction, characterized as "charming and courteous" ("piacevole e costumato ciascuno," I.Intro.79, my translation). We thus witness a polarization between a negative Cecco (Fortarrigo), associated to the example of malice found in Cepparello, and a positive one (Angiolieri), who shares the virtues of the three male members of the *brigata*. In this respect, the two antagonists represent an oppositional pair, thus providing the foundation of what Katherine Brown has called a "narrative reversal" (*Boccaccio's Fabliaux*, 16–20), that is to say the systematic

15 The word *malizia* is used by Cecco Angiolieri himself to describe the heart of the indifferent lady in sonnet XXI, vv.1–4: "– Oncia di carne, libra di malizia, / per che dimostri quel che 'n cor non hai? – Se' tu sì pazzo, ch'aspetti divizia / di quel che caramente comparrai?" ["An ounce of flesh for every pound of spite, / Your heart can't mean all that your words declare." / "Are you so mad to think I mean to share / What I have bought so dear and hold so tight?" (XXVII)].

16 See Surdich, "La 'varietà delle cose,'" 243.

inversion of logically opposed qualities, such as male and female, rich and poor, or good and bad.

From the very beginning, the two Ceccos are indeed presented as two opposing selves, only bound together by an antisocial hatred for their respective fathers:

> Erano, non sono molti anni passati, in Siena due già per età compiuti uomini, ciascuno chiamato Cecco, ma l'uno di messere Angiulieri e l'altro di messer Fortearrigo. Li quali, quantunque in molte altre cose male insieme di costume si convenissero, in uno, cioè che ammenduni li loro padri odiovano, tanto si convenieno, che amici n'erano divenuti e ispesso n'usavano insieme. (IX.4.5)
>
> [In Siena, not many years ago, there lived two young men, who had both come of age and were both called Cecco, the one being the son of Messer Angiulieri and the other of Messer Fortarrigo. And whilst they failed to see eye-to-eye with each other on several matters, there was one respect at least – namely, their hatred of their respective fathers – in which they were in such total agreement that they became good friends and were often to be found in one another's company.]

According to Alberto Asor Rosa's calculations, this tale is one of only twenty-seven stories in the *Decameron* that is totally devoid of erotic themes (*"Decameron" di Giovanni Boccaccio*, 533). In a narrative with no female characters, the core of the tale is a peculiar homosocial relationship, in which two unlikely friends become rivals, if not enemies, at the very moment in which their belongings and identities are swapped.[17] In spite of their presentation as two fundamentally opposite personalities, it is interesting that the two Ceccos of Boccaccio's tale are bound together by a paternal hatred often thematized in the work of the historical Angiolieri.[18]

---

17 Getto reads the tale as a typical example of a story based on a rivalry, a notion of friendship in which two friends end up embodying an antithetical role with respect to each other (*Vita di forme* [1972], 225). For comments on the exclusion of female characters, see Migiel, *A Rhetoric*, 59. For more on the topic of friendship and a reading of IX.4 in relation to tale I.2, see Cottino-Jones, *Order from Chaos*, 163.

18 Anti-paternal sentiments not only bring together, under the aegis of the Sienese poet's lyric persona, the two opposing Ceccos in the tale, but also establish a possible connection between Angiolieri's sonnets and Boccaccio's works. Scholars have, indeed, found traces of a similar disposition, potentially autobiographical, in Boccaccio's corpus through the recurrent depiction of father figures as stingy old men. See Bruni, *Boccaccio*, 405–6, and Tufano, "Il regime comico," 55n3.

As Cecco himself affirms, loathing for his father is one of the defining features of his poetics, explicitly acknowledging the predominance of this theme in two metaliterary sonnets, respectively LXII and LXXXV in Lanza's edition: "Babb'e Becchina, l'Amor e mie madre" [Dad, my Becchina, Love and then my mother (LXXXV; the numbers in parentheses with the translations are Mortimer's)] and "Tant'abbo di Becchina novellato" [I've written so much of Becchina dear (XCVIII)]. In the latter, the author goes so far as to playfully say that he is afraid of having exhausted the audience's interest: "Tant'abbo di Becchina novellato, / e di mie madr'e di babbo e d'Amore, / ch'una parte del mondo n'ho stancato" [I've written so much of Becchina dear, / Of mother, father, and the god of Love, / I'm tiring half the readers that I have (vv. 1–3)]. This aversion takes a variety of forms, including the bemoaning of his father's avarice,[19] the cursing of his longevity,[20] and, perhaps most famously, the fervently expressed desire for his death: "S'i' fosse morte, andarei da mio padre; / s'i' fosse vita, fuggirei da lui" [LXXXII, vv. 9–10; If I were Death, I'd pay my Dad a visit; / If I were Life, he'd get what he deserved (LXXXVI)].[21] This paternal hatred is so relevant in Cecco's corpus that it even generates an antiphrastic, self-deprecating palinode in sonnet LXXXIX, "Chi dice del suo padre altro ch'onore" [A man who speaks no good about his sire (XCVII)].

If the two Ceccos in IX.4 are united by a shared paternal hatred, well documented in Angiolieri's sonnets, it is remarkable that the dividing line between the two characters should be their differential dispositions toward gambling and drinking:

> Al quale l'Angiulieri rispose che menar nol volea, non perché egli nol conoscesse bene a ogni servigio sufficiente, ma per ciò che egli giucava e

19 See sonnet XXXI, "S<e> i' non torni ne l'odio d'Amore" [Unless I risk Love's enemy once more (XXXXVI)]; LXXIV, "Tre cose solamente mi so' in grado" [There are three things that give me great delight (LXXXVII)].

20 See sonnet LIX, "Non potrebb'esser, per quanto Dio fece" [In spite of God, there seems but little doubt (XCV)]; LXXVI, "I' potre' anzi ritornare in ieri" [It's far more likely that I shall return (XC)], LXXVII, "Sed i' credesse vivar un dì solo" [If I felt sure to live a full day longer (LXXXIX)]; LXXVIII, "Il pessimo e 'l crudele odio ch'io porto" [The bitter hatred that I bear today (XCIV)]; LXXIX, "I' ho un padre sì compressionato" [My father's constitution is so blessed (XCI)]; LXXXI, "Sed i' avesse mille lingue in bocca" [If I possessed a thousand tongues, and each (XCIII)].

21 For the expression of a similar desire, see also LVIII, "Qual è senza danari 'nnamorato" [A man who has no cash and falls in love (LXXXVIII)]; LXXX, "Morte, merzé, se mi' prego t'è 'n grato" [Now Death, if it should please you, deign to take (XCII)].

> oltre a ciò s'inebriava alcuna volta; a che il Fortarrigo rispose che dell'uno e dell'altro senza dubbio si guarderebbe e con molti saramenti gliele affermò, tanti prieghi sopragiugnendo che l'Angiulieri, sì come vinto, disse che era contento. (IX.4.8)

> [But Angiulieri refused his offer, not because he had the slightest doubt of his ability to perform these duties, but because Fortarrigo was an inveterate gambler and furthermore he occasionally got very drunk. Fortarrigo assured him that he would guard against both these weaknesses and swore repeatedly that he would keep his promise, to which he added such a torrent of entreaties that Angiulieri finally yielded and agreed to take him.]

Although surely not as omnipresent as the hatred for his father, love for drink and the dice is considered by many modern readers to be among the most prominent features of Cecco Angiolieri's poetic voice,[22] thanks perhaps to the enduring popularity of sonnet LXXIV:

> Tre cose solamente mi so' in grado,
> le quali posso non ben ben fornire:
> ciò è la donna, la taverna e'l dado;
> queste mi fanno'l cor lieto sentire. (vv. 1–4)

> [There are three things that give me great delight, / And none of them come at a handy price; / Woman, the tavern and a game of dice; / And these alone can make my heart feel light. (LXXXVII)]

The celebration of an irregular lifestyle and the pleasure of over-imbibing is also present in sonnet LXXV, vv. 1–3: "Tutto quest'anno ch'è, mi son frustrato / de tutti i vizi che solia avere; / non m'è rimaso se non quel di bere" [Throughout this year I duly have restrained / Every habitual vice excepting drink, / From which, it's true, I have not quite refrained (LXV)].

It is curious, then, that at the beginning of Boccaccio's tale, the character of Cecco Angiolieri explicitly objects to the bad habits associated with the persona of the historical poet and instead attributed in this tale to his alter ego, Fortarrigo. In this way, the lyric identity of Cecco Angiolieri is assessed negatively within Boccaccio's universe,

---

22 As Alfie remarks, only two of Angiolieri's sonnets are fully given over to the theme of tavern culture; see "Poetics Enacted," 178, and *Comedy*, 96.

not merely by its association with the villain of the tale, Cecco di Fortarrigo, but also more ironically by the value judgments of the character of Cecco Angiolieri himself. Boccaccio creates a double, Cecco di Fortarrigo, who has the characteristics of Angiolieri's persona in his sonnets, while the character of Angiolieri rejects those celebrated features and the person who now embodies them, resisting Fortarrigo's offer to be his servant on account of his penchant for drinking and gambling.

In Boccaccio's tale, we witness the displacement and performative dismantling of Cecco Angiolieri's authorial identity. Although Boccaccio never refers to Cecco as a poet, in this most literary day of the *Decameron*, readers would have no difficulty in identifying the popular Tuscan writer as such.[23] Nevertheless, by the end of the tale a certain equilibrium is reached: the man named Cecco Angiolieri is left in shirtsleeves, like a man who has lost all his clothes gambling, while the inveterate gambler, Cecco di Fortarrigo, assumes the outward markers of Cecco Angiolieri's identity. In a sense, the character named Cecco Angiolieri only coincides with the lyric persona of the poet of the same name, once he has been robbed by his doppelgänger.

Since the rediscovery of Cecco Angiolieri's poetry in the late nineteenth century, early literary scholarship established a clear and perhaps obvious connection between IX.4 and two specific sonnets by Angiolieri, "Se Die m'aiuti, a le sante guagnele" and "Non si disperin quelli de lo'nferno," poems XXXII and LXXXIII, respectively. In the former, without questioning the historicity of the tale told by Boccaccio, early readers of Angiolieri's work discovered a first allusion to the poet's departure from Siena; in the later, a *unicum*, critics found explicitly named both Ceccos present in IX.4 (D'Ancona, *Cecco Angiolieri da Siena*, 176–82 and 196; Massèra, *I Sonetti di Cecco Angiolieri*, 110–11, 141–2, and 179–80). If early critics of Angiolieri read Boccaccio to find historical information about the life of the Sienese poet, whose sonnets were read autobiographically, more recent scholarship of the *Decameron* has done much the opposite, looking to Angiolieri's corpus to better understand Boccaccio's tale.

Drawing on Massèra, for example, Vittore Branca in his commentary uses the sonnet "Non si disperin quelli de lo'nferno" to introduce the main characters and their unusual relationship (1054–5). Having established a case of intertextuality, Fabian Alfie considers the same sonnet

23 Aside from Cecco Angiolieri's presence in IX.4, there are also many references to Dante's work in IX.8. See Surdich, "La 'varietà delle cose,'" 239.

"crucial to an analysis of this *novella*" ("Poetics Enacted," 179). For its undeniable importance, this last text is worth quoting at length:

> Non si disperin quelli de lo'nferno
> po' che n'è uscito un che v'era chiavato,
> el quale è Cecco, ch'è così chiamato,
> che vi credea istare in sempiterno.
> Ma in tal guisa è rivolto il quaderno
> che sempre viverò grolificato,
> po' che messer Angiolieri è scoiato,
> che m'affliggea e di state e di verno.
> Muovi, nuovo sonetto, e vanne a Cecco,
> a quel che giù dimora a la Badia:
> digli che Fortarrigo è mezzo secco,
> che non si dia nulla maninconia;
> ma di tal cibo imbecchi lo suo becco
> ch'e' viverà più ch'Enoch ed Elia. (LXXXIII)
>
> Let not the devils and the damned despair,
> For someone has escaped who lay in chains;
> Cecco, I mean, a soul who shared their pains
> And thought he'd have to stay for ever there.
> The tide has turned, and turned in such a way
> That I shall live in glory from now on;
> The skinflint's skinned, Old Angiolieri's gone,
> My bane through summer and winter, night and day.
> Then rise, new sonnet, find that Cecco out
> Who lives down at the Abbey; tell him how
> Old Fortarrigo's almost dry,[24] and now
> He need not be downcast but have no doubt
> That if he feeds on hope, as he should do,
> He'll outlive Enoch and Elijah too. (XCVI)

This sonnet is the only work of Angiolieri's production to mention Cecco di Fortarrigo by name. This proves to be particularly compelling given not only the hatred shared by both Ceccos for their respective fathers but also the presence of a kind of friendly prank played, in this case, not by Fortarrigo at the expense of Angiolieri, but rather by

24 Although not evident in the English translation, "dry," the Italian "secco," like "stecchito," indicates not merely the lack of moisture but the condition of being bony and rigid like a dead body or even Death itself, often represented as a skeleton.

the author Angiolieri on his correspondent Fortarrigo. Whereas Angiolieri's sonnets with no other exception complain of the almost demonic longevity of his father or wish for his quick demise, this one celebrates the long-anticipated moment of his death. Diverging from Lanza, who attributes the promise of a miraculous longevity to the soon-to-be-orphaned Cecco di Fortarrigo (in Angiolieri, *Le rime*, 166), many critics, including Alfie, Bentivogli, Branca, and Contini,[25] read the sestet instead as a taunting prediction of a long life for a half-dead Fortarrigo *père*. In other words, Cecco is finally emancipated from Angiolieri but gleefully notes that the same cannot be said for his homonymous friend. This reference to the death of Angiolieri's father situates the action of the sonnet temporally after the *beffa* depicted in the *Decameron*, where Angiolieri's return to Siena is made possible thanks to his father's continued good health.

Boccaccio's tale follows the sonnet in restating the odd friendship between the two Ceccos, their common anti-paternal disposition, and a mocking antagonism. Because of the similarities between this poem and *Decameron* IX.4, it is not unreasonable to imagine that Boccaccio might have resurrected these two characters for the purposes of his story. Contini was persuaded that this sonnet provided the foundation for Boccaccio's tale (*Poeti del Duecento*, 381). More recently, Bruno Bentivogli has questioned its attribution to Cecco Angiolieri and its availability as a source for Boccaccio. "Non si disperin quelli de lo'nferno" is represented in only one extant manuscript from the fifteenth-century (MS Riccardiano 1103), which falsely attributes several other poems, although none of them by Cecco. For this reason, among others, Bentivogli hypothesizes that the sonnet could actually have been written *after* Boccaccio's tale, rather than vice versa; according to this line of reasoning, a counterfeiter would have forged a sonnet after the *Decameron* in order to provide an appendix to Boccaccio's tale, along with the much-coveted news about the death of Cecco's father ("Sospetti di falsificazione," 17). Alfie finds Bentivogli's thesis unconvincing. Drawing on a marginal gloss in the manuscript Chigiano L.VIII.305, he even goes so far as to attribute a little-known anonymous sonnet to Cecco di Fortarrigo as part of a non-existent *tenzone* with Angiolieri's "Non si disperin quelli de lo'nferno" ("Cecco vs. Cecco," 125–7). As there is no philological consensus about the sonnet that reports the names of Boccaccio's two protagonists, one can only regret the lack of an

25 For Alfie's interpretation, see "Cecco vs. Cecco," 124–5; for Banca's, see 1055n3; for Bentivogli's, see "Sospetti di falsificazione," 12–13n1; for Contini's, see *Poeti del Duecento*, 381.

authoritative critical edition of Cecco Angiolieri's poetry as promised by Luigi Pirandello more than one century ago in 1896 ("Un preteso poeta umorista," 258).

Regardless of the relationship between "Non si disperin quelli de lo'nferno" and Boccaccio's authorial imagination, however, a series of thematic and linguistic overlaps between the two texts suggests an intertextual reading of IX.4 and Angiolieri's sonnets. Scholars like Branca, for instance, have already pointed out the thematic connection between the scene at the inn, with an inebriated Fortarrigo looking for his pawned doublet, and a sonnet often attributed to Cecco Angiolieri (1058).

The tale could be divided into four narrative sequences: the two Ceccos' life in Siena (IX.4.5–8), their departure and stay at the inn in Bonconvento (IX.4.9–18), Fortarrigo's act of malice on the road to Torrenieri (IX.4.19–23), and Angiolieri's final humiliation in Corsignano, where he awaits his father's aid and a future revenge (IX.4.24–5). In the second one, the longest, Cecco di Fortarrigo appears in his shirt, having lost his own clothing and money, and Angiolieri's money as well, at the gaming table. Before an infuriated Angiolieri, in a last desperate attempt to delay his departure, Cecco di Fortarrigo explains that he has pawned his doublet, and that he hopes to win it back with the financial help of the other Cecco whom he had just robbed. The scene takes an almost surreal turn as Fortarrigo skilfully manipulates the truth to his own advantage, acting as though nothing had happened in front of the innkeeper's household. The repeated detail of the lost doublet, its pawning out of necessity, and Fortarrigo's request for money in a state of intoxication echo a sonnet traditionally ascribed to Cecco Angiolieri, "I' son venuto di schiatta di struzzo" [I have become an ostrich in my need (CXXI)].[26] Massèra was the first to notice that the initial part of Fortarrigo's prank can be possibly linked to the sonnet (*I Sonetti di Cecco Angiolieri*, 196). In this poem, the word "farsetto" [doublet], *hapax legomenon* in Cecco's poetry, appears in a situation that closely resembles Boccaccio's tale. Having pawned his doublet and eaten his corselet out of hunger, the speaker in Cecco's sonnet is now about to pawn his gorget as well.

26 The sonnet features anonymously in Chig. L.VIII.305 and was included by Massèra in Angiolieri's corpus. However, both Contini and Lanza express doubts about the authenticity of this attribution (Contini, *Poeti del Duecento*, 392; Lanza's edition of *Rime*, 240–1).

In the same scene at the inn in IX.4, during the altercation that follows his discovery of being robbed, Angiolieri is allowed his only direct speech:

> "Che ho io a fare di tuo farsetto, che appiccato sie tue per la gola? ché non solamente m'hai rubato e giucato il mio, ma sopra ciò hai impedita la mia andata, e anche ti fai beffe di me." (IX.4.16)
>
> ["What the hell do I care about your doublet?" he yelled. "May you be hanged by the neck. Not only do you rob me and gamble away all my money, but you prevent me from leaving as well. And now you stand there making fun of me."]

This single instance of direct discourse, compared to the six given to Cecco di Fortarrigo, creates an uneven distribution of power between the two characters. As Max Alexander Staples remarks, almost all of Cecco Angiolieri's speeches are reported indirectly to "emphasise the point that he is passive even when he talks. 'L'Angiulieri diceva egli altressì ma le sue parole non erano ascoltate'" [Angiolieri also was speaking but his words remained unheard (*The Ideology of the Decameron*, 34, my translation)].

From the linguistic point of view, direct speech in this text is particularly marked with terms coming from the Sienese area and oral language.[27] Drawing on Branca's study of Boccaccio's expressionism (*Boccaccio medievale* [1996], 362–4), in which IX.4 is defined as a tale "resonant of literary echoes," Paola Manni has recently linked the language of Fortarrigo's second direct speech to a particular sonnet by Cecco Angiolieri – number LXI in Lanza's edition – "Lo mi' cor non s'allegra di covelle" [Today no joy unto my heart accrues (XXIV)] (*La lingua di Boccaccio*, 160–1).

In IX.4 Fortarrigo's words are coloured by a mimetic use of Sienese vernacular: "Deh, Angiulieri, in buonora lasciamo stare ora *costette* parole che non montan *cavelle*" [Come now, Angiolieri, let's forget about these words that do not mean anything (IX.4.15, my translation and emphasis)]. If, as Branca has noticed, the idiomatic Sienese term "costette" brings the reader back to tale VII.10.22 (1058), which also features two protagonists from Siena, the word "covelle" – from the Latin *quod velles* – is present not only in two other tales, VIII.3.17 and IX.3.12,

27 On this topic, see also Alfie, "Poetics Enacted," 183 and 185–6.

but also in the aforementioned poem "Lo mi' cor non s'allegra di covelle" and in another sonnet, "L'altrier sì mi ferìo una tal ticca" [The other day a certain itching will (CXX)], once attributed to Cecco and now ascribed to another Sienese poet, Meo dei Tolomei.

The linguistic connection between the two Ceccos' direct discourse in the *Decameron* tale and Angiolieri's poetic corpus is highlighted by a further analysis of the specific vocabulary which they share. To return, for example, to the only speech by the character of Cecco Angiolieri, not only the substantive "farsetto" but, with the single exception of the verb "impedire" [to prevent], every other word as well can be found in the language of the sonnets. For instance, the term "appiccato," in reference to the act of hanging oneself, appears in sonnet LXXXVIII, "Un danaio, non che far cottardita" [If only I had one last coin to spare (LXX)]. A similar turn of phrase is also used in the first two lines of sonnet LXIII: "Or odite, signor', s'i' ho ragione, / ben di dovermi empiccar per la gola" [Now listen, gentlemen, if I am right, / that I should be strung up by the neck (my translation)], in which the apostrophe "signor'" anticipates the *captatio benevolentiae* employed by Fortarrigo with the farmers at the end of the tale.[28] The word "beffa" [mockery], for its part, is used in three poems: sonnet V, "Amor, poi che'n sì greve passo venni" [Love, when you brought me down to such a state (XV)], sonnet LXIV, "Se l'omo avesse'n sé conoscimento" [A man who truly knows what's for the best (LXVIII)], and a sonnet dubiously ascribed to Cecco Angiolieri, "Salute manda lo tu' buon Martini" [Berto Rinier, your Buon Martini sends (CXXIX)]. Interestingly, the word "andata" [going, journey] appears in sonnet LXXXIV, "Chi dice del suo padre altro ch'onore [A man who speaks no good about his sire (XCVII)], in which the author ironically condemns those who express hatred for their fathers.

It is not only a linguistic connection that has led critics to link Fortarrigo's trick, in the third sequence of the tale, to a dialogic sonnet from Angiolieri's corpus, "Accorri, accorri, accorri, uom, a la strada!" (Branca, 1059). In his final act of malice, Fortarrigo, having chased Angiolieri's palfrey on his nag, calls for some farmworkers' help, pretending that it is in fact he who has been robbed. Fortarrigo's guile is represented through three other instances of direct speech. In the first, he addresses the workers with a simple imperative, "Pigliatel, pigliatelo!" [Get him, get him! (IX.4.21, my translation)]. In the second, he

28 Branca links what he refers to as "almost a *captatio benevolentiae*" to the sermon of Frate Cipolla in VI.10.37 (1059).

feigns anger toward Angiolieri in a performance that is directed only at the workers. Finally, Fortarrigo speaks to the crowd of peasants bringing his scheme to completion by spinning a false narrative, in which he is the first to attribute his own actions to the character of Cecco Angiolieri: "Vedete, signori, come egli m'aveva lasciato nell'albergo in arnese, avendo prima ogni sua cosa giucata! Ben posso dire che per Dio e per voi io abbia questo cotanto racquistato, di che io sempre vi sarò tenuto" [Gentlemen, you can see the sort of state he left me in, sneaking off from the inn as he did, after gambling away everything he possessed! But with God's help and your own, I can say that I've salvaged something at least, and I shall always be grateful to you for your timely assistance (IX.4.22)]. Thus, before the final exchange of clothes, this factitious rendition of the tale's events inaugurates the concluding reversal of the characters' identities.

Cecco Angiolieri's sonnet "Accorri, accorri, accorri, uom, a la strada!" features a similarly lively dialogue, set in the street, in which the lover enacts a contrived robbery, the common trope of the stolen heart:

"Accorri, accorri, accorri, uom, a la strada!".
"Che ha', fi' de la putta?". "I' son rubato".
"Chi t'ha rubato?". "Una che par che rada
come rasoi', sì m'ha netto lasciato".
"Or come non le davi de la spada?".
"I' dare' anzi a me". "Or se' 'mpazzito?".
"Non so che'l dà". "Così mi par che vada:
or t'avess'ella cieco, sciagurato?".
"E vedi che ne pare a que' che'l sanno?".
"Di' quel che tu mi rubi!". "Or va' con Dio;
ma anda pian, ch'i' vo' pianger lo danno".
"Ché ti diparti con animo rio?"
"Tu abbi'l danno con tutto'l malanno!".
"Or chi m'ha morto?". "E che diavol sacc'io?". (XVI)

"Help, help! For God's sake, help! Hi, here in the street!"
"What's up, you whoreson?" – "I've been robbed, I swear."
"Who's robbed you then?" – "A wench who does it neat,
And cleaner than a razor shaves your hair."
"But where's your sword? To kill her would be sweet."
"I'd rather kill myself." – "You're mad, then." – "Yea,
I'm mad, but don't know why" – "So, I repeat,
That wretched girl would take your sight away!"
"A madman, yes, we see you know that part!"

> "What have you plundered from me?" – "Go in peace,
> But slowly, give me time to mourn this woe
> And see your leaving." – "With a bitter heart!"
> "Now may your loss with every curse increase!"
> "Who killed me?" – "How the devil should I know?" (XVI)

The sonnet unfolds as a dialogue between three parties: the lover, the lady, and a passerby. It is exactly the presence of a third party that makes the comparison compelling, because the reader at first is forced to identify with the passerby, who takes at face value the lover's cry for help. It is only after the ninth verse of text, with the intervention of the lady's voice, that the metaphorical nature of the robbery becomes apparent. In this respect, the reader is the dupe of Cecco's narrative trick in the sonnet.

In IX.4 too, as Mario Baratto has pointed out, the role of a third party is crucial in a tale otherwise dominated by only two male characters. Baratto specifically emphasizes the role played by the crowd in this tale of deception. After all, the one Cecco who is defeated, Angiolieri, is not actually deceived by the other Cecco, Fortarrigo; it is only because of the participation of others, first the innkeeper's household and then the farmworkers, that Fortarrigo's mystification of truth can be successful: "While Angiolieri does not want to play a part and expresses genuine emotions, Fortarrigo consciously uses language not so much to establish dialogue, communication, complicity between two individuals, but rather as an instrument of play and deception" (*Realtà e stile* [1993], 236).

In spite of its relatively low profile in modern literary criticism,[29] for Baratto, IX.4, which he defines as "a perfect mechanism" (ibid.),[30] is symptomatic of an important development in Boccaccio's narrative mode, from the binary pattern of a tale based on the tension between its protagonists to a more complex form of comedy, in which "the reader of *The Decameron* ideally becomes a spectator" (ibid., 241). The dialogic form provided by some of Cecco's sonnets like "Accorri, accorri, accorri, uom, a la strada!" and his debate poetry surely could have

29 Despite the "historical literary interest" (see Bergin, *Boccaccio*, 320) that can be found in the tale owing to the presence of one of the few writers in the whole *Decameron*, the story of Cecco Angiolieri has received little critical attention, in comparison to the popularity of Guido Cavalcanti's tale in Day Six, to the point that Fabian Alfie has even defined this paucity of scholarship as "tragic" ("Poetics Enacted," 171).

30 For a similar, positive evaluation, see also the commentary by Attilio Momigliano: "The tale is one of the most balanced and the most perfect" (Boccaccio, *Il Decameron. 49 novelle*, 299n2).

supplied Bocacccio with an important vernacular model for his own comic style.[31]

The ambiguity of the tale and its puzzling treatment of the historical character of Cecco Angiolieri may explain the difficulty scholars have encountered in addressing what only has the appearance of one of the many trickster narratives present in the book. *Decameron* IX.4 is, indeed, a tale that is very difficult to classify, characterized by an unusual peculiarity. As Asor Rosa points out, even given the thematic hybridization of many of the *Decameron*'s tales, of the entire collection of one hundred stories, only eight, including IX.4, do not fit easily into the eight fundamental subjects supplied in the rubrics (*"Decameron" di Giovanni Boccaccio*, 481). Asor Rosa argues that, more than the theme of trickery, what defines this story is "the inscrutable and slightly foolish strangeness of Cecco di Fortarrigo" (ibid.). For this exceptional state of freedom and thematic openness, along with two other stories from the same day (IX.6 and IX.10), Asor Rosa regards the tale of the two Ceccos not only as beautiful and possibly underappreciated but also as an anticipation of the "forms and trajectories of the modern short story" (ibid., 482).

If the *Decameron* is written in response to the havoc wreaked by the Black Plague, the reverse world of comic poetry described in Cecco Angiolieri's sonnets exemplifies a carnivalesque threat to the restoration of social order. The final defeat of the alter ego of Cecco Angiolieri created by Boccaccio and his failed journey seem to be a literary rejection of his poetics and the values they represent. By displacing the rascal persona of the poet to the character of Cecco di Fortarrigo, Boccaccio enacts a scenario in which the Sienese author, in the form of the intradiegetic Cecco Angiolieri, is paid back with his own coin, as he becomes the butt of a hard-drinking gambler's trickery. In this way, Boccaccio does not so much appropriate Cecco's poetics as he subverts them. Although the historicity of IX.4, or lack thereof, cannot be stated with any certainty, the dynamics between the two Ceccos provide a metaliterary dramatization of the poet's lyric corpus. In this respect, the theme of the double becomes the narrative equivalent of the intertextual device at play in the tale. By enacting the conflict between two opposing selves, Boccaccio effectively parodies their extratextual referent, the poet Cecco Angiolieri.

31 For comments on the importance of the "poeti giocosi" in informing Boccaccio's comic tone, see Mazzotta, *The World at Play*, 161.

Art, Nature, and Reality in Boccaccio's Giotto: *Decameron* IX.5

MARCELLO CICCUTO

On many occasions in his critical works, Giovanni Boccaccio sought to explicitly draw attention to the relation between artists of his time and nature (or, if one prefers, reality). He saw it as an evolution with respect to the late medieval principles of aesthetics, as witnessed by what the new pictorial schools, which would later associate themselves with the Giotto period, had brought to light, most notably in the transitional years between the thirteenth and the fourteenth centuries.[1] For example, the words written as a commentary to Dante's *Commedia* reveal an author intent on indicating just how much this relation had become complex compared with the older criteria of pure *imitatio naturae*:

> ... secondo che ne bastano le forze dello 'ngegno, c'ingegnamo nelle cose, le quali il naturale esemplo ricevono, fare ogni cosa simile alla natura, intendendo, per questo, che esse abbiano quegli medesimi effetti che hanno le cose prodotte dalla natura, e se non quegli, almeno, in quanto si può, simili a quegli, sì come noi possiamo vedere in alquanti esercizi meccanici. Sforzasi il dipintore che la figura dipinta da sé, la quale non è altro che un poco di colore con certo artificio posto sopra una tavola, sia tanto simile, in quello atto ch'egli la fa, a quella la quale la natura ha prodotta e naturalmente in quello atto si dispone, che essa possa gli occhi de' riguardanti o in parte o in tutto ingannare, facendo di sé credere che ella sia quello che ella non è. (*Esposiz*. XI.I, 68–9)[2]

1 For a more detailed description of this gradual legitimization of a new aesthetic within the cultural panorama between the thirteenth and fourteenth centuries, see Ciccuto, "Il novelliere en artiste" and "Un'antica canzone." A more developed view with respect to these earlier studies is amply described in Ciccuto, "Petrarca e le arti."

2 Boccaccio, *Esposizioni sopra la Comedia di Dante*. The English translation is by Papio, from *Boccaccio's Expositions on Dante's Comedy*.

> [[Art] follows Nature, inasmuch as we strive, to the extent that the power of our intellect allows, to make everything that emulates the natural model in a way that is similar to Nature's. What the author means is that we do this so that what we make possesses the same characteristics as the things produced by Nature or, if it does not, so that it at least appears as similar to them as possible, just as we see in several mechanical activities. The painter seeks to have the figure he is depicting (which is nothing other than a bit of colour placed with a certain amount of technique upon a panel) turn out as similar as possible to the model that Nature had made, and he does this in such a way that his painting is naturally able, in full or in part, to deceive the eyes of the viewer, making him believe it to be something that it is not.]

Even earlier, however, *Decameron* VI.5.5–6 had confirmed, this time in narrative form, the consolidation of this aesthetic stance in the cultural landscape of the time, in parallel with the legends that had begun circulating about various artists, all operating within the context of innovations initially introduced by Giotto, the "master of the seven liberal arts":

> Giotto, ebbe uno ingegno di tanta eccellenzia, che niuna cosa dà la natura, madre di tutte le cose e operatrice col continuo girar de' cieli, che egli con lo stile e con la penna o col pennello non dipignesse sì simile a quella, che non simile, anzi più tosto dessa paresse, in tanto che molte volte nelle cose da lui fatte si truova che il visivo senso degli uomini vi prese errore, quello credendo esser vero che era dipinto. (VI.5.5)[3]

> [Giotto, was a man of such outstanding genius that there was nothing in the whole of creation that he could not depict with his stylus, pen, or brush. And so faithful did he remain to Nature (who is the mother and the motive force for all created things, via the constant rotation of the heavens), that whatever he depicted had the appearance, not of a reproduction, but of the thing itself, so that one very often finds, with the works of Giotto, that people's eyes are deceived and they mistake the picture for the real thing.]

Here one also recognizes in the figure of the artist a model for a new, entirely earthly, creator, an *artifex* of images – and more generally, of a

3 Quotations are from Boccaccio, *Decameron*, ed. Branca (1992). The English translation is by McWilliam (1995). See Sacchetti, *Il Trecentonovelle*, 146–7, as well as the relevant discussion in Ciccuto, "Un'antica canzone," 114–20.

new and different reality – that went so far as to replace the older ones. These earlier images, as is known, claimed to be derived from a linear, unproblematic relation between appearance and identity, guaranteed in all respects by the indisputable equivalence between the *figura hominis* and the *imago Dei*.[4] The whole semiotic system of correspondences had been based on the deceptiveness of visible appearances, physical identity, and the centuries-old certainties regarding the perfect and univocal relation between *figurae* and *veritas*, rooted in the principle of Adam and human creation being the equivalent of the *imago Dei*. It is precisely this system that Boccaccio's genius begins to gradually undermine, enlisting the help of those new gods – the artists – who recurrently make appearances at the narrative level. Perfectly aware of the role of *deceptio* in everyday happenings and human perception, they become the intellectually qualified and emancipated subverters of this system which presupposes a perfect correspondence between absolute truth and living semblances.

To tell things as they truly are, beyond their deceitful appearances, becomes the ambition of the storyteller and the various artist-characters placed on the stage of the *Decameron*, all involved in the creation of an alternative reality (and vision) in opposition to the older, real one. Within this new approach, the gifts of *inventio*, intellectual creativity, and inquiring language oppose all mimetic relations – that is, any inert mirroring of the human world's limited manifestations. They go so far as to conjure up a new conception of reality that is almost the opposite of the conventional one: a true *regio dissimulitudinis* within which operate the agents of an *ars* that is no longer a detached "observation" of existence but rather the systematic infraction of the ordinarily visible world by means of imaginative (and verbal) acts.

The *beffa* driven by wit, the verbal staging of a creative faculty, therefore acts as the complete opposite of every passive or thoughtless relation of mirroring with respect to the visible surface of the world. In all of the *novelle* of the so-called "Calandrino cycle," it is in fact the artists-painters who take on the duty of trying new and unusual ways of approaching and interacting with the everyday visible.[5] In particular, it is through the resources of an inventive wit that the *beffa* verbally takes shape and is realized in the creation of one or more imaginative illusions. These, in turn, are precisely what constitutes the *beffa*, which creates an alternative factuality, a mental dimension that is only

---

4 I am not going into much detail here concerning this issue, which I hope is sufficiently explained in Ciccuto, "Un'antica canzone," 114–20.

5 For this point, see specifically Picone, "L'arte della beffa," 213–14.

measurable in terms of the critical distance that separates it from the ordinary and passive conditions of human existence.[6] Painting acts as a conceptual model for an entirely new attitude that one cannot help but call epistemological, and that participates in the function of cultural renewal that Boccaccio himself is integrating into the literary/narrative genre. The artist-characters he casts in his *novelle* (Giotto, Bruno, Buffalmacco, Calandrino, but also at a metanarrative level giving another example of fiction making with the recurring prankster-character Maso del Saggio) embody this function.

Given the choice of painting (along with its most lively and inventive representatives) as the basis on which the *Decameron* self-consciously re-establishes every act of cognition and perception, we may consider the extent to which the character of Calandrino constitutes the cornerstone of the whole system of the *Decameron*, which revolves around the question of perceiving and representing reality. Calandrino's nature as a passive imitator, if not a sterile copier, of ordinary appearances is revealed in several narrative episodes. It transpires first in his "simple" observation of others' artwork[7] and then in the internal workings of

6 "Il beffatore dimostra attraverso la sua azione di saper dominare la realtà circostante, trasformando in evento la quotidianità: fa sentire al beffato di star vivendo un'avventura straordinaria, salvo poi a farlo risvegliare con i frammenti del sogno infranto … la beffa è qui diventata una creazione personale, quasi un duplicato dell'invenzione letteraria. E il regista della beffa si pone allo stesso livello dei narratori della cornice e dell'autore dell'opera" [The trickster's actions demonstrate that he is in control of the circumstances, when he transforms daily occurrences into an event. The person tricked feels that they are living an extraordinary adventure, save for being forced to wake up holding the shreds of the broken dream … The *beffa* becomes a personal creation, almost a duplicate of literary invention. As a *metteur en scène*, the trickster rises to almost the same level as the narrators in the frame and the author of the work (Picone, "L'arte della beffa," 206, my translation)]. Precisely this notion of a constant "comparison with reality" has led some critics to assert the substantial historical truthfulness of the events narrated by Boccaccio within the Calandrino cycle (as Picone mentions, ibid., 211). But as has recently been proven by Santagata (see "Un tassello per Calandrino pittore") precisely concerning the stories that have Calandrino as their protagonist, we are dealing with an entirely literary *fictio*.

7 "E per avventura trovandolo un dì nella chiesa di San Giovanni e vedendolo stare attento a riguardare le dipinture e gl'intagli del tabernaculo il quale è sopra l'altare della detta chiesa, non molto tempo davanti postovi, pensò essergli dato luogo e tempo alla sua intenzione" [So one day, happening to find him in the church of San Giovanni staring intently at the paintings and the bas-reliefs of the canopy that had recently been erected above the high altar, he decided that this was the ideal time and place for doing what he had in mind (VIII.3.6)] For this element, see also Surdich's findings in "La 'varietà delle cose,'" 234–6.

the *novella* of the heliotrope, which is entirely based on the contrast between an (unproductive) culture of the visible and an (imaginatively fruitful) culture of the invisible.[8] It surfaces once again in the attempts at elevating the modest status of Calandrino *qua* artist as one of those who "schiccherare le mura a modo che fa la lumaca" [daub walls all the time like a lot of snails (VIII.3.29)], which are inextricable for that same character from the "lies" (but for him, "certainties") that are based on outdated conceptions of visual culture.[9] It is also at the core of the game of substitutions between appearances and reality around which the whole story of the "porco imbolato" [stolen pig (VIII.6)] revolves.[10] Lastly, it appears in the grandiose and brilliant representation of the overturning of cognitive conventions orchestrated in the *novella* that has as the butt of its joke an alter ego of Calandrino's, Simone da Villa.[11]

It is precisely by turning to the undercurrents of the plot of our *novella* that we may find a confirmation of these interpretative formulations, which because of spatial constraints must here be limited to a cursory outline. A particular interpretative itinerary has nevertheless emerged from these few scattered indications. Right at the outset of the narrative one notices the author's insistence on the "verità del fatto" (IX.5.5), whose meaning is then immediately overturned and displaced

8 For a reading of the "heliotrope" *novella* in line with this interpretation, see Marcus, *An Allegory of Forms*, as well as Picone's notes in "L'arte della beffa," 216–17.

9 It seems evident that the products of this new culture – identifiable, for example, with the famous tabernacle by Lippo di Benivieni observed by Calandrino – are of little interest to the character: when Maso begins to speak "delle virtù di diverse pietre" [of the virtues of different stones], bringing ancient lapidary culture into the conversation, Calandrino's attention is immediately drawn away from the new artwork he has been observing, and which obviously represents the possibility of a jump into the novel world represented by the new school. Instead, all of the character's certainties are based on the efficacy of the old culture of the visible and the relations arising from it: "noi la troverem per certo, per ciò che io la conosco; e trovata che noi l'avremo, che avrem noi a fare altro se non mettercela nella scarsella e andare alle tavole de'cambiatori, le quali sapete che stanno sempre cariche di grossi e di fiorini, e torcene quanti noi ne vorremo? Niuno ci vedrà; e così potremo arricchire subitamente" [We'll find it without a doubt, because I know what it looks like; and once we've found it, all we have to do is to put it in our purses and go to the money-changers, whose counters, as you know, are always loaded with groats and florins, and help ourselves to as much as we want. No one will see us; and so we'll be able to get rich quick (VIII.3.29)]. For Calandrino, a change of status would therefore arise not from a renewal of his own art – which remains a pitiful scribbling on walls – but from a repetition of century-old clichés based on an outdated, mechanical relation between the visible and the invisible.

10 See again Ciccuto, "Il novelliere en artiste," 126–7.

11 See ibid., 127–30 as well as Surdich, "La 'varietà delle cose,'" 236–8.

by the staging of the credulity of Calandrino, who mistakes for real and concrete "facts" the inventions and illusory appearances placed before his eyes by the prankster-artists. The fiction of Niccolosa "sì forte innamorata" [so much in love] is seen by the middling artisan as a certainty, "un gran fatto" [an astonishing deed (IX.5.15)], after a series of exchanged *sguardi* in paragraphs 9–11 which do not connote any recognition of reality but rather the beginning of the contrary: the creation of a fantastic alternative to the facts themselves. It is worth noting that Bruno immediately offers to "fix things up for him," that is, to arrange the "fatti suoi" (IX.5.18). These "facts" are both the ones invented by the words of the artists-tricksters – "Calandrino udendo queste parole gli pareva essere a' fatti" [on hearing these words, Calandrino felt as though he was already getting down to business (IX.5.38)] – and also the circumstances which Bruno and Buffalmacco find so amusing – "traevano de' fatti di Calandrino il maggior piacere del mondo" [being hugely entertained by Calandrino's antics in the affair (IX.5.41)].[12] At a certain point in the story these same facts come to coincide with the giving of fake trinkets: "quando un pettine d'avorio e quando una borsa e quando un coltellino e cotali ciance, allo'ncontro recandogli cotali anelletti contraffatti di niun valore, de' quali Calandrino faceva maravigliosa festa" [such as an ivory comb, a purse, a small dagger, and other such trifles, in return bringing him some worthless little rings, which sent Calandrino into raptures (ibid.)].[13]

The whole process of Calandrino's falling in love, during which he is led by the artificers of the prank into a state of absolute credulity vis-à-vis the exterior appearances of events, becomes emblematic of his own inability to use speech in order to control the development of those very same events. Employing one of the most conventional expressions of the lyric love genre, that of ineffability, the hapless painter declares that "ella mi piace tanto, che io nol ti potrei dire" [I am so wild about her that I can't begin to tell you how I feel (IX.5.17)]. In fact, the situation ends

12 Later on, Calandrino will claim control of the circumstances of his affair, boasting that he would have no qualms offending with "sì fatte cose" a higher power than Filippo: the prank he would not hesitate to play on Christ is, literally, "such a thing" (neither "a factual thing" nor "a thing like that").

13 The courtly ritual of accompanying the act of falling in love with the giving of gifts becomes based on ostensible and false values, both on the part of the addressee (in the form of feigned love) and on the part of the giver (the pinchbeck jewels). A pact between parties of this sort becomes entirely artificial, because it has been deprived of the authentic rationale that is supposed to regulate the exchange of values in a more typical gift-giving scenario. On this topic during a time close to that of Boccaccio, see the plentiful documentation offered by Buettner, "Past Presents."

up being such that all Calandrino *can* say is that he is *morto* – "ella m'ha morto" [she struck me all of a heap (IX.5.23)] – thereby recognizing the condition in which he has always been as a result of his approach to his work. He relies precious little on the imagination – that very faculty which is as little present in his painterly production as in his rather limited verbal mastery of reality.[14]

In fact, Calandrino's tendency to stop at the superficial appearances of situations (e.g., Niccolosa's being evidently enamoured with him) mirrors the basic behaviour of a character who, being inclined toward a pure, simple, and passive observation of circumstances, uncritically recognizes as a *fact*, and therefore as a definite certainty, anything that he *sees*. In other words, he is emblematic of a type of perception that is reduced to a purely mimetic or superficially visual reproduction of happenings. Consequently, the character of Calandrino is at the mercy of the fantastical construction of appearances put in place by his artist friends. Not only does he himself consider it "un gran fatto" (IX.5.15), but he also interiorizes it and it becomes part of him to the extent that he considers himself capable of reversing the usual order of things – "Io la fregherei a Cristo *di così fatte cose*" [for a girl like that, I'd slip one over on Jesus Christ (IX.5.17, emphasis added)] – or even more fittingly to declare himself equal to the situation facing him: "io so meglio che altro uomo far ciò che io voglio" [when it comes to obtaining what I want, I know better than anybody else how to go about it (IX.5.34)]. He further internalizes the situation to such an extent that he himself, rather than Bruno, Filippo, or Buffalmacco, ultimately pretends to be capable of asserting a youthfully active identity which corresponds perfectly to the image constructed by his friends: "E intendi sanamente che io non son vecchio come io ti paio: ella se ne è ben accorta ella; ma altramenti ne la farò io accorgere se io le pongo la branca adosso, per lo verace

14 As will be considered later, this reuse of the Dantean verse "Io non mori' e non rimasi vivo" (*Inferno* 34) unites the violent transformation of Calandrino's identity (or characterization) with his state of being "né morto né vivo" (IX.5.65) in reference to certain key points of the aesthetic debates of the thirteenth and fourteenth centuries regarding the role of the "arte nuova," and in particular that of Giotto and his school. This opposition between a new, "living" art and a superseded "dead" one had been the focal point of several ekphrases in the *Commedia*, and had been present more broadly in the Dantean discussion of the "plastic" values of poetic writing, especially developed in the episode of the purgatorial encounter with the poet Statius. For more on this topic, see Ciccuto, "All'ombra della Garisenda" and "Trattando l'ombre come cosa salda" as well as the forthcoming article "*Saxa loquuntur*. Aspetti dell'*evidentia* nella retorica visiva di Dante."

corpo di Cristo ..." [You needn't think I'm past the age for this sort of thing, because I'm not, and she knows it. And once I lay my paws on her, she'll know it even better – for Christ's truthful body! (IX.5.36)].

To furthermore render themselves coherent with the fiction created by the labour of the artists' verbal construction, we find Filippo and Buffalmacco pretending "not to notice" the fact that Niccolosa is taking "il miglior tempo del mondo ... de' modi di Calandrino" [the greatest delight in Calandrino's eccentricities (IX.5.30)]. While she is apparently participating wholly in the fanciful separation from reality just orchestrated by the group of tricksters, they turn a blind eye to it: "Filippo con Buffalmacco e con gli altri faceva vista di ragionare e di non avvedersi di questo fatto" [And whilst all this was going on, Filippo was in deep conversation with Buffalmacco and the others, pretending not to notice]. Nor, of course, does Boccaccio neglect the opportunity to insert certain signals into the verbal plot of invention which are meant to function as points of reference for the reader (and obviously for the complicit protagonists of the narrative), marking the stages of this constructive itinerary of invention. Bruno goes so far as to say that "per lo corpo di Dio" (IX.5.31) – that is, a non-existent reality – the song and sounds of Calandrino could make Niccolosa "gittare a terra delle finestre" [hurl herself bodily through the window], which literally means they would make her die, according to a "deviated" meaning of the expression which Calandrino obviously is incapable of grasping. For his part, Calandrino himself maintains that he could possess the woman "per lo verace corpo di Cristo" [for Christ's truthful body (IX.5.36)], in line with the "real" circumstances of which the poor artisan has become the credulous interpreter.[15]

We must also recognize a further indication of a special relation between artistic activity and the ability to deviate imaginatively from reality in the location where the artists are working, the villa of Camerata, belonging to Niccolò Cornacchini (IX.5.6). This dwelling is one of the places where Buffalmacco has been able to show his qualities as a fanciful painter, beyond the bounds of the representational conventions of his time, as I have had the chance to note elsewhere.[16] For Calandrino as well, the *novella* remarkably and unambiguously reveals

15 Calandrino's exclamation "per l'amor di Dio" [for the love of God (IX.5.44)] corresponds perfectly to Tessa's intention to make her husband suffer the torments of a true "passion": "Alla croce di Dio, ella non andrà così, che io non te ne paghi" [By God's cross, it won't end without you paying for that (IX.5.53)].

16 See Ciccuto, "Gli anticlassici di Vasari."

the connection between his humble decorative work at the villa and the possibility of a love which he considers real but which is in fact entirely fictive: "Vedendo Calandrino che il lavorio si veniva finendo e avvisando che, se egli non recasse a effetto il suo amore prima che finito fosse il lavorio, mai più fatto non gli potesse venire" [Calandrino, seeing that the work was nearing completion, and realizing that unless he gathered the fruits of his love before the frescoes were finished he would never have another opportunity (IX.5.42)].

Once again, through the character of Bruno, Boccaccio pushes the fiction of the joke well beyond the limits of any *effet du réel,* to which only Calandrino's credulity remains bound. To make the story proceed toward the final unravelling of the ever-tighter knot of fiction and reality, the *novella* has recourse to the ploy of the magical scroll, the "brieve" (IX.5.45–9). The object becomes a document meant, paradoxically, not to ascertain or guarantee a certain state of things but rather to shift the level of signification of every presumed *fact* of Calandrino's story toward an even more radical condition of delirium and abstraction, related in this case to the deceptive "magical" power of the instrument brought into play. It is this brief interlude that serves as the precondition for the appearance of Tessa, who is also fully inscribed in the unreal world conjured by the tricksters. Thus, she "non le parve giuoco" [was not at all amused (IX.5.53)] to accept as real the fake love story woven around the figure of her husband. In fact, she sees it as an opportunity for resolution and revenge for the concrete effects produced by that other figment of the imagination conjured up by the artists in the story of the heliotrope, which Nello explicitly recalls at this point – "Tessa, tu sai quante busse Calandrino ti diè senza ragione il dí che egli ci tornò con le pietre di Mugnone, e per ciò io intendo che tu te ne vendichi" [You remember the hiding Calandrino gave you, Tessa, for no reason at all, on the day he came home from the Mugnone with all those stones? Well, now's your chance to be even with him (IX.5.52)]. The interlude concomitantly serves to introduce the words of Filippo, who involves Calandrino even more in this fiction by calling him "maestro" (IX.5.55), before quickly leaving the imaginary world constructed around the joke's victim to enjoy a "new" view of events. This type of vision becomes symbolic of the entire "Calandrino cycle" in the sense of providing a "view" beyond conventions, one that can overturn the ordinary perception of facts to which Calandrino is consigned as the butt of the joke: Filippo "S'andò a nascondere in parte che egli poteva, senza esser veduto, veder ciò che facesse Calandrino" [concealed himself in a place from which, without being observed, he would be able to see what Calandrino was doing].

In truth, Niccolosa plays the role of an additional signpost for the reader, given her sceptical questioning regarding the possibility that the entire story might be nothing other than a gigantic fantastical invention: "Può egli esser vero che io ti tenga?" [Is it really possible that I am holding you in my embrace? (IX.5.58)]. At the same time, she firmly demands, as she explicitly states, that no concrete proposals of the lover be realized, limiting them purely (and this will not surprise us) to an exercise in exchanging superficial glances: "O tu hai la gran fretta! Lasciamiti prima *vedere* a mio senno: lasciami *saziar gli occhi* di questo tuo viso dolce!" [Oh, but you are too hasty … First let me have a good look at you: let me feast my eyes upon your dear, sweet face (IX.5.60, emphasis added)]. It will therefore be the three artist-jokers who will *see* the real unfolding of the situation: "Bruno e Buffalmacco n'erano andati da Filippo, e tutti e tre vedevano e udivano questo fatto" [Bruno and Buffalmacco saw and heard everything that passed between them, having meanwhile joined Filippo (IX.5.61)]. Until the intervention of Monna Tessa brings about *en abyme* the recognition of the truly pitiful and pained nature of the *novella*'s protagonist-victim,[17] Calandrino is lulled into recognizing himself in the image of the *free lover* conjured up by his friends' fiction.

The narrative insists, in contrast to the image of the feigned lover, on the image of the fake singer of serenades and the fake orchestrator of a love affair, on the "filthy reviled dog" and "old fool" that in fact correspond more to Calandrino's true nature. This true nature is that of the sterile imitator, of one who is faithful to the commonplaces of artistic thinking (as opposed to the imaginative explorer of the world's new interpretive boundaries *sub specie artis*), which also makes a reappearance thanks to the notable metaphorical twisting of "premendoti tutto, non uscirebbe tanto sugo che bastasse a una salsa" [if they were to squeeze you from head to toe, there wouldn't be enough juice to make a sauce (IX.5.64)]. Here, the image of obtaining so little sap that it would not suffice even for a small amount of sauce indirectly tells us a great deal about the inherent sterility of Calandrino's nature. In fact, it aligns itself above all with the action of "schiccherare" [scribbling] on the walls meant for frescoing, which constitutes the only

17 Thus in IX.5.65 ("Or non ti conosci tu, tristo? Non ti conosci tu, dolente?" [Don't you know yourself, villain? Don't you know you, scoundrel?]) we find a reversal of Calandrino's earlier declaration in IX.5.34 – "io so meglio che altro uomo far ciò che io voglio" [I know better than anybody else how to go about it] – and finally at the end when he is returned to his niggardly nature, "Così adunque Calandrino tristo e cattivo" [And so … Calandrino … all forlorn and dejected (IX.5.67)].

distinguishing feature of Calandrino's art (and which literally corresponds, on his part, to "staining" or "obscuring"; in other words, to his inability to create something as complex as it is clear and concretely expressive). The metaphor further underlines the pervasive return in the text of the motif – already present in Dante – which compares a lack of creativity to death, or at least to uncertainty between life and death: "Calandrino, vedendo venir la moglie, non rimase né morto né vivo" [When he first saw his wife coming in, Calandrino was unsure whether he was dead or alive (IX.5.65)]. This "dead painting" corresponds to the inertia of artistic schools still focused on the passive cult of imitation as opposed to the creative "vitality" of newer movements, including Giotto's school, which were capable of imparting life to the inanimate, as Boccaccio himself had noted on several occasions in his aesthetic reflections.

Calandrino's uncertain state "between life and death" therefore precisely (as well as metaphorically) describes his situation as an artist caught between the archaic status of the imitator and the new imagined reality as the *fictor* of an adventure that would require much greater intellectual gifts than he usually displays. And so his fake identity as a shrewd womanizer – created of course not by him but by the imaginative talents of his painter-colleagues – is suddenly diminished, if not entirely dismissed, at the end. Once a reality closer to the concrete truth of the characters and the situation erupts onto the scene alongside Tessa, even Calandrino himself has no means of contradicting it: he "né ebbe ardire di far contro di lei difesa alcuna" [hadn't the courage to defend himself against her onslaught (IX.5.65)]. Calandrino's persona as a skilful lover, acquired thanks to the fiction of his artist-friends and suddenly revealed as so improbable that it no longer corresponds in any way to the "real" aspect of one who at most could repeat – and therefore, in essence, imitate *ad infinitum* – his initial, limited identity, is effectively crossed out, cancelled, brought back to its original state by means of scratches and scoldings: "Monna Tessa corse con l'unghie nel viso a Calandrino … e tutto gliele graffiò" [Monna Tessa pounced upon him and attacked him with her nails, clawing his face all over]; "ma pur così graffiato e tutto pelato e rabbuffato … Così adunque Calandrino tristo e cattivo, tutto pelato e tutto graffiato, a Firenze tornatosene, più colassù non avendo ardir d'andare …" [All torn, and bleeding, and disheveled … And so, scratched and torn to ribbons, Calandrino made his way to Florence, and not having the courage to return there … (IX.5.63–7)]. Nor will the unfortunate man find the strength any more to return to that place, the villa of Camerata, where, lacking adequate resources, he had in vain attempted to transform his identity for the better.

In the end, Calandrino is brought back to a form of self-knowledge that is more appropriate to his identity as nothing more than a *tristo e cattivo*, a sad and shoddy artist. This is indeed the meaning of Tessa's exclamation "Or non ti conosci tu, tristo? Non ti conosci tu, dolente?" (IX.5.64). The adventure of passion and intellect devised for him by his artist colleagues could no longer be supported by an identity inherently incapable of imaginative creativity and tied to a relation with reality which, for Calandrino, cannot be other than that of repetitive, thoughtless respect for every convention and the *status quo*. This theme will be taken up soon after this *novella*, once the "execution" of Calandrino's cycle has come to an end; specifically, in the story of Talano da Imola, *Decameron* IX.7, where the excessive realism of the distrustful Margherita is what once again indicts within the narrative world of the *Decameron* any principle of a non-negotiable reality based on the supposed, unchanging value of that which is available to the all too simplistic and ordinary *visible sense* of common people.[18] In the *novella*, Margherita appears incapable of recognizing the superior significance of "verità dimostrate da' sogni" and is furthermore "ritrosa in tanto che a senno di niuna persona voleva fare alcuna cosa, né altri far la poteva a suo" [the most argumentative, disagreeable and self-willed creature on God's earth, for she would never heed other people's advice and regarded everyone but herself as an incompetent fool].[19] But the adventures staged by Boccaccio's artists have by now established at the

---

18 Possibly to be considered a form of "blindness," which allows one to relate the phrase "se ne sarebbe avveduto un cieco" of Calandrino's *novella* to the proud words of Margherita in *Decameron* IX.7.10: "egli avrebbe buon manicar co' ciechi" [he'd do well for himself at a supper for the blind].

19 See IX.7.3–4. It seems, indeed, that Margherita has no intention of trusting the *senno* involved in oneiric or even just imaginary occurrences, which she considers deceptive – "ma tu sogni di me quello che tu vorresti vedere" [you only dream these horrid things about me, because you'd like to see them happen (IX.7.8)] – and lacking any basis for belief. This opens the door for a very real intrusion of reality, which will end up concretely and violently transforming the very identity of the woman – "fu guerita, ma non sì che tutta la gola e una parte del viso non avesse per sì fatta maniera guasta, che, dove prima era bella, non paresse poi sempre sozzissima e contraffatta" [her recovery was not complete … for the whole of her throat and a part of her face were so badly disfigured that whereas she was formerly a beautiful woman, she was thenceforth deformed and utterly loathsome to look upon (IX.7.13–14)] – who at the end of the tale is forced to pay with her appearance for "non avere, in quello che niente le costava, al vero sogno del marito voluta dar

work's horizon the importance of a new way of "seeing" the world. This vision extends well beyond the coordinates of the purely visible, arising specifically from a productive use of the intellective faculties. The figures of Bruno, Buffalmacco, Giotto, and, *e contrario*, Calandrino thereby play a central role in the *Decameron*'s project to enact an imaginative transformation of the real.

fede" [her refusal to give credence, when it would have cost her nothing, to her husband's prophetic dream (IX.7.14)].

The Tale of Pinuccio and Niccolosa: *Decameron* IX.6

SIMONA LORENZINI

The sixth tale of the Ninth Day of the *Decameron* tells the story of Pinuccio, a young nobleman from Florence who has fallen in love with Niccolosa, the young daughter of a countryside host who is used to lodging acquaintances and people he knows well. In order to make love with an only seemingly hesitant Niccolosa, Pinuccio goes to her father's inn with his friend Adriano asking to be given a place to spend the night, as if they were returning to Florence from another city. The innkeeper, who knows the two young men well, welcomes them in his modest house. After the dinner, the host takes the two gentlemen to the bedroom. In the bedroom there are three beds, one for the two young men, one for Niccolosa, and one for the host and his wife; there is also a cradle for their little boy. When everyone is in bed, Pinuccio goes to the bed of Niccolosa, who at first is frightened, but then welcomes him "lietamente" [gladly]. During the night, awakened by noises that eventually she will discover were made by a cat, the host's wife gets up to investigate. Adriano gets up too, since he needs to relieve himself, and in so doing casually moves the cradle aside. When he returns to his bed, however, he forgets to move the cradle back. Returning from her investigation and confused by the cradle's new placement, the host's wife accidentally gets in bed with Adriano, who gives her great pleasure. After having enjoyed himself with Niccolosa, Pinuccio wants to return to his bed, but instead, in turn confused by the moved cradle, he gets into the host's bed. Believing himself to be in bed with Adriano, Pinuccio boasts about the pleasure he enjoyed with Niccolosa. The host gets up angrily and the two men start quarrelling. To the host, who threatens him for having seduced his daughter, Pinuccio aggressively replies, "What can you do to me?" Hearing them arguing, the host's wife wakes up and turns to Adriano believing he is her husband and asking what is going on between their guests. Adriano, laughing, replies that they must have had too much to drink the night before. As soon as she hears Adriano's voice, the host's wife realizes what has happened, and she immediately gets into her daughter's bed. Pretending she has just been awakened by the dispute, she asks her husband why he is quarrelling with Pinuccio. When the host tells her that Pinuccio has spent the night with Niccolosa, she promptly replies that it is impossible and that Pinuccio is lying, since she herself was in bed with her daughter the entire night. Both men, she chides, must still be under the influence of wine, if they are wandering around the bedroom and imagining things. The woman's pretence is immediately supported by Adriano, who suggests to Pinuccio that he should quit once and for all his habit of getting up and sleepwalking around telling fables as if they were true stories. Entrapped by this chaotic situation, the host believes his wife's and Adriano's words and, taking Pinuccio by the shoulders, starts shaking and calling him in order to wake him up. Taking on Adriano's cues, Pinuccio plays along, pretending he is a sleepwalker and acting accordingly, so that the host ends up laughing at him. He finally arises from the host's bed and returns to Adriano's with a great show of drowsiness. The morning after, the innkeeper continues laughing at Pinuccio and his dreaming. Then, having saddled their horses and drunk a cup with the host, the *gentili uomini* leave the inn satisfied. Pinuccio finds other ways to meet with Niccolosa, and, since she swears to her mother that Pinuccio had certainly dreamed, the *buona donna*, remembering Adriano's embraces, believes herself to have been the only one awake.

This very simple but well-crafted tale about deception and illusion – "un rapido racconto, tra i migliori di Boccaccio anche per lo svolgimento dell'intreccio" [a fast-paced story, among the best by Boccaccio, when it comes to the unfolding of the action], as Mario Baratto has defined it (*Realtà e stile* [1996], 109) – has received little critical attention. Scholars have usually approached this novella from two different perspectives, some by discussing the Boccaccio–Chaucer connection and their individual relationships with the *fabliau* tradition, others by pointing out Boccaccio's use of *ars combinatoria* as narrative technique. As for the first approach, while some scholars still hesitate to recognize Boccaccio's influence on Chaucer or at least to admit Chaucer's familiarity with Boccaccio,[1] others have argued strongly in favour of Boccaccio

1 For Chaucer's acquaintance with Boccaccio's tale, see Peter Beidler, "Chaucer's *Reeve's Tale*" (and 250n6 for a bibliography on this question) and "The Reeve's Tale." According to Beidler, Chaucer probably knew Boccaccio's *Decameron* – what Beidler called a "hard" analogue; in particular, Chaucer would have found in Boccaccio's tale details not available in other French and Flemish sources of the cradle-trick story.

being a model for the *Canterbury Tales*. More important than establishing the link between Boccaccio and Chaucer is, however, to observe what happens when the topoi of a widespread *fabliau* are inflected in two texts that are not necessarily designed to be read together. The personal re-elaboration of the cradle-trick motif relies on Boccaccio's and Chaucer's different sensibilities and creativity as well as on the different functions each tale assumes within its narrative organism.[2] Chaucer's Reeve's Tale has been read as an angry response to the previous Miller's Tale, the point of the story being the Reeve's narrative revenge upon the Miller, a point he scores by depicting a duped miller in his story, and it is an integral part of the broader antagonism between these particular pilgrims to Canterbury (Giaccherini, "*The Reeve's Tale*," 109n18). Boccaccio's purpose appears to be quite different and emerges immediately when we think of the active role taken by the host's wife – one of the main differences between Boccaccio's and Chaucer's tales.[3] That highlighting the woman's role was Boccaccio's main intention may be inferred from the rubric preceding the novella: "La donna, ravedutasi, entra nel letto della figliuola e quindi con certe parole ogni cosa pacefica" [the good woman, apprehending the circumstances, gets her to bed with her daughter, and by divers apt words re-establishes perfect accord].[4] Similarly, Panfilo's introductory words insist on her active intervention, responsible for impressing a positive narrative turn on the plot. In Boccaccio's tale, the woman, the real protagonist of the plot's solution, discovers the deception into which she herself has fallen, but, as "savia," she can cover both her own and her daughter's "vergogna."

For a comparison between the two medieval authors, see Boitani, *Chaucer and Boccaccio*; and the more recent essay collection edited by Koff and Schildgen, *The Decameron and the Canterbury Tales*. On the literary sources of Boccaccio's tale and on how he rewrites his models, especially Jean Bodel's *Gombert*, see also Morosini, "La 'Bele Conjunture'" and the bibliography in Vittore Branca's 1992 edition.

2 Enrico Giaccherini has insisted on the reciprocal independence of the two texts by identifying peculiarities of both authors in dealing with a common matter. He has also stressed Boccaccio's modern overcoming of some elements typical of the *fabliau* tradition thanks to narrative techniques meant to exalt human agency and *ingenium* ("*The Reeve's Tale*"). See also Heffernan, "Chaucer's 'Miller's Tale'" (with a thorough review of the bibliography on Chaucer's and Boccaccio's comic tales' relationship and their personal indebtedness to the *fabliau* tradition).

3 Beidler lists all the unique similarities in the two texts, supporting the thesis of IX.6's direct influence on Chaucer's Reeve's Tale ("Chaucer's *Reeve's Tale*," 240–5).

4 Unless otherwise indicated, Italian quotations are from Branca's 1985 edition of Boccaccio's *Decameron*. English translations are J.M. Rigg's.

At the other end of the scholarship spectrum, Italian scholars have underlined the geometric precision of this novella as an example of Boccaccio's predilection for the *ars combinatoria* as narrative technique and of his use of *ars combinatoria* in configuring space, time, characters' relationships, and speeches.[5] Building upon the plots he found in the probable sources of the cradle-trick story, Boccaccio takes the movements of the beds and the cradle to the extreme by adding further movements and displacements. Paolo Divizia has recently argued that all possible combinations of beds and exchanges are experienced in a way that makes the novella almost impossible ("Una doppia forzatura logica," 407–10). In the novella, Boccaccio exploits to the fullest the combinatorial potential of mistaken identities and misunderstandings which occur among the various characters. He emphasizes the potentially dangerous effects of the sexual inter-combinations by staging the action in the restricted space of a crammed bedroom and the pitch-black atmosphere of nighttime. The *brevitas* of the novella thus becomes a metaphor of temporal and spatial constraints and reflects, in its narrative perfection, the perfect geometry of both physical and verbal exchanges. The *ars combinatoria* as narrative strategy also works outside the novella, suggesting that the sequence of stories in the day is far from being random.

The reading I propose will correlate the narrative strategy, based on an exploration of all possibilities to achieve a positive outcome, and the central message Boccaccio conveys, the therapeutic power of words to heal disorder and prevent scandal. As the novella dramatizes the ambiguous relation connecting actions to words and appearance to truth, the power of storytelling to transform dreams into reality and vice versa emerges as its central theme.

Significantly enough, the novella is told by Panfilo, whose name is associated, from the very beginning of the *Decameron*, with novellas that urge both readers and characters to look deeper into the stories and to go behind appearances.[6]

---

5 For an analysis of Boccaccio's narratological techniques, see Almansi, "Lettura della quarta novella," 310–13, and Branca, *Boccaccio medievale* (1956), 104. About this novella, Baratto speaks of "una perfezione quasi geometrica" (*Realtà e stile* [1996], 109).

6 According to Victoria Kirkham, Panfilo allegorically represents "reason" (*The Sign of Reason*, 14, 142–5); Boccaccio's choice would therefore seem appropriate for a tale dominated, structurally and linguistically, by chaos. More important is, however, to remember how Panfilo's first story is explicitly concerned with the impossibility of going beyond appearances ("il giudicio … degli uomini," [the judgment of man]) coupled with the necessity to interrogate ourselves about their interplay with truth ("il giudicio di Dio," [the judgment of God]), as per *Decameron* I.1.6. I want to thank

It is also significant that the only characters endowed with a name that should convey, at least apparently, the idea of a well-defined individuality and narrative agency are the two young men, Pinuccio and Adriano, and the host's daughter, Niccolosa. While the name of Niccolosa – as well as the location "pian di Mugnone," which is the setting of all Calandrino's stories – creates a structural bond with the previous novella ("il nome della Niccolosa amata da Calandrino m'ha nella memoria tornata una novella d'un'altra Niccolosa" [this Niccolosa, that Calandrino loved, has brought to my mind a story of another Niccolosa (IX.6.3)]), the naming of Pinuccio and Adriano complicates the characters' relationships. Names give people individuality, agency, and an active role.

Adriano is Pinuccio's "fidato compagno" who knows about Pinuccio's love for Niccolosa. Adriano's description is minimal; he acts more as right-hand man for Pinuccio and then for the host's wife. As for Pinuccio, the name (and Boccaccio insists on this element: "che così avea nome il giovane" [such was the gallant's name (IX.6.6)]) concludes the presentation of the character whose desire to have a sexual encounter with Niccolosa moves the tale. Pinuccio's presentation is the more detailed of the story: "un giovinetto *leggiadro* e *piacevole* e *gentile uomo* della nostra città, il quale molto usava per la contrada, e focosamente l'amava" [a goodly and mannerly young gentleman of our city, who was not seldom in those parts, and loved her to the point of passion (IX.6.6, emphases added)]. Boccaccio insists on the pleasantness of Pinuccio's appearance and on his social preeminence, since they provoke Niccolosa's own falling in love with him: "e ella, che d'esser da un così fatto giovane amata forte si gloriava … di lui similmente s'innamorò" [and she, being mightily flattered to be loved by such a gallant … grew likewise enamoured of him (IX.6.6)]. From this presentation, readers would expect an active role for Pinuccio; instead, what will emerge is that Pinuccio represents the pole of opposition to the prudent and wise behaviour of the woman, as the narrator clearly states later on in the novella: "che non era il più savio giovane del mondo" [who was not the most discreet of gallants (IX.6.21)]. In contrast, the narrator twice underlines the foresightedness of the woman: "per che, come savia, senza alcuna parola dire, subitamente si levò"; "Adriano, veggendo che la donna saviamente la sua vergogna e quella della figliuola ricopriva" [being a discreet woman, she started up, and saying never a word …

Susanna Barsella and Simone Marchesi for having pointed out to me this aspect of Panfilo's storytelling, which is so relevant for the novella of Pinuccio and Niccolosa and its interplay between reality and appearance.

Adriano, in his turn, seeing how adroitly the good woman cloaked her own and her daughter's shame (IX.6.24, 27)]. Though sexual content is present and, to some extent, constitutes the element from which the story springs, the emphasis is more on quick retorts and ingenious trickeries shifting the interest toward intelligence and resolve. In the novella, love is just a functional element of Boccaccio's narrative strategy: readers already know that Niccolosa is a willing partner, so no courting seems to be in order there.

The other two characters, the host and his wife, are not given any names; yet they are the two most important characters in the plot, when we consider the main purpose of the novella. Nameless as they are, they stand for concepts that transcend individualities and, eventually, gender roles: the creative and misleading power of language and the practice of good reading/interpretation. We know nothing of the host's wife except that she was an "assai bella femmina," but she is the hub of the story and reveals herself in the promptness of acting, in the excitement of words, in taking charge of the situation. She knows how to use words to re-establish order, to secure the outcomes she wants, to save her family from scandal. Her mastery of words and rhetoric can be compared to the storytelling art, to the very idea of storytelling as *poiesis*, creation. What the wife eventually does in the novella is to create, in fact, a different story, and through that a different reality. On the other hand, acting as a foil to his wise wife, the host, "un buono uomo," constitutes an example of a bad reader. As we shall see, through the host and his naïvety, Boccaccio-Panfilo warns against the dangers of deceptive rhetoric when accompanied by inadequate skills in interpretation.

As noted, that the wife plays a crucial role in this tale is established in Panfilo's opening words: his story will concern "un subito *avvedimento* d'*una buona donna* avere un grande scandalo tolto via" [how a good woman by her quick apprehension avoided a great scandal (IX.6.3, emphasis added)]. At the beginning of the following tale, the next narrator remarks, in a confirmatory statement, that the audience appreciated specifically that feature in the story they just heard: "Essendo la novella di Panfilo finita e l'*avvedimento* della donna *commendato* da tutti" [all had commended the good woman's quick perception (IX.7.1, emphasis added)]. It is the only example within the *Decameron* when Boccaccio uses the word "avvedimento" twice for a female character, in a markedly circular and cohesive structure. By using the word "avvedimento" at the beginning of the seventh novella, Boccaccio also creates a sharp contrast with the female character of that story, Margherita, who is all but prudent.

But what does this "avvedimento" consist of, precisely? The term has already appeared in the *Decameron*. In the conclusion of the Fifth Day, Elissa says:

> Noi abbiamo già molte volte udito che con be' motti o con risposte pronte o con avvedimenti presti molti hanno già saputo con debito morso rintuzzare gli altrui denti o i sopravegnenti pericoli cacciar via; e per ciò che la materia è bella e può essere utile, voglio che domane con l'aiuto di Dio infra questi termini si ragioni, cioè di chi, con alcun leggiadro motto tentato, si riscotesse, o con pronta risposta o avvedimento fuggì perdita o pericolo o scorno. (V.Concl.3)
>
> [Ofttimes, said she, have we heard how with bright sallies, and ready retorts, and sudden devices, not a few have known how to repugn with apt checks the bites of others, or to avert imminent perils; and because it is an excellent argument, and may be profitable, I ordain that tomorrow, God helping us, the following be the rule of our discourse; to wit, that it be of such as by some sprightly sally have repulsed an attack, or by some ready retort or device have avoided loss, peril or scorn.]

A quick overview of other novellas can cast some light on the meaning of Boccaccio's *avvedimento*. The sixth tale, like the others that follow and precede it, reproduces, in a different way, motifs that have appeared in previous novellas (Branca, *Boccaccio medievale* [1956], 17). Some of these motifs are bed tricks (III.2, 6, and 9; VII.4); nighttime and chance (II.2 and 5, IV.10, IX.1); illicit sexual intercourse with alleged husbands (III.2 and 6); substitution of illusion for reality (VII.4, 8, and 9); dreams and visions (V.8; VII.10; IV.5 and 6; IX.7); wine as a means for accomplishing personal interests (II.7; VI.2; VII.4; VIII.6; IX.4). As for the dreaming motif, I will discuss the thematic contiguity between IX.6 and IX.7 at the end of this *lectura*. Here, I want to pause briefly on women's wise use of rhetoric, which is another crucial element that the tale of Pinuccio and Niccolosa shares with previous novellas.

At the end of Day One, in her introduction to the novella of Mastro Alberto, Pampinea complains that women have lost the ability to use wit and skilful conversation; women prefer to paint themselves and show off their bodies and clothes out of vanity rather than their cleverness.[7]

7 "Valorose giovani, come ne' lucidi sereni sono le stelle ornamento del cielo e nella primavera i fiori ne' verdi prati, così de' laudevoli costumi e de' ragionamenti piacevoli sono i leggiadri motti; li quali, per ciò che brievi sono, molto meglio alle

Pampinea herself uses wit as a woman and encourages women to use wily remarks in order to show that they are not merely passive objects; furthermore, as she explains, witty conversation is not in contradiction with female modesty; on the contrary, what women sometimes project as modesty is only stupidity. In the *Decameron*, many female characters benefit from their wit and cleverness to get out of an unpleasant situation: the marchioness of Monferrato and the inappropriate advances of the king of France (I.5); the Lady from Gascony and her clever speech in front of the king of Cyprus to get justice for a personal outrage (I.9); Madonna Oretta and her pleasant but caustic retort to the rough storytelling of a knight (VI.1); Madonna Filippa and her successful argument against the validity of man-written laws (VI.7); Ghita and the trick played upon her husband Tofano through a skilful eloquence that substitutes illusion for reality (VII.4). In these two latter stories, other elements are worth noting in relation to the tale of Pinuccio and Niccolosa.

In VI.7, Madonna Filippa wins over her male audience by making the assembly laugh at the humoristic justification for her adultery (VI.7.17–18). Lisa Perfetti underlines how Quintilian and Cicero recommend the use of laughter and jest to win over a reluctant audience and to dispel unpleasant circumstances (*Women and Laughter*, 85–6).

---

donne stanno che agli uomini, in quanto più alle donne che agli uomini il molto parlare e lungo, quando senza esso si possa far, si disdice, come oggi poche o niuna donna rimasa ci sia la quale o ne 'ntenda alcun leggiadro o a quello, se pur lo 'ntendesse, sappia rispondere: general vergogna è di noi e di tutte quelle che vivono. Per ciò che quella vertù che già fu nell'anime delle passate hanno le moderne rivolta in ornamenti del corpo; e colei la quale si vede indosso li panni più screziati e vergati e con più fregi si crede dovere essere da molto più tenuta e più che l'altre onorata … e fannosi a credere che da purità d'animo proceda il non saper tralle donne e co' valenti uomini favellare, e alla lor milensaggine hanno posto nome onestà … È il vero che, così come nell'altre cose, è in questa da riguardare e il tempo e il luogo e co cui si favella" [As stars in the serene expanse of heaven, as in spring-time flowers in the green pastures, so, honourable damsels, in the hour of rare and excellent converse is wit with its bright sallies. Which, being brief, are much more proper for ladies than for men, seeing that prolixity of speech, when brevity is possible, is much less allowable to them; albeit (shame be to us all and all our generation) few ladies or none are left to-day who understand aught that is wittily said, or understanding are able to answer it. For the place of those graces of the spirit which distinguished the ladies of the past has now been usurped by adornments of the person; and she whose dress is most richly and variously and curiously dight, accounts herself more worthy to be had in honour … And we make believe, forsooth, that our failure to acquit ourselves in converse with our equals of either sex does but proceed from guilelessness; dignifying stupidity by the name of modesty … True it is that in this, as in other matters, time and place and person are to be regarded (I.10.3–7)].

In the tale of Pinuccio and Niccolosa, the narrator insists twice on the host's laughs: "di che l'oste faceva le maggior risa del mondo" [whereat the host laughed amain (IX.6.29)]; "e venuto il giorno e levatosi, l'oste incominciò a ridere e a farsi beffe di lui e de' suoi sogni" [the host fell a laughing and making merry touching Pinuccio and his dreams (IX.6.31)]. The host's wife and Adriano's pretence that Pinuccio is a habitual sleepwalker makes the host laugh, thus dispelling his anger and upset. The host's final laughter relieves a tense situation where at stake, as I will discuss later on, are not only two cases of illicit intercourse but also a likely socially marked confrontation between him and Pinuccio.

In VII.4, Tofano pretends to be drunk to reveal his wife's misconduct, but Ghita cleverly overturns the situation. Through her control over domestic space and language, she locks Tofano out of their house, and turns all the blame on him by accusing him of being a drunk and wicked man in front of relatives and neighbours:

> La donna co' suoi vicini diceva: "Or *vedete* che uomo egli è! Che *direste* voi se io fossi nella via come è egli, e egli fosse in casa come sono io? In fé di Dio che io *dubito* che voi non *credeste* che egli *dicesse* il *vero*: ben potete a questo *conoscere* il senno suo! Egli *dice* a punto che io ho fatto ciò che io *credo* che egli abbia fatto egli. Egli mi *credette* spaventare col gittare non so che nel pozzo, ma or volesse Iddio che egli vi si fosse gittato da dovero e affogato, sì che egli il *vino, il quale egli di soperchio ha bevuto*, si fosse molto bene inacquato." (VII.4.26–7, emphases added)
>
> [Whereupon: "Now mark," quoth the lady to the neighbours, "the sort of man he is! What would you say if I were, as he is, in the street, and he were in the house, as I am? God's faith, I doubt you would believe what he said. Hereby you may gauge his sense. He tells you that I have done just what, I doubt not, he has done himself. He thought to terrify me by throwing I know not what into the well, wherein would to God he had thrown himself indeed, and drowned himself, whereby the wine of which he has taken more than enough, had been watered to some purpose!"]

Ghita exploits a weakness of her husband, the inclination for wine, to create an alternative reality. Her convoluted speech, focused on the semantic fields of believing, seeing, and knowing, replaces the actual truth of facts with a fictitious one, as the host's wife will do at the end of IX.6 by displaying a similar ability to manipulate domestic space and linguistic signs. However, unlike the tale of Pinuccio and Niccolosa, in VII.4 the substitution of illusion for reality is valid only for the neighbours and the relatives of the woman, since Tofano remains aware of the alternative reality created by his wife.[8]

When in control of language, space, and wit, women can therefore demonstrate superior ability to respond to and solve a situation unpleasant for them, or to pursue a personal goal. The use of a well-timed response is therefore legitimate, in a domestic as well as in a public space, as Pampinea suggested in her remarks at the beginning of I.10. Anyway, we do not have to look further than the Ninth Day to find other examples of women's cleverness and eloquent speech. In IX.2, a young nun, Isabetta, "da un soprastante pericolo leggiadramente parlando diliberò" [by a happy retort, and the favour of Fortune, delivered herself from imminent peril (IX.2.4)]. In this novella, the main action takes place during the night, as in IX.6, and, as in the tale of Pinuccio and Niccolosa, the darkness is crucial for the dénouement of the plot. Informed by a group of nuns who are knocking insistently at her door that Isabetta is with her lover, the abbess – who in turn is entertaining a priest in her bedchamber –

> spacciatamente si levò suso e come meglio seppe *si vestì al buio*; e credendosi torre certi veli piegati, li quali in capo portano e chiamangli il saltero, le venner tolte le brache del prete; e tanta fu la fretta, che *senza avvedersene* in luogo del saltero le si gittò in capo. (IX.2.9–10, emphases added)
>
> [rose in a trice; and huddling on her clothes as best she might in the dark, instead of the veil that they wear, which they call the psalter, she caught up the priest's breeches, and … clapped them on her head.]

Because of the darkness, the abbess Madonna Usimbalda wears the wrong garments, thus making possible the clever remark of Isabetta: "*avvisando* ciò che era, tutta rassicurata disse: 'Madonna, se Dio v'aiuti, annodatevi la cuffia e poscia mi dite ciò che voi volete'" [the significance whereof being by no means lost upon her, she quite plucked up heart, and: "Madam," quoth she, "so help you God, tie up your coif, and then you may say what you will to me" (IX.2.15, emphasis added)]. Isabetta's promptness ("avvisando") clearly contrasts with the inadvertence ("senza avvedersene") of the abbess, who, however, at the end of the story, "*avvedutasi* del suo medesimo fallo e *vedendo* che da tutte *veduto* era né aveva ricoperta, *mutò sermone* e in tutta altra guisa che fatto non aveva cominciò a parlare" [finding herself detected by all in the same

8 For a detailed analysis of this novella, see Getto, *Vita di forme* (1986), 165–75.

sin, and that no disguise was possible, changed her tone, and held quite another sort of language than before (IX.2.18, emphases added)].

Not only does the abbess realize she is wearing her lover's clothes, but she recants her previous hypocrite position and through a different speech she gets out of an unpleasant situation. Thanks to her *mutato sermone*, Madonna Usimbalda allows herself to continue enjoying her lover's encounters and, at the same time, she safeguards her own and the convent's good reputation. The abbess can now rightfully enter the group of wise and prudent women, alongside Isabetta and the host's wife.

As for IX.6, the "avvedimento" of the host's wife is the well-crafted speech that helps her to preserve her family and her own honour. Her words function as the climax of the story, and everything in the novella is functional to spotlight the linguistic strategies she adopts to re-establish a social and moral order that overcomes the threat to her and her daughter's reputation. Her words also prevent her husband from a violent confrontation with Pinuccio, whose retort to the host insists on a social dissymmetry between the *gentili uomini* of the city and the *buon uomo* of the countryside that the story establishes from the very beginning:[9] "e come che *povera persona* fosse e avesse *piccola casa*, alcuna volta per un bisogno grande, *non ogni persona ma alcun conoscente* albergava" [and, for that he was in poor circumstances, and had but a little house, gave not lodging to every comer, but only to a few that he knew, and if they were hard bested (IX.6.4)]; "Pinuccio, tu sai bene come io sono agiato di poter così *fatti uomini, come voi siete*, albergare" ["Pinuccio," replied the host, "thou well knowest that I can but make a sorry shift to lodge gentlemen like you" (IX.6.10, emphases added)].

Boccaccio forces his characters into a delimited spatial and temporal framework in a rapid exchange of lines, movements, and relocations in the darkness that reward the intuitive skills of the host's wife. We can easily recognize two parts in the novella. In the first part, the narrator insists on the social and geographical context, briefly introduces the characters, and describes the inn and the disposition of the bedroom. By insisting on a meticulous description of the rooms and furniture arrangements in the home, Boccaccio emphasizes the importance that the environment will have for the story, the novella being almost an issue of bed arrangements and ingenious stratagems that create a potentially

9 Pinuccio ironically replies to the host, who wants to punish him for having seduced his daughter: "Di che mi pagherai? Che mi potrestù far tu?" [And how wilt thou pay me out? What canst thou do? (IX.6.21)]; similarly, when he arrives at the inn, Pinuccio does not ask but rather orders the host: "Vedi, a te conviene stanotte albergarci" [Thou must even put us up to-night (IX.6.9)].

tense situation.[10] The insistence on the motif of the house and lodging creates the idea of a domesticity and familiarity that emphasizes the extraordinary nature of the nighttime exchanges. These elements define a situation of normality and daily life where the unpredictability of chance and the readiness of a simple wife's answer stand out. As Mario Baratto has pointed out (*Realtà e stile* [1996], 106), what is striking is the appearance of normality, everydayness in which the "caso" manifests itself: the stirring of a cat, people moving the cradle. The extraordinary event – Pinuccio and Niccolosa's lovemaking in a dark room where other people are sleeping – is cleared in a few sentences:

> Pinuccio avendo ogni cosa veduta, dopo alquanto spazio, parendogli che ogni uomo adormentato fosse, pianamente levatosi se n'andò al letticello dove la giovane amata da lui si giaceva, e miselesi a giacere allato: dalla quale, ancora che paurosamente il facesse, fu lietamente raccolto, e con essolei di quel piacere che più disideravano prendendo si stette. (IX.6.13)

> [Pinuccio, who had taken exact note thereof, waited only till he deemed all but himself to be asleep, and then got softly up and stole to the bed in which lay his beloved, and laid himself beside her; and she according him albeit a timorous yet a gladsome welcome, he stayed there, taking with her that solace of which both were most fain.]

Simultaneously, another couple is enjoying having sex: Adriano and the host's wife. After having insisted on the prior events that make possible the lovers' intercourse – the stirring of a cat and the changing position of a cradle – the narrator again devotes only a couple of sentences to the actual fact: "Adriano, che ancora radormentato non era, sentendo questo la ricevette bene e lietamente, e senza fare altramenti motto da una volta in sù caricò l'orza con gran piacere della donna" [Adriano, who was still awake, received her with all due benignity, and tackled her more than once to her no small delight (IX.6.17)]. While the narrative structure persists – a detailed description of the backstory, a short description of the sex scene – there the similarities end. Both couples enjoy lovemaking, but in one case, the lovemaking is the direct consequence of premeditation, in the other, it is only the fortuitous result of the accidental movement of a cradle. Adriano helps Pinuccio to have sex with Niccolosa; by accident, Adriano helps himself to have intercourse with Niccolosa's mother. The symmetry of the situation is only

10 On the importance of the inn as setting for the unfolding of the story, see Getto, *Vita di forme* (1986), 204.

apparent. Both Pinuccio and Niccolosa are aware of what is happening and their enjoyment is reciprocal; they are both emotionally involved in the pleasure: "dalla quale, ancora che paurosamente il facesse, fu lietamente raccolto, e con essolei di quel piacere che più disideravano prendendo si stette" [and she according him albeit a timorous yet a gladsome welcome, he stayed there, taking with her that solace of which both were most fain (IX.6.13)]. As for the other coupling that is happening in the same room, there is, instead, only the satisfaction of a purely physical urge, however enjoyable; and while we know something about the woman's pleasure ("con gran piacer della donna" [to her no small delight (IX.6.17)], nothing is said about Adriano's. Moreover, what is more important, only Adriano knows what is happening; the host's wife is, temporarily, disoriented by the darkness "Oimè, cattiva me, vedi quel che faceva! in fé di Dio, che io me n'andava dirittamente nel letto degli osti miei!" [Alas! blunderer that I am, what was I about? God's faith! I was going straight to the guests' bed (IX.6.16–17)]. The *buona donna*, who has got up in the night, is about to re-enter the bed where her husband is sleeping but then catches herself in what she thinks is a mistake and speaks aloud about almost jumping into bed with her guests. Disoriented by the cradle and by her own words, the host's wife eventually does what she is saying and ends up going to their guests' bed. This episode further complicates the already confusing play of appearance and reality, since the wife's words describe what she is actually doing, even if she does not know it. The content of the words is the reality but the wife is not able to grasp it; here words designate as true something – going to the guests' bed – that is not true, since she is actually going to the right bed. The fact that the Italian word for "guest" and "innkeeper" is the same – *oste* – complicates even more Boccaccio's narrative strategy.

More poignantly, the woman's utterance contrasts with Adriano's silence ("senza fare altramenti motto"). Adriano understands how words can be dangerous and, in this specific case, threaten the achievement of unexpected sexual gratification; he knows the importance of well-timed and measured words. On the contrary, Pinuccio's self-gratifying words provoke a situation of tension that could jeopardize the future pursuit of the same pleasure.[11] Silence is here functional to the erotic achievement; together with darkness, it clouds the truth and allows the fulfilment of erotic desire. Silence, darkness, and the narrowness of the space are required to compromise truth and allow deception.

11 On the interweaving of silence, eloquence, and making love, see Myriam Swennen Ruthenberg's analysis, "The Tale of Ricciardo and Catella," 115–18.

If, by establishing the inn as the proper setting for this tale, Boccaccio makes more reasonable and easily acceptable the wife's words on Pinuccio's and her husband's abuse of wine, even insisting on the nighttime frame is functional to Boccaccio's purposes. The night confuses, arouses the unexpected, the fears, and the wonders; it is the background of intrigues and subterfuges, which favours the action of Fortune. The night is a time for not only intrigues and deceptions but also dreams and illusions; the night complicates the relationships between reality and appearance, between what we think we see and what is real; finally, night and obscurity set the stage for easy deception through rhetoric. If the inn setting for the story makes the motif of drunkenness more plausible, the night makes more plausible the wife's and Adriano's playing with the motif of dreaming.

In the second part of the tale the focus is, instead, on the urgency of quick decisions and well-thought words. The events begin to happen rapidly, and dialogue prevails over description. Attention shifts from action to words that must support and integrate action. The performance of the wife is an excellent combination of words and deeds: first, a gesture that would intend to bring the cradle back to its proper position (IX.6.24); then, the intervention of the words (IX.6.25), further demonstrating their inherent inescapability. Through the movement of the cradle and then through her going to her daughter's bed, the wife translates words into deeds and vice versa. The moving of the cradle becomes a metaphor of her strong agency and freedom of speech. By moving the cradle, by moving herself into her daughter's bed, she demonstrates the power that facts have to manipulate reality.

The axis of deception and truth, of appearance and reality reaches its synthesis in the proper use of the motifs of wine and dreams as narrative strategies that the story reserves for the "buona donna." Adriano tells the wife that Pinuccio and her husband are arguing because they had much to drink the night before. She picks up on that idea and accuses them of drinking so much that they wander around and don't know what they are doing. According to Monica Balestrero, dreams in Boccaccio have a strongly negative connotation, as they are fiction, lies, often generated by corporal excesses (*L'immaginario del sogno*, 40).[12] Since corporal excesses like drunkenness and/or gluttony cause it, the dream is considered false and therefore prevents separation of reality and imagination. That is the case of this novella:

12 On the assimilation of dream and drunkenness in other tales, see Balestrero, *L'immaginario del sogno*, 38–9.

> La donna disse: "Egli [Pinuccio] *mente ben per la gola*, ché con la Niccolosa non è egli giaciuto: ché io mi ci coricai io in quel punto che io non ho mai poscia potuto dormire; e tu se' *una bestia che gli credi. Voi bevete tanto la sera*, che poscia sognate la notte e andate in qua e là senza sentirvi e parvi far meraviglie: egli è gran peccato che voi non vi fiaccate il collo! Ma che fa egli costì Pinuccio? perché non si sta egli nel letto suo?" D'altra parte Adriano, *veggendo* che la donna saviamente la sua vergogna e quella della figliuola ricopriva, disse: "Pinuccio, io te l'ho detto cento volte che tu non vada attorno, ché questo *tuo vizio del levarti in sogno* e *di dire le favole che tu sogni per vere* ti daranno una volta la mala ventura: torna qua, che Dio ti dea la mala notte!" (IX.6.26–7, emphases added)

> ["Tush! he lies in the throat," returned the good woman: "he has not lain with Niccolosa; for what time he might have done so, I laid me beside her myself, and I have been wide awake ever since; and thou art a fool to believe him. You men take so many cups before going to bed that then you dream, and walk in your sleep, and imagine wonders.'Tis a great pity you do not break your necks. What does Pinuccio there? Why keeps he not in his own bed?" Whereupon Adriano, in his turn, seeing how adroitly the good woman cloaked her own and her daughter's shame: "Pinuccio," quoth he, "I have told thee a hundred times, that thou shouldst not walk about at night; for this thy bad habit of getting up in thy dreams and relating thy dreams for truth will get thee into a scrape some time or another: come back, and God send thee a bad night."]

The excess of wine creates a bedrock for both Pinuccio's lies and the host's gullibility. The woman accuses both men of being too drunk to know what they are talking of. By involving the husband in her speech ("Voi bevete tanto la sera"), she makes her explanation more plausible; even her husband is subject to the same type of behaviour as Pinuccio. Drinking as a cause of visions is easily accepted in its verisimilitude by the host, who really works with wine ("un buono uomo, il quale a' viandanti dava pe' lor danari mangiare e bere" [a good man that furnished travellers with meat and drink for money (IX.6.4)]). The *insomnium* that Pinuccio invents to justify his actions, false even if it were real because caused by excessive drinking, as taught in the classical and medieval tradition known to Boccaccio, becomes a narrative ploy.[13] Even her husband might have dreamed because of an excess of wine; consequently,

---

13 According to the medieval classification descended from Macrobius, dreams caused by physical alterations do not contain any message, do not need interpretation, and are therefore false (see Cappozzo, "Delle verità dimostrate da' sogni," 203–7, with an

she argues, the words he could have heard are false. The good woman resorts to a persuasive rhetoric grounded on realistic motives.

Both Adriano and the host's wife insist on the effects of drunkenness, dreaming and sleepwalking, which associate the host and Pinuccio. The explanations the host receives from the woman and Adriano, all resting on the correlation between drinking, sleepwalking, dreaming, and confusing fables and true stories, finally convince him. If sleepwalking, dreaming, and mistaking dreams for realities assimilate both the host and Pinuccio (as the use of identical images seems to suggest: "*sognate* la notte e *andate in qua e in là* ... parvi far *meraviglie*"; "Pinuccio, io te l'ho detto cento volte che tu non *vada attorno* ... questo tuo vizio del *levarti in sogno* e di dire le *favole che tu sogni per vere*," emphases added), the woman's insistence on drunkenness eventually affects only her husband's behaviour. Initially, Adriano tells the wife that the two men are arguing because "essi bever troppo iersera" [they drank too much yestereve (IX.6.23)]; then the wife accuses both men of being too drunk ("*Voi* bevete," emphasis added). However, Pinuccio never pretends to be drunk: "Pinuccio, avendo raccolto ciò che detto s'era, cominciò a guisa d'uom che sognasse a entrare in altri farnetichi" [Pinuccio, taking his cue from what he had heard, began as a dreamer would be like to do, to talk wanderingly (IX.6.29)]. It seems that drinking is connected with the host's social characterization as innkeeper, but that seems also to suggest a social, moral, and, eventually, intellectual inferiority. Even if he is not "il più savio giovane del mondo," Pinuccio is, nevertheless, smart enough to understand what Adriano and the host's wife are saying. He takes on the cue of dreaming and sleepwalking, thus differentiating himself from the host's credulity and adulterated state of mind as caused by inebriation. Because of his inclination for drunkenness, the host can be easily mocked by the clever eloquence of his wife.

According to the medical knowledge of the time, the state of drunkenness was considered a humoral imbalance, an alteration of the drinker's complexion. Wine acts as a means of both physiological and moral corruption, causing states of alteration and disinhibition, affecting intellectual faculties and creating a confused state (Spani, "Il vino di Boccaccio"). Too much drink distracts the mind of a man who no longer knows how to distinguish between dream and reality. In the novella, the wife exploits the widespread idea of wine's inebriating power – which in this case is not true – to make her husband take as

---

extensive bibliography on this topic). For the theme of fake sleep and its narrative possibilities, see also Getto, *Vita di forme* (1986), 245–6.

false (Pinuccio's words on his night intercourse with Niccolosa) what is actually true. The motif of wine is, in sum, just a rhetorical device used to persuade her audience. The explanation of the facts she is proposing is so verisimilar and logical that her husband cannot but accept it (as do the other characters). Eventually, the woman's capacity to manipulate her uncritical audience, her husband, succeeds, thanks also to the perfect orchestration with Adriano's words.

The narrative situation resembles the fiction-making act at the core of *Decameron* VII.9, where Lidia, Nicostrato's wife, and her lover Pyrrhus make love in front of the husband and convince him that what he thought he saw did not happen. In both novellas, Panfilo shows each woman's ability to make her husband believe that his claims are false because of the hallucinatory effects of a pear tree or of wine, respectively. Both stories show how deception can be so entrenched in the real world that its detection becomes difficult in the acknowledged system of morality; they again demonstrate the polyvalent nature of storytelling and the questionable social uses to which it can be put. In the Pinuccio and Niccolosa novella, the host's wife has Pinuccio considered drunk, saving her and her daughter's reputation and her husband from an asymmetrical social confrontation.

The novella ends with a general reconciliation; the host's anger is diverted and the love affair concealed. However, the work of human intelligence restores only partially the social order threatened by adultery, since we know that Pinuccio and Niccolosa will continue meeting. The final equilibrium is, therefore, only apparent and somehow ironically limited by the host's laugh, since the final happy ending relies on a thread of lies. Boccaccio never ridicules the goodness and naïvety of the host, as is the case with other characters (like Calandrino in the previous tale). There is never any sarcasm or irony toward the host; he is an honest man who reacts with bitterness and amazement in front of Pinuccio. His final laughing spell ("l'oste incominciò a ridere e a farsi beffe di lui e de' suoi sogni" [the host fell a laughing and making merry touching Pinuccio and his dreams (IX.6.31)]) casts an ambiguous light on the finale and problematizes the relation between reality and appearance. The host's laughter resonates bitterly and emphasizes his inadequacy, his separateness from the others, from the world of his wife, Adriano, and Pinuccio. He thinks of mocking Pinuccio when, instead, he has been mocked. He remains metaphorically and physically entrapped in the close and obscure space of the bedroom.

It is not just the host who is being mocked, however: all the characters have been surprised by the darkness and by the nipping in and out of bed (Baratto, *Realtà e stile* [1996], 110). The woman reacts promptly to the misunderstandings by creating new ones, which allow an acceptable (and accepted) truth from everyone to be re-established. The mischievous conclusion of the narrator (Niccolosa's denials)[14] also brings the host's wife into the world of nightly misunderstandings, "per la qual cosa la donna, ricordandosi dell'abracciar d'Adriano, *sola seco* diceva d'aver vegghiato" [For which cause the good woman, calling to mind Adriano's embrace, accounted herself the only one that had watched (IX.6.33, emphasis added)]. For a moment, that insistence on the oneness of her vigilant experience isolates the host's wife from the others; eventually, she seems entrapped by her own storytelling. The ironic final line invites us, as readers, not to admire the successful lie so much as to eventually believe in it; at the same time, the word "vegghiato" alludes again to her unique watchfulness. As always, Boccaccio separates the level of narrative from that of the reader's interpretation; conclusions are always debatable and never definitive.

Through her witty rhetoric and quick agency, the host's wife constructs a different world that her husband takes for reality by accepting her words without investigating further. This last aspect points to the other central issue of the novella, the characters' and reader's responsibility to interpret correctly, being especially mindful of how language can be manipulated to create an appearance of truth. Through this novella, and especially through the character of the host who takes verbal appearances for reality, Boccaccio-Panfilo warns against the relative reliability of perception and the deceptive aspect of appearance.

As Roberta Morosini observes ("La 'Bele Conjunture,'" 263), the insistence on verbs such as *credere* and *vedere* emphasizes the ambiguous relationship between reality and appearance on which the inmost meaning of the story relies. While the host is unable to correctly interpret the ambiguous sentence of his wife ("con la Niccolosa non è egli [Pinuccio] giaciuto: ché io mi ci coricai io in quel punto che io non ho mai poscia potuto dormire" [he has not lain with Niccolosa; for what time he might have done so, I laid me beside her myself, and I have been wide awake ever since (IX.6.26)]), the "avvedimento" of the woman – a word that contains the verb *vedere* – hints

14 A further complication of the relationship between reality and fiction occurs at the end of the story when the daughter wants to convince her mother that Pinuccio really only dreamed of lying with her: "E poi appresso, trovati altri modi, Pinuccio con la Niccolosa si ritrovò, la quale alla madre affermava lui fermamente aver sognato" [Nor, afterwards, did Pinuccio fail to find other means of meeting Niccolosa, who assured her mother that he had unquestionably dreamed (IX.6.33)].

also at her insightfulness and capacity to interpret reality correctly and promptly: "La donna, parendole avere *udito* il marito garrire e *udendo* Adriano, *incontanente conobbe* là dove stata era e con cui: per che, *come savia*, senza alcuna parola dire *subitamente* si levò" [The good woman had already half recognized her husband's angry tones, and now that she heard Adriano's voice, she at once knew where she was and with whom. Accordingly, being a discreet woman, she started up, and [said] never a word (IX.6.24, emphases added)]. As an uncritical reader, the host misinterprets reality and remains definitely entrapped in the darkness of the bedroom – that is, in the darkness of falsehood. On the other hand, again the host's wife reveals her promptness in understanding what has happened by interpreting words correctly, since she realizes she has enjoyed sex with Adriano all night when she hears her husband's and Adriano's voices. At least in two circumstances, Adriano seems to show a command of words superior to that of the woman. First, when through silence – as a way of not *saying* the truth – he allows himself an unexpected pleasure (IX.6.17). Then, when through his words he reveals to the host's wife what happened during the night. It seems that not only was the woman awake during the night ("sola seco diceva d'aver vegghiato" [accounted herself the only one that had watched (IX.6.33)]), but Adriano was as well ("che ancora radormentato non era" [who was still awake (IX.6.17)]). Words can be deceptive and create a false reality, but they can also tear up the veil of darkness and dreaming when interpreted correctly, as the host's wife does.

Through the character of the host who believes to be true what is actually false, Boccaccio conveys his ironic attitude toward a canonical definition of truth. "Human truth does not exist as an abstract form. Instead, it is contingent on circumstance ... The power of truth, indeed its human essence, depends on its delivery and its reception. Thus, the clever lie can win the day over artless honesty. Similarly, the ethos of a given person or culture often determines both delivery and reception" (Grudin and Grudin, *Boccaccio's "Decameron,"* 126). Truth is relative and needs to be supported by foresight, imagination, eloquence, and good listening. "For Cicero and Boccaccio, eloquence – the ability to move minds with truthful words – has as its corollary eloquent listening – the skill of judging the words of others. Day IX of the *Decameron* provides us with lessons, both positive and negative, concerning both of these skills" (ibid., 122–3). The "buona donna" triumphs since she can control, through eloquence, the flow of information; by employing deception rather than truth, her rhetoric prevaricates on her husband's naïvety. The social and cultural environment of the host – the countryside inn where he works with wine – makes him believe promptly in his wife's words. The woman uses the realistic (but, this time, false) motifs of drunkenness and dreaming to create a story; wine and dream, hence, act as rhetorical devices. She is an eloquent speaker, whereas her husband is not an eloquent listener. Hinging on the inverted relationship between appearance and reality, the novella marks the triumph of concealment where reality reconciles or coincides with appearance.

So far, the novella has entrusted the host's wife with a great power, the ability to use language to create an alternative reality.[15] Pinuccio and Niccolosa's tale has shown that those who can manipulate language have agency and can take control of situations. According to Teodolinda Barolini, Boccaccio does not "subscribe to suspicion of language or suspicion of women, nor to the reifying of the divide between words and deeds." Instead, the "*Decameron* depicts *parole/femmine* as conduits to *fatti/maschi* and *fatti/maschi* resulting in *parole/femmine* in a mighty interwoven skein of word and deed, male and female, interconnected and unsunderable" ("Le parole son femmine," in *Dante and the Origins of Italian Literary Culture*, 302). For Barolini, women appropriate the world of men, the dimension of *fare*, through their words. Barolini's reading of the gender poetics of the *Decameron* can be applied also to IX.6.

In the novella, we see how women's words can restore the disorder caused by men's deeds. The words of the host's wife constitute the determining *fatti* that re-establish a social order. "Dir delle parole" really becomes "far de' fatti": the wise wife "con certe *parole* ogni cosa *pacefica*," where *pacificare* means literally "to make peace." Not only do her words become deeds, but also her very deeds lead to words: "come savia, *senza alcuna parola dire* subitamente si levò, e presa la culla del suo figlioletto, come che *punto lume nella camera non si vedesse*, per *avviso* la portò allato al letto dove dormiva la figliuola e con lei si coricò" [being a discreet woman, she started up, and saying never a word, took her child's cradle, and, though there was not a ray of light in the room, bore it, divining rather than feeling her way, to the side of the bed in which her daughter slept (IX.6.24, emphases added)]. The moving of the cradle and the getting into her daughter's bed – *fatti* – constitute the necessary backdrop for her words. Through her ability at using

15 For Boccaccio's attitude toward and treatment of female characters, see Marilyn Migiel's Introduction to her book *A Rhetoric of the "Decameron"*. On feminine rhetoric in the *Decameron*'s frame, see also Susanna Barsella, "Travestimento autorale e autorità narrativa." In particular, Barsella highlights the rhetorical importance of Pampinea as a narrative figure who somehow mirrors and complements the narrative voice of the author.

rhetoric and eloquence, through her ability at seeing/reading correctly even through the darkness of the bedroom, the "buona donna" reverses gender relationships and takes agency.

The relationship between genders and words and deeds is, however, more complex than we can suppose, especially if we read this novella together with the following one. The boundary that sets women and words on the one side and men and deeds on the other is much less rigid than it first appears. While the novella of Pinuccio and Niccolosa gives us readers a positive example of women's agency, the following one reverses this outcome.[16] Boccaccio's *ars combinatoria* juxtaposes tales that reverse any perspective and deny any easy resolution, demonstrating how for each element we can always find the exact opposite. The internal correlations between the two novellas stress their textual interdependence and their thematic importance.

Decameron IX.6 deals with the reception of discourse where lies are interpreted as truth. *Decameron* IX.7 is, instead, about the outcome of a prophetic dream and the reception of truth as lies. Margherita's mischievous and suspicious susceptibility leads her to invent a different narrative, a different interpretation of her husband's dream, a plausible and verisimilar interpretation, but a false one (Botti, "A proposito del sogno di Talano," 180–7). She does not have any faith in her husband's dream and the outcome is tragic for her. In this novella, what seems prodigious is eventually true; what is false in the previous one, namely Pinuccio's feigned dream state, becomes true. The deceiving of Margherita and the host depends on their being bad interpreters and failing readers. In the two tales, dreams function as a *mise en abyme* of the narrative system, of the fictional creation, although at different degrees of complexity owing to their different status (one is a *visio*, the other one an *insomnium*).[17] In IX.6, the act of dreaming functions as a rhetorical device around which it is possible to create a different but false narrative. In IX.7, the oneiric image actually works as a story inside the story. Again, the insistence on verbs like *vedere* and *parere* is crucial for the story:

> dormendo egli, gli *parve* in sogno *vedere* la donna sua andar per un bosco assai bello, il quale essi non guari lontano alla lor casa avevano; e mentre

16 For a reading of IX.7 as an instalment of Boccaccio's treatment of women's agency throughout the *Decameron*, see Grace Delmolino's essay, "The Tale of Margherita, a Self-Willed Wife: *Decameron* IX.7," in this volume.

17 Boccaccio entrusts a detailed and technical exposition of the dream theory to Panfilo, the narrator of this novella (IV.6.3–7).

così andar la *vedeva*, gli *parve* che d'una parte del bosco uscisse un *grande* e *fiero lupo*, il qual *prestamente s'avventava alla gola* di costei e *tiravala in terra* e lei gridante aiuto *si sforzava di tirar via*; e poi di bocca uscitagli, tutta *la gola e 'l viso pareva* l'avesse *guasto*. (IX.7.6, emphases added)

[he, sleeping, saw in a dream a very beautiful wood that was on the estate at no great distance from the house, and his lady there walking. And as she went, there leapt forth on her a huge and fierce wolf that griped her by the throat, and bore her down to the ground, and (she shrieking the while for succour) would have carried her off by main force; but she got quit of his jaws, albeit her neck and face shewed as quite disfigured.]

The boundary between what is real and what is not real (as in the previous novella) is blurred, and truth and falsehood are set in a disorienting relationship. In this case, however, the prophetic nature of the dream involves a true narrative, even if Margherita considers it false.[18]

The opposite treatment of dreams as rhetorical device in these novellas entails a radical upturning also in gender relationships: by showing what the woman incurs because she does not believe in her husband's dream (thus contradicting the previous novella), the story makes the reversal of roles the most radical possible. Whereas the host's wife is truly "savia" and "avveduta" [prudent, wise], Margherita, who believes she is "savia" in not believing her husband's words ("e io sarei bene sciocca se io nol conoscessi e se io il credessi!" [what a fool were I to believe him! (IX.7.10)]), eventually acts as "sciocca" and regrets miserably her lack of belief: "miseramente pianse la sua ritrosia e il non avere … al vero sogno del marito voluto dar fede" [she did many a time bitterly deplore her perversity, in that … she would nevertheless pay no heed to the true dream of her husband (IX.7.14)].

The act of seeing as a way of knowledge and foresight denotes the way the host's wife acts in IX.6. I have already mentioned that the word "avvedimento" belongs to the semantic field of *vedere* (seeing); we can find other examples throughout the novella. Initially, the woman "disavedutamente" sleeps with Adriano, but then she "ravedutasi," solves the situation; "per avviso," she carries the cradle to the side of her

18 On the contraposition between *vedere* and *parere* in Talano's dream, see also Delmolino, "The Tale of Margherita," 166–7.

daughter's bed. What is more striking is the fact that the woman can move and arrange things in the darkness of the bedroom:

> per che levatasi temendo non fosse altro, così *al buio levatasi* come era se n'andò là dove sentito aveva il romore … La donna, avendo cerco e trovato che quello che caduto era non era tal cosa, *non si curò d'altramenti accender lume per vederlo*, ma garrito alla gatta nella cameretta se ne tornò e *a tentone dirittamente* al letto dove il marito dormiva se n'andò … per che come savia, senza alcuna parola dire subitamente si levò, e presa la culla del suo figlioletto, *come che punto al lume nella camera non si vedesse*, per avviso la portò allato al letto dove dormiva la figliuola. (IX.6.14, 16, 24, emphases added)

> [the good woman, who, fearing that it might be a matter of more consequence, got up as best she might in the dark, and betook her to the place whence the noise seemed to proceed … The good woman searched till she found that the accident was no such matter as she had supposed; so without troubling to strike a light to investigate it further, she reproved the cat, and returned to the room, and groped her way straight to the bed in which her husband lay asleep … Accordingly, being a discreet woman, she started up, and saying never a word, took her child's cradle, and, though there was not a ray of light in the room, bore it, divining rather than feeling her way, to the side of the bed in which her daughter slept.]

Even in the darkness of the bedroom, she goes directly and rightly to her husband's bed, as stressed by the almost oxymoronic phrase "a tentone dirittamente." Anyway, at least for a moment, the host's wife is entrapped in the same network of night misunderstandings that deceives the other characters, as she is diverted from her foresightedness by quite a fortuitous accident, Adriano's moving of the cradle.

From this perspective, the night frame of the novella functions as metaphor for the ability/inability to read correctly beyond appearances. If, mocked as he is, the host remains entrapped in the darkness of his credulity, the freedom of moving in the darkness is, by contrast, a *mise en abyme* of his wife's instantaneous self-recognition, of her ability to understand immediately what is happening and to act consequently: "*incontanente* conobbe … *subitamente* si levò" [she at once knew … she started up (IX.6.24, emphasis added)]. In IX.7, Margherita pretends she is able to see through what she thinks are the mendacious words of her husband: "Oh! egli avrebbe buon manicar co' *ciechi*, e io sarei bene *sciocca* se io nol *conoscessi* e se io il *credessi*! Ma per certo e' non gli verrà fatto: e' convien pur che io *vegga*, se io vi dovessi star tutto dì, che mercatantia debba esser questa che egli oggi far vuole" [Ah! he would sup well with the blind, and what a fool were I to believe him! But I warrant he will be disappointed, and needs must I, though I stay there all day long, see what commerce it is that he will adventure in today (IX.7.10, emphases added)]. The blind one here is Margherita, not the husband, who actually *sees* in the appearances of his dream what will happen.[19] And the subjunctive mode of her discourse ("conoscessi," "credessi") contrasts with the assertive and definitive mode of the past tense connoting the actions of the host's wife.

Boccaccio's *ars combinatoria* has mixed up beds, roles, stereotypes, narrative techniques, gender relationships, medieval definitions (*insomnium* vs *visio*), and rhetorical devices. Acting also at the macrotextual level, this set of narrative elements has established a continuity between this novella and the following one. The message embedded in both stories emerges in a sharper light through their juxtaposition; the dynamic of narrative correlations and oppositions raises wider ethical and social questions, which might have been lost without those references. By playing on different levels of interpretation and perception, both novellas deal with misinterpretation, misreading, and good vs. bad reading practices, and they echo each other. Male credulity contrasts with female unbelief; the wise words of a wife with a husband's sage recommendation; the *visio* in its classical and medieval definition of a dream image that is true and has no need for interpretation with Pinuccio's *insomnium* that can never be true because it is false (but eventually becomes true through the woman's words).

The two novellas share a last aspect, the conclusion, in which, so to speak, the two female figures get the closing say: "la Niccolosa … alla madre affermava lui fermemente aver sognato; per la qual cosa la donna, ricordandosi dell'abbracciar d'Adriano, sola seco diceva d'aver vegghiato" [Niccolosa … assured her mother that he had unquestionably dreamed. For which cause the good woman, calling to mind Adriano's embrace, accounted herself the only one that had watched (IX.6.33)]; "Laonde ella [Margherita] … assai volte miseramente pianse la sua ritrosia e il non avere, in quello che niente le costava, al vero sogno del marito voluta dar fede" [Wherefore … she did many a time bitterly deplore her perversity, in that, when it would have cost her nothing, she would nevertheless pay no heed to the true dream of her

19 According to Delmolino, Margherita eventually "resolves not to blindly accept what Talano has told her of his vision. Instead, she wants to see for herself"; Margherita's desire to see becomes, therefore, a means to exert her own agency (ibid., 167).

husband (IX.7.14)]. Both conclusions are moments of retrospectively debating and questioning what Panfilo and Pampinea have just narrated and leave us readers with a sort of unease. Glancing back at the central actions in the stories functions as a retrospective judgment, if not a moral one. Boccaccio seems to suggest that, in the end, even fiction is only a verbal appearance.

The Tale of Margherita, a Self-Willed Wife: *Decameron* IX.7

GRACE DELMOLINO

In *Decameron* IX.7, Pampinea recounts Talano d'Imolese's dream of his wife Margherita venturing into the woods near their home, where she is attacked by a wolf. When he warns her of his dream, she scorns his warning, ventures into the woods, and is attacked by a wolf. The story is one of the shortest in the *Decameron*, and the *brigata*'s immediate reaction is to declare it truly a prophetic dream; critics have mostly followed suit in focusing their interpretation on the predictive qualities of Talano's dream.[1] I centre my reading on the concept of *ritrosia*, Margherita's quality of powerful self-willedness, in order to reframe *Decameron* IX.7 as the story of Margherita's agency and the suppression of her will through violence.

Margherita is a *ritrosa moglie*, a wife who defies her husband's will. She is described as "sopra ogni altra bizzarra, spiacevole e ritrosa, in tanto che a senno di niuna persona voleva fare alcuna cosa, né altri far la poteva a suo" [the most argumentative, disagreeable and self-willed creature on God's earth, for she wished to do nothing at another's direction, nor could others make her do it at her own (IX.7.4)].[2] The concept of *ritrosia* undergirds this tale's treatment of female agency. Forms of "ritrosia/ritroso" appear seldom in the *Decameron*: apart from one use of the diminutive "ritrosetto" in *Decameron* V.4, the word appears only

1 See Balestrero, *L'immaginario del sogno*, ch. 4; Botti, "A proposito del sogno di Talano"; Canovas, "Forme et fonction de l'énoncé onirique"; Selig, "Decameron IX/7 and X/4 and the Text Within." On dreams in the *Decameron* more broadly, see Cappozzo, "Il *Decameron* e il *Libro dei sogni di Daniele*"; Cardini, "Sognare a Firenze fra Trecento e Quattrocento"; Marchesi, "Dire la verità dei sogni."

2 The *Decameron* is cited from Branca's 1992 edition. I use the English translations of McWilliam (1995), with occasional adaptations to preserve a more literal reading. Emphasis within quotations is mine.

in IX.7 and IX.9 (three times and five times, respectively).[3] The adjective "ritrosa" describes only two characters in the *Decameron*, both of them wives who disobey their husbands: Giosefo's unnamed wife in *Decameron* IX.9 and Margherita in *Decameron* IX.7.

What exactly does it mean to be *ritrosa*? Etymologically, the word evokes backwardness and opposition, in both a moral and physical sense: the Italian *ritroso* derives from the Latin *retrorsum* (*retro* + *versum*, "turned backwards"). To give an example roughly contemporary to Boccaccio, Brunetto Latini describes as "ritroso" a person who breaks his promises, causing upset to a friend who expected him to keep his word, and Jacopo Alighieri describes the "ritroso affetto" of Dante's Simonists, whose bodies are turned physically upside down to mirror an approach to religious office that runs contrary to the rightful order of divine will.[4] The *Tesoro della lingua italiana delle origini* defines *ritrosia* as "Atteggiamento o carattere proprio di chi è poco disposto ad acconsentire alle richieste altrui" [Behaviour or character of one who is ill disposed to consent to the requests of others], citing *Decameron* IX.7 as an example of the word's usage. Although a corpus search shows a broad and gender-neutral range of usages in the Trecento, Boccaccio restricts his application of the term *ritrosia* to women.

A passage from the *Corbaccio* illustrates how *ritrosia*, in this restricted sense, describes women's exercise of agency in a misogynistic context where that agency is read as disobedience and presumption: "sono generalmente tutte presuntuose, e a se medesime fanno accredere che ogni cosa lor si convenga, ogni cosa stia lor bene, d'ogni onor, d'ogni grandezza sian degne, e che senza loro gli uomini niuna cosa vagliano, né viver possano; *e sono ritrose e inobedienti*" [they are generally all presumptuous, and convince themselves that they deserve everything, that it is fine for them to do anything, that they are worthy of every

3 These statistics are taken from the concordance available on *Decameron Web* (http://www.brown.edu/Departments/Italian_Studies/dweb/). I am counting instances of the noun "ritrosia" and the adjective "ritrosa" together.

4 In the *Favolello*, Brunetto Latini writes "Altretal ti redico / de lo ritroso amico, / ched a la comincianza / mostra grande 'bondanza, / poi a poco a poco alenta" [I will tell you again of the contrary friend, who at the beginning shows great generosity then bit by bit diminishes his giving (lines 63–7)]. Jacopo Alighieri writes that the Simonists' bodies are inverted "a dimostrare il ritroso loro affetto, sommettendo lo spirituale dovere della misericordia alle terrestre e temporali ricchezze" [to show their backwards behaviour, putting their spiritual obligation of mercy beneath terrestrial and temporal wealth (*Chiose all''Inferno'*, 19.1–3)]. These citations and my claims about the usage of "ritroso"/"ritrosia" are drawn from searches of the database available at the *Corpus OVI dell'italiano antico*.

honour, of every greatness, and that without them men are worth nothing, and are not even capable of survival; and they are contrary and disobedient (246)].[5]

Ritrosia, as Boccaccio uses it, is a gendered quality: it is *women's* disobedience in a misogynist system defined by women's subordination to men, where female submissiveness is axiomatic and women are expected to accept men as their governors and leaders. In such a system, a woman who acts contrarily to men's wishes – as though her own free will could be worth following even when the men in her life disagree – transgresses against the accepted order of things. Thus, the best translation of *ritrosa* as Boccaccio uses it is "contrary" or "self-willed," with the same negative and gendered cast those words maintain in English.[6] The *Merriam-Webster Dictionary* defines "self-willed" as "governed by one's own will; not yielding to the wishes of others." The "simple definition" makes things even clearer: to be self-willed is to be "determined to do what you want even though other people may not want you to do it." Likewise, a person who is "contrary" is "temperamentally unwilling to accept control or advice." *Ritrosia* captures these overlapping meanings of "contrariness" and "self-willedness": it is the quality of exercising one's own will in opposition to the will of others. For Margherita, that means exercising her will in opposition to her husband's. Because she asserts her will within the patriarchal structure of marriage, in defiance of her husband, her self-willedness is cast negatively, as *ritrosia*. In this essay, I read *Decameron* IX.7 through the lens of *ritrosia* in order to liberate Margherita's resistance from its negative encoding and position this novella as a keystone for the *Decameron*'s treatment of agency.

Pampinea narrates only one act of resistance by Margherita, and that is her refusal to obey Talano when he warns her not to venture into the forest near their house. She disregards the warning, and the dreamed-of wolf attack comes to pass. What could have been interpreted as a coincidence – wolves constituted a real and present danger in the Middle Ages – is instead presented in retrospect as the inexorable hand of

---

5 The other appearance of the word in the *Corbaccio* is in one of many lists of unpleasant adjectives used to define the widow the narrator formerly loved: "golosa, *ritrosa*, ambiziosa, invidiosa, accidiosa e delira" [gluttonous, self-willed, ambitious, envious, slothful, and delusional (270)]. Translations of the *Corbaccio* are mine.

6 One definition of "contrary" in the *Oxford English Dictionary* is "Of antagonistic or untoward disposition, perverse, obstinately self-willed; contrarious." A citation from *Uncle Tom's Cabin* illustrates the negatively gendered cast of the adjective when used in this sense: "Gals is nat'lly made contrary; and so, if you thinks they've gone one road, it is sartin you'd better go t'other" (cited in *Oxford English Dictionary*, "Contrary," 2b).

fate reaching down to smite Margherita.[7] Thus is the tale read by the *brigata*, who declare "universalmente … quel che Talano veduto avea dormendo non essere stato sogno ma visione, sí appunto, senza alcuna cosa mancarne, era avvenuto" [universally … that what Talano had seen in his sleep was no dream, but rather a vision, as it corresponded so exactly with what had actually taken place (IX.8.2)]. To make Talano's dream a prophetic vision is to suggest that the events could have been avoided, had the prophecy only been heeded. So Pampinea frames her story: she will narrate what happened to Margherita "*per* non crederne uno [sogno] di lei dal marito veduto" [*because* she did not believe a dream about her that her husband had seen (IX.7.3)].[8] Other than this simple synopsis, Pampinea offers little moralizing judgment, leaving readers to interpret the tale in the absence of authorial commentary.

Pampinea introduces her tale as a true event that befell a neighbour of hers, "una mia vicina" (IX.7.3). She even floats the possibility that other members of the *brigata* might know this neighbour's husband, Talano d'Imolese, as she casually wonders, "Io non so se voi vi conosceste Talano d'Imolese" [I don't know whether any of you were ever acquainted with Talano d'Imolese (IX.7.4)]. To specify the historical reality of characters is to resist giving them the status of universal examples. In her *proemio* to *Decameron* IX.9, Emilia will extrapolate a universalizing moral from Pampinea's tale, effectively translating it from anecdote to exemplum, but Pampinea makes no such sweeping claims for her own story. At the same time, the hyperbolic description of Talano's wife is indeed characteristic of exemplary tales that exaggerate vices in order to caution against them. Margherita is "una giovane, bella tra tutte l'altre … ma sopra ogni altra bizzarra, spiacevole e ritrosa" [an exceedingly beautiful young woman … but the most argumentative, disagreeable and self-willed creature on God's earth (IX.7.4)].

---

7 Modern hunting and agricultural practices have practically eradicated wolves in Europe, but the threat of a wolf attack would have been very real in medieval Italy when the animal population was less controlled. Lords frequently offered hunters monetary rewards for killing a wolf. The sum depended on the kind of wolf, with females often earning a larger reward, given their importance for the reproduction of the species. See Ortalli, "Natura, storia e mitografia" (273–5).

8 The authorial rubric of IX.7, in slight contrast to Pampinea's summary, offers only coordinate clauses to describe the plot: "Talano d'Imolese sogna che uno lupo squarcia tutta la gola e 'l viso alla moglie; dicele che se ne guardi; ella nol fa, *e* avviene" [Talano d'Imolese dreams that his wife is savaged all about the throat and the face by a wolf, and tells her to take care; but she ignores his warning, *and* the dream comes true (IX.7.1)]. The conjunction *e/and* suggests only temporal succession, unlike *per/because*, which implies causality.

Two traits are fundamental to Margherita's character: her exceptional beauty and her exceptional *ritrosia*. We might reasonably assume that Talano married her for the former quality, like any number of husbands in the *Decameron* who select wives for their youth and beauty.[9] Marriage is not enough to curb her other defining characteristic. She does not follow her husband's commands, resulting in behaviour that is "gravissimo ... a comportare a Talano" [enormously difficult ... for Talano to bear (IX.7.4)].

The trope of an outspoken woman – what R. Howard Bloch terms "woman as riot" – whose disobedience to male command results in some kind of ill event befalling her is hardly unique to Boccaccio (*Medieval Misogyny*, 17). Although no direct source exists for Boccaccio's story, many traditions (from literary narratives to popular tales to mainstays of medieval preaching) rely on a similar linkage of a wife's disobedience to a violent, sometimes fatal, accident.[10] *Decameron* IX.7, however, should not be read as a straightforwardly misogynist exemplum, because Boccaccio's insistence on the concept of *ritrosia* offers a key to unlocking a more complex reading of the story. Pampinea links gender and *ritrosia* (defined as resistance to the control or guidance of others) in her opening remarks, though she does not use the word *ritrosia* until later. She tells the *brigata* she has been inspired by other stories of true dreams and women's refusal to heed them: "Altra volta, piacevoli donne, delle verità dimostrate da' sogni, *le quali molte scherniscono*, s'è fra noi ragionato" [Delectable ladies, we have talked on previous occasions about the truths embodied in dreams, *which many of us women refuse to take seriously* (IX.7.3)]. Her *inciso*, that women scorn the predictive value of dreams, has no apparent precedent in the other stories to which she alludes. These are *Decameron* IV.5, in which Lisabetta dreams of her dead lover's burial place, and IV.6, in which Andriuola dreams of her lover's impending death.[11] Both of these Day Four stories depict women who have and believe true dreams of the past and future respectively. While Lisabetta and Andriuola dream their

9 *Decameron* II.10 offers, in the character of Bartolomea, a prime example of a wife selected for her youth and beauty. Her marriage comes to ruin because her husband fails to take into account other aspects of her personality.

10 Boccaccio, *Decameron*, ed. Branca, 1273n1; Lee, *The Decameron, Its Sources and Analogues*, 287–9.

11 *Decameron* V.8 and VII.10 can also be placed into the same broad category of paranormal phenomena as IV.5 and IV.6, though neither features a dream. In *Decameron* V.8, Nastagio witnesses an apparition in the daytime, and though Meuccio in *Decameron* VII.10 is sleeping when the ghost of his friend Tingoccio comes into his room, the ghost wakes Meuccio up in order to deliver his message.

own dreams, Margherita is faced with the decision of whether to trust a dream she experiences only at second hand, through her husband's account of it. Pampinea's point, it would seem, is not that women do not trust dreams broadly speaking. It is that women do not trust other people's dreams, and perhaps men's dreams in particular. In *Decameron* IX.7, Margherita's determination to follow only her own will and her unwillingness to trust her husband's dream result in her physical disfigurement. That stubbornness is presented both as a unique feature of her personality that she exhibits more than any other woman, and as an innate attribute of her gender. The contradiction forces readers to consider which interpretation might have more merit, and we find far more evidence of Margherita's individual agency than of her conformity to a misogynist stereotype.

Margherita's will clashes with Talano's in their first spoken interaction. After dreaming his dream, Talano tells his wife that, although he is pained by her self-willed behaviour, he still feels an obligation to keep her from harm: "Donna, ancora che la tua ritrosia non abbia mai sofferto che io abbia potuto avere un buon dí con teco, pur sare' io dolente quando mal t'avvenisse" [Woman, your contrariness has been the bane of my life since the day we were married; but all the same I should be sorry if you came to any harm (IX.7.7)]. Margherita, primed by the statement that her husband has suffered every day of his marriage to her, hesitates to take his statement of good intentions at face value. She responds: "Chi mal ti vuol, mal ti sogna: tu ti fai molto di me pietoso ma tu sogni di me quello che tu vorresti vedere" [Evil wishes beget evil dreams. You pretend to be very anxious for my safety, but you only dream these horrid things about me because you'd like to see them happen (IX.7.8)]. Reading his dream in a proto-Freudian light, Margherita suspects that Talano's dream might be less a vision from God and more a manifestation of Talano's own desires. Margherita, self-willed in all things, attributes volition rather than prophecy to her husband's dream.

She responds forcefully, informing her husband that "per certo io me ne guarderò, e oggi e sempre, di non farti né di questo né d'altro mio male allegro" [you may rest assured that I shall never give you the satisfaction of seeing me suffer any such fate as the one you describe, whether on this day or any other (IX.7.8)]. Talano accuses Margherita of making him suffer; she in turn accuses him of wishing suffering on her. In previous days of the *Decameron*, men have reacted violently to perceived or real slights from women in their lives. The dark knight of *Decameron* V.8, for instance, cites "la letizia avuta de' miei tormenti" [the happiness she took in my torments (V.8.22)] as cause for his punishment of the woman who once rejected him. We might also recall

Bernabò's attempt to have his wife murdered in response to a false claim of adultery (II.9): his will to violence is no less though his wife has, in reality, done nothing wrong. Similar rhetoric around delight in another's suffering appears in the *Corbaccio*. The narrator tries to calm the devastation of rejection by reminding himself that his pain will be pleasure to his beloved: "tu dunque, piangendo, attristandoti, rammaricandoti, sommo piacere fai a questa tua nemica" [with all your sadness and crying and self-flagellation, you are providing immense pleasure for this enemy of yours (37)]. When men believe that women have made them suffer, vitriol and suffering are revisited upon the women on an amplified scale. If Talano truly means it when he says his marriage to Margherita has caused him daily pain, Margherita has grounds to be wary.

Though Margherita responds logically, Talano claims to have known she would react the way she did because she is by nature ungrateful for counsel given by others. He tells her, "Io sapeva bene che tu dovevi dir cosí, per ciò cotal grado ha chi tigna pettina" [I knew you would say that. A mangy dog never thanks you for combing its pelt (IX.7.9)]. The *Vocabolario degli Accademici della Crusca* glosses this proverb (literally, "that's what you get for scratching ringworm") as meaning "chi fa servigio a ingrati, o a chi non merita, ne riceve ma' gradi" [whoever does a favour for an ingrate, or for someone who doesn't deserve it, receives no appreciation].[12] To say "I knew you would say that" denies Margherita the agency of reacting to a particular situation, because her reaction – according to the proverbial logic – has already been determined by an ingratitude and resistance that she exhibits indiscriminately.

Boccaccio alludes to an essentialist rhetoric of female stubbornness in the *De mulieribus claris*, writing in the biography of Sempronia Gracchi that

> Erunt forte qui dicant … non tamen hanc ob constantiam inter claras fuisse ponendam, eo quod, quodam innato sibi more, mulieres in quocunque proposito obstinate opinionis atque inflexibilis pertinacie sint. (LXXVI.6–7)[13]
>
> [Perhaps some will object that, nonetheless, she should not have been included among famous women on the grounds of constancy, since by inborn habit women are obstinate and unbending in their opinions in everything.]

12 *Vocabolario degli Accademici della Crusca*, "Pettinare."

13 I cite the Latin text and English translation of the *De mulieribus claris* from Virginia Brown's edition and translation, *Famous Women*.

The essentializing axiom strips women of their ability to make individual decisions based on agency and contingency. Their constancy cannot be ascribed to their conviction on a particular issue, but rather to their innate tendency to be unbending in their opinions. They can be right as the proverbial stopped clock is right: because even an arbitrarily fixed position will sometimes happen to coincide with the truth.

Many women find their place in Boccaccio's *De mulieribus* because of their constancy of will. We might think of Gualdrada (CIII), who states her absolute refusal to kiss an emperor after her father offers her to him, or the Hebrew queen Mariamme (LXXXVII), who spurns and rebukes her husband Herod for his unwarranted jealousy, not wavering in her condemnation of him even when faced with death.[14] Throughout the *De mulieribus*, Boccaccio portrays a number of exemplary women who exercise agency and constancy in very individualized situations. In fact, when he narrates Mariamme's steadfastness in the face of her execution, he describes her as "vilipensa morte … nec ulla ex parte femineo ritu flexa" [scorning death … she did not give way at all, as women are wont to do (LXXXVII.9)]. The word "flexa" [bent], which Mariamme is markedly not, recalls the "inflexibilis" [unbending] in Sempronia's earlier biography, where women are supposedly "obstinate opinionis atque inflexibilis pertinacie" [instinctively obstinate and unbending in their opinions (LXXVI.6)]. Sempronia is praised for her inflexibility (even though "some say" women are unbending in everything). Mariamme too is praised for her inflexibility (even though it is feminine nature to be "flexa," to bend). In the biography of Sempronia, Boccaccio distances himself from the essentialist claims about women's inflexibility by attributing them to a hypothetical "some": "Erunt qui forte dicant …" [Perhaps there will be some who say … (LXXVI.6)]. The rest of the *De mulieribus* offers example after example of positively encoded female steadfastness and *fermezza*.[15]

The constancy in the face of adversity exhibited by Sempronia, Gualdrada, Mariamme, and others in the *De mulieribus* is a positive counterpart to the negatively encoded *ritrosia* exhibited by Margherita in *Decameron* IX.7. Both describe a person who remains committed to their

14 A version of Gualdrada's steadfastness appears in the *Decameron*, too: the character Violante/Giannetta in II.8 offers a defence of her honour in a situation very similar to Gualdrada's (II.8.59–64).

15 Elsa Filosa argues that Boccaccio was heavily influenced by political events in his own life when writing the *De mulieribus*, which contains strong praise of women who are steadfast, loyal, and true in their resistance to tyrannical rulers and governments. See Filosa, "Motivi anti-tirannide e repubblicani."

own will even in opposition to the will of others. Yet one is a valued quality, and one is despised. In Margherita's case, little else than her social status as a married woman – one who uses speech to assert her own will in opposition to her husband's – renders her *ritrosa*. She violates the Pauline dictum that "man is the head of woman" and refuses to blindly accept her husband's counsel. Her suspicion of his motives is evident in her internal dialogue as she speculates, "Hai veduto come costui maliziosamente si crede avermi messa paura d'andare oggi al bosco nostro? là dove egli per certo dee aver data posta a qualche cattiva e non vuole che io il vi truovi" [Here's a crafty fellow! Do you see how he tries to frighten me out of going near the woods today? He's doubtless planned a tryst there with some strumpet or other, and doesn't want me to find him (IX.7.10)]. Margherita is jealous, and she wants to know the truth. Whether her jealousy might have any basis in fact is left unspecified, but we do know that jealousy has had unfortunate consequences for women in other *Decameron* stories. Catella in III.6, for example, finds herself raped and blackmailed as a result of her suspicion that her husband is sleeping with another woman. *Decameron* VII.8 suggests that when it is the husband who becomes jealous, his wife can pay the price for that too: Sismonda only barely escapes being beaten and having her hair cut off by a husband driven to fury by his jealousy. IX.7 does not give us enough evidence to determine whether Margherita's jealousy might be founded, but her inclination to believe the worst of her husband recalls yet another proverb, referenced by Pampinea herself in I.10: "le femine in ogni cosa sempre pigliano il peggio" [women always choose the worst in everything (I.10.8)].[16] Women's jealousy can be explained by an essentialist, misogynistic proverb: women will always believe the worst, and so even if they are right, it is only by chance.[17] Once again, the rhetoric of misogyny denies a woman agency,

16 Pampinea's first story, perhaps not coincidentally, also deals with a "Margherita": Malgherida dei Ghisolieri mocked old Maestro Alberto's love for her, but in the end, "credendo vincer fu vinta" [thinking to conquer, she was conquered (I.10.20)]. Malgherida's playful insubordination in mocking an older man, and her comeuppance in the form of a witty verbal rebuke, have morphed into something much more sinister by Day Nine.

17 Though he plays with misogynist logics whereby women are taken as a universal category and men as individuals, Boccaccio tends to complicate gender stereotypes by showing examples of the same behaviour in men and women alike. In *Decameron* VII.4, Tofano d'Arezzo becomes irrationally jealous of his wife Ghita. When he locks her out of the house at night – even though by this point, he *is* correct that she's been with a lover – the town believes her word over his and condemns him for telling lies about his wife. Riccardo tells Catella in III.6 that his word would

suggesting that her choice was determined by her gender rather than by her individual will.

Convinced that her husband harbours ill intent, Margherita exclaims internally, "Oh! egli avrebbe buon manicar co' ciechi, e io sarei bene sciocca se io nol conoscessi e se io il credessi!" [Ah, he'd do well for himself at a supper for the blind, but knowing him as I do, I should be a great fool to take him at his word (IX.7.10)]. Talano would "do well at a supper for the blind," in the sense that he would easily be able to put one over on them and take their food without them realizing. At this metaphorical supper, Margherita would be in the position of a blind person, to whom Talano could do whatever he wanted because she cannot "see" what he is doing. Yet she resolves not to blindly accept what Talano has told her of his vision. Instead, she wants to see for herself: "e' convien pur che io *vegga*, se io vi dovessi star tutto dí, che mercatantia debba esser questa che egli oggi far vuole" [I shall have to *see*, even if I have to wait there the whole day, what business takes him to those woods today (IX.7.10)]. Her desire to see stands in tension with the visionary qualities of Talano's dream. As Talano dreams, the visionary verbs *vedere* and *parere*, to see and to seem, appear repeatedly: "gli *parve* in sogno *vedere* la donna sua andar per un bosco … e mentre cosí andar la *vedeva*, gli *parve* che d'una parte del bosco uscisse un grande e fiero lupo [he *dreamt* that he *saw* her wandering through the woods … and as he *watched*, an enormous and ferocious wolf *seemed* to emerge from a corner of the woods (IX.7.5–6)].[18] But a visionary *vedere* is not enough for the empirical Margherita, who wants to see with her own eyes. The novella stages a conflict between the passive transmission of prophecy and the active exercise of agency, between Talano's vision and Margherita's sight.

When Margherita enters the forest, although she is "stando attenta e guardando or qua or là se alcuna persona venir vedesse" [keeping

---

be believed over hers if she tried to denounce him, but it is not universally the case in the *Decameron* that a man's word is given more weight than a woman's.

18 According to Dino Cervigni, the modal verb *vedere* "implies an active participation (at least on a physical level) on the part of the beholder" (*Dante's Poetry of Dreams*, 46). He further argues that "Whereas personal involvement would seem to denote imaginings, in which the subject seeks to project his own phantasizing outside of himself, passivity seems rather to pertain to experiences in which the subject is basically receptive, such as in prophetic dreams" (49). The description of Talano's dream uses an active *vedere* with Talano as the subject and Margherita as the object ("la vedeva") as well as the more passive *parere* with Talano as an indirect object ("gli parve"). Boccaccio's mixed use of visionary language allows for both readings: Talano as active agent or as passive receptor.

a sharp lookout on all sides so that she could see if anyone was coming], she is utterly "senza alcun sospetto di lupo" [without any fear of a wolf (IX.7.11–12)] when one leaps out of the underbrush and attacks her.[19] For all her determination to see with her own eyes, she does not see the wolf coming. As it turns out, and despite what the *brigata* later claims about Talano's visionary accuracy, the dream does not precisely match the attack as it happens in life. In the dream, Margherita struggles and screams, managing to tear herself away from the wolf's jaws: "lei gridante aiuto si sforzava di tirar via; e poi di bocca uscitagli, tutta la gola e 'l viso pareva l'avesse guasto" [she struggled to free herself, screaming for help, and when at length she managed to escape from its clutches, the whole of her throat and face appeared to be torn to ribbons (IX.7.6)]. When she is actually attacked, she submits immediately: "né poté ella, poi che veduto l'ebbe, appena dire 'Domine, aiutami', che il lupo le si fu avventato alla gola, e presala forte la cominciò a portar via come se stata fosse un piccolo agnelletto" [she scarcely had time to exclaim "Lord, deliver me!" before the wolf hurled itself at her throat, seized her firmly in its jaws, and began to carry her off as though she were a new-born lamb (IX.7.12)]. Previous descriptions of Margherita suggest minimal resemblance to a little lamb. She is beautiful, but far from meek. When the wolf has seized her in its jaws and her throat is about to be ripped out, she finally becomes docile and submissive, such that "essa non poteva gridare, sí aveva la gola stretta, né in altra maniera aiutarsi" [she was unable to scream for help, so tightly was the wolf holding on to her throat, nor could she help herself in any other way (IX.7.13)]. The violence of a wolf attack – which targets her throat, a physical locus of speech – overcomes her refusal to comply with the will of anyone but herself, and literal strangulation silences her sharp tongue.

The emphasis on Margherita's docility as soon as the wolf is upon her recalls a popular tradition around the sighting of wolves in the wild. Bestiaries from the Middle Ages report the belief, traceable back to Pliny's *Historia naturalis*, that if a man encounters a wolf and is seen by the wolf before seeing it, he will be rendered speechless. Conversely, if he sees the wolf first, the animal will be the one rendered docile

19 The phrase "senza alcun sospetto" immediately recalls *Inferno* 5, conjuring a feeling of dread: Francesca too was "sanza alcun sospetto" [suspecting nothing] (129) right before her husband murdered her. I cite the *Commedia* from the Petrocchi edition with translations by Allen Mandelbaum available at *Digital Dante* (http://digitaldante.columbia.edu/).

and submissive.[20] Although the power dynamics mirror each other, with first sight leading to dominance, the nature of submission differs between animal and human. Submission, for an animal, means that it will not attack; for a human, it means that the person will not *speak*. The ultimate submission of Margherita's will is not her physical vulnerability to the wolf, but her inability to even cry out or use her voice. The wolf would have strangled her to death, "se in certi pastori non si fosse scontrato, li quali sgridandolo a lasciarla il costrinsero" [but for the fact that it ran towards some shepherds, who yelled at the beast and forced it to release her (IX.7.13)]. Perhaps Talano, dreaming of the independent and resistant Margherita he knew, could only imagine that she would use her own voice ("lei gridante aiuto") to free herself. But in a perfect *contrapasso* against Margherita's *ritrosia*, she is denied even the agency of saving herself from death. Instead, male shepherds save her and male doctors cure her. She must rely on men's voices in order to preserve her life, since it is the act of their yelling, "sgridando," that makes the wolf let her go, while her own voice is silenced.

Female submission brought about by animal violence links this story to the tale of Nastagio degli Onesti. *Decameron* V.8 stages a more domesticated version of the savage wolf attack that befalls Margherita. In that earlier story, Nastagio witnesses a pack of dogs, incited by a knight on horseback, chasing down and tearing apart a naked lady. The knight explains that they are both spirits and that the ritualistic mangling of the woman's body, which recurs every Friday in that very spot, punishes her transgressions against him in life: her mutilation is "quello che questa malvagia femina ha meritato" [what this wicked woman has earned (V.8.19)]. The knight describes her "fierezza e crudeltà" [pride and cruelty] in refusing to reciprocate his love when he was alive, which eventually drove him to suicide: "per la sua fierezza e crudeltà andò sí la mia sciagura, che io un dí con questo stocco, il quale tu mi vedi in mano, come disperato m'uccisi" [her pride and cruelty led me to such a pass that, one day, I killed myself in sheer despair with this rapier that you see in my hand (V.8.21)]. The knight is damned because of his suicide; the lady because of "lo peccato della sua crudeltà e della letizia avuta de' miei tormeti" [the sin of her cruelty and the happiness

20 Ortalli, "Natura, storia e mitografia," 280–2. Additional advice was often given that, should one encounter a wolf in the wild, one ought to remove one's clothes and bang two rocks together to scare it away. For more extensive treatments of wolves in the Middle Ages, see Ortalli, *Lupi genti culture*; Pluskowski, *Wolves and the Wilderness*; Trin, *Les loups*; Levalois, *Le symbolisme du loup*; Salisbury, *The Beast Within*; Rowland, *Animals with Human Faces*.

she took in my torments (V.8.22)].[21] The nature of her cruelty prior to the knight's death is left unspecified, but it is nonetheless deemed a sin and she is sentenced to a purgatorial *contrapasso* because of it.

While her would-be lover lived, she failed to bend her will toward his, eschewing Francesca's courtly dictum of *Inferno* 5.103 that "Love pardons no beloved from loving" and deciding not to love a man just because he loved her. Her punishment takes the form of a hunting scene where two mastiffs subdue her so that the knight can cut out her heart and feed it to the animals. The dogs reduce her to a degree of servility she never showed in life, bringing her finally under the knight's control, "inginocchiata e da' due mastini tenuta forte" [kneeling before him and held in place by the two mastiffs (V.8.29)], naked and crying for mercy in the ultimate expression of servitude to another human being. The story ends with Nastagio taking advantage of this weekly performance to subdue the will of a contrary woman in his own life, an unnamed woman from the Traversari family who does not return his love. He plans a banquet in the woods, inviting his unwilling beloved and her companions, knowing that partway through their meal they will witness the hunt. The sight of another woman being torn apart by dogs as punishment for her "cruelty" in not reciprocating a man's love results in not only the Traversari lady but all the ladies of Ravenna becoming "sempre poi troppo piú arrendevoli a' piaceri degli uomini … che prima state non erano" [much more tractable to men's pleasures … than they had ever been in the past (V.8.44)]. By threat of physical mutilation, their wills are contorted into alignment with those of men.

The dogs in *Decameron* V.8 serve as an extension of the knight's own will: they are a manifestation of physical violence that, although sent by "fate" or "God" or "divine order," nevertheless aligns perfectly with the man's personal desire for revenge on a woman who scorned him. They are the domesticated counterpart to the wolf in *Decameron* IX.7, a wild and untamed animal whose violence nevertheless channels Talano's own desire for his wife to be more submissive. In fact, that is exactly how Margherita reads his dream, accusing him of dreaming what he wishes would befall her. In a chiasmus of symbolism, the literal wolf represents Talano, while the literal Margherita becomes a symbolic lamb, an "agnelletto" who cannot move or speak of her own volition.

21 Simone Marchesi sees the infernal hunt of *Decameron* V.8 as part a tradition of "courtly" texts in which "la pena inflitta punisce la ritrosia (nel Boccaccio, 'la crudeltà') della donna amata" [the suffering inflicted serves to punish the beloved woman's *ritrosia* (in Boccaccio, "cruelty")] (Marchesi, "Intenzionalità tragica," 36).

Even once she has been rescued from the wolf, she remains quiet and voiceless. Nor does her beauty emerge unscathed. The doctors cure her in the sense that she does not die from the attack, but her face is left "sozzissima e contrafatta" [deformed and disfigured (IX.7.13)], and she is ugly to look upon. To be "contrafatta," literally made opposite, is the physical analogue to the psychic quality of *ritrosia*: both are perversions of a presumed natural order.[22] And so it would seem that her physical disfigurement "cures" the mental disfigurement: she experiences both regret for not listening to her husband and shame at the sight of her appearance by others. In one fell swoop, she is silenced in the domestic sphere and banished from the public one. She is made ashamed of her appearance, or, more precisely, ashamed to appear where others might see her. She weeps at the now-physical manifestation of her *ritrosia*, a trait that, together with her beauty, had defined her identity. The wolf attack has made her not just a docile "agnelletto" but ashamed of being *herself*. And the quality that led to the wolf attack was precisely her determination to be herself, to heed only her own volition, to exercise self-will in all matters.

Two stories later, Emilia, the queen of the Ninth Day, tells a tale of another *ritrosa moglie*: her tale of Solomon's advice to Melisso and Giosefo, the latter of whom seeks counsel regarding his contrary wife. Emilia claims to have been inspired by Pampinea's tale, and she takes the occasion of her *proemio* to transform the story of Margherita from an anecdote about Pampinea's neighbour into a parable illustrating how even God will punish women who deviate from the "natural" order in which women are subservient to men. Her decision to begin with a lengthy gloss on a previous tale is singular in the *Decameron*, and it is Emilia's unique choice that makes it possible to talk about Margherita's "punishment" for her *ritrosia*. Pampinea uses no vocabulary of justice, retribution, or punishment in *Decameron* IX.7. Although she describes Margherita's regret at not having listened to her husband, there is no narrative moralization to suggest that she necessarily deserved what

22 The idea that "right order" is for women to be beautiful (though of course without the use of "trickery" like makeup, condemned in the *Corbaccio* as deceit practised upon unwitting men) is another form of misogyny. As the old woman in *Decameron* V.10 explains to a young wife, women are valued for their youth, beauty, and suitability for child-bearing. Now that she is old, she bears her evident age as a social burden, just as Margherita does her disfigurement: "veggendomi fatta come tu mi vedi," the woman explains, "non troverei chi mi desse fuoco a cencio" [in this sorry state I'm in now, if I wanted to light a fire, I couldn't find anyone to lend me a poker (V.10.17)]. On this story see Barolini, "'Le parole son femmine,'" in *Dante and the Origins of Italian Literary Culture*, 293–5.

happened to her. Emilia, by contrast, summarizes IX.7 in morally judgmental terms: "Idio quello gastigamento mandò che il marito dare non aveva saputo" [God sent the punishment that her husband was unable to visit upon her (IX.9.6)]. The freak occurrence of a wolf attack becomes, unambiguously, a "gastigamento": a punishment for Margherita's transgression.

The word "gastigamento" connects Pampinea's tale in Day Nine to her tale in the previous day, also in seventh position: *Decameron* VIII.7, the novella of the scholar and the widow. The story describes Rinieri's brutal revenge against Elena, the woman who subjected him to a freezing night locked in her courtyard while she cavorted with her lover and mocked Rinieri's infatuation with her. Pampinea introduced that tale with a clear authorial judgment, claiming to present "una giusta retribuzione" [a just retribution (VIII.7.3)] rendered unto a fellow Florentine citizen. Pampinea defines this "just retribution" as a "vendetta," which she classifies as a sub-type of the *beffe* that are the theme of Day Eight: "Noi abbiamo per piú novellette dette riso molto delle beffe state fatte, delle quali niuna vendetta esserne stata fatta s'è raccontato" [Many of the stories already narrated have caused us to laugh a great deal over tricks that people have played on each other, but in no case have we heard of the victim avenging himself (VIII.7.3)]. Yet within the story, Pampinea has Rinieri offer a different definition of *vendetta* when Elena pleads with him to cease tormenting her. Rinieri explains to her, "questo che io fo non si possa assai propriamente vendetta chiamare *ma piú tosto gastigamento, in quanto la vendetta dee trapassar l'offesa*, e questo non v'agiugnerà" [to call what I am doing revenge [vendetta] is a misuse of words, for it is rather a punishment [gastigamento], inasmuch as revenge must exceed the offence and this will fall short of it (VIII.7.87)]. Rinieri defines *vendetta* as a retribution that exceeds the original crime, while a *gastigamento* is punishment that does not surpass the offence.

Rinieri positions himself as an accurate judge of the severity of Elena's offence as well as the degree to which he punishes her, claiming that he is indeed, as Pampinea suggests at the beginning of the tale, visiting a "just retribution" upon Elena. Yet by his own definition, the *brigata* judges him to have enacted a *vendetta*, not a *gastigamento*. They find that only part of Elena's suffering was delivered "giustamente" [justly], implying that the rest was unjust, and they condemn Rinieri as "rigido e costante fieramente, anzi crudele" [excessively severe and relentless, not to say downright cruel (VIII.8.2)].[23] Nor does the reception of VIII.7

23 Ullrich Langer argues that "The point of the novella can be seen as the negotiation of distributive justice, and the commentary of the narrator Pampinea seems to underline the fact that it is less a matter of an interesting sequence of events than of

conclude in Day Eight. Ten stories later, the spectre of VIII.7 rises again when the narrator, Lauretta, directly contradicts Rinieri's claim that his actions constituted a fitting retribution for Elena's treatment of him. In her introductory remarks to IX.8 – the story that bridges Pampinea's tale of Margherita and Emilia's tale of another *ritrosa moglie* – Lauretta explains that she takes her inspiration from the scholar's *vendetta*: "me muove la rigida vendetta, ieri raccontata da Pampinea, che fé lo scolare, a dover dire d'una assai grave a colui che la sostenne, quantunque non fosse per ciò tanto fiera" [I am prompted, by the account Pampinea gave us yesterday of the scholar's bitter vendetta, to tell you of another vendetta, which, whilst it was no laughing matter for its victim, was at the same time rather less brutal (IX.8.3)]. Lauretta does not accept Rinieri's explanation that his torture of Elena constitutes a *gastigamento* or a deserved punishment, nor does she echo any vocabulary of justice. She calls Rinieri's actions a "rigida vendetta" [rigid vendetta], a harm that exceeds the original offence, and condemns his *vendetta* as "fiera" [brutal, prideful].

The framework of revenge and punishment that Pampinea used in VIII.7 is absent in the framing of IX.7, until Emilia, in her introduction to IX.9, returns to the language of "gastigamento." The rubric already prepares readers to expect a discussion of punishment: "Due giovani domandan consiglio a Salamone, l'uno come possa essere amato, *l'altro come gastigare debba la moglie ritrosa*" [Two young men ask Solomon's advice, the first as to how he may win people's love, the second as to *how he should punish his obstinate wife* (IX.9.1)]. Emilia summarizes her story as a tale of how "fu gastigata la ritrosa" [the contrary lady was punished (IX.9.35)]. She repeats the word "gastigamento" three times in her introduction, twice when describing the qualities in women that make them worthy of punishment and once to describe the wolf attack that befell Margherita in IX.7. Because Pampinea did not narrate IX.7 as a tale of punishment, the role of Margherita's punisher – analogue to Rinieri in VIII.7 and Giosefo in IX.9 – must be retroactively cast by Emilia. She appeals to the highest possible authority. God himself, she says, punished Margherita for disobeying her husband: "Idio quello gastigamento mandò che il marito dare non aveva saputo" [God sent the punishment that her husband was unable to visit upon her (IX.9.6)].

---

finding the equal proportion of injuries" ("The Renaissance Novella as Justice," 322). For Langer, the scholar's attempt at justice is "unsatisfactory" because it is deemed by the *brigata* to have exceeded Elena's original crime (323). Teodolinda Barolini reads VIII.7 as a tale of Rinieri's excess, in an Aristotelian sense, and his utter failure to put his intellectual training to humane and compassionate use (Barolini, "The Scholar and the Widow").

Emilia transforms Margherita not only into the object of a punishment but into a negative example, representative of all other women who transgress as she did.

Pampinea's story was specific and historically rooted in a way that resists exemplarity. Even in VIII.7, when Pampinea makes a more explicit authorial judgment of her female protagonist, Elena remains a distinct individual: she has a name and she is "una nostra cittadina" [a fellow townswoman of ours (VIII.7.3)], part of a group that includes Pampinea herself. Emilia's female character, the wife of Giosefo, is nameless and of unspecified origin. She serves as a universal example, an animated archetype. Emilia emphasizes universality from the very start, saying that should anyone of sound mind consider the "ordine delle cose" [order of things], they will recognize "tutta la universal moltitudine delle femine dalla natura e da' costumi e dalle leggi essere agli uomini sottomessa" [that the universal multitude of women are through nature and custom, as well as in law, subservient to men (IX.9.3)]. Women have become a "universal multitude," a group that, however large, remains homogeneous. And the universal role of women, Emilia states, is to be subservient to men.

Even without the proof of law and custom, nature alone offers sufficient evidence of women's inferiority, according to Emilia:

> la natura assai apertamente cel mostra, la quale ci ha fatte ne' corpi dilicate e morbide, negli animi timide e paurose, nelle menti benigne e pietose, e hacci date le corporali forze leggieri, le voci piacevoli e i movimenti de' membri soavi: cose tutte testificanti noi avere dell'altrui governo bisogno. (IX.9.4)
>
> [Nature proves this lesson to us very plainly, for she has made us soft and fragile of body, timid and fearful of heart, compassionate and benign of disposition, and has furnished us with meagre physical strength, pleasing voices, and gently moving limbs. All of which shows that we need to be governed by others.]

Women's physical weakness "testifies" to their need of governance by others, but one might wonder whether women's fearful hearts and benign dispositions could be secondary qualities that follow from the vulnerability in their "weak and delicate" bodies. Without the recourse of physical self-defence, what choice does one have except to accommodate the wishes of others?[24] Accommodation of the will of men,

24 In the Introduction to Day One, Pampinea tells the *brigata* that "Natural ragione è, di ciascuno che ci nasce, la sua vita quanto può aiutare e conservare e difendere" [Every person born into this world has a natural right to sustain, preserve, and

according to Emilia, will result in harmonious coexistence with those men: "a ciascuna, che quiete, consolazione e riposo vuole con quegli uomini avere a' quali s'appartiene, dee essere umile, paziente e ubidiente" [it behoves any woman who seeks consolation and tranquility with the men to whom she belongs, to be humble, patient, and obedient (IX.9.3)]. The adjectives "umile, paziente e ubidiente" are all words for submission of the will, deriving etymologically from words for lowness, suffering, and listening to another.

The idea that "peace" or "consolation" can be achieved by a woman submitting her will completely to the will of a man – even to the point that it causes her suffering – reaches its peak articulation in *Decameron* X.10. Gualtieri puts Griselda through increasingly brutal trials, he explains at the end of the story, "vogliendoti insegnar d'esser moglie" [because I wanted to teach you how to be a wife (X.10.61)]. After she has suffered through each in turn, Gualtieri decides that he has achieved "quella consolazione che io desiderava" [that consolation I desired (X.10.62)]. What he means, as Teodolinda Barolini puts it, is the total submission of Griselda's will to his own: with Griselda, he achieves his desire for "the other to be present without being present, without registering any sign of a separate will, without, in fact, being other" ("The Marquis of Saluzzo," 43). Emilia seems to suggest that the erasure of a woman's will is inevitable, because "chi ha bisogno d'essere aiutato e governato, ogni ragion vuol lui dovere essere obidiente e subgetto e reverente all'aiutatore e al governator suo" [it stands to reason that those who need to be aided and governed must be submissive, obedient, and deferential to their benefactors and governors (IX.9.5)]. Again, the adjectives she chooses are revealing: *obidiente* (from Latin *ob* + *audiens*, listening to another), *subgetto* (from *subiectus*, placed beneath), *reverente* (from *revereri*, to respect or fear another). If women need governance, then they must place themselves beneath their governors. They should listen, they should submit, they should fear. After all, Emilia asks her audience, "e cui abbiam noi governatori e aiutatori se non gli uomini?" [and who do we have to be our governors and benefactors, if not men? (IX.9.5)]. What other choice is there?

---

defend his own life to the best of his ability (I.Intro.53)]. Despite this resounding advocacy of self-defence, the other women hesitate to move off the mark until men show up to accompany them. Yet the men of the *brigata* will be, Pampinea declares, "e guida e servidor" [both guides and servants (I.Intro.80)]. The men's role in the *brigata* is much more nuanced than that of a man who is a woman's absolute "aiutatore e governatore" [helper and governor (IX.9.5)] as Emilia describes.

Her question goes unanswered, but the unspoken response is deafening: a woman could govern herself. *Decameron* IX.7 depicts a woman who refuses to accept her husband as her "governatore e aiutatore," a wife whose assertion of her self and her separate will, whose presence as an other, disrupts her husband's "quiete, consolazione e riposo." The result is violence. And so the story of Margherita has inspired Emilia's reflections:

> A cosí fatta considerazione, come che altra volta avuta l'abbia, pur poco fa mi ricondusse ciò che Pampinea della ritrosa moglie di Talano raccontò, alla quale Idio quello gastigamento mandò che il marito dare non aveva saputo. (IX.9.6)
>
> [I have expressed views of this kind on previous occasions, and I was confirmed in them a little while ago by what Pampinea told us about Talano's obstinate wife, to whom God sent the punishment that her husband was unable to visit upon her.]

Emilia confirms the reading of Talano-as-wolf, which Margherita herself initially proposes. The wolf attack is not a freak accident, but the expression of her husband's desire to punish her even though he does not know how to do it himself. And, according to Emilia, Pampinea's historically rooted tale about her neighbour can function as a universal exemplum for all women:

> e per ciò nel mio giudicio cape tutte quelle esser degne, come già dissi, di rigido e aspro gastigamento che dall'esser piacevoli, benivole e pieghevoli, come la natura, l'usanza e le leggi voglion, si partono. (IX.9.6)
>
> [and therefore, in my judgement, all those women should be harshly and rigidly punished, who are other than agreeable, kindly, and compliant, as required by nature, custom, and law.]

Emilia here offers a third series of adjectives with etymological roots in the vocabulary of the will: *piacevole* (from the verb *piacere*, to please); *benivola* (from *volere*, to want); and *pieghevole* (from *piegare*, to bend). All three indicate a direction of the will. Women should be pleasing *to* another, they should be well-wishing *to* another, they should bend their will *to* the will of another. A woman becomes *ritrosa*, backward and resistant to the natural order, when she does not bend her will to accommodate the will of someone else. And when a woman is *ritrosa*, she is worthy of punishment, of "rigido e aspro gastigamento."

To say that a wolf attack constitutes a "gastigamento," a just punishment measured precisely to the crime of Margherita's *ritrosia*, requires an equivalence to be drawn between women's transgressive speech or behaviour and men's physical violence. Emilia concludes her *proemio* with a misogynistic proverb to illustrate the concept: "Buon cavallo e mal cavallo vuole sprone, e buona femina e mala femina vuol bastone" [Good steed, bad steed, alike need the rowel's prick; good wife, bad wife, alike demand the stick (IX.9.7)].[25] She clarifies that the proverb should be interpreted not just "sollazzevolmente" [humorously], but also "moralmente" [morally (IX.9.8)] in its literal sense. Women "want the stick" not just as a sexual metaphor, but as a technique of discipline to maintain an orderly coexistence with the men in their lives. The verb *vuole*, as used in the proverb, expresses the subjugation of women's "will" to men's desires: *volere*, here, indicates not the direction of an individual's will, but the imposition of an other's will on a self whose will may or may not align with that of the other. Emilia suggests, in very literal terms, that women who have transgressed require "il baston che le punisca" [the rod to punish them], while women who have not nevertheless require "il bastone che le sostenga e che le spaventi" [the rod to encourage and frighten them (IX.9.9)].

Michael Sherberg interprets the apparent misogyny of Emilia's *proemio* to IX.9 as ironic, citing the contradiction between her happy facial expression (she begins "lieta" [happy (IX.9.2)]) and the disturbing content of her speech. He suggests that Emilia's argument "is not exclusively moral, if indeed at all: rather, it is fundamentally practical. Emilia offers such advice because, as she well knows, women live surrounded by violence" (*The Governance of Friendship*, 102). A more explicit contradiction of Emilia's words is Emilia herself: both a woman and a queen, one who currently has governance over the rest of the *brigata*. In her governance, she imposes a rule of law that allows for all persons, male and female, to govern themselves. When selecting the theme for her day, she chooses the freedom to choose: "non intendo di ristringervi sotto alcuna spezialità, ma voglio che ciascuno secondo che gli piace ragioni, fermamente tenendo che la varietà delle cose che si diranno non meno graziosa ne fia che l'avere pur d'una parlato" [I do not propose to confine you to any particular topic; on the contrary, I desire that each of us should speak on whatever subject he or she may choose, it being my firm conviction that we shall find it no less rewarding to hear

25 I cite the 1903 translation of J.M. Rigg available at *Decameron Web* as it better captures both the rhyme and sexual implications of the Italian proverb.

a variety of themes discussed than if we had restricted ourselves to one alone (VIII.Concl.5)]. Emilia argues for the restorative benefits of liberty and diversity. She encourages her companions to speak "secondo che gli piace," in accordance with their will. The diversity of subjects that will result – for of course each individual's will inclines toward different topics – will make their coexistence *more* pleasant, not less. The liberty enjoyed in Day Nine will prepare the *brigata* for a return to the rule of law in Day Ten: "chi appresso di me nel reame verrà, sí come piú forti, con maggior sicurtà ne potrà nelle usate leggi ristrignere" [we shall all recruit our strength, and thus my successor will feel more justified in forcing us to observe our customary rule (VIII. Concl.5)]. Emilia suggests that the exercise of individual freedom will strengthen the *brigata* when they return to stricter governance in Day Ten. In direct contradiction of the system she describes in IX.9 – where strong leadership is achieved by weakening the individual freedom of women – Emilia's government as queen of the *brigata* creates strength by encouraging individuals to exercise their will.

Like Emilia, Pampinea is queen of an unthemed day. In fact, she institutes the practice of having governed days of storytelling in the first place, explaining that "estimo che di necessità sia convenire esser tra noi alcuno principale, il quale noi e onoriamo e ubidiamo come maggiore, nel quale ogni pensiero stea di doverci a lietamente vivere disporre" [I consider it necessary for us to choose a leader, drawn from our own ranks, whom we would honour and obey as our superior, and whose sole concern will be that of devising the means whereby we may pass our time agreeably (I.Intro.95)]. Pampinea argues that having a "principale," a ruler who is obeyed as authority, will facilitate the "continuar della nostra letizia" [continuation of our happiness (I.Intro.95)]. But she does not propose a tyrannical leadership that erases conflicting wills. Instead, the "principale" should have as their ultimate objective the happy coexistence of all their subjects. Furthermore, she decrees that all should experience the positions of both ruler and ruled, "acciò che ciascun pruovi il peso della sollecitudine insieme col piacere della maggioranza" [so that each will experience the burden of responsibility and the pleasure of command associated with sovereign power (I.Intro.96)]. Pampinea recognizes that all are inclined to delight in the "piacere della maggioranza," in the pleasure that comes from bending others to your will. And thus a weight of responsibility, the "peso della sollecitudine," comes with ruling in such a way as to take others' interests and desires into account. In the *brigata,* not even a king's or queen's will is accommodated absolutely, nor is any individual will absolutely suppressed.

On the cusp of Day Four, the first day to be governed by a man, the incumbent queen Neifile transfers her crown to Filostrato and quips, "Tosto ci avvedremo se il lupo saprà meglio guidar le pecore, che le pecore abbiano i lupi guidati" [Now we shall discover whether the wolf can fare any better at leading the sheep than the sheep have fared in leading the wolves (III.Concl.1)]. Her metaphorical sheep and wolves anticipate the animal symbolism of *Decameron* IX.7: men are aggressive and powerful, like wolves who attack livestock, while women are docile and meek, like flocks of sheep who must be guided by others. In medieval Italian as in modern English, "sheep" describes humans who cannot or do not follow their own will, but move with a crowd of nearly identical companions guided by the design of a higher power.[26] Neifile already subverts the conventional metaphor, however, because she places the sheep in the role of guides. Filostrato calls her out for suggesting what is clearly untrue, namely that the female members of the *brigata* resemble sheep in any way:

> Se mi fosse stato creduto, i lupi avrebbono alle pecore insegnato rimettere il diavolo in inferno, non peggio che Rustico facesse ad Alibech, e perciò non ne chiamate lupi, dove voi state pecore non siete. (III.Concl.2)
>
> [Had you listened to me, the wolves would have taught the sheep by now to put the devil back in Hell, no less skilfully than Rustico taught Alibech.

---

26 The repentant sinners in Dante's purgatory are described positively as sheep who move without knowing why: "Come le pecorelle escon del chiuso / a una, a due, a tre, e l'altre stanno / timidette atterrando l'occhio e 'l muso; / e ciò che fa la prima, e l'altre fanno, / addossandosi a lei, s'ella s'arresta, / semplici e quete, e lo 'mperché non sanno" [Even as sheep that move, first one, then two, / then three, out of the fold – the others also / stand, eyes and muzzles lowered, timidly; / and what the first sheep does, the others do, / and if it halts, they huddle close behind, / simple and quiet and not knowing why (*Purg.* 3.79–84)]. Their mindlessness is cast positively because they follow God, the only true arbiter of "right order." In *Paradiso* 5, on the other hand, Beatrice condemns as "pecore matte" [sheep gone mad] the men on earth who follow "mala cupidigia" [evil greed] (*Par.* 5.79–80). Beatrice echoes Dante's negative use of "pecore" in the *Convivio*, where he writes of the common people that "Questi sono da chiamare pecore, e non uomini; chó se una pecora si gittasse da una ripa di mille passi, tutte l'altre l'andrebbero dietro; e se una pecora per alcuna cagione al passare d'una strada salta, tutte l'altre saltano, eziandio nulla veggendo da saltare" [These people should be called sheep, not men, for if a sheep were to cast itself over a cliff a thousand feet high, all the others would follow after it; and if while crossing the road a sheep for any reason leaps, all the others leap, even though they see nothing to leap over (*Convivio* I.11.9)]. I cite from the Italian text and Richard Lansing's English translation available at Digital Dante.

> But you have not exactly been behaving like sheep, and therefore you must not call us wolves.]

Filostrato suggests that, had the *brigata* indeed held true to their roles as women-sheep, they would have yielded by now to the desires of the men-wolves in the group. But they have not, and therefore cannot be called sheep, just as the men cannot be called wolves when they have not "preyed" on malleable young ladies as Rustico preyed on Alibech in *Decameron* III.10. Neither the men nor the women of the *brigata* have given in to their animalistic drives.

The *brigata* is a social unit that accommodates both the order that comes from having a single guide and the diversity that comes from different individuals exercising their will even within a hierarchical system. The marriage of Margherita and Talano in *Decameron* IX.7 (together with the marriages in V.8, IX.9, X.10, and others) is a social unit that seeks to achieve the order of a single will by permanently suppressing the will of another. The violence that achieves such suppression is bestial in nature: savage dogs subdue the lady in V.8, a wolf-husband attacks a sheep-wife in IX.7, a mule in IX.9 is interpreted as a metaphor for a *ritrosa moglie*, and Gualtieri's actions are condemned as "matta bestialità."[27]

Pampinea ends her story in Day Nine with the comment that Margherita "miseramente pianse la sua ritrosia e il non avere, *in quello che niente le costava*, al vero sogno del marito voluto dar fede" [shed many a bitter tear for her petulant ways and her refusal to give credence, *when it would have cost her nothing*, to her husband's prophetic dream (IX.7.14)]. But it is not true that it would have cost her nothing to simply follow her husband's warning. To surrender one's will to another, to become a mindless sheep, is too high a price to pay for marital harmony. The *Decameron* advocates for compromise and tolerance over submission and degradation, because when humans become animals, the social contracts that hold society together collapse. Boccaccio condemns humans behaving like animals in the Introduction to Day One, when people die "non come uomini ma quasi come bestie" [not like men but almost like beasts (I.Intro.44)], abandoning or abandoned by those humans around them, while the animals act "quasi come razionali" [almost like rational beings (I.Intro.46)]. The members of the *brigata* avoid the societal collapse depicted in the Introduction by creating their

27 On the violent wife-battering depicted in *Decameron* IX.9, and the dehumanizing animal metaphors applied to women across various times and cultures, see Vasvári, "'Buon cavallo e mal cavallo.'"

own law, a law that allows for both a single ruler and individual will to coexist. The result is such a state of peace and contentment that, in the Introduction to the Ninth Day, the narrator claims an outside observer could only have remarked that "O costor non saranno dalla morte vinti o ella gli ucciderà lieti" [Either these people will not be vanquished by death, or they will welcome it with joy (IX.Intro.4)]. In *Decameron* IX.7, Boccaccio shows us the grim outcome when women's agency is restricted or eliminated so that masculine authority can reign supreme. In that story, we find not consolation but tyranny, not harmony among differing wills but suppression of one self in service of another. When women become sheep, men become wolves, and the *Decameron* shows us that neither bestial servitude nor bestial violence should be tolerated as the foundation of social order.

A Metaphor Unveiled? Wine, Wrath, and the Bible in *Decameron* IX.8

JOHNNY L. BERTOLIO

The eighth novella of the Ninth Day is probably the one most evidently permeated by Dantean references in the entire *Decameron*. In such "a true party of Dantean archetypes, as Umberto Eco would say" (Fido, "Dante personaggio mancato del libro galeotto," 118), the majestic and dreadful figure of Filippo Argenti emerges: he is dragged into the plot by the lust for vengeance of another character taken from the *Divine Comedy*, to wit Ciacco.

Wrathful Filippo and gluttonous Ciacco are the protagonists of a new *comédie humaine* that starts with a prank organized on the historical (and again densely Dantean) background of late medieval Florence. Ciacco runs into his friend Biondello while the latter is buying some lampreys on behalf of Vieri de' Cerchi (of the *White* Guelph faction), but he tells Ciacco that said purchase was requested by Corso Donati (of the *Black* Guelph faction), who had asked for fish because it was Lent.[1] As an ancient Roman *cliens*, Ciacco already foretastes a delicious meal that his wallet and the prescribed abstinence could not have otherwise offered him. But when he arrives at Corso's, he finds that dinner is very frugal, and does not include lampreys at all.

Ciacco realizes that he has been the victim of a trick and is now eager for vengeance against Biondello: as the first prank had implied the proverbial gluttony of the cheated, the new one will call into question Biondello's passion for always being "più pulito che una mosca" [cleaner

1 The presence of these two pivotal political leaders in the novella has been examined by Olson, *Courtesy Lost*, 65–97. The scholar suggested that here Boccaccio "rewrites" the Dantean view of Florentine history in terms of individual personalities lacking "courtesy."

than a fly (IX.8.5)].[2] The plan is more elaborate and involves another proverbial character vice, that is, Filippo Argenti's wrath. Ciacco sends a huckster, who acts as a middleman, or a helper, to provoke Filippo by asking him to pour his wine into a wicker bottle supposedly on Biondello's behalf: "Messere, a voi mi manda Biondello, e mandavi pregando che vi piaccia d'arubinargli questo fiasco del vostro buon vin vermiglio, ch'e' si vuole alquanto sollazzar con suoi zanzeri" [Sir, I've been sent to you by Biondello who asks if you would be so kind as to rubify this flask for him with some of your fine red wine because he wants to have a good time with his little[3] drinking buddies (IX.8.14)].

No translation will do justice to the original text, which contains some rather obscure expressions: in particular, "ar[r]ubinare" and "zanzeri/zanzari." According to the commentaries, these words belong to contemporary gangster jargon. The fact that they are incomprehensible and rare bothers Argenti more than their actual meaning (Goldberg, "'La vita serena'," 49). "Ar(r)ubinare" (with a single or double "r") should mean "to make red as a ruby," while "zanzeri" ("zanzari" at IX.8.25: the autograph waves between these two forms)[4] could derive from the Venetian dialect, where "zanza" (="ciancia") means "gossip," "trifle," and so "zanzeri" would mean "tittle-tattle friends," "comrades."[5]

Aside from the general tone, and from the not irrelevant fact that it is Lent, the request sounds inappropriate because both the middleman and Biondello belong to a much lower class than Argenti, who is a noble knight and should be addressed accordingly. Quick to anger, Argenti does not understand the exact meaning of the question that he repeats parrot-fashion back to his interlocutor: "Che 'arrubinatemi' e che 'zanzeri' son questi?" [What's this stuff about "rubifying the flask" and "little drinking buddies"? (IX.8.17)]. Argenti seems to understand

2 Here and below quotations from the *Decameron* are from Branca's 1976 edition and translations are by Rebhorn. Unless otherwise noted, other translations are mine.

3 Rebhorn adds the adjective "little" on purpose because a modern (and not very medieval) meaning of "zanzero" is "rent boy."

4 See Boccaccio, *Decameron*, ed. Branca (1976), 621.

5 "*Zanzeri*: evidente è il senso di amici, compagnoni; ma questa parola si trova soltanto qui, e non è neppur certo se si pronunzi sdrucciola, come vogliono, o piana; si potrebbe pensare a parola non fiorentina, ma veneziana, *zanza*, ciancia, (sicché *zanzèri* burloni); e messer Filippo non se ne sarebbe irritato di meno per la sua stranezza: forse una parola di gergo" [*Zanzeri*: the meaning of "friends, companions" is clear; but this word can be traced only here and it is not even sure if it is proparoxytone, as they prefer, or paroxytone. We could speculate that it is a not a Florentine word but Venetian, from *zanza*, "tittle-tattle" (and *zanzèri*, "jokers," thereof); and Sir Filippo would have not got less angry for its weirdness: maybe a jargon word (Zingarelli in *Le opere di G. Boccaccio*, 430–1)].

that underneath the question lies a provocative tone: as Mario Baratto pointed out, these Florentine characters share a sort of "philological complicity" based on the various levels of the language they speak (Baratto, *Realtà e stile* [1984], 265).

As Ciacco had imagined, Argenti flies into a rage. When he runs into Biondello, whom he considers the author of the request, the counter-prank reaches its peak: Filippo vents his anger on the unaware Biondello, who is made mincemeat and only survives thanks to some passers-by who intervene.

The architecture of the first and of the second prank is clear: Ciacco's gluttony and Biondello's impudence are punished according to a desire for justice that belongs to the narrator of this novella, Lauretta.[6] Even Ciacco's promise to wreak vengeance "Avanti che otto giorni passino" [Before a week's gone by (IX.8.12)] sounds like one of Dante's prophecies in the *Divine Comedy*, especially the one uttered by the other literary Ciacco in *Inferno* 6.67–8 (Surdich, "La 'varietà delle cose,'" 239). Two other characteristics are emphasized: Ciacco's ability to make biting remarks ("morditore," IX.8.4) – the reason why rich and noble men seek his company during meals – and Biondello's true obsession with cleanliness, which is punished when he is thrown into the mud in the street and his clothes are torn during Argenti's attack.

When commenting on the request that the middleman addresses to Argenti, all past and recent editors of the novella underline two aspects: (1) the daring tone, based on the "carnival" violation of social hierarchy, and (2) the usage of a lower-class, if not criminal, slang that Argenti is not able to decode. By a man chronically prone to wrath any odd request could have been seen as an assault. Yet, it is likely that Boccaccio constructed the entire verbal sequence intentionally. How intentionally is what we will examine in the following paragraphs.

One of the most evident symptoms of anger is facial colour, red, just as paleness is a symptom of fear. When the devils prevent Dante and Virgil from entering the city of Dis, Virgil's face grows red with anger while Dante the pilgrim's face turns pale with fear (*Inf.* 9.1–3). According to the Aristotelian phenomenology accepted by Dantean commentators (e.g., Francesco da Buti, and Boccaccio himself), fear causes blood to gather around the heart, while anger makes blood boil and spread across all the veins and organs, including the face.[7] When, in the third

6 See Kirkham, "An Allegorically Tempered *Decameron*," 14.

7 The same opposition pale/red is in *Teseida* VII.33: "videvi l'Ire rosse come foco, / et la Paura pallida in quel loco" (the house of Mars). In his glosses Boccaccio explains

novella of the Fourth Day, Lauretta (the same narrator as IX.8) describes anger, she says:

> E tra gli altri [vizi] che con più abbandonate redine ne' nostri pericoli ne trasporta, mi pare, che l'ira sia quello; la quale niuna altra cosa è che un movimento subito e inconsiderato, da sentita tristizia sospinto, il quale, ogni ragion cacciata e gli occhi della mente avendo di tenebre offuscati, *in ferventissimo furore accende* l'anima nostra (IV.3.4, emphasis added)

> [Furthermore, in my opinion, the one [vice] that we control the least as it leads us into danger is anger. For anger is nothing other than a sudden, thoughtless impulse, prompted by a feeling of resentment, that banishes reason, shrouds the eyes of the mind in darkness, and *sets* our souls *on fire with raging fury.*]

As Lauretta maintains afterwards – "più leggiermente in quelle s'accende e ardevi con fiamma più chiara e con meno rattenimento le sospinge" [not only do they [women] catch fire more easily, but their anger burns in them with a fiercer flame, and meeting less resistance there, carries them away with it (IV.3.5)] – and as the character of Catella had already offered proof of in the Third Day ("di subita ira accesa" [all of a sudden she flared up in anger (III.6.21)]; "di fervente ira accesa" [blazing with passionate anger (III.6.33)]), women are deemed to be more prone to irascibility.[8] Here we observe that red is associated not simply with boiling blood but especially with burning fire.

Boccaccio notices this inner fire in Dante's description of the wrathful in the fifth circle of *Inferno*, where Argenti is punished: they are depicted restlessly tormenting each other. According to Boccaccio's gloss in the *Esposizioni sopra la Comedia di Dante*, this behaviour "niuna altra cosa è che un disegnare gl'impeti furiosi degli iracundi, quando dal focoso accendimento dell'ira sono incitati" [is nothing but the depiction of the furious instincts of the wrathful when they are spurred by the ardent outburst of wrath (*Esp. all., Inf.* 7.126)]. Boccaccio later adds that the swamp where they boil in Hell is steaming in conformity with the

all the details of the description and confirms that red recalls the appearance of a wrathful person.

8 On this female attitude, see also *Elegia di Madonna Fiammetta* V.8–10 and VI.22.1, and *Corbaccio* 158. The idea that irascibility runs deeper in women and in general in weak beings (sick people, elders, and children) can already be found in classical authors (e.g., Plutarch, *Moralia* 457b).

"choleric humor, which is hot and dry" ("omore collerico, il quale è caldo e secco," 134).

Another trait of this category of sinners emerges in the third terrace of Purgatory, where Dante meets the wrathful enveloped in thick black smoke (*Purg.* 15.142–5 and 16.1–9). This induced blindness clearly reflects the lack of judgment of these sinners, ready to get mad at anyone without reason. In a famous passage of Seneca's *De ira*, wrath itself appears immersed in a thick fog (II.35.5) precisely like Mars's house in Boccaccio's *Teseida* (VII.30).

The same characteristics of the wrathful to be found in both *Inferno* and *Purgatorio* are evident in Filippo Argenti. When he listens to the middleman's request, he appears "tutto tinto nel viso" [all red in the face (IX.8.17)], a description that corresponds to Latin *accensus* (Fornaciari), and that scholars have glossed as "infocato di sdegno" (Fanfani), "rosso, quasi paonazzo per l'ira grande" (Lipparini), "infiammato" (Segre), and "*rosso, infocato* per la rabbia" (Branca).[9] Some *loci paralleli* identified by Branca confirm such a meaning: "tutto tinto nel viso" (*Filostrato* V.13.2); "con viso tinto" (*Elegia di Madonna Fiammetta* VI.20.10).[10] In *Purgatorio* the killers of Saint Stephen, a champion of docility, move against him "acces*i* in foco d'ira" (15.106).[11] The metaphor wrath equals fire, thus, moves the colour red from the metaphoric object (fire) to the person that experiences the emotion. The expressions "ar(r)ubinargli" and "vin vermiglio" in Boccaccio's sequence belong precisely to this chromatic scale.

At this point a second metaphor overlaps with the first one: wrath and wine make up in fact a frequent and natural pair, the former being

9 Fornaciari in *Novelle scelte dal Decamerone*, 237; Fanfani in *Il Decameron*, 2:324; Lipparini in *Il Decameròn*, 275; Segre in *Opere di Giovanni Boccaccio*, 1299; Branca in Boccaccio, *Decameron* (1976), 1088.

10 In his edition of Boccaccio, ibid., Branca also mentions *Inferno* 3.29, where the colour of the "aura sanza tempo" has got a darker nuance – still alive in Spanish *tinto* (referred to wine as well) and in the Sicilian dialect adjective *tintu* (Varvaro, *Vocabolario Storico-Etimologico del Siciliano* [*VSES*], 1077–8). We could add *Inferno* 9.38 and Petrarch, *Rerum vulgarium fragmenta* XXXVI.11, where it is blood that determines the participle. See also *Filocolo* IV.96.8: "cominciasi a crucciare e a tignersi nel viso."

11 In the New Testament: "Audientes autem haec dissecabantur cordibus suis et stridebant dentibus in eum" (Acts 7:54), with the typical attitude of the wrathful grinding their teeth. See also *Filocolo* IV.145.1: "L'amiraglio ascolta queste cose, e infiammasi, udendo, d'ardentissima ira … turbato si leva … e andando sanza riposo per la sua camera torcendosi le mani e strignendo i denti, giura …" [The admiral listens to these words and, hearing them, is inflamed … gets up all troubled … and while pacing restlessly his room, wringing his hands and gnashing his teeth, swears that …].

one of the consequences of excessive consumption of the latter. As Seneca mentions in his *De ira*,

> vinum incendit iras, quia calorem auget; pro cuiusque natura quidam ebrii effervescunt, quidam saucii. Neque ulla alia causa est cur iracundissimi sint flavi rubentesque, quibus talis natura color est qualis fieri ceteris inter iram solet; mobilis enim illis agitatusque sanguis est. (*De ira* II.19.5)

> [wine kindles anger because it increases the heat; some boil over when they are drunk, others when they are simply tipsy, each according to his nature. And the only reason why red-haired and ruddy people are extremely hot-tempered is that they have by nature the colour which others are wont to assume in anger; for their blood is active and restless.][12]

More than any other literary or even medical source, however, it is a biblical image, something that Northrop Frye would have called an archetype, that seems to be a vital element in Argenti's reaction and in the architecture of the entire novella. Scholars have demonstrated the paramount role of the Bible as *the* book of reference for literary works during the Middle Ages, when it served as a treasure trove of quotations, images, and inspiration as well as a key to reading, understanding, and interpreting reality.[13] Both the Old and the New Testaments use the metaphor of "the cup of the Lord's wrath," implying that wrath can be drunk as a beverage. Psalms (74:9), Isaiah (51:17), and Jeremiah (25:15), to mention only the major books, speak about this unusual cup from which the impious draw. A passage from Revelation on the damnation of idolaters is extremely instructive because it connects all the elements examined above (wine, wrath, and fire):

> Si quis adoraverit bestiam et imaginem eius et acceperit caracterem in fronte sua aut in manu sua et hic bibet *de vino irae Dei* qui mixtus est mero *in calice irae ipsius* et cruciabitur *igne* et sulphure in conspectu angelorum sanctorum et ante conspectum agni et fumus tormentorum eorum in saecula saeculorum ascendit nec habent requiem die ac nocte qui adoraverunt

12 Seneca, *Moral Essays*, 206–7; trans. Stewart. The same image in Sirach 31.29–30 as well as in Plutarch, *Moralia* 68d. An overview of the presence of wine in Boccaccio's *Decameron* has been offered by Spani, "Il vino di Boccaccio."

13 See Bragantini, "Premesse sull'ascolto decameroniano," 72–3, and Battaglia Ricci, "La Bibbia nelle opere di Giovanni Boccaccio."

> bestiam et imaginem eius et si quis acceperit caracterem nominis eius. (*Nova Vulgata*, Revelation 14:9–11, emphasis added)
>
> [Anyone who worships the beast or its image, or accepts its mark on forehead or hand, will also drink *the wine of God's fury,* poured full strength *into the cup of his wrath,* and will be tormented in *burning* sulphur before the holy angels and before the Lamb. The smoke of the fire that torments them will rise forever and ever, and there will be no relief day or night for those who worship the beast or its image or accept the mark of its name].[14]

The metaphor wine equals wrath emerges in high relief from this passage, as do the punishments that idolaters will suffer: fire and smoke, tortures, and perennial restlessness. We find the latter element in Dante's description of the wrathful, who keep moving and never rest, and address their impulses, if not against others, then against themselves by grinding their own teeth or biting their own lips. The smoke from fire and sulphur comes, instead, from biblical references to Sodom and Gomorrah. As we noticed, Dante places the wrathful expiating in Purgatory in a thick cloud of smoke, where the dark haze is also a reflection of these sinners' mental blindness.

Frye locates the corresponding New Testament passage for the grape harvest of wrath mentioned by Isaiah[15] in the same apocalyptic context of Revelation (14:18–20): here the colour red, wine, blood, and the grape harvest are bound together and associated with God's wrath and indignation.[16]

These references strongly suggest that the counter-prank planned by Ciacco on Biondello is founded on the biblical metaphor of wine equals wrath, which is visibly alluded to by the use of an actual flask into which Filippo is to pour his vermilion liquor. The bottle is an emblematic object that participates in the literal level of the metaphor

---

14 In the same chapter (14:8) the author applies to Babylon the image of "the wine of her licentious passion" (see also 16:19 and 19:8.5).

15 "Torcular calcavi solus, et de gentibus non erat vir mecum; calcavi eos in furore meo et conculcavi eos in ira mea. Et aspersus est sanguis eorum super vestimenta mea, et omnia indumenta mea inquinavi" [The wine press I have trodden alone, and of my people there was no one with me. I trod them in my anger, and trampled them down in my wrath; their blood spurted on my garments; all my apparel I stained (Isaiah 63:3)].

16 See Frye, *The Great Code*, 153–4. Frye also reminds us how vital was such an image: it reaches "The Battle Hymn of the Republic," whose famous line "He is trampling out the vintage where the grapes of wrath are stored" inspired the title of a novel by John Steinbeck, *The Grapes of Wrath* (217–18).

and then leaves the scene relatively quickly. In other novellas, instead, real objects are part of the puns and innuendos, and remain present: for instance, in *Decameron* VIII.2.41–4, Lady Belcolore and the priest from Varlungo build their erotic language around a real mortar and a real pestle that, alluding to their sexual counterparts, are exploited at the second level of the metaphor as well.[17]

What confuses the issue in *Decameron* IX.8 is the fact that the real meaning of the metaphor remains veiled from most of the actors at play. Only Ciacco possesses the key to decoding the riddle. The middleman simply repeats, without thinking, what he was told, and Argenti smells only the provocative sense of challenge present in the jargon words that he cannot understand. The same can be said of poor Biondello, who barely hears part of the request before being beaten almost to death. Only Ciacco as the screenwriter, who was presented at the beginning as a word creator, the narrator, and the readers are aware of everything. To adopt Saussure's and Genette's terminology, for the various addressees the signified has a different meaning or no meaning at all.

addressor		*message*		*addressee*
	signifier	*signified*	*referent*	
Ciacco	wine	?	?	middleman/ Argenti/ Biondello
Ciacco	wine	wrath	wrath-in-action	brigata/readers

The presence of a metaphor renders the communication process more complicated. As I.A. Richards would say, Argenti grasps only the superficial side of the metaphor, that is the "vehicle," whose "tenor" remains veiled, and therefore he unleashes his irrational outburst because of a failure in logic (Richards, "Metaphor," 87–138).

A possible parallel can be found in the above-mentioned novella of Ricciardo and Catella (III.6). In that story, Catella thinks that her husband (Filippello) is cheating on her, and she plans to join him in the

17 On the importance of metaphors and emblems in the *Decameron*, see Fido, "Retorica e semantica nel 'Decameron,'" 94–9.

public baths where he is supposed to meet with his lover. Filippello is, however, unaware of everything and the whole thing has been arranged by Ricciardo, who is in love with Catella and manages to have sex with her precisely because she believes that the man in the bathroom is Filippello. In this instance, too, there is need for a dark fog that makes the misunderstanding successful: the room has no windows, and Catella does not speak because she fears that her (alleged) husband might discover her identity. Here the exchange is not a verbal one: *two people* (Ricciardo and Filippello) are mistaken for one another, whereas Argenti (like Biondello) fails to recognize the metaphorical link between *two things* (wine and wrath). Yet, Argenti and Catella share the same degree of wrath and blindness and cannot see what their eyes are supposed to see. When Catella vents her anger on the person she thinks is Filippello (but who in fact is Ricciardo), she calls him three times a "dog" (III.6.34–6), the typical animal counterpart for a wrathful person.[18] The fact of the matter, however, is that *she* is the real wrathful dog, and her very name, Catella, an affectionate diminutive for Caterina, is also the Latin word for a female puppy. Because of her anger, Catella is as blind as Argenti: she confuses people, attributes, and words.

If we look for similar procedures and results in terms of metaphors and linguistic puns in the *Decameron*, the novella of Alibech (III.10) can be of invaluable help. The sexual experience of Alibech with a monk called Rustico is described as a pleasing exorcism through the metaphor of the Devil that has to be put back into Hell. In that story, the girl experiences the substance of the metaphor (having sex with a man) but is not able to decode it because she does not know what sex is. Rustico, the women in Capsa, the narrator Dioneo, the listeners, and the readers, all of whom know what sex is, possess the key to interpreting the two levels of the message. Alibech's naïve ignorance reappears in Biondello, who has no opportunity to understand the message because he hears it from Argenti only an instant before tasting his wine (that is, being beaten by him). Ciacco, on the contrary, who is present at the scene, the narrator who tells the story, and the audience who hears or reads it have in their hands the key to understanding what the metaphor refers to, that is Argenti's wrath. The opposite situation – one, that is, in which the characters using metaphors are very conscious of their meaning – is in the above-mentioned novella of Belcolore and the priest from Varlungo: although in the presence of other characters who ignore

18 See the analysis of the novella by Swennen Ruthenberg, "The Tale of Ricciardo and Catella (III.6)," 126.

their allusions, the woman and the priest adopt erotic innuendos, and even actual objects, to convey a sexual message that they both perfectly understand.

Alibech cannot grasp the metaphoric sublimation of sex because she is a pure and naïve virgin girl and therefore does not know what sex consists of. On the contrary, Biondello only misses the link between the metaphor and its meaning, because (we can assume) as a man he must have experienced wrath on other occasions. In both cases, the senses and meanings (through sex or wrath) triumph over the letter – no matter what their verbal equivalent is. This reminds us of the Introduction to the Fourth Day, where Filippo Balducci tries to repress his son's sexual appetite for the women they encounter by calling them "goslings." In spite of that degrading term, the young boy would like to take one of those "goslings" with him. The word gimmick, a not-functioning metaphor with a euphemistic nuance from Balducci's point of view, collapses again under the pressure of carnal reality.[19]

This procedure of saying something that entails a different degree of awareness among the listeners is very similar to so-called tragic irony, where the audience already knows an event that the protagonists do not yet know but refer to with ambiguous words. When Argenti speculates about the person behind the odd request ("a instanzia di cui che sia" [by someone or other (IX.8.23)]), he in fact enacts an ironically tragic pattern: as the audience already knows, it was somebody else (Ciacco, and *not* Biondello) who formulated the question.

The novella of Ciacco and Argenti can be therefore labelled as a new version of "the parody of the *adaequatio rei et intellectus*."[20] From the point of view of Argenti, of Biondello, and of the middleman, the words in question do not have any particular logical relation but are merely used to provoke a negative reaction. More broadly, it is the same characterization of Filippo Argenti that places the plot in the list of the novellas that tell stories of pranks against gullible people, who are easily swayed also for their innate instability of character. On top of being wrathful, Filippo is described as "come colui che *piccola levatura* avea" [short tempered by nature (IX.8.17, emphasis added)]; that is, he was "di mente corta, di poca riflessione e giudizio."[21] Such a portrayal perfectly matches naïve people (often women, like Catella and Alibech, as well as children), who end up being the butt of puns and practical

19 See Duyos Vacca, "Converting Alibech," 222–6, and Baxter, "*Turpiloquium* in Boccaccio's Tale of the Goslings," 822–5.

20 This formula derives from Sinicropi, "Il segno linguistico del 'Decameron,'" 195.

21 Zingarelli in *Le opere di G. Boccaccio*, 431.

jokes – as Argenti himself notes: "paioti io fanciullo da dovere essere uccellato?" [do you think you can make a fool out of me as if I were some kid? (IX.8.25)]. For instance, Boccaccio says that Lisetta "*piccola levatura* avea" [got all worked up very easily (IV.2.41, emphasis added)] precisely when she confided to a close friend what happened to her (that the Archangel Gabriel had fallen in love with her), and in doing so she revealed that she had been deceived. Frate Alberto, the trickster in that novella, exploits both her simplicity and her vanity. The same happens with Lady Agnesa and friar Rinaldo, when the latter tries to demonstrate through scholastic logic how obliged she is to him for his being godfather of her child, which soon leads Agnesa to yield to Rinaldo's sexual request because she "loica non sapeva e di *piccola levatura* aveva bisogno" [was no logician and needed very little to be persuaded (VII.3.22, emphasis added)].[22]

The naïvety of the deceived as well as a certain degree of vanity are thus prerequisites to the success of a prank. In the novella in question, we find gullibility in Argenti, whose wrathful behaviour makes him unable to reflect – his mind is as blurred as that of the wrathful in Purgatory. Vanity, on the other hand, belongs to Biondello, described at the beginning of the novella as "something of a dandy."[23] The beating he receives and his fall in the mud remind us of the gluttonous in *Inferno* 6: not only Ciacco but also Biondello, always eager to enjoy a free meal from his upper-class friends, can be considered a glutton worthy of the same punishment.[24]

This web of connections among the characters of the novella, who mirror and counterbalance one another, has a further twist. Ciacco and Argenti share some remarkable traits: when Ciacco realizes that he will not have the delicious dinner his stomach was expecting, Boccaccio says that he "in sé non poco *turbatosene*, propose di dovernel pagare" [got really upset and resolved to pay him back (IX.8.11, emphasis added)]; when Argenti cannot catch the middleman, he "era rimaso fieramente *turbato*" [was left in an absolute fury (IX.8.23, emphasis

---

22 According to Fanfani (in Boccaccio, *Il Decameron*, 2:137), this expression hides a "metafora presa da arche o pietre, o simili, le quali sono murate, o fissate così leggermente che poco ci vuole a smuoverle" [metaphor taken from tombs or stones that are walled up or fixed so lightly that they are easily shifted] as in *Decameron* III.8.68. See also Fontes-Baratto, "Le thème de la 'beffa' dans le 'Décameron,'" 29.

23 As Rebhorn wittily comments in Boccaccio, *The Decameron*, 933.

24 As underlined by Ferreri, "Ciacco, Biondello e Martellino," 232–3. The critic also illustrates the similarities between this prank and the episode of Ciampolo (who was a "barattiere" like the middleman in our novella) in *Inferno*.

added)]. Afterwards, as Ciacco, the "morditore," "tutto pieno di belli e di piacevoli *motti*" [always had a wealth of witty, amusing things to say (IX.8.4)], Argenti "non era uomo da *motteggiar* con lui" [was not the sort of man to joke around with (IX.8.28, emphasis added)]. The first linguistic symmetry implies that both Ciacco and Argenti suffer from the same disease, to wit anger, which twice becomes the reason for the prank that follows. The second symmetry is based on Ciacco's ability to shape language, and on Argenti's attempt to defy it. For the *motto* hits the nail on the head, and Argenti's reaction against the "motteggiare" of his counterpart implicitly confirms the success of Ciacco's endeavour.

The entire weight of the misunderstanding, or rather, of the failed understanding of the metaphoric *motto*, falls physically back on Biondello, who does not have a chance to defend himself from Ciacco's vengeance. Biondello must have forgotten his colleague's prophecy and, failing to heed the suggestions Machiavelli was to give, he did not try to prevent the downturn of fortune with his own skills and actions. In addition, the counter-prank's results are much heavier than the first one's: Ciacco simply did not have the opportunity to taste the lampreys, whereas Biondello only apparently did not drink Argenti's wine – in fact he has a feeling that he had a lot of it (IX.8.31). When Argenti bursts out with "Che 'arrubinatemi' e che 'zanzari' mi mandi tu dicendo a me?" [Why did you send somebody to me talking about "rubifying the flask" and "little drinking buddies"? (IX.8.25)], and Biondello, caught unawares and soundly beaten, continues to ask what those words mean, the "good vermillion wine" has already overflowed from the barrel, but neither of the two characters seems to have realized it.

Solomon and Emilia, or the King and I: A Reading of *Decameron* IX.9*

ALBERT RUSSELL ASCOLI

Queen Solomon

In a very short story from *Decameron* Day Six – which, however, has remarkably expansive thematic-structural implications – the narrator, Emilia, fourth of seven female members of the "lieta brigata," briefly satirizes the pretensions of a young girl named "Cesca," who was, and still is, "più che una canna vana e a cui di senno pareva pareggiar Salamone" [vainer than a reed, to whom it seemed that in wisdom she was the equal of Solomon (VI.8.10)].[1] Characteristically sly, Boccaccio here anticipates another, much longer, story of that same Emilia, which follows the fortunes of two young men who "domandan consiglio a Salamone" [ask Solomon for counsel (IX.9.1)], told in the penultimate position of Day Nine, the day over which she rules as queen.[2] In the latter and later case, however, it is Emilia herself who apparently identifies with the wisdom of Solomon, whose enigmatic counsel she invokes in order to illustrate her thesis that "la universal moltitudine delle femine dalla natura e da' costumi e dalle leggi [deve] essere agli uomini sottomessa" [the universal multitude of women is subordinate to men, by nature, by customs, and by laws (IX.9.3)], and that said men

* My thanks to Martin Eisner, Corey Flack, Ronald Martinez, Roberta Morosini, Regina Psaki, Barbara Spackman, and especially Susanna Barsella and Simone Marchesi for suggestions that have made this essay better.

1 My reading here of Emilia and problems of gender, governance, and epistemology that cluster around her builds on an earlier essay, Ascoli, "Auerbach fra gli Epicurei," esp. 149–51. This and all citations of the *Decameron* throughout the essay are to Branca's 1980 edition. Translations are my own.

2 In addition to IX.9, Solomon's name appears in only two other stories – first in VI.8, then twice in VI.10 (par. 16 and 47).

should use both the threat and the reality of violent beatings in order to enforce their legitimate and necessary dominion. Although in one sense the story told in IX.9 is consonant with the underlying anti-feminism of VI.8 – and the recourse to physical violence an extreme alternative to the failed attempt by Cesca's uncle to cure the silly girl of her narcissistic foolishness with a witty *motto* – from another perspective, as we shall see, it is Emilia herself who, both in her story and in her rule of the *brigata* in Day Nine generally, invites derision in her willingness to appropriate the stature of the traditional paragon of earthly wisdom in the domain of human governance.

The title I have given to this *lectura*, in fact, calques a traditional debate, variously represented in the later Middle Ages and Renaissance, between "Solomon and Marcolf," the former, in this instance, the spokesperson of, among other things, a learned (and qualified) philogyny which is repeatedly and thoroughly routed by the earthy wisdom of a canny peasant.[3] While Boccaccio may or may not have been familiar with some version of this dialogue, and while his, and Emilia's, "Salamone" draws, as we will see, on a patchwork tradition in which the name of Solomon and the biblical and post-biblical texts associated with it are invoked for both pro- and anti-feminist purposes, I evoke it heuristically to give a sense of the deep complexities and ambiguities invested in IX.9. As we will also see, these complexities emerge in the relationships that exist between the story of Solomon's counsel told in IX.9 and the figure of Emilia,[4] most especially the

3 Bose, "From Exegesis to Appropriation," 189, 193–198; Ziolkowski, ed., *Solomon and Marcolf*. The earliest extant manuscripts of the dialogue date from the fifteenth century, though references to the pairing of Solomon and Marcolf go back to the eleventh and there was wide diffusion of the text in the later Middle Ages (Ziolkowski, "Introduction," in *Solomon and Marcolf*, esp. 6–16). I am indebted to Martin Eisner for calling this tradition to my attention.

4 The name Emilia, and the variant Meliana, or Emiliana, was used by Boccaccio in four works prior to the *Decameron* (*Comedia delle ninfe fiorentine*, 20.5–6; 21 (all); 44.3; 47, ll. 19–21 [Emilia, a former nun, now married to someone "grazioso" – etymon of Giovanni, as in *Paradiso* 12.80 – then allegorically identified with Astrea and Justice]; *Amorosa visione*, 44.25–30 [identified allusively only, but again as a former nun now married "tal che me' saria non fosse"]; *Teseida, o delle nozze di Emilia* [a principal character throughout]; *Rime* 69, "Contento quasi," ll. 35–6 ("e Meliana [or "emiliana"] è colei, / Di Giovanni di Nello, ch'è dop'ella"). See the lucid summary of Francesco Tateo, *Boccaccio*, 8–9. These recurrences have sometimes been used to find a thread linking all the works in which the name appears, as well as to identify a person from Boccaccio's biography. For the biographical question, see Billanovich, *Restauri Boccacceschi*, 105–26. The key to making the connection between at least some of these earlier Emilias and the Decameronian Emilia is the reference in her *novella* of Gianni

extraordinary, polemical preamble on gender politics (or gender and politics) with which she introduces the tale (IX.9.3–9), which in turn is linked to the larger context of her role as queen of Day Nine,[5] and indeed to a number of prior appearances in the *Decameron*. Thus understood, this *novella*, most commonly dismissed, when considered at all, as crassly repugnant in subject matter, or as thoroughly inept in the manner in which it is told, or both, nonetheless casts considerable light, and shadow, back over all of the preceding. And, as I will only be able to hint at here, the link between Emilia and Solomon, beyond even its centrality in the late medieval version of the "woman question," is the final instalment in a series of reflections, most visibly beginning with Emilia's "mirror-song" of self-love and/or self-knowledge in the first *ballata* of the *Decameron*, in which the structural, narrative-thematic, function known as "Emilia" becomes a privileged Boccaccian vehicle for assessing key problems of epistemology.

Lotteringhi to an alternate version in which the protagonist's name, like [e]Meliana's consort in "Contento quasi," is Giovanni di Nello (VII.1.33; cf. VII.2.10). While any naïve biographism has been discredited, the persistent Emilia/Meliana/Emiliana–Giovanni di Nello connection is clear, though its significance in the *Decameron* is not. An interesting attempt to define Emilia's identity in specific historical terms is in Richardson, "The 'Ghibelline' Narrator in the *Decameron*." The Decameronian Emilia has also been interpreted allegorically: by Ferrante, "The Frame Characters of the *Decameron*," 214, 224 (Emilia is said to be Prudence, which Ferrante conflates with Wisdom more generally, but which is in fact foresight or practical intelligence, the form of knowledge embodied by Solomon; see also n. 54 below) and by Kirkham, "An Allegorically Tempered *Decameron*", 131–71 in *The Sign of Reason in Boccaccio's Fiction*, esp. 149, 161, 168–9 (Emilia is the theological virtue of Faith ["the evidence of things unseen"]), followed by Smarr, *Boccaccio and Fiammetta*, 199–201. While I do not accept Emilia as an allegorical cypher, both of these identifications do point to the epistemological dimension of the character with which I am concerned here. Directly relevant to this study is Markulin, "Emilia and the Case for Openness in the *Decameron*," who sees a recurrent focus on problems of interpretation in some of the stories told by Emilia (I.6, IX.9, X.5, and esp. VII.1), and assigns her a key structural-thematic role in the book, a role that, he notes, is signalled by her speaking "baldanzosamente," boldly and aggressively, in both her first appearance (I.6.2) and her last (X.6.2; on the latter, see n. 47 below). Kircher, *The Poet's Wisdom*, 133–43, 251–6, sees her as "the most perplexing and intriguing of the *Decameron* narrators" (252). In a recent cluster of six essays in the 2013 special issue of *Annali d'Italianistica* dedicated to the macrotext of the *Decameron*, with special attention to the role of the ballads, Dino Cervigni assigns a key place to Emilia in the work's system of values. See, especially, "The *Decameron*'s Ballads" (see also n. 64 below).

5 Day Nine as a whole has generally received less attention than other days, for reasons addressed below. For overviews of the day, see Peirone, "Per aver festa"; Cleaver, "Authorizing the Reader," 11–18 et passim (her specific analyses concentrate on IX.3, 5, 9, 10) (see also note 34 below); and Gittes, "'Dal giogo alleviati.'"

All that said, it should already be clear that the object of this *lectura*, known as *Decameron* IX.9, should be read not simply as "a story," but as a complex textual unit, which includes not only the twenty-six conventional paragraphs of the *novella* proper (IX.9.10–35) but also the seven introductory paragraphs (IX.9.3–9; by far the longest narrator's introduction in the *Decameron*),[6] not to mention the initial summarizing rubric (IX.9.1) and the response of the *brigata* to the preceding story (IX.9.2). What is more, to appreciate fully the significance of "IX.9" means grasping, as just suggested, its role within the "macrotext" of the *Centonovelle* as a continuation of and gloss on much that has gone before and as a precursor and foil to some of what comes after.[7] I will, however, begin by rehearsing the story and the critical controversies that have surrounded it, offering some thoughts of my own about how to read the tale, with a focus on the enigmatic and enigma-generating figure of Solomon. I will then proceed to survey a series of primarily intratextual contexts against and within which it should be read, with a view both to providing additional instruments for interpreting IX.9 and to demonstrating the crucial role it plays in the larger economies of the *Decameron*, including the overarching problem of gender politics, the tale's situation within the series of stories told in Day Nine and (to a certain extent) in Day Ten, and, finally, its intrication with the figure of Emilia as it appears throughout, in the ways already sketched above.

Emilia's Tale of Solomon

The story told in the final twenty-six paragraphs of *Decameron* IX.9 is one of the relatively rare examples of historical-mythical narrative that

---

6 At seven paragraphs and 438 words, the two closest are both in stories of Panfilo – in I.1 (Ciappelletto/Cepparello; five paragraphs, 343 words) and VI.5 (Giotto; six paragraphs, 319 words).

7 On Emilia as queen of the day, see also the Introduction to this volume by Barsella and Marchesi. Other readings I have done of single *novelle* (conspicuously IV.2 and VII.9) have similarly moved between the story's diegesis (its plot) and "metadiegetic" or "(pseudo-)paratextual" features that surround and condition the telling of the tale. See "Boccaccio's Auerbach" and "Pyrrhus' Rules," first published, respectively, in 1992 and 1999. I say "pseudo" because while the passages that describe the activities of the *brigata*, the preambles of the narrators, the responses of the listeners, and so on, are paratextual vis-à-vis the stories, they are themselves part of a framing story, a *diegesis*, to which the interventions of the Boccaccian "I" (especially in the *Proemio*, the Introduction to Day Four, and the Author's Conclusion) in turn stand as paratexts. On the complexities of the *Decameron*'s structure from this perspective, see especially Fido, *Il regime delle simmetrie imperfette* and "Architettura"; and Picone, "Autore/narratori."

abandons the present and immediate past of Boccaccio's own world for an ancient setting, in this case, presumably, the time and place of Solomon, the Old Testament king.[8] The tale recounts the intertwined *vicende* of two men, Melisso and Giosefo,[9] who, for different reasons, are seeking out Solomon to see if his famed wisdom will provide an answer for their respective problems. Melisso's problem is that he is unloved and apparently unlovable despite vast expenditures on the entertainment of prospective friends. Giosefo's problem is that he has an intractably contrarian wife, "più che altra femina ritrosa e perversa" [more than any other woman, obstinate and perverse (IX.9.12)], who systematically refuses to do his bidding.

Having met, as if by chance, on the road to Jerusalem from Antioch, the two strike up a provisional friendship (curiously at odds with Melisso's problem of friendlessness) and proceed to Solomon's court, where each receives a brief and enigmatic response from Solomon, who is not otherwise explicitly characterized, although he clearly brings some complex biblical and medieval baggage with him. Giosefo is told: "Va al Ponte all'Oca" [Go to the Goose-Bridge]; more concisely still, Melisso is told imperatively: "Ama" – i.e., "Love" (IX.9.14–15). Neither is immediately enlightened by what he hears, and they return homeward, together, in disappointment. Each, subsequently, comes to an understanding of what he believes Solomon's hidden message to him to have been, Giosefo at far greater length than Melisso.

In a two-part narrative sequence, then, Giosefo decides he has found the key to Solomon's words and puts his newfound knowledge into

8 Baratto, *Realtà e stile* (1970), 24, notes three others (V.1, VII.9, and X.8), plus four set in the earlier/legendary Middle Ages (I.3, III.2, X.9, and X.10).

9 The names Melisso and Giosefo also have associations with an ancient past, though specifically *not* with the time of Solomon, thus reinforcing a timelessly legendary quality in the story. Melissus/Melisso was known to Boccaccio as a member of the fifth-century-BCE Eleatic school of philosophy, which rejected sense experience as a basis for knowledge and preferred rational argumentation. Melisso the philosopher is mentioned in *Amorosa Visione*, 4.45–8, without being assigned specific ideas, in the company of a long list of great thinkers. Boccaccio has a known propensity both for giving characters Greek or pseudo-Greek names (Filostrato, Panfilo, Pirro, Nicostrato, et alii; see again my "Pyrrhus' Rules") and for introducing characters with the names of classical philosophers, as in V.1 (Aristippo; possibly also Cimone alluding to Timon) and X.8 (Aristippo again; possibly also Gisippo, alluding to Chrisyppus; and Sofronia, named after the philosophical concept of Temperance), and so on. As we will see (esp. n. 16 below), there is also a Dantean connection. Giosefo's name, while clearly carrying Jewish associations, is harder to pin down, with possible links to Jacob's youngest son, the Virgin Mary's earthly husband, or the historian Flavius Josephus (on this last see n. 23 below).

action, thus apparently solving his marital problems. This sequence takes up the majority of the story proper (eighteen out of twenty-six paragraphs), and its contents have rendered the story profoundly repellent to most modern readers, sponsoring the savage beating of first a mule and then a wife as the means of imposing the male will to domination on animal and woman alike. Arriving at a bridge, name at first unknown, the two men witness a muleteer beating his animal with a *stecca* or *bastone* to make it cross said bridge. The two young men, on their horses, invite the man to use his "ingegno" [wit] to "menarlo bene e pianamente" [lead him along nicely and easily], but the muleteer replies, "Voi conoscete i vostri cavalli e io conosco il mio mulo" [you know your horses, and I know my mule], continuing to beat the animal until it finally consents to cross the bridge (IX.9.19–20). Upon then learning that the bridge is called "Ponte all'Oca" (IX.9.21), Giosefo believes he has now grasped the lesson Solomon intended him to learn, namely that he should beat his wife into submission, like the muleteer his mule. This he does, at length and in reasonably graphic detail, with his own "baston tondo d'un querciolo giovane" [rounded rod from a young oak tree (IX.9.28)],[10] after his wife, showing her usual arrogant disobedience, fails to prepare the meal he wished to serve Melisso. The result is that the following day, as Melisso again witnesses, and clearly approves, she now does as she is bid, with a further result for the two men: "il consiglio [di Salamone] prima da lor male inteso sommamente

10 "Giosefo … se n'andò in camera, dove la donna, per istizza da tavola levatasi, brontolando se n'era andata; e presala per le trecce, la si gittò a' piedi e cominciolla fieramente a battere con questo bastone. La donna cominciò prima a gridare e poi a minacciare; ma veggendo che per tutto ciò Giosefo non ristava, già tutta rotta cominciò a chieder mercé per Dio che egli non l'uccidesse, dicendo oltre a ciò di mai dal suo piacer non partirsi. Giosefo per tutto questo non rifinava, anzi con più furia l'una volta che l'altra, or per lo costato, ora per l'anche e ora su per le spalle battendola forte, l'andava le costure ritrovando, né prima ristette che egli fu stanco: e in brieve niuno osso né alcuna parte rimase nel dosso della buona donna, che macerata non fosse" [Giosefo … went into the bedroom, where the woman, having left the table grumbling in vexation, had gone. Taking her by the braids, he threw her down at his feet and commenced to beat her with this rod. The woman first began to shout and then to threaten, but seeing that for all of that Giosefo wasn't letting up, already thoroughly pounded, she began to beg for mercy in the name of God that he might not murder her, adding that she would never again do anything that wasn't pleasing to him. But Giosefo was having none of it, rather, with still greater fury than before, he went on beating her roundly now on her ribs, now on her hips, now on her shoulders, seeking out the seams in her body, nor did he stop until he was exhausted. In short, no bone, nor any other part on the backside of the good dame remained that was not beaten to a pulp (IX.9.28–30)].

lodarono" [the counsel of Solomon, at first poorly understood by them, they now praised most highly (IX.9.33)].

In a very brief concluding paragraph, the problem of Melisso is ostensibly resolved as he consults another wise man as to the meaning of Solomon's advice to him:

> E dopo alquanti dì partitosi Melisso da Giosefo e tornato a casa sua, a alcun, che savio uomo era, disse ciò che da Salamone avuto avea; il quale gli disse: "Niuno più vero consiglio né migliore ti potea dare. Tu sai che tu non ami persona, e gli onori e' servigi li quali tu fai, gli fai non per amore che tu a alcun porti ma per pompa. Ama adunque, come Salamon ti disse, e sarai amato." Così adunque fu gastigata la ritrosa, e il giovane amando fu amato. (IX.9.34–5)
>
> [After some days Melisso left Giosefo and returned to his home, and told to a wise man what he had heard from Solomon, who then replied to him: "No truer nor better counsel could he have given you. You know that you love no one, and that the honours and services that you do for others are done not for love that you bear anyone, but for show. Love, therefore, as Solomon told you, and you will be loved." Thus was the obstinate wife punished and the young man in loving became beloved.]

In this almost comically abbreviated form, the case of Melisso has largely been treated as a foil to that of Giosefo – and in fact I too will treat it in that light, though with a different emphasis.

The tale of Solomon's advice and its aftermath has been among the least studied *novelle* of the *Decameron*,[11] notwithstanding its length, its position within its day and within the work as a whole, not to mention the virulence with which it rehearses and develops the topic of female inferiority and subjection. It may be that this very virulence – and specifically the repugnant doubling of scenes of extreme physical violence against an animal and a woman, subscribed to as morally acceptable by both male characters as well as by the narrator – has led critics to avert their gaze from the tale.[12] If that interpretation is apparently

---

11 As far as I know, there is not a single critical essay devoted exclusively to this *novella* in the last one hundred years (see Branca, "Introduzione," cxiv–cxv, in Boccaccio, *Decameron* [1980]); the most extensive treatments of it are those of Cleaver, "Authorizing the Reader," chap. 4; Gittes, "'Dal giogo alleviati,'" 402–6; and Cervigni, "The *Decameron*'s Ballads," 164–70. See also n. 5 above.

12 Typical of this reaction are Baratto, *Realtà e stile* (1970), 386–7; Cazalé Bérard, "Filoginia/Misoginia," 125–6; and Vasvári, "'Buon cavallo e mal cavallo,'"

belied by the attention paid to "The Scholar and the Widow" (VIII.7) and, in its own way, the tale of Griselda (X.10), it might be because those tales lend themselves more easily to a recuperative allegorization that at least partially neutralizes the significance of the violence done to women in them. It may also be that the quality of the story *as story* has been deemed poor, a judgment in keeping with the general lack of interest in Day Nine. In any event, the story has received somewhat more attention recently, for three different, though closely interrelated, reasons. In the first place, the increasingly sharp focus on questions of gender in the *Decameron* and elsewhere in the Boccaccian oeuvre has made it much, much harder to ignore this story, and has in fact solicited a number of "reparative" or "recuperative" readings designed to suggest that, at the very least, Boccaccio problematizes, if he does not in fact ironically reverse, the story's surface misogyny.[13] In the second place, in part overlapping with the first critical theme, an interest in the problematics of interpretation as a central concern of the *Decameron* has also led critics to gravitate to the issue of how Solomon's advice is interpreted by the characters, as well as by the work's internal (the *brigata*) and external ("us") readers and, to a certain extent, by the story's narrator, and, again, to seek to re-valorize the story along with its author.[14]

---

esp. 330–5. Vasvári (334) does note that the responses to the story are divided by gender (women muttering, men laughing, IX.10.2), but still sees Boccaccio's tale as essentially anti-woman. See also the incisive comment on the story and the *brigata*'s divided response to it in Savelli, "Riso," 368.

13 The first critic to make this argument was Shirley S. Allen, "The Griselda Tale and the Treatment of Women in the *Decameron*," 9. The current version of this strategy of reading can be traced back to Millicent Marcus, "Misogyny as Mis-reading," though she does not mention IX.9. And it has been developed repeatedly in attempts to counter the apparently pervasive misogyny of the *Corbaccio*, for example by Hollander, *Boccaccio's Last Fiction*, and Psaki, "'Women Make All Things Lose Their Power.'" For the application of this strategy to *Decameron* IX.9, see again Psaki, ibid., 7, 9, and "Voicing Gender in the *Decameron*," esp. 103, as well as Migiel, *A Rhetoric*, 148–59. On the notion of "reparative" reading as an antidote to what Paul Ricoeur and many others since have called "the hermeneutics of suspicion," see Sedgwick, "Paranoid Reading and Reparative Reading." I prefer "recuperative" here because the movement in question lacks the theoretical grounding that Sedgwick invokes, and instead seems to be motivated by a desire to make a favourite author and a contemporary ideology coincide.

14 Both Psaki, "Women Make All Things Lose Their Power" (7, 9) and "Voicing Gender in the *Decameron*" (esp. 103), and Migiel, *A Rhetoric* (148–59), make problematization of Giosefo's interpretation the key to their readings. While acknowledging the importance of gender in IX.9, Cleaver, "Authorizing the Reader" (75–88, 92–3), focuses exclusively on hermeneutic issues. Kircher, *The Poet's Wisdom* (254–5), and Sherberg, *The Governance of Friendship* (100–6), also note the focus on interpretation,

Finally, growing attention to Emilia's role in the *Centonovelle* generally has led a number of critics to consider the story, however grudgingly, with the aim of superimposing a positive image on this figure derived from readings of her song and some of her earlier stories on her role here and throughout Day Nine.[15]

To the question of how seriously we should take Emilia's assertion that "Buon cavallo e mal cavallo vuole sprone, e buona femina e mala femina vuol bastone" [Both good and bad horses want the spur, and good and bad girls both need the rod (IX.9.7)] – anticipating in figure the impending equation of "moglie ritrosa" and obstinate mule, as well as the *bastoni* that the muleteer will use on his animal and that Giosefo will apply to his wife – we will return a little later on. For now, let us consider three of the more interesting and compelling versions of the claim that the story resists or even subverts its apparent legitimation of the violent domination of women, and animals, by men, those of Marilyn Migiel, Natalie Ann Cleaver, and Regina Psaki.

Both Migiel and Cleaver argue that Giosefo's interpretation of Solomon's words through the scene at Goose-Bridge is questionable if not in fact erroneous. Migiel's argument (*A Rhetoric*, 152–6, 199n15) begins by connecting Boccaccio's Solomon to Dante's representation of the Old Testament king's status as the paragon of earthly judicial wisdom, which is linked to a discourse on the necessity of making rational distinctions rooted in human realities rather than abstract logic (*Paradiso* 13.103–26), a practice for which the ancient philosopher Melissus, to whom Melisso presumably owes his name, stands as a counter-example.[16] And she further connects Dante's representations

---

and both see Emilia as deliberately problematizing Giosefo's reading of the scene at Goose-Bridge.

15 This seems to be true of Markulin, "Emilia and the Case for Openness," who, as noted above (n. 4), was a pioneer in exploring the problem of interpretation in the *Decameron*, but who speaks very briefly about IX.9 despite its relevance to his argument (197), and even more so of Cervigni, "The *Decameron*'s Ballads," whose constant focus on Emilia's exemplary positive role in the book does not stand up well to a reading of IX.9 (164–70). Kircher, despite insisting on her "perplexing and intriguing" qualities (*The Poet's Wisdom*, 252) in the context of this story, also seems insufficiently attentive to the problems presented by the misogynist "preamble" to IX.9.

16 See also Cleaver, "Authorizing the Reader," 79–80. In Dante's account, Melisso (following an Aristotelian critique in the *Physics* [1.3]) is numbered among those who "andaro e non sapean dove" [set out, without knowing where they were going (13.125–6)] as far as the truth is concerned, and "sanza distinzione afferma e nega" [affirm and deny without making distinctions (13.116)], as against the very specifically defined wisdom of Solomon in matters pertaining to earthly governance and adjudication. Citations from *Paradiso*, as well as translations, are taken from *The*

to the biblical Solomon's request to God for the discriminating wisdom necessary for just rule and God's response:

> [Solomon:] dabis ergo servo tuo cor docile ut iudicare possit populum tuum et discernere inter malum et bonum…
> [God:] quia postulasti … tibi sapientiam ad discernendum iudicium ecce feci tibi secundum sermones tuos et dedi tibi cor sapiens et intellegens in tantum ut nullus ante te similis tui fuerit nec post te surrecturus sit (3 Kings 3:9–12)

> [Give your servant an understanding heart so that he can judge your people, and distinguish between evil and good … Because you asked … for the wisdom to exercise discerning judgment, I have done as you have requested, and I have given you a wise and understanding heart. Before you there has never been anyone like you, nor after you will anyone like you come forth.]

She then argues that Giosefo clamorously fails to live up to this standard of discerning judgment in his interpretation of the scene at Goose-Bridge, a failure highlighted by his connection with the Greek philosopher's namesake, Melisso.

Cleaver makes an intriguing argument, namely that in Solomon's most famous judgment – between two women each claiming a baby as her own – the Hebrew king deliberately proposes a violent and unacceptable solution, which would result in the baby's death, in order to elicit an empathetic and self-effacing response on the part of the true mother, after which he renders a final, just, judgment (1 Kings 3:16–28). On this reading, Giosefo's literalizing interpretation of what he sees at Goose-Bridge amounts to taking Solomon's judgment at face value and missing the opportunity to find a more humane solution to his problem (Cleaver, "Authorizing the Reader," 77, 80–4). Like Migiel's, then, Cleaver's argument ultimately depends on retaining a belief in the authority of Solomon as judge and counsellor, while undermining the use to which his counsel is put, at least by Giosefo.

Psaki, briefly but compellingly, goes a step further, to ask whether, if Giosefo had applied the imperative "Ama" ostensibly directed at Melisso to his own relationship with his wife, would that not have been a better solution than the one he adopted? Subsequently, other critics,

---

Divine Comedy of Dante Alighieri, Volume 3: Paradiso, ed. and trans. Durling, notes by Durling and Martinez. On Melisso as Melissus, see n. 9 above.

in apparent ignorance of Psaki's essay, have made points similar to this, and in particular expand the interpretation of "Ama" by linking it to a Christian "caritas," set in opposition to what they see as the literalist, legalistic interpretation of the Jewish Giosefo.[17]

As we proceed, I will suggest that there are, indeed, a number of ways in which Boccaccio hints that the story, and indeed the complex of "IX.9" as a whole, should not be taken at face value, even as he positions it as a kind of climax (or, perhaps, better, "ante-climax," since it precedes and prepares Day Ten) and a turning point within the themes and structures of the *Decameron*. First, however, there are some questions to be posed to the reading of the story as internally "self-subverting," and specifically to the two characters and the two pieces of advice Solomon gives them. That there is a wide gap between the command "Va al Ponte all'Oca" and the example of the mule being beaten, and a further gap between the example and the moral drawn from it, is unquestionable. However, for me there is a nagging suspicion that the story does in fact push the reader in the direction that Giosefo then takes, a point borne out by the "murmuring" of the women after hearing it (IX.10.2). One problem is that in the magical world of fiction there is no such thing as coincidence, so it is not really possible to assume that the Solomon of this tale did not "foresee" or entail a specific encounter at "Goose-Bridge" that would, in some way, constitute the answer to Giosefo's question, though of course not necessarily in the way Giosefo thinks it does. Second, why would Solomon go out of his way to tempt Giosefo with a solution that would result in grievous bodily harm to his wife, since the remedy of beating for stubbornness is, if not the correct interpretation of what is seen, surely the most obvious? Most important, for our purposes, is the name of the bridge, which has, in fact, not been interpreted by critics, despite some obvious connotations, along with a rather unexpected and significant intertext not previously identified. The first of these connotations is that of animality in general, which, we have already begun to see, is a theme central to the story (Emilia's equation of women and horses; Giosefo's equation of

17 Kircher, *The Poet's Wisdom*, 255, and Cleaver, "Authorizing the Reader," 80–1, simply point to the contrast between the recourse to violence and the counsel to love. Cervigni, "The *Decameron*'s Ballads," 166–9, and Gittes, "'Dal giogo alleviati,'" 404–5, develop the Jewish vs. Christian reading, ostensibly elaborating a suggestion of Janet Smarr in a rather different context ("Altre razze ed altri spazi nel *Decameron*," 144) and have begun to advance the idea that the episode stages a confrontation between Jewish law and Christian charity. For the difficulties with using the imperative "Ama" to support this reading, see nn. 19, 20 and 21.

his wife and a mule), and which recurs at critical points throughout Day Nine.[18] The second, more particularly, is that of a noisy intrusive goose as potentially a stereotypical representative of female behaviour, along the lines of the "papere" in the Boccaccian narrator's story in the Introduction to Day Four. What is perhaps most remarkable about the passage is that it appears to have its origins in the prior Solomonic tradition, and there in a context that is clearly relevant to the use Emilia and/or Boccaccio are making of the Old Testament king in IX.9. And this in turn will point us to the question of exactly how much we can rely upon Solomon's authority to underpin a recuperative interpretation of the story at whose centre he sits, also given the fact that the first person to invoke and to rely upon that authority is Emilia, and for purposes very different from those of the above-cited critics.

What, then, about Melisso's "Ama"? The deliberate combination – whether by Emilia or Boccaccio or both – of the two different types of *quaestio*, one modelled generically on a widely diffused variant of the topos of the "taming of the shrew," the other narrativizing a commonplace of classical philosophy,[19] would suggest that we are deliberately invited to compare the two cases. This is also suggested by the carefully opposed outcomes in violent domination, on the one hand, and, presumably if not demonstrably, a turn to self-effacing love, on the other.

18 On the importance of animals and animal imagery throughout the *Decameron*, see Stoppino, "Contamination, Contagion and the Animal Function in Boccaccio's *Decameron*," esp. 99–103, on Simona and Pasquino (IV.7), a story told by Emilia, and 111–12 on the tale of Talano's wife (IX.7), which Emilia says inspired her choice of this *novella*. See also Ó Cuilleanáin, "Man and Beast in the *Decameron*," as well as Gittes, "'Dal giogo alleviati,'" esp. 285–7, and the essays by Grace Delmolino and Max Matukhin in this volume. Animals and animal imagery are featured prominently in Emilia's definition of her queenship (VIII.Concl.3–5) and again in IX. Intro.2–3 (and at least two other stories she tells feature animals and animality: II.6 and VII.1). The two most important stories of this kind in Day Nine, both closely connected to IX.9, are IX.7 and IX.10. The presence of a leading character name "hog" (Ciacco) in IX.8 may also be relevant. See also n. 55 below.

19 As Kircher, *The Poet's Wisdom*, 252n67, also points out, the locution's proximate source is clearly a topos of classical philosophy, "si vis amari, ama" [if you wish to be loved, love], a phrase found in Seneca and by him attributed to a Greek philosopher, the Stoic Hecato of Rhodes (Seneca, *Epistolae ad Lucilium* 1.9.6). The connection is made crystal clear in the reformulation of the Solomonic imperative by the wise man at the end of the story: "Ama adunque, come Salamone ti disse, e sarai amato" [Love, therefore, as Solomon said to you, and you will be loved (IX.9.34)]. Branca's note to this passage in the cited edition mentions Seneca, Ovid, Martial, and echoes of these in a number of late medieval texts (2:1099). The Senecan *motto* may in fact be compatible with Christian *caritas* as a love that grows by being shared (cf. *Purg.* 15), but the story does not emphasize this fact.

The added, apparently gratuitous association of both stories with Solomon seems further to push the reader in the direction of seeing them as alternatives to one another.

On the other hand, we should, solomonically, make some distinctions as to how far the parallelism between the two cases can be taken. Giosefo's issue is heterosexual – how to make male-female relationships work; Melisso's is, at least implicitly, homosocial: he seeks the "love" of his peers among the citizenry, which means, in the social world of fourteenth-century Florence, Boccaccio's mixed-gender company notwithstanding, an all-male world. From this point of view, one might well argue that he has, in effect, solved his problem before he ever hears the wise man's interpretation of Solomon's word.[20] Melisso's already friendly relationship with Giosefo is consummated in a male bonding, which in this case specifically takes place around the successful subjugation of a woman. This reading is further strengthened if we recognize that in the original Senecan context, the phrase "si vis amari, ama" is specifically deployed in a discussion of (male-male) friendship, not sexual or marital love.[21] And, in fact, the origin of "Ama" in Seneca, as against, say, the Gospel of John (13:34), should also and a fortiori lead us to doubt attempts to turn Giosefo and Melisso and/or the two pieces of advice they receive into representatives of the old dispensation and the new, Judaism and the punitive law vs Christianity and the loving spirit. On the same point, as already noted, Melisso himself is nominally linked to a Greek philosopher – and one whose abstract rationalism Dante sets in specific opposition to Solomonic judiciousness – with no substantive indications that he is a Christian and no real follow-up

20 It is especially telling that Giosefo specifically addresses Melisso as "amico" just as he is about to batter his wife (IX.9.26–7). Given the stress on Melisso's problem, it is hard not to see this use of the word as deliberate. And, further, given their laughter at the beaten woman's expense, it is even harder to see Melisso representing a real alternative to Giosefo: "[Giosefo] di ciò insieme ridendosi con Melisso, il divisò; e poi, quando fu ora, tornati, ottimamente ogni cosa e secondo l'ordine dato trovaron fatta: per la qual cosa il consiglio prima da lor male inteso sommamente lodarono" [[Giosefo], laughing together with Melisso about it, [laid out for his wife how he wanted dinner prepared]; and then, when it was time, they returned and found everything to have been done perfectly according to the orders given: on account of which, the counsel [of Solomon], which at first they had not understood, they now praised most highly (IX.9.32)]. It is worth adding that the laughter of the men of the *brigata*, as against the murmuring of the women, puts them on the side of Giosefo and Melisso (IX.10.2) – and perhaps recalls Dioneo's stricture that we tend to laugh at the harm of others, especially when we feel we are exempt from it ourselves (V.10.3).

21 Petrarch cites Seneca in the *De Remediis Utriusque Fortunae* (Dialogue I.50); on this see Fenzi, "Petrarca e la scrittura dell'amicizia," 564.

to show what he does with the interpretation of Solomon's counsel that he has received.[22] If anything, Giosefo, whose name might link him to Jesus' foster-father or to the Christianizing author of the *Jewish Antiquities*, has a somewhat more obvious associative connection to Christianity and its complex relation to the Jewish tradition.[23]

Of course, the real key to recuperative readings of the story told in IX.9 is the enigmatic figure of Solomon/Salamone, whose authoritative wisdom is seen by so many recent critics to be misinterpreted by Giosefo (and with him Melisso) or indeed to have already supplied, hidden in plain sight, the kinder, gentler alternative to the *bastone* deployed at Ponte all'Oca in his command to Melisso. I have pointed to the convergence of questions of gender relations and of interpretation at the heart of the story. It is obvious that Solomon produces difficult utterances in need of being interpreted by the two men, on one hand, and the audience of the story, on the other. Though less explicit, it should also be clear that this Salamone, like Solomon, the judging king of the tradition, is himself an interpreter par excellence, whose reputed "sapientiam ad discernendum iudicium" [wisdom to exercise discerning judgment] is what draws Giosefo and Melisso to him and then permits him to judge the circumstances and needs of the two men and to provide them with their respective imperatives. In other words, in order to render judgment, a discerning, or critical, understanding of presented evidence, which I would call a form of interpretation, is required. Considerably less clear, however, is how the story's audience, its readers, are to interpret this Salamone in himself and, more specifically, how, if at all, he may be implicated in the problematic representation of gender relations that dominates both the story and Emilia's preamble to it.

The fundamental issue faced in trying to interpret the figure of Solomon in Boccaccio is the radical slippage between the very limited information we are given by the story and the wealth of competing accounts of Solomon available in the later Middle Ages. In the first instance,

22 Saint Paul has almost as low an opinion of the Gentile philosophers as he does of the stony-hearted Jews. See Colossians 2:8; 1 Timothy 6:20; 1 Corinthians 1:20.

23 See n. 9 above. The historian is particularly intriguing because of his role in rewriting the history of the Jews from a Christian perspective in a text central to medieval culture. Bose, "From Exegesis to Appropriation," 193–5, 197 and notes, assigns Josephus a pivotal role in the transmission of the Solomon story and specifically those aspects of it concerning the king's importance in debates over the character of women (and over men's attitudes toward women). In his *Genealogia Deorum Gentilium*, Boccaccio cites Josephus as an *auctor* among others on four occasions (I.iv.8, IV.lxviii.12, XIII.ix.1, x.1). See also Gittes, "'Dal giogo alleviati,'" 403–4.

already in the Bible there are multiple texts in which this personage appears (1 Kings; 3 Kings; 1 Chronicles) and of which he is said to be the author (Proverbs; Ecclesiastes; Song of Songs); there are Jewish and Christian commentaries on those texts; controversies over specific episodes in those texts; as well as the appropriation of the biblical figure in non-theological venues including collections of moral exempla like the *Disciplina Clericalis*,[24] in pre-Boccaccian *novella* compilations like the *Novellino* (*novella* 7), and in the Solomon and Marcolf dialogue tradition mentioned earlier. As has been amply demonstrated in relation to the medieval tradition as a whole, and to Dante in particular, Solomon's moral and theological status is quite uncertain, oscillating between the exalted vision of him as the paragon of earthly wisdom and the condemnation of him for his uxorious attachment to foreign women, an attachment which led him into idolatry and even put into question his ultimate salvation.[25]

Because of the Dantean connection, because of the structural role that Solomon plays in the story, and because of the emphasis on the problem of governance in Emilia's preamble (of which more anon), what interpretations of this figure there have been to date have emphasized Solomon as king, judge, and interpreter.[26] However, the two pieces of advice given can be seen as alluding to the negative counter-tradition of Solomon both as lover and, I will add, as uxorious, even idolatrous, husband.[27]

Boccaccio's awareness of the ambiguities surrounding Solomon, at least within a few years after writing this story, can be seen in the following passage from the *Genealogia Deorum Gentilium*, which has not previously been connected to IX.9, where Boccaccio uses the example of the Hebrew king to illustrate the proposition that even the wisest of humans are subject to weakness and error, even while defending

24 Alfonsi, *Disciplina Clericalis*. I thank Stefano U. Baldassari for suggesting the relevance of this latter text. On Boccaccio's relationship to the "wisdom" tradition generally, see Andrei, *Boccaccio the Philosopher*, esp. his "Introduction." See also n. 28 below.

25 On the medieval Solomon, see esp. Bose, "From Exegesis to Appropriation." See also Nasti, *Favole d'amore e "saver profondo"*, both on the medieval tradition generally and on its relevance for Dante's representation of Solomon in *Paradiso* 10–14, as well as Scancarelli Seem, "*Nolite iudicare*." Cleaver, "Authorizing the Reader," 77–80, gives a useful account of the figure's traditional ambiguities.

26 Typical are Gittes, "'Dal giogo alleviati,'" 404: "Solomon … appears as he does in Dante's *Convivio* 'in persona della Sapienza' (*Convivio* 4.5.2)," and Cleaver, "Authorizing the Reader," 80: "[t]his is Solomon the King and Judge."

27 See Cleaver, "Authorizing the Reader," 80.

himself from the hypothetical claim that his defence of pagan poetry is an example of such error:

> Salomon tamen adest, testis certissimus imbecillitatis humane. Huic scientia omnis concessa est [a Deo], divitie omnes et imperium grande, summa cum iustitia populos subditos tenuit, Deo templum edificavit mirabile, multa bona composuit, et tandem, iam etate maturus, tot honorum largitore postposito, conscenso offensionis monte, Maloch, Egyptiorum ydolum, flexis genibus adoravit. Quid ergo? Tu ne eris fortior Salomone aut circumspectione plenior? Fallimur de nobis nimium confidentes! Hec quidem negari non possunt, vera sunt! Attamen aliud belli genus michi cum erroribus gentilitiis est, quam Salomoni fuerit cum Egyptiaca coniuge, que, astu femineo advertens quoniam infelicis viri animam formositate sua laqueasset, et suos deos extollere avida, nunc amplexu venereo, nunc mellitis saviis, nunc blandiciis muliebribus, nunc petulca lasciviis, nunc precibus, nunc lacrimis, quas obsequiosissimas habent femine, nunc indignatione composita absque intermissione non diebus omnibus tantum, sed noctibus amantis viri animum impugnabat. O quam gravia et intolerabilia sunt dilectarum mulierum, et potissime nocturna, certamina! Hic tandem, dum timeret mulieris, quam summe diligebat, gratiam amictere, terga dedit, et viribus armate femine inermis succubuit. (*Genealogia*, 14.9.14–16)
>
> [Even if examples did not abound, Solomon is certainly a convincing proof of human weakness. He enjoyed at God's hand all wisdom, all wealth, great empire, held the Gentiles in just tribute, built a wonderful temple to God, wrought many good works; and yet in his old age forgot the Giver of so many honors, went up into the mountain of offence, and adored the Egyptian idol Moloch on bended knee. And will you prove stronger or more circumspect than Solomon? True, we deceive ourselves who trust too much in our own strength; the fact is true and undeniable. But my contention with paganism differs from that between Solomon and his Egyptian wife. Well aware in her woman's guile that she had ensnared the soul of an unhappy man with her beauty, and eager to glorify her own gods, she proceeded to ply him incessantly with amorous embraces, honeyed kisses, a woman's flattery, wantonness, prayers, and tears – a very ready means with her sex – nay, with assumed indignation; and thus kept up the attack upon her lover day and night as well. Ah, how strong and irresistible are the love assaults of women, especially at night. For fear of losing her favor whom he loved above all the rest, Solomon turned and succumbed without defense to the armed force of a woman's wiles.]

This Boccaccian Solomon, while he is indeed the wisest of humans (see also *Genealogia* 14.9.14), is not infallible, not above committing the gravest of spiritual errors. Here, it is true, Solomon is not himself seen as misogynist – quite the opposite, since he is uncritically philogynist – but he does become the *occasion* for Boccaccio's own fairly violent anti-woman outburst.

It is, however, the case that in the medieval misogynist tradition, Solomon does play a part, with various of his biblical utterances deployed on both sides of the question.[28] And, of course, the Solomon-Marcolf tradition tends to pit Solomon's judicious distinction between the goodness of some wives and the badness of others (e.g., *Solomon and Marcolf*, 54–7, Pt. 1, Dialogus 9a, 10a) against Marcolf's indiscriminately virulent attacks on all women and on wives in particular. Why is this particular tradition especially cogent in the present case? Because, in fact, it is a possible, tellingly symptomatic, and previously unidentified, source of the suggestive place-name, "Ponte all'Oca," which plays such a pivotal role in the story. In the version of the dialogue edited and translated by Jan Ziolkowski, we find the following, at the very beginning of the exchange between the two figures:

> SOLOMON: "Bene iudicavi inter duas meretrices que in una domo oppresserant infantem"
> MARCOLF: "Ubi sunt auce, ibi sunt cause, ubi mulieribus, ibi parabole"
> SOLOMON: "Dominus dedit scienciam in ore meo, ut nullus sit similis mei in cunctis finibus terrre" (*Solomon and Marcolf*, 54–5, Pt. 1, Prologue, 5a–6a)

> [SOLOMON: "I judged well between two prostitutes who had suffocated a baby in one house."
> MARCOLF: "Where there are geese there are disputes; where women there are words"
> SOLOMON: "The Lord gave me wisdom in my mouth, such that no one is like me in all the ends of the earth"]

28 Bose, "From Exegesis to Appropriation," esp. 196–8 and 201–3. Cazalé Bérard, "Filoginia / Misoginia," 125, links IX.9 to a misogynist tradition dating back to Solomon's Proverbs, without making specific intertextual connections. The pro- and anti-woman Solomons can often be found together in a single text. For instance, Alfonsi, *Disciplina Clericalis*, ch. 9, "de mala femina," cites Solomon as an authority for instructing men on the depravity of their wives (40, 42); while in ch. 14, "exemplum de puteo" (54), the misogyny of the story told (which in fact is a primary source of *Dec.* VII.4) is offset with a philogynist proverb of Solomon.

Now, this Solomon immediately recalls, in a boastful mode, the two episodes – the divine gift of a wisdom unique on earth and the Judgment between the women (the latter significantly rewritten, as the women become prostitutes and are guilty of infanticide) – with which the most authoritative version of the Hebrew king is identified throughout the tradition, while it is Marcolf who dismisses women as querulous geese. However, the connection to "Ponte all'Oca," which the Emilian Solomon indicates as the locus where Giosefo's problems will be solved, couldn't be more obvious, with the implication that, in fact, Giosefo's interpretation of what he sees is the one most likely intended by Solomon. How does Solomon mutate into Marcolf? Perhaps because he is a character in the story of a narrator who, like her Cesca before her, here fancies herself another Solomon, but has a world-view not unlike that of Marcolf (whose aphoristic syntax she may appear to echo in her own proverb: "Buon cavallo e mal cavallo vuole sprone, e buona femina e mala femina vuol bastone").

The Tale of Solomon and the *Novelle* of Day Nine

The reading I have just given of the story told in IX.9 emphasizes just how difficult it is to find an intrinsic remedy to the problem of the *novella*'s assertion not only of the hierarchical mastery of men both over the animal kingdom and over women, but also of the use of brute force as the best means of enforcing that mastery. As we have seen, recuperative readings of the story tend to emphasize the possibility that there is a discrepancy between the enigmatic counsel of Solomon and the interpretations given to it by the two principal characters, not to mention the reader; but we have now also seen that there is significant evidence to suggest that the misogynist interpretation is sponsored by the story itself, and especially by the "figure of the interpreter," Salamone/Solomon.[29] I have also suggested that – whatever the results of a reading of the story in isolation – the intertwined problems of interpreting its misogynistic violence, of interpreting the problem of interpretation itself, and of interpreting Solomon as "figure of the interpreter" all point toward the necessity of considering the figure of Emilia and the ambitious justification she gives for telling the story.

29 While the question of Solomon's second imperative, "Ama," still remains somewhat in abeyance, I do think I have shown that it is at least as easy to read it as a sign of a homosocial complicity among men as it is to take it as a real alternative to Giosefo's recourse to violence against his wife.

Before we turn to a detailed analysis of Emilia's preamble, seen in the light of her queenship in Day Nine, however, I want suggest that the meaning of the story is both reinforced and significantly qualified if we consider it in relation to evidently comparable *novelle* that come both before and after in Day Nine.[30] This detour is doubly sponsored by a general knowledge of how the *novelle* talk to one another throughout the *Decameron*, and Day Nine especially, and by the fact that in her preamble to IX.9 Emilia positively insists upon making such comparisons, when she states that "a così fatta considerazione [both her anti-woman screed and the subsequent illustrative story], come che altra volta avuta l'abbia,[31] pur poco fa mi ricondusse ciò che Pampinea della ritrosa moglie di Talano raccontò" [I was brought back to such-like considerations only a little while ago, although I have had them on other occasions, by that which Pampinea recounted of the stubborn wife of Talano (IX.9.6)]. The horrendous disfigurement of Margherita, "bizzarra, spiacevole, e ritrosa" [bizarre, unpleasant, obstinate (IX.7.4)], who perversely refuses to credit her husband's well-intentioned warning, in turn must be seen in relation to perhaps the most famously misogynist story in the *Decameron*, that of the scholar Rinieri's deliberate torture and disfigurement of the widow Elena in the previous day.

That further connection could be made simply in virtue of Pampinea's role as narrator of both stories, not to mention the similar numerical placement (VIII.7; IX.7), but becomes obligatory after we read Lauretta's comments as she introduces the next story:

> quasi tutti da alcuna cosa già detta mossi sono stati a ragionare, così me muove la rigida vendetta, ieri raccontata da Pampinea, che fé lo scolare, a dover dire d'una assai grave a colui che la sostenne, quantunque non fosse per ciò tanto fiera. (IX.8.3)

30 For instance, Cleaver's association of IX.9 with the story of Cavalcanti (VI.9) ("Authorizing the Reader," esp. 93–5). On the "connectivity" among stories in this day and with those in other days, see also the essay by Maria Pia Ellero in this volume.

31 This qualification, "come che altra volta avuta l'abbia," suggests one might think to look for other Emilian tales that reflect this perspective, but, unlike Pampinea, she is not consistently associated with anti-feminist narratives. The most likely candidate, as already noted, is the Cesca story (VI.8). Other possibilities are the Tedaldo story (III.5) and Madonna Dianora's well-intentioned but failed attempt to rid herself an unwanted suitor in X.5, discussed below. On IX.7, and its connection to Emilia and IX.9, see also the essay by Grace Delmolino in this volume.

> [almost all of us have been prompted to speak by something previously said, and so I am moved by the rigid vengeance of the scholar related yesterday by Pampinea to speak about another [example of vengeance] quite serious to him who suffered it, even if it was not so fierce [as the scholar's].]

Lauretta not only refers the *brigata*, and the reader, back to Pampinea's prior story, but also offers a version of the principle that each new story responds to and should remind us of earlier stories, a notion that evidently applies as much if not more to IX.7 and to IX.9 than to her own *novella*. In fact, as is well known, the misogynist ideology that Emilia affirms in her preamble, and that is illustrated variously by Pampinea in her two stories and Emilia in hers, was first advanced, in less violently disciplinary terms, as the *brigata* was being constituted as a socio-political entity, when Pampinea's initial proposal for forming the group was modified by Filomena and Elissa to ensure that what they identified as the native weaknesses of the seven women would be supported by male strength.[32] This perspective was then reinforced, and specifically linked to the activity of narration itself, by the comments with which Pampinea introduced her very first story, later to be echoed verbatim by Filomena, concerning the suitability of briefer stories to the limitations of female temperament and intellect.[33] In other words, IX.9

32 "Ma Filomena … disse: '… Noi [femine] siamo mobili, riottose, sospettose, pusillanime e paurose; per le quali cose io dubito forte, se noi alcuna altra guida non prendiamo che la nostra, che questa compagnia non si dissolva …' Disse allora Elissa: 'Veramente gli uomini sono delle femine capo e senza l'ordine loro rade volte riesce alcuna nostra opera a laudevole fine …' [Filomena said, "… we women are inconstant, riotous, suspicious, pusillanimous, and fearful, on account of which, I greatly fear that, if we do not have any other guidance than our own, this company will quickly disband …" And then Elissa said, "truly, men are the heads of women, and without the order they bring, rarely does any work of ours lead to a praiseworthy outcome" (Intro.74–6)]. On Pampinea as stand-in for, and dialogic interlocutor of, the Boccaccian narrator, see Barsella, "Travestimento autoriale e autorità narrativa nella cornice del *Decameron*." Emilia's abdication of authority near the end of the book stands in clear contrast with Pampinea's role as law-giver at its beginning. Nonetheless, as we shall see, Emilia too is in a complex relationship to the Boccaccian narrator and she is not wrong to see in IX.7 a precedent for her harsh view of female sovereignty. See also n. 33 below.

33 Pampinea speaks of "*i leggiadri motti; li quali, per ciò che brievi sono, molto meglio alle donne stanno che agli uomini, in quanto più alle donne che agli uomini il molto parlare e lungo*, quando senza esso si possa far, *si disdice*, come che oggi poche o niuna donna rimasa ci sia la quale o ne 'ntenda alcun leggiadro o a quello, se pur lo 'ntendesse, sappia rispondere: general vergogna è di noi e di tutte quelle che vivono. Per ciò che quella vertù che già fu nell'anime delle passate hanno le moderne rivolta in

is by no means an isolated and aberrant textual moment, as it has often been considered, but something very like a logical, if extreme, climax of a work-long thematics, to which it adds Emilia's "theorization."

On the other hand, Day Nine even more obviously provides a series of *novelle* that might well seem designed to counterbalance and implicitly critique Emilia's (and Pampinea's) attacks on their own gender. Though not in reference to IX.9, Tobias Gittes has recently pointed out that earlier in the day we were treated to three stories of especially clever and independent women (IX.1, IX.2, IX.6; Gittes, "'Dal giogo alleviati,'" 389–92, 398–9). Even more directly relevant is the thematic cluster constituted by the two Calandrino stories – IX.3 and IX.5 – with reference back to the first in the series, VIII.3, as well.[34] IX.3, the story

---

ornamenti del corpo; e colei la quale si vede indosso li panni più screziati e più vergati e con più fregi si crede dovere essere da molto più tenuta e più che l'altre onorata, non pensando che, se fosse chi adosso o indosso gliele ponesse, *uno asino* ne porterebbe troppo più che alcuna di loro: né per ciò più da onorar sarebbe che *uno asino. Io mi vergogno di dirlo, per ciò che contro all'altre non posso dire che io contro a me non dica'"* [graceful turns of phrase; which, because they are brief, are much better suited to women than to men, in as much as speaking at length is, when they can do without it, much less indicated in women than in men; even though today few women or even no woman at all remains who knows any graceful turn of phrase, or, to such a quip, even if she were to understand it, would she be capable of responding: it is the collective shame of us and of all women who are alive. And this is because that virtue which once in the past was in the souls of women, modern women have turned into ornamentation of the body; and she who is seen wearing the most dappled and adorned clothing believes she ought to be held to be worth more and to be honoured more than other women, never thinking that, if such praise were to belong to whoever put more on or upon herself, an ass would carry much more than any of one of them, nor would such a one be more worthy of being honoured than an ass. I am ashamed to say it, since I cannot say against other women what I do not say against myself (I.10.4–6, emphasis added; cf. VI.1.2–4)]. The critique of women who indulge in "molto parlare e lungo" resonates with the Marcolfian "ubi mulieribus, ibi parabole" cited above. It should be said that Pampinea herself tells the longest story in the *Decameron* (VIII.7) and that, while Emilia tells one of the shortest (VI.8), in IX.9 she too goes on at considerable length. Note that the twice-repeated comparison of an overdressed woman to an "asino" anticipates distantly the comparisons of women to horses and mules in IX.9 as well as IX.10. After all this, the story she tells involves the shaming of a Bolognese woman who attempts to use such a *motto* against her elderly lover, and so I.10, preamble and tale, ends up being doubly anti-woman. Note also that the woman's name, "Malgherida," anticipates that of Talano's wife (IX.7.4), and that, being Imolese, she is also from the Emilia-Romagna region, is an "emiliana" (see again n. 4).

34 Perhaps the most complete reading of the four-story Calandrino suite (despite the apparent limitation to the first tale) is in Martinez, "Calandrino and the Powers of the Stone," which has telling things to say about Calandrino and Tessa's relationship. Marchesi examines the interconnections between VIII.3 and IX.3

of Calandrino induced to believe he is pregnant, reinforced by IX.5, the *novella* in which his companions convince him that with the aid of a love-philtre he will succeed in winning the love and sexual favours of the beautiful Niccolosa, together propose a gender inversion that implies a rethinking of gendered identities and attendant roles. In contemplating the painful consequences of his supposed pregnancy, Calandrino is placed in the position of identifying with female corporality, and particularly with the dangers of labour, and his fantasy that it is Tessa's predilection for woman-on-top sex that has produced his dilemma completes the symbolic reversal of roles. The direct relevance of this story to Emilia's advocacy and positive representation of wife beating then emerges in the following story when Tessa finds the prostitute Niccolosa astride her husband, "a cavalcione," as if riding a *horse* – in anticipation of an image that we already have seen is fundamental to IX.9 both in Emilia's preamble and in the story itself and that will become even more so in IX.10 – in the very position he claimed his wife preferred (IX.5.56–62). This leads to the exceptional, if not entirely unprecedented in the *Decameron*, representation of husband beating,[35] with specific allusion to Calandrino's claim about the supposed origin of his "pregnancy":

> Monna Tessa corse con l'unghie nel viso a Calandrino, che ancora levato non era, e tutto gliele graffiò; e presolo per li capelli e in qua e in là tirandolo cominciò a dire: "Sozzo can vituperato, dunque mi fai tu questo? … Or non ti conosci tu, tristo? non ti conosci tu, dolente? che premendoti tutto, non uscirebbe tanto sugo che bastasse a una salsa. Alla fé di Dio, egli non era ora la Tessa quella che t'impregnava …" Calandrino, vedendo venir la moglie, non rimase né morto né vivo, né ebbe ardire di far contro di lei difesa alcuna: ma pur così graffiato e tutto pelato e

around the problem of interpretation (*Stratigrafie decameroniane*, 108–14) and focuses attention on the inverted sexual relationship of Calandrino and Tessa (esp. 132–4). In the run-up to her reading of IX.9, Cleaver also considers the Calandrino cycle around a problematics of interpretation ("Authorizing the Reader," 38–74). On Calandrino in Day Nine, see also the essays by Marcello Ciccuto (IX.5) and, especially, Federica Anichini (IX.3) in this volume.

35 Getto, *Vita di forme* (1966), 257–9, gives a list of husbands who are maltreated at the behest of their wives throughout the book, unhappily referring to the representation of the abuse of spouses of both sexes as "questo motivo scherzoso" [this humorous motif (259)]. Migiel specifically cites VIII.3 and IX.5 together with IX.9 as examples of spousal abuse, though she does not develop the implications of the sequence (*A Rhetoric*, 147). Her essay, however, was the first to pose the problem of "domestic abuse" as a category in the *Decameron* and IX.9 specifically (147–59).

> rabbuffato, ricolto il cappuccio suo e levatosi, cominciò umilmente a pregar la moglie … (IX.5.63–5)

> [Monna Tessa ran with her fingernails at the face of Calandrino, who had not yet been able to get up [from where Niccolosa had been astride him], scratched him all over with them; and grabbing him by the hair, and shaking him here and there, she began to say, "You dirty contemptible dog, so you do this to me … Don't you know who you are, wretch? Don't you know who you are, miserable man? Who, if you were squeezed out completely couldn't produce enough juice to make a sauce? God's faith, in this case it wasn't Tessa the one who was impregnating you …" Calandrino, seeing his wife coming … dared not defend himself against her at all; but, even as scratched and flayed and disarrayed as he was, grabbing his cloak and standing up, he began humbly to beg his wife …]

In other words, Giosefo's violence against his wife is closely anticipated by a more than justified instance of a wife's against her husband. In addition, both IX.3 and IX.5 specifically recall a prior example of wife beating (VIII.3.51–4) in the story of the "heliotrope." That beating, of course, was motivated not by any real fault of Tessa, but by Calandrino's need for a scapegoat to cover his own folly, which he (assisted by Bruno and Buffalmacco) justifies under cover of the clichéd generalization, with which the Emilia of IX.9 would be quite comfortable, that "le femine fanno perdere la virtù a ogni cosa" [women make everything lose its power (VIII.3.61)].[36] Calandrino, "little, fallen man," may, in retrospect, suggest the unreadiness and bad faith of the male sex more generally in claiming the responsibility that Emilia in her preamble and then in her story wishes to attribute to them.

Finally, at least as far as Day Nine is concerned, there is the story of Donno Gianni, Compar Piero, and Comar Gemmata told by Dioneo immediately after Emilia's *novella*,[37] implicitly but clearly responding to it, in the mode of parody and indeed of ridicule.[38] The triangular structure of men collaborating and/or competing around a woman's body is

---

36 This line of argument was suggested to me by Psaki's discussion of the quoted phrase (which she translates as her title), in "Women Make All Things Lose Their Power," 11.

37 This story has, if anything, been interpreted less frequently than IX.9. See, however, Matukhin's treatment of the tale in this volume, with his broad survey of work that has touched on it in one way or another.

38 See also the brief but cogent reading of IX.10 as response to IX.9 in Hollander and Cahill, "Day 10 of the *Decameron*," 122–3.

reasonably common in the *Decameron*, and in fact proliferates through Day Nine, beginning with the first story, but IX.10 does mirror the homosocial situation of Melisso, Giosefo, and Giosefo's wife in IX.9.[39] More importantly, the main plot point, the attempted metamorphosis of Gemmata into a "cavalla," parodically literalizes both Emilia's metaphorical equation of "buon cavallo e mal cavallo" with good and bad women and, of course, Giosefo's (mis)treatment of his wife as if she were a mule. In the process Dioneo turns back to what Emilia has just called the "sollazzevole," i.e., sexual, reading of the women's "need" for the *bastone*, i.e., the penis.[40]

Queen for a Day

By placing the tale of Solomon's counsel in the context of the other *novelle* of Day Nine, we have also begun to see how it stands in complex relation to two thematic strands that traverse much of the *Decameron*: one that subscribes to the reigning gender hierarchy of the late Christian Middle Ages, and one that implicitly contests and critiques that hierarchy. By turning now to examine more closely the figure of Emilia, the *novella*'s narrator, who is also queen of Day Nine, we will see that through her, and in particular through her deployment of and confused identification with the enigmatic character of Solomon, these two strands converge so as to starkly dramatize the failure of the *Decameron*, and presumably its author, to make a clear and morally efficacious distinction between them.

Despite the biographical, allegorical, and now interpretative-epistemological readings that have successively attached themselves to the name of Emilia in her recurrent appearances from Day One forward (see again note 4), the significance of her role as narrator of IX.9 has not been as carefully studied as it could be, nor, conversely, has the story been primarily read, as it seemingly demands to be, as a product of her highly motivated narration.[41] Emilia, to the extent that she appears

---

39 Migiel, *A Rhetoric*, 59, points out that IX.4 and IX.8 involve male-male rivalries, to which we could add IX.1 (the two frustrated lovers), not to mention both Calandrino stories (Bruno, Buffalmacco, and Maestro Simone).

40 Migiel, *A Rhetoric*, 143, argues, improbably, that Donno Gianni is not necessarily planning a sexual conquest from the beginning.

41 Only partial exception can be made for Migiel, *A Rhetoric*, 157–8. Kircher, *The Poet's Wisdom*, 252–3, 255; Sherberg, *The Governance*, 100–2; and Cleaver, "Authorizing the Reader," 75–95 passim (esp. 82) all refer to the preamble in subordinate relation to their analyses of the story Emilia tells and without analysing it in its entirety. As we will see, Kirkham, "Morale," esp. 249–50, 253, discusses Emilia's use of the

at all in readings of the story told in IX.9, has played an essentially passive and subordinate, one might even say "feminized," role, as one who serves as a relay between the subject of the tale and the Subject (i.e., author) of the *Decameron*, whether that relation is of (1) a misogynistic tale and narrator both directly attributable to a misogynistic streak in the book's author; (2) a misogynistic tale and a misogynistic narrator to an author who subverts both, or (3) an apparently misogynistic tale to a narrator who subverts that misogyny in harmony with the views of the author.

This does not mean, to be clear, that the "Emilia" who reigns in Day Nine and speaks in IX.9 is a fully realized character consistent and continuous with all other appearances of that name in the *Decameron cornice*. It would be folly to seek absolute continuity and consistency in any of the members of the "lieta brigata" as they appear throughout the *Decameron*, with the inevitable exception of Dioneo.[42] Yet, there are notable, if intermittent, textual signals, both explicit and implicit, which appear to attach individualizing identifiers to characters – and this, I claim, is true of this instantiation of "Emilia," who, in her dual role as queen of Day Nine and introducer-teller of IX.9, is as extreme and polarizing a character, in her own way, as Dioneo, with whom, crucially, she shares a subversive relationship to the exercise of authority.[43] Indeed, as already noted, the two are both paired and opposed in Day Nine, a connection that then continues into Day Ten.

In point of fact, Emilia's role as queen of Day Nine can be directly connected to her narration in IX.9. Most notably, her story has at its centre, projected as an emanation of the wisdom she intends to deliver, Solomon, *the* paragon of kingship in the Judeo-Christian tradition. Her reign is a very unusual one by the standards set over the first eight days. From the outset, a reader is invited to pay particular attention to it and to recognize that both she, as ruler, and the day as a whole over which she presides are heavily qualified in advance, even as the question and the problem of rule are forcefully posed.[44]

categories of moral allegory in the preamble, but then does not address the story itself.

42 Hollander, "The Struggle for Control," investigates what the text gives us to go on as concerns relations between the ten members of the *brigata* and cites several previous attempts at studying them singly and in relation to one another (see esp. 249n10). For previous discussions of Emilia in particular, see again n. 4.

43 An exception is Rumble, "Framing Boccaccio," 112–14.

44 It should be noted that readers of the day rather consistently take at face value and as a positive Emilia's claim to be conferring needed "liberty" on the *brigata*

To begin with, from Day One on, every prior designation of the "queen [or king] for a day" has been in some sense a real choice on the part of the outgoing sovereign. We might think, for instance, of Elissa's choice of Dioneo.[45] In this case, however, Lauretta's apparent choice between two (Emilia and Panfilo) is effectively reduced to one, both by the pressures of gendered numerology (the three men are distributed 4–7–10) and by a certain privilege that Panfilo has been accorded from the first story of the First Day on. Panfilo's special role is then ratified by the newly crowned Emilia's selection of him to sing the final song of Day Eight,[46] and in her anticipation of his "emendation" of her reign both as she assumes the crown herself and then in crowning him at day's end.

That Lauretta is not choosing a successor in accordance with her own better judgment becomes obvious immediately. Her coronation of Emilia is grudging at best, openly hostile at worst:

> Lauretta, conoscendo il termine esser venuto oltre al quale più regnar non dovea … levatasi la laurea di capo, in testa a Emilia la pose donnescamente dicendo: – Madonna, io non so come piacevole reina noi avrem di voi, ma bella la pure avrem noi: fate adunque che alle vostre bellezze l'opere sien rispondenti – ; e tornossi a sedere. (VIII.Concl.1)
>
> [Lauretta, recognizing the moment having arrived beyond which she was no longer to rule … lifting the laurel crown from her brow she placed it, in lordly fashion, on Emilia's head saying, "My Lady, I do not know how pleasant a queen we will have in you, but we will certainly have a pretty one: do therefore make it so that your works correspond to your beauties." And so she returned to her seat.]

Lauretta's haughty dismissal of Emilia as a vacuous beauty queen, negative in a way that no previous transition of this kind has been, is given substance immediately thereafter by her successor's eminently girly reaction:

> Emilia, non tanto dell'esser reina fatta quanto del vedersi così in publico commendare di ciò che le donne sogliono esser più vaghe, un pochetto

(most recently see Gittes, "'Dal giogo alleviati'"). Compare the introduction to this volume by Barsella and Marchesi.

45 See Ascoli, "Pyrrhus' Rules," 107–11.

46 Panfilo's song evidently contains a hidden meaning, which the *brigata*, however, is unable to ferret out (VIII.Concl.13), perhaps anticipating the foregrounding of allegory in Emilia's preamble to IX.9.

si vergognò e tal nel viso divenne quali in su l'aurora son le novelle rose; ma pur, poi che tenuti ebbe gli occhi alquanto bassi e ebbe il rossor dato luogo ... cominciò a parlare. (VIII.Concl.2)

[Emilia, not so much because she had been made queen, but seeing herself so praised in public for that of which women are usually most desirious, became a little embarrassed, and in her face she turned the colour that we see in newly bloomed roses at dawn. But then, after she had held her eyes down for a little while, and her blush had faded ... she began to speak.]

In missing Lauretta's overt scepticism regarding her potential for a rule that is "piacevole," not to mention intelligent and just, Emilia focuses exclusively on the compliment directed at her outward appearance.[47]

Her immediately subsequent definition of how the day's stories will be organized (or not) and her rationale for that definition may be read as giving further substance to Lauretta's thinly veiled contempt:

Dilettose donne, assai manifestamente veggiamo che, poi che i buoi alcuna parte del giorno hanno faticato sotto il giogo ristretti, quegli esser dal giogo alleviati e disciolti, e liberamente dove lor più piace, per li boschi lasciati sono andare alla pastura: e veggiamo ancora non esser men belli ma molto più i giardini di varie piante fronzuti che i boschi ne' quali solamente querce veggiamo; per le quali cose io estimo, avendo riguardo quanti giorni sotto certa legge ristretti ragionato abbiamo, che, sì come a bisognosi, di vagare alquanto e vagando riprender forze a rientrar sotto il giogo non solamente sia utile ma oportuno. E per ciò quello che domane, seguendo il vostro dilettevole ragionar, sia da dire non intendo di ristrignervi sotto alcuna spezialtà, ma voglio che ciascuno secondo che gli piace ragioni, fermamente tenendo che la varietà delle cose che si diranno non meno graziosa ne fia che l'avere pur d'una parlato; e così avendo fatto, chi appresso di me nel reame verrà, sì come più forti, con maggior sicurtà ne potrà nell'usate leggi ristrignere. (VIII.Concl.3–5)

47 If Emilia seems unaware of Lauretta's evident contempt for her, there is evidence that she has taken note: in Day Ten, her story of Madonna Dianora and the garden comes immediately after Lauretta's, and there she cuttingly dismisses Lauretta's claim to have offered an incomparable example of "magnificenza" (X.5.2–3 and 26). Emilia's polemic then sets off an intense interpretive *querelle* among the members of the *brigata* (X.6.1, 3–4). As noted earlier (n. 4 above), Markulin, "Emilia and the Case for Openness in the *Decameron*," 191–5, sees this sequence as a key part of the problematics of interpretation that attaches itself to Emilia.

[Delightful ladies, quite clearly we see that, after the oxen have laboured for part of the day under the restraint of the yoke, they are then loosed from under it, and freely are left to go where they please through the woods to batten. And we also see that gardens containing plants with various foliage are not less but indeed much more beautiful than the woods in which we see only oaks growing. On account of these things I estimate, taking note of how many days during which we have spoken under the constraint of specific laws, that, as those in need, it will not only be useful but opportune for us to wander freely, and in wandering renew our strength in order then to enter again beneath the yoke. And thus concerning that which is to be said tomorrow in your delightful narrations, I do not intend to restrain you under any special topic, but I wish that each one of you may speak about that which pleases you, firmly believing that the variety of things about which you will speak will be no less gracious than if you had spoken about one only. And having thus done, the one who comes after me as ruler will with greater confidence restrain you, who have been made stronger by this freedom, under the customary laws.]

Dioneo in his day (VII) had made an elaborate joke, containing a serious analysis, of the problem he faced in assuming the role of king after having successfully claimed exemption from obeying the laws of the daily sovereign.[48] Emilia, by contrast, simply abdicates responsibility,[49] noting, in anticipation of her discourse on male governance, that the ruler, by default male, who comes after her will then be able to restore the order she has refused to impose.[50] Even more to the point, her analogy equating her fellows in the "lieta brigata" with oxen anticipates the key references to beasts of burden scattered throughout the day (see again note 18 above), notably, of course, the degrading equation of women with horses and mules in IX.9 and IX.10, and it may suggest a degraded and dehumanizing conception of the group's activities.[51]

---

48 Ascoli, "Pyrrhus' Rules," esp. 103–7, as well as Sherberg, *The Governance of Friendship*, esp. 153–8, 179–80.

49 For a very different reading of this passage, and of Emilia, see Gittes, "'Dal giogo alleviati,'" esp. 381–3. See also the essay by Maria Pia Ellero in this volume.

50 That she relies on Panfilo to make all right again is clear enough from the language she uses here ("chi appresso [etc.]"), and then from her charge to him at the end of the day (IX.Concl.2, cited in the text below).

51 Note that Emilia's characterization of the activities of the *brigata* as a kind of labour runs generally counter to the "recreational" and playful definitions much more often assigned to them, definitions that will be widely reaffirmed during Day Ten, notably by Panfilo in X.9, with phrasing that seems to target specifically not only Filomena (the preceding speaker) but also Emilia: "E se noi qui per dover correggere

In fact, the stories that follow in Day Nine clearly bear the stamp of the queen's un-ruly, unstructured regime, with several of the *novelle* either explicitly referring back to prior tales or evidently employing narrative formulas already tried, thus suggesting a generalized failure of creative imagination, rather than the liberating effect Emilia promises.[52] Whether this phenomenon is more reflective of the fact that the *inventio* of the storytellers (or of Boccaccio himself) is nearing exhaustion as the stock of tales to be told runs low, or of Emilia's failure to provide creative stimulus and guidance, is uncertain. Nonetheless, the manner in which her queenship is presented allows us seriously to entertain the latter possibility. In either case, Day Nine clearly serves as a necessary if generally underappreciated prelude both to the triumphal Day

---

i difetti mondani o per riprendergli fossimo, io seguiterei con diffuso sermone le sue parole; ma per ciò che altro è il nostro fine, a me è caduto in animo di dimostrarvi … una delle magnificenze del Saladino" [and if we were here to rebuke or to correct worldly faults, I would follow [Filomena's] words with ample speech; but since our goal is another, it has come into my mind to show you one of the magnificent acts of the Saladin (X.9.4)]. Panfilo seems here to step away from Emilia's charge to him at the end of Day Nine (IX.Concl.2; cited and translated below).

52 In Day Nine, repetitiveness is perhaps most obvious in the two Calandrino stories (IX.3 and IX.5), although both Filostrato and Fiammetta make a case that familiarity is a source of pleasure (IX.3.3; IX.5.3–5). IX.8 is explicitly connected by Lauretta to VIII.7, but is also linked to earlier stories (esp. V.8, VI.5, and VI.9) that include Dantean characters (cf. Olson, *Courtesy Lost*, 65–88 passim). Other examples are the descent into the tomb of Scannadio in IX.1, reminiscent of the latter part of the Andreuccio saga (II.5; as well as, as Migiel points out in *A Rhetoric*, of VIII.4); the story of the abbess and the nun (IX.2), which is a remake of the abbot and the monk (I.4), with allusion to the "pantsing" of the judge by Maso del Saggio in VIII.5; the story of the two Ceccos in IX.4, which is a less engaging version of the Giotto story (it actually bores the audience [IX.5.2]); the *novella* of Talano's dream, which is explicitly linked to earlier prophetic tales (esp. IV.5 and IV.6), and may recall the threat of wolves in V.3, and is also indebted to earlier examples of Pampinea's misogyny (I.10 and VIII.7); Dioneo's tale, finally, which is not only a parody of Emilia's horsification of women, but also of other tales told in which a hapless husband witnesses his wife having sex with another man (e.g., V.10, VII.2, VII.9, VIII.8, cf. II.10; on VIII.8's relation to other stories, see Holmes. "Doing unto Others"). The repetitive features of the day have long been recognized, without necessarily being cast in a primarily negative light. Peirone, "'Per aver festa,'" 149, speaks of Boccaccio's choice, through Emilia, of "liberty" in theme as a pretext for replication of prior themes, motifs, and locales. Migiel, *A Rhetoric*, 59, gives a cogent list of prior stories recalled, to which my own is partially indebted. See also Gittes, "'Dal giogo alleviati,'" 388–9, 400–2. Barolini, succinctly, says "more of the same" ("The Wheel of the *Decameron*," 538). See also Cleaver's discussion of the day's "crisis of creativity" ("Authorizing the Reader," 11–12, 16–17, 41–7, et passim). The editors of this volume, with equal persuasiveness, argue, as does Gittes, for the enabling power of the freedom Emilia confers.

Ten and the subsequent return to Florence,[53] whether as a much-needed moment of relative repose before returning to the "harness" or yoke of regulated storytelling or as a clamorous failure against which to measure the narrative successes to come.

From this point of view, then, the passing of the crown from Emilia to Panfilo at the end of the day is fraught with significance. At first, the transition seems to bear out Emilia's positive rationale for abandoning the "leggi" of thematic coherence, as well as confirming her assessment of the complementary and climactic role to be played by Panfilo:

> Ma essendo le novelle finite e il sole già cominciando a intiepidire, e la reina conoscendo il fine della sua signoria esser venuto, in piè levatasi e trattasi la corona, quella in capo mise a Panfilo … e sorridendo disse: "Signor mio, gran carico ti resta, sì come è l'avere il mio difetto e degli altri che il luogo hanno tenuto che tu tieni, essendo tu l'ultimo, a emendare: di che Idio ti presti grazia, come a me l'ha prestato di farti re." Panfilo, lietamente l'onor ricevuto, rispose: "La vostra virtù e degli altri miei subditi farà sì, che io, come gli altri sono stati, sarò da lodare"; e … disse: "Innamorate donne, *la discrezion d'Emilia*, nostra reina stata questo giorno, per dare alcun riposo alle vostre forze arbitrio vi diè di ragionare ciò che più vi piacesse; per che, già riposati essendo, giudico che sia bene il ritornare alla legge usata …" (IX.Concl.2–4, emphasis added)

> [But the *novelle* having been finished and sun already beginning to cool off, the queen, recognizing that the end of her reign had come, stood up and took off the crown, putting it then on the head of Panfilo. Smiling, she said, "My Lord, a great burden remains for you, namely that of having to make amends, you being the last, for my faults and those of the others who have occupied the place that you now hold. In this may God lend you grace, as he lent it to me in making you king." Panfilo, happily having accepted the honour, responded: "Your virtue and that of my other subjects will make it so that I, as the others have been, will be worthy of praise"; and, he then said, "Enamoured ladies, the discreet judgment of Emilia, who has been our queen this day, in order to give respite to your forces, gave you freedom to speak about that which pleased you most; so that, now being rested, I judge that it will be good to return to the customary law …"]

---

53 Cervigni, "Making Amends," 417–421, goes so far as to suggest that Panfilo's choice of topic is motivated specifically by Emilia's call for him to "make amends" for what has gone before. Cf. Hollander, "The Struggle for Control," 280.

While Emilia acknowledges that her "rule" may have been defective, she generalizes that defect to the other past queens and kings, and Panfilo brushes past the idea that amends must be made, attributing "virtù" to all of them and "discrezione" to Emilia in particular. In praising Emilia, however, he is also contradicting her, since he attributes to her precisely the faculty of judiciousness ("discrezione") she herself had just said in the preamble to IX.9 is proper to men alone in their capacity as natural rulers of women.[54]

Shortly thereafter, the new king specifically sets a topic for Day Ten, one that may be read as a polemical response both to Emilia's rule in Day Nine generally and to IX.9 in particular:

> "... voglio che domane ciascuna di voi pensi di ragionare sopra questo, cioè: di chi liberalmente o vero magnificamente alcuna cosa operasse intorno a' fatti d'amore o d'altra cosa. Queste cose e dicendo e faccendo senza alcun dubbio gli animi vostri ben disposti a valorosamente adoperare accenderà: ché la vita nostra, che altro che brieve esser non può nel mortal corpo, si perpetuerà nella laudevole fama; il che ciascuno che al ventre solamente, *a guisa che le bestie fanno*, non serve, dee non solamente desiderare ma con ogni studio cercare e operare." (IX.Concl.4–5, emphasis added)
>
> ["I wish that tomorrow each of you ladies think of speaking about the following, namely: about whoever has acted generously or indeed magnificently concerning the facts of love or some other thing. Speaking of and doing these things will doubtless incite your well-disposed souls to act valorously; because this life of ours, which can be nothing other than brief in the mortal body, will perpetuate itself in praiseworthy fame; which is what anyone who does not merely serve the belly, as the animals do, must not only desire, but with all zeal seek and carry out."]

---

54 "Discrezione" is a technical term allied to the practical virtues of justice and especially prudence (on Emilia and prudence, see n. 4 above), and thus aptly associated with governance. The cited uses represent two of three in all of the *Decameron*. Dante in *Convivio* defines the word thus: "la parte razionale ha suo occhio, con lo quale apprende la differenza de le cose in quanto sono ad alcuno fine ordinate: e questa è la discrezione" [the rational part of the mind has its eye with which it perceives the difference between things in so far as they are ordered to some goal: and this is discretion (I.xi.3:)]; see IV.viii.1, where he attributes the definition to Aquinas's commentary on Aristotle's *Ethics*. See also Ascoli, *Dante and the Making of a Modern Author*, 153 and n40.

In light both of Emilia's imagination of the *brigata* as oxen and of her conflation of women with horses and then mules, Panfilo's choice of a topic that serves to distinguish human beings from those who follow their appetites, "as the animals do," seems pointed indeed.[55] Day Ten will continue to offer responses to Emilia. Her own story provides a far milder version of Emilian anti-feminism, as Madonna Dianora tries to do the right thing in defence of her marital chastity, but errs in not turning the matter over to her husband, while her husband reproves her verbally, without any recourse to or even threat of the "bastone," and is ready to tolerate an offence to his honour in order to keep her from breaking her promise. In the very last story, of course, Dioneo dexterously manages to critique both Panfilo's ennobling "humanism" *and* Emilia's anti-feminism, with a story that features a husband's "matta bestialitade" [mad bestiality] contrasted with the implied "magnanimitade" [magnanimity] of his ever and overly patient wife – in what we can also now see is at once the apotheosis of Emilia's ideally subservient woman and a final refutation of IX.9's ideology of wise male governance.[56]

Emilia as and against Solomon

We now turn, at last, to a closer examination of Emilia's role in IX.9. As suggested from the outset, IX.9 is not just "a story" among others, but rather a larger textual unit containing the story of a story being told and of its teller, a teller who clearly enunciates not only the meaning that she intends her *novella* to communicate, but also principles of textuality and of interpretation that she applies, and expects her readers

55 The turn from animal to human as a reply to both IX.9 and IX.10 is noted by Cervigni, "The *Decameron*'s Ballads," 170.

56 Bruni, *Boccaccio*, 272n30, notes that Griselda's behaviour fulfils Emilia's strictures ("dee essere umile, paziente e ubidente oltre all'essere onesta" [she must be humble, patient and obedient, in addition to being virtuous (IX.9.4)]) to the letter. Cervigni, "The *Decameron*'s Ballads," 166, says that Giosefo's treatment of his wife is a "matta bestialità," comparing Giosefo to Gualtieri; he does not, however, hold Emilia as narrator as responsible for endorsing such behaviour. A more comprehensive comparison is in order, one that takes into account the structural-thematic relationship between Emilia's exaltation of male governance and Dioneo's ferocious critique of patriarchal tyranny. On the latter, and its relationship to the broader tradition of "law, nature and custom," with which we have seen here Emilia is also engaged in her preamble, see Barsella, "Boccaccio, i tiranni e la ragione naturale," esp. 149–59.

to apply, to that tale. Indeed, no story in the *Decameron*, this side of Dioneo's tales, is more ostentatiously bound up with the perspective of its narrator than that of Solomon's advice to Giosefo and Melisso. To put it more concretely, IX.9 not only is a viciously anti-woman story but also is told by a female character who demonstrates a violent antipathy for the female sex, and deliberately proposes to illustrate that antipathy for pedagogical purposes, using a radically distorted version of the pervasive late medieval model – what Judson Allen called the "ethical poetics" – of allegorical writing and reading.[57]

In addition to creating a general predisposition to suspicion regarding Emilia's storytelling in IX.9, the introduction to her queenship also prepares two topics that are central to IX.9: first, in general, the question of good and especially bad government, and second, and more specifically, the problem of women's fitness or lack thereof for (self-) rule. Both of these topics, of course, are tightly linked to the choice of Solomon as her protagonist and alter ego in the *novella*. At the same time, given her "hands off" approach to her role as queen, and what will become clear are her views of women's intrinsic intellectual limitations, Emilia's preamble to her story is extraordinarily ambitious and polemical. As noted earlier, it is longer than any other narrator's preamble in the *Decameron* by nearly one hundred words. Leaving aside the symptomatic importance of this "quantitative" indicator, I want to stress that in the attempt to define the subject of the story, the mode of signification that it uses, and the effect it is meant to have on readers, Emilia's preliminary remarks are comparable only to the Boccaccian narrator's reflections on his book (far more extensive, of course) in the *Proemio*, the Introduction to Day Four, and the Author's Conclusion. It is all the more curious then how little these seven paragraphs have figured in readings of the story, much less in any larger attempts to understand the "poetics" of the *Decameron* more generally.

Emilia's preamble is divisible into two parts, the first of which gives a rationalized justification for the need of women to be governed by men and the second of which supplies an allegorizing gloss of the proverb comparing women and horses. Both of these, as will be seen, align her in complicated ways with different aspects of the Solomonic tradition. She begins by offering the longest and most elaborate version in the

57 Allen, *The Ethical Poetic of the Later Middle Ages*. This is what Dante in a famous, if controversial, passage calls the "allegory according to the poets" as against "allegory according to the theologians" (*Convivio* 2.1). In the *Genealogia Deorum Gentilium*, Boccaccio's defence of poetry (including moderns as well as ancients) deploys a version of this model (14.10). See also nn. 59 and 61 below.

Decameron of the oft-repeated claim that women by law, custom, and nature are rightfully subject to male rule:[58]

> se con sana mente sarà riguardato l'ordine delle cose, assai leggermente si conoscerà tutta la universal moltitudine delle femine dalla natura e da' costumi e dalle leggi essere agli uomini sottomessa e secondo la discrezione di quegli convenirsi reggere e governare, e però, a ciascuna che quiete, consolazione e riposo vuole con quegli uomini avere a' quali s'appartiene, dee essere umile, paziente e ubidente oltre all'essere onesta, il che è sommo e spezial tesoro di ciascuna savia. E quando a questo le leggi, le quali il ben comune riguardano in tutte le cose, non ci ammaestrassono, e l'usanza, o costume che vogliamo dire, le cui forze son grandissime e reverende, la natura assai apertamente cel mostra, la quale ci ha fatte ne' corpi dilicate e morbide, negli animi timide e paurose, nelle menti benigne e pietose, e hacci date le corporali forze leggieri, le voci piacevoli e i movimenti de' membri soavi: cose tutte testificanti noi avere dell'altrui governo bisogno. E chi ha bisogno d'essere aiutato e governato, ogni ragion vuol lui dovere essere obediente e subgetto e reverente al governator suo: e cui abbiam noi governatori e aiutatori se non gli uomini? Dunque agli uomini dobbiamo, sommamente onorandogli, soggiacere. (IX.9.3–5)
>
> [If the order of things is considered with a sound mind, it will be very easy to understand that all the universal multitude of women is subordinate to men, by nature, by customs, and by laws, and that it is fitting that women be governed and ruled by them. Therefore, any woman who wishes quiet, consolation, and repose with those men to whom she belongs, must be humble, patient, and obedient, as well as being virtuously chaste, which is the highest and special treasure of any wise woman. And when to this end the laws – which are concerned with the common good in all things – do not instruct us, nor use, or custom as we may wish to call it, whose powers are great and worthy of reverence, then nature shows it to us quite openly, the which nature has made us delicate and soft in our bodies, in our souls timid and fearful, in our minds benign and pious, and which has

58 A number of critics have pointed out the close ties of Emilia's discourse to legal categories, traced back to Cicero through Aquinas (Kirkham, "Morale," 252–3, and esp. Sherberg, *The Governance of Friendship*, 100–2). I hasten to point out that the texts cited by these critics are rhetorical, philosophical, and/or theological and do not derive directly from the works (esp. Justinian; Gratian) being used in applied jurisprudence. Recent work of Justin Steinberg has, instead, begun to situate a number of Boccaccian *novelle* in relation to rapidly evolving practices of adjudication and law enforcement: see his "Mimesis on Trial."

> given us little bodily strength, pleasurable voices, and gentle movements of our limbs: all these things testifying to the fact that we are in need of being governed by others. And whoever is in need of being helped and governed, all reasons argue that they should be obedient, subject, and reverent before their governor: and to whom do we have as governors and helpers if not men? Therefore to men must we, honouring them in the extreme, submit.]

Note, the carefully rationalized, if somewhat repetitive, argumentative structure adopted by Emilia, which, from one perspective, seems to contradict her claims about the need wisely to submit to the greater wisdom of male governance. Emilia's apparent "philosophical" bent previews both the allusive recourse to the name "Melisso" and, again, the emblematic figure of Solomon as epitome of earthly wisdom and wise government.

Having given her own theoretical rationale for the subordination of women to men in all things, she then moves on to the practical problem of enforcing this regime upon "la universal moltitudine delle femine," whether they think they need it or not, with an authoritarian emphasis that is in stark contradiction to the "libertarian" regime she announced at the beginning of her rule. To this end, she introduces the previously cited illustrative proverb that at once previews the key animal metaphor – here equating women and horses, there women and mules – that will dominate Giosefo's story and spill over into Dioneo's parodic response, and then she aligns her tale with the pedagogical force of moral allegory.[59]

> Gli uomini un cotal proverbio [usano]: "Buon cavallo e mal cavallo vuole sprone, e buona femina e mala femina vuol bastone." Le quali parole chi volesse sollazzevolemente interpretare, di leggier si concederebbe da tutte così esser vero; ma pur vogliendole moralmente intendere, dico che è da concedere. Son naturalmente le femine tutte labili e inchinevoli, e per ciò a correggere la iniquità di quelle che troppo fuori de' termini posti loro

---

59 See again n. 57 above. Before Kirkham ("Morale," 249–50, 253) used this passage to claim that Boccaccio deploys moral allegory throughout the *Decameron*, it had gone virtually untouched. Since then, Migiel has treated it briefly (*A Rhetoric*, 157–8), while Cleaver, "Authorizing the Reader," 18, 81–8 passim, convincingly positions the story itself in a relation of critique to the tradition of moralizing allegoresis but does not discuss Emilia's words in detail. As Simone Marchesi has pointed out to me, the phrase "sana mente" in particular might recall *Purgatorio* 6, verse 36 ("se ben si guarda con *la mente sana*") in a context which also involves a question of interpretive difficulty.

si lasciano andare si conviene il baston che le punisca; e a sostentar la vertù dell'altre, ché trascorrer non si lascino, si conviene il bastone che le sostenga e che le spaventi. (IX.9.7–9)

[Men use a proverb such as this: "Both good and bad horses want the spur, and good and bad girls both need the rod." The which words, for whoever wanted to interpret them in a pleasurably amusing way, would easily be admitted by all women to be true. But if one wishes to understand them morally, I say that this too is to be conceded. Women are all naturally flighty and inconstant and for this reason the rod is needed to punish those who let themselves go beyond their proper limits; and to sustain the virtue of the others, in order that they may not let themselves transgress, the rod is necessary to support them and to frighten them.]

Having thus, to a degree virtually unprecedented in the *Decameron*, both pre-defined the meaning of her *novella* and previewed a mode of signification in relation to which it is to be understood, Emilia then states that she will tell the tale of Solomon's "consiglio" "sì come utile medicina a guerire quelle che così son fatte da cotal mal [i.e., disobedience]" [as a useful medicine for curing of such evil those with a like disposition (IX.9.7)],[60] though whether she does this in order to teach men to beat their wives or in order to frighten women into obeying their husbands, or both, is not entirely clear. What *is* evident is that she has explicitly abandoned the *brigata*'s primary goal of giving pleasure through storytelling for a rigidly didactic purpose.

It is, in fact, in relation to the framing recourse to the structure and language of moral allegory that we need to consider the problematics of interpretation *within* the story. More specifically, Emilia approximates the twofold structure of the moralizing allegory used primarily in the interpretation of non-biblical and especially classical texts – by assigning two meanings to the proverb.[61] The first, obviously, is sexual, and

60 It is noteworthy that Emilia focuses exclusively on what will become the Giosefo portion of the tale, opening the way to scholarly claims that her story contains a counter-narrative of which she is not in full control. As noted, however, I believe that it is possible to read the Melisso story as at least partially reinforcing that of Giosefo rather than of contradicting it.

61 Kirkham, "Morale," 249, invokes the fourfold model of biblical exegesis, as does Migiel, *A Rhetoric*, 258, in relation to this passage, without noting the inversion of literal and allegorical. In fact, as we have seen (nn. 57, 59 above), Boccaccio seems to be invoking the twofold "allegory of poets" rather than the biblical model. Later, in the *Genealogia*, he is careful to distinguish between the sacred theology of the Bible and the "physical theology" of poets (15.8), and specifically avoids the four

she quickly concedes its universal truth without further comment (and with no obvious resonance in this story – though, again, Dioneo at least alludes to it in the next one): all women, good and bad, want sex. The second, which is "moralmente da intendere," is that *both* good and bad women need either to be beaten (the latter) or to be in constant fear that they will be beaten (the former).

In the movement from one meaning to the other we might see a deliberate staging of an encounter between those readers, like those who have seen the *Decameron* as a delightfully salacious "pleasure craft" ("dulcis") and those, like Kirkham, who find in it an elaborate moral allegory of some kind ("utilis"),[62] although we would have to admit that the "useful" "moral" reading, at least in the case at hand, is quite unlike the usual form such readings take, and indeed seems quite perverse. And there is more: the passage gestures, in a curious and contorted way, toward the problem of literal vs. figurative language that is a, if not the, central concern of the Boccaccian narrator in both the Introduction to Day Four and in the upcoming Author's Conclusion. What is most striking (pun intended) is that the first meaning, structurally associated with the "letter" in moral allegory, is actually figurative: "bastone" stands in for the penis, while the second meaning, associated with the figurative meaning in moral allegory, is actually literal: a "bastone" is a "bastone," *punto e basta*.[63] The story, as we have already seen, then illustrates this point very specifically, and *literally*, by putting

---

senses of the biblical exegetes, although in the case of Dante, but not of himself or Petrarch, there is a sense that a comparison to the Bible might be in order (see Ascoli, "Blinding the Cyclops," 119–20 and nn 22–3, 125 and nn 42–3.

62 Cf. Kirkham, "Morale," esp. 252–5.

63 From one perspective, the first meaning is actually not so different from the second – in the world of the *Decameron*, that is – since the need for sex (the voracious need of, say, an Alibech) also implies both a subjection to the male member and an untrammelled desire in need of violent discipline. Interestingly, Baratto, *Realtà e stile* (1970), 386–7, notes the affinities, reading III.10 as "sollazzevole" in Emilia's sense; cf. Migiel, *A Rhetoric*, 157–8. On this reading it is noteworthy that, in the proverb, "vuol" in the "sollazzevole" sense designates active desire in a woman (a male member is what she truly *wants*), while in the moral sense it mandates her passive subjection to male power (a drubbing with a club is what she *is in need of*, whatever she may think or want). For a reading of Boccaccio's representation of disruptive female sex drive as liberating rather than confining, an expression of female agency rather than a projection of male fantasy (with specific reference to II.10), see Barolini, "'Le parole son femmine'" in *Dante and the Origins of Italian Literary Culture*, 281–303, 442–47, this essay first published 1993. Barolini's astute discussion of the function of sexual metaphors in the *Decameron* (297–302) could be applied in this case to explain Emilia's movement from figurative to literal as mapping onto her apparent desire to contain the "mobility" of her sex.

bastoni in the hands first of the muleteer and then of Giosefo (IX.9.17, 20, 28, 30). And it is from this perspective that it becomes almost impossible to deny that Salamone/Solomon is present in the story, at least according to the intention of Emilia, to lend his authority in support of the violent subordination of women to and by men.

In confirmation of this association, finally, we should note that Emilia's inversion of poetic allegory may, perhaps, have at least one specifically biblical original in mind. As is very well known, Solomon's Song of Songs presented exegetes and theologians with ongoing problems regarding both its highly charged sexual content and the apparent highlighting of its putative author's lascivious and uxorious character. In that case, of course, it is the literal sense that matches up to the "sollazzevole" interpretation, which in Emilia's hands becomes figurative, but remains first in order of exposition. The second, "moral" meaning is far from the Christological and ecclesiological meanings that the exegetical tradition assigned to the Song, but it too, as we have already seen, matches up with the misogynistic uses to which the figure of Solomon was sometimes put, and in particular to the Solomon and Marcolf tradition.

It is, then, as necessary as it is impossible to take Emilia's *predica* and her following tale seriously as representatives of the thematics and the poetics of the *Decameron*. It is *necessary* because of clearly delineated connections to (1) a dominant thematic strand that is common to all three narrative levels of the book and (2) the problematics of polysemous signification, made possible by the figurative quality of Boccaccio's language, to which the book's author returns again and again. It is all the more necessary because of the culminating position of the story both in Day Nine and in the economy of the *Decameron* as a whole. But it is *impossible* because Emilia herself is a personified contradiction, and deeply confused to boot. She is a female ruler (however temporary) who uses her reign as a bully-pulpit to advocate for female submission and to propagate the virulent dehumanizing topoi of misogyny. She deploys rational argument to prove female irrationality. Perhaps most notably, she makes a total hash of her attempt to claim for her discourse the force of moral allegory, by inverting the hierarchical relationship between literal and figurative on which allegory is founded.

Now all this might be taken as an argument in favour of seeing IX.9 as a whole, if not the story taken in isolation, as a self-subverting critique of misogyny, were it not for the fact that in so doing we apparently end up affirming Boccaccio's apparent attitude of contempt toward his female mouthpiece. At the heart of this muddle is Emilia's Cesca-like identification with her personal version of Salamone/Solomon: Emilia not only appropriates the authoritative figure of Solomon in support of her exemplary illustration of male governance of women, but also aligns herself with key, heterogeneous, elements of the Solomonic tradition, including both a claim to special wisdom concerning the legal, customary, and natural basis of gendered hierarchies and the deployment of allegorical interpretation to transform an erotic proverb into a "moral" lesson. In so doing she reveals her own great distance from the best features of an idealized Solomon. As governor she oscillates between abdication of responsibility and violent authoritarianism. As gender theorist she is self-subverting, advancing a theory of female incompetence that undermines her authority to articulate such a theory. As allegorist, she produces a travesty of medieval allegory and allegoresis, confusing literal and allegorical and promoting a "moral" justification for male violence against women. At the same time, I would argue, both her preamble and the story it introduces bring out the contradictions and confusions that in fact surround the figure of Solomon in medieval culture, making of him/it, as it were, and in a double anachronism, an ideological Rorschach test.

The Importance of Being Emilia

This reading, while affirming the crucial structural and thematic significance of Emilia, of the story she tells, and of the day over which she reigns, seen within the larger economy of the *Decameron*, has, by and large, taken a very negative view of all three. One of my aims here has been to counter the neglect, benign or otherwise, that both story and day have, both understandably and unjustly, suffered in Boccaccio scholarship, despite a few recent steps to reverse the trend. As for Emilia, the story is more complicated. On one hand, it seems to me that the infrequent, generally laudable efforts, especially by Joseph Markulin, Timothy Kircher, and Dino Cervigni, to give Emilia a more prominent role in our understanding of the *Decameron*'s ideology, have wilfully ignored the extraordinarily problematic light in which this character is placed during what is by far her most prominent appearance in the work. On the other hand, it is also true that there is more to Emilia than her turn as vehement and vacuous anti-feminist in Day Nine suggests. In point of fact, it can be argued that as functional marker of the narrative and conceptual concerns of the *Decameron* she is indeed one of the most crucial, if undervalued, presences in the work. This essay began by observing how the story of the vain, narcissistic girl Cesca, whose misplaced sense of intellectual superiority leads her to fancy herself another Solomon, anticipates both the return of Solomon in IX.9 and the negative representation of Emilia both as queen and as narrator of that story. But Emilia is the narrator of that story as well and in that context is presented as both deeply self-reflective and keenly aware of the failings of her protagonist (Ascoli, "Auerbach fra gli Epicurei"). And that story, in turn, as several critics have observed, points back to Emilia's song at the end of Day One, which, in my view, leaves her ambiguously suspended between superficial self-love and the self-reflexivity of a philosopher:[64]

Io son sì vaga della mia bellezza,
che d'altro amor già mai

64 Silber, *The Influence*, 69–70, first pointed out the obvious echoes of Dante's Rachel, figure of the contemplative life: "*Rachel mai non si smaga / dal suo miraglio*, e siede tutto giorno. / Ell' è d'i suoi belli occhi veder vaga" [*Rachel is never distracted from her looking glass*, and sits there all day long. She is ... desirous to see her lovely eyes (*Purg*. 27.97–108, esp. 103–5, emphasis added)], and subsequent critics have followed him in linking this Emilia to philosophical contemplation (e.g., Smarr, *Boccaccio and Fiammetta*, 179–80, 200; Kircher, *The Poet's Wisdom*, 133–9; Hollander, "The Struggle for Control," 270–1, 293–4). Others have observed that, in the absence of Dante's eschatological framework, the song seems to reflect (pun intended) a jejune female narcissism, not unlike that of Cesca. For this reading, see the brief comments of Van der Voort, "Convergenze e divaricazioni," 217n24, and C.M. [Carrie Murphy], "Emilia," *Decameron Web*. Most notable, however, is the extensive exploration of Boccaccio's appropriations, here and elsewhere, of the Narcissus myth, by Raffaela Zanni, "La 'poesia' del *Decameron*," 129–39, although I cannot fully subscribe to her claim that Boccaccio is here unequivocally affirming an autonomous and positive version of female sexuality (66–7). Another extraordinarily ambitious attempt to make the *ballata* a figure for a core humanistic value of the *Decameron* in general is Cervigni, "The *Decameron*'s Ballads," esp. 152–71 (see also Cervigni, "Fiammetta's Song of Jealousy," 484–6). I cannot, however, find a textual basis for Cervigni's claim that "she [Emilia] contemplates in herself the good present in every human being and in creation at large," thus unequivocally establishing a "lofty ideal" against which everything else in the book should be measured (154). From the perspective of this paper, another notable problem with Silber and followers' reading of the song is that in IX.9 Emilia's connection is not to contemplation but to the active life and practical wisdom (of which, again, Solomon is the outstanding representative). Already in the *ballata*, I would argue, Emilia is linked not only to Rachel at the mirror of speculation but also to her sister in allegory Lia, who is the *singer* of the song that Emilia [Emi-Lia?] so clearly echoes, and who also speaks, in the first person, of admiring herself in a mirror ("i' mi son Lia, e vo movendo intorno / le belle mani a farmi una ghirlanda. / *Per piacermi a lo specchio, qui m'addorno*" [I myself am Lia; and I go moving my lovely hands to make myself a garland. To please myself at the mirror I here adorn myself (*Purg*. 27.100–2, emphasis added)]. On this point, Zanni ("La 'poesia' del *Decameron*," 136) has rightly pointed to an earlier Boccaccian Lia, who is described in terms that echo Dante's entrance into the Earthly Paradise, and is elaborately identified as the "in bono" sister of Narcissus (*Comedia delle ninfe fiorentine*, ch. 4). The many complexities of Emilia's entanglement with good and bad forms of human knowledge cannot be fully described, much less further unravelled, here, though I intend to confront them in future work.

> non curerò né credo aver vaghezza.
> Io veggio in quella [la mia bellezza], *ognora ch'io mi specchio,*
> *quel ben che fa contento lo'ntelletto*:
> né accidente nuovo o pensier vecchio
> mi può privar di sì caro diletto. (I.Concl.18–19, emphasis added)
>
> [I am so enthralled by my own beauty that I shall never care nor have desire for any other love. I see in that beauty, whenever I gaze in the mirror, that good which renders the intellect content. Neither any new occurrence nor any old thought may deprive me of such a dear delight.]

From this perspective, whose development will have to wait for another occasion, I believe it is fair to say that Emilia becomes a figure for the possibilities and limitations of human knowledge within the confines of the natural world, the restricted domain concerning which, in fact, Solomon, for all his many frailties, is said to have possessed a wisdom second to none. That Boccaccio articulates these issues through the figure of a woman, and systematically entangles epistemology with gender and vice versa, is another, and not the least important, of the defining and yet enigmatic traits of his *Decameron*.

Natura contra naturam: Sins against Nature in *Decameron* IX.10

MAX MATUKHIN

The plot of the tenth *novella* of the Ninth Day is unusually straightforward with respect to other stories in the *Decameron*: there are almost no *peripeteia*, the action is limited to a single place and time, fortune plays no part in it, it does not revolve around a *motto* or *beffa*, and by the end the situation of its protagonists remains seemingly unchanged. Indeed, the structure of the *novella* is such that it would have been out of place in any of the thematic days of the *Decameron*, rendering it therefore a story peculiar to Day Nine. The *novella* goes more or less as follows: Donno Gianni di Barolo, a priest in a small village in Puglia, in order to supplement his miserly church income, takes up selling wares and becomes friendly with another poor peddler by the name of Pietro da Tresanti. And just as Donno Gianni offers Pietro lodging every time he ends up in the village of Barletta, so Pietro puts up Donno Gianni every time the latter stops by Tresanti. The only issue is that Pietro's house is so small that the priest has to sleep in the stall beside his horse. Being rather embarrassed by this situation, Pietro's wife, Gemmata, offers to stay with a friend so that the priest may share their bed with her husband. Donno Gianni, not wishing to disturb, jokingly tells her that he quite enjoys the company of his mare during the night, since he turns her into a beautiful young woman. Pietro's wife takes the statement literally and asks Donno Gianni to transform her into a horse so that she might help her husband carry additional wares and thereby earn more. After much convincing, the priest, knowing not what else to do, finally agrees, though he warns Pietro that the most difficult stage of the transformation is the attachment of the tail. At dawn, he makes the naked Gemmata stand on all fours while he recites the enchantment and in the process becomes aroused. To attach the tail, he proceeds to have intercourse with Piero's wife before the latter's very eyes, at which point the merchant begins to protest, saying that he doesn't want a tail on the horse after all. Donno Gianni, having climaxed, tells Pietro that he has ruined the enchantment and Gemmata, in perfect innocence, rebukes her husband for having interrupted the spell. From that day onwards, Pietro never asks Donno Gianni for the same service again, and the poor merchant goes on selling his wares with only his donkey to carry them.

The simplicity of the *novella* may account for the fact that it has largely been disregarded by critics, though by contrast Pier Paolo Pasolini did decide to include it in his 1971 film, *Il Decameron*. Mario Baratto has interpreted the story primarily in terms of its unique setting (it is the only *novella* that takes place in Puglia) as well as the characters' poverty and primitive nature.[1] Enchantments thus take the place of intelligent *beffe* in a story where motivations are more instinctive than conscious or rational. John Ahern goes still further along this interpretive line, seeing the tale as one of "inconsequential ineptitude" and "ludicrous incompetence" ("Dioneo's Repertory," 53), in which none of the protagonists learn anything. In a way, the *novella* thereby acts as a foil for the *brigata*'s own world, since it portrays a milieu that not only differs radically from their own but in which "their brilliant narrations and the values which they dramatize have no place" (ibid.). It is in this sense a *novella* that, according to Ahern, seeks to disrupt the fictive world that the young men and women have constructed over the course of the preceding nine storytelling days.[2] Franco Fido has additionally noted that the association between lady and steed is originally a courtly, chivalric one: the *novella* therefore stages a demystification, a parodic literal re-enactment that abases the original chivalric image, converting the courtly into the sexual.[3] Just as *novella* III.5 had already transformed a courtly motif into a mercantile one, so IX.10 further transforms a magical world (that of Donno Gianni's enchantment) into a purely physiological one. While the story's setting is indeed at odds

1 See Baratto, *Realtà e stile* (1984), 360–3.

2 See also Bàrberi Squarotti, "Le antifrasi di Dioneo." Bàrberi Squarotti also sees the *novella* as effectively antithetical both to the world of the *brigata* and to their storytelling. For him, as for Baratto, it is "la rappresentazione, antifrastica nei confronti degli schemi consueti del narrare utilizzati dalla brigata, di un mondo assolutamente privo di 'intelligenza', di abilità, di sapienza del vivere" [the representation, contrary to the usual narrative patterns adopted by the *brigata*, of a world completely deprived of any ethical "intelligence," ability, and wisdom (73)].

3 See Fido, "Silenzi e cavalli nell'eros del *Decameron*." It must be noted, though, that the association between lady and steed does not seem to be as common as Fido would have one believe. Aside from III.5, it does not reappear anywhere else in the *Decameron*, and the association is not particularly prevalent in Old French courtly literary forms (such as Chrétien de Troyes's romances).

both with the *brigata*'s world and that of numerous other *novelle*, these interpretations do not entirely account for the uniqueness of IX.10: after all, both socially and geographically, the *Decameron* is highly heterogeneous, and by the end of the Ninth Day there have already been stories such as that of Simona and Pasquino (IV.7), which opens the domain of infelicitous love to the lower strata of society,[4] or those of Calandrino (VIII.3, VIII.6, IX.3, IX.5), where the painter often interprets all too literally the tales woven by his more astute companions.[5] In other words, the lower social classes and their potential credulity vis-à-vis the symbolic order have already been amply displayed, just as the *novelle* have ventured a great deal further abroad than Puglia (though this does not diminish the importance of the setting).

This scarcity of critical interpretations and the seeming simplicity of the *novella* are in fact at odds with its highly significant position within the frame-structure of the *Decameron*. First of all, it is a story told by Dioneo, who is responsible for some of the most famous, bawdy, and provocative tales of the *Centonovelle*, such as those of Frate Cipolla (VI.10) and Griselda (X.10), and whose stories are always in a semantically privileged position, given that they are the last of each day (with the exception of I.4). Dioneo is thus able to comment on all of the day's preceding *novelle* (as he does in Day Ten by proposing a story that is seemingly the opposite of the exemplary narratives that have come before it, disclosing thereby their potentially problematic nature),[6] and to serve as a link between one day and the next (thus, the felicitous ending of IV.10 prefigures the theme of Day Five). Second of all, IX.10 concludes the main "body" of the *Decameron*, bookended as it is by the two free thematic days (Day One and Day Nine), before the *brigata* switches, upon Panfilo's bidding, to the radically different stories of Day Ten. The tenth *novella* of the Ninth Day could therefore be considered the last true hermeneutically open *novella* of the *Decameron*, seeing as the stories of the subsequent *giornata* are more akin to the medieval

4 As Panfilo says, prefacing the *novella*, "quantunque Amor volentieri le case de' nobili uomini abiti, esso per ciò non rifiuta lo 'mperio di quelle de' poveri" [whilst Love readily sets up house in the mansions of the aristocracy, this is no reason for concluding tha he declines to govern the dwellings of the poor (IV.7.4)]. All quotations of the *Decameron* are from Branca's 1992 edition. Translations are from McWilliam (1995).

5 On the topic of Calandrino's credulity, see Marcus, "Mischief and Misbelief: The First Tale of Calandrino (VIII.3)" in *An Allegory of Forms*, 79–92; Mazzotta, *The World at Play*, 186–212; Martinez, "Calandrino and the Powers of the Stone."

6 On the problems of interpretation surrounding Day Ten, see Hollander and Cahill, "Day Ten of the *Decameron*."

genre of exempla, where the interpretive coordinates of the work are determined in advance. Tzvetan Todorov has furthermore noted that the tale constitutes an *unicum* in the *Decameron* because it stages a form of vision (on Pietro's part) that is neither true nor false but "prétendue." Its special status is due to the fact that "on pourrait dire que Gianni faisait précéder ses actes de l'expression 'je prétends que ...' suivie de la description d'un acte autre que celui, perçu par les assistants. Par le fait que le curé prétend faire autre chose, il ne peut être accusé de commettre un méfait" [one could say that Gianni preceded his acts with the phrase "I pretend that ..." followed by the description of an act which differed from the one perceived by those present. Because the priest is pretending to do something entirely different, he cannot be accused of committing a misdeed (*Grammaire du Décaméron*, 72)]. No other *novella* presents an identical mode of vision. Lastly, the importance of interpreting the story is underscored by the text itself, since in the conclusion to the Ninth Day, which directly follows it, the author remarks, "Quanto di questa novella si ridesse, meglio dalle donne intesa che Dioneo non voleva, colei sel pensi che ancora ne riderà" [How the ladies laughed to hear this tale, whose meaning they had grasped more readily than Dioneo had intended, may be left to the imagination of those among my fair readers who are laughing at it still (IX.Concl.1)].[7] There is therefore more than one way of understanding the tale, or rather its narrator seems to be speaking on several levels at once.[8] In order to better understand what Dioneo (and Boccaccio) are doing in this story, it may therefore serve to consider its sources: specifically, its most direct precedent, which is the French *fabliau* "De la pucelle qui vouloit voler," an exemplum derived from the *Vitae Patrum* by Jacques de Vitry, as well as the Apuleian world that Gemmata's failed metamorphosis evokes.[9] The variety of the *novella*'s sources already delineates three distinct levels of meaning intended for varying audiences, depending on their linguistic

7 Ahern for some reason interprets this reaction as indicating a misinterpretation of the story on the ladies' part ("Dioneo's Repertory," 52), but it is not to be excluded that Dioneo meant for different members of the *brigata* (the seven women as opposed to the two other men) to comprehend the *novella* on different levels.

8 Bàrberi Squarotti believes that the women only understand the "risvolto puramente osceno" [purely erotic side] ("Le antifrasi di Dioneo," 73)] of the *novella*, bringing it back into the sphere of the erotic, but there is no reason to believe that this is necessarily the case. The laughter of the women may be attributed to the paradoxical meeting of the natural and what is considered unnatural, which will be considered below, or else to the sexual ignorance displayed by both Gemmata and her husband.

9 For other possible sources, see Vittore Branca's note *ad locum*.

and cultural competency: a vernacular French one, a Latin one, and a classical one.[10]

The *fabliau* in question belongs to the same tradition as better-known *fabliaux* such as "La damoisele que ne pooit oïr parler de foutre," "Cele qui fu foutue et desfoutue por une Grue," and "De l'Escuiruel," where the sexual act is metaphorically redefined by the male lover in order to render it acceptable to the woman he is attempting to seduce (much like *Decameron* III.10).[11] As in Dioneo's tale, the young lady is "De grant biauté" [of great beauty], but the setting is entirely different: she is courted by rich clerks, bourgeois, and knights, but refuses to listen to their entreaties. One day, she decides that she wishes to learn how to fly, "comme fist Dedalus" [as Dedalus did], and a clerk tells her that in order to do so she will require both a beak and a tail.[12] Having agreed to being endowed with them, the young lady is taken to a room where the priest first kisses her, explaining that that is how beaks are made, and then proceeds to have sexual intercourse with her "par darriere" [from behind] for the sake of the tail, while the young lady encourages him to do a thorough job of attaching it. In so doing, the clerk demonstrates a desire to seduce the *pucele* and an ingeniousness which Donno Gianni by contrast entirely lacks. Dioneo's priest makes an innocent joke which he is pressed to literally enact without initially wishing to do so. Fittingly, unlike Donno Gianni, the clerk will not be satisfied by a single such encounter and explains that an entire year of such treatment will be necessary for the tail to grow. The expected happens, and the *pucele* becomes pregnant, at which point she finally realizes that she has been "gabée" or tricked. The clerk responds to her accusations by defending his actions: "Se grosse estes, ce est nature; / Mais ce estoit contre nature / Que par l'air voliez voler" [If you are pregnant, then

10 On the "layered" or stratigraphic nature of the *Decameron* and its intertextual allusions, see Marchesi, *Stratigrafie decameroniane*, esp. xiii–xxii.

11 The *fabliau* in question is number 108 in Montaiglon and Raynaud, *Recueil général et complet des fabliaux*, 4:208–11.
On the presence of *fabliaux* in the *Decameron*, see Brown, *Boccaccio's Fabliaux*. On "La pucelle qui voloit voler," see 18, 38–9.

12 Could this *fabliau* be what Dante is referring to in *Inferno* 29, where Griffolino recounts how "quei, ch'avea vaghezza e senno poco, / volle ch'i' li mostrassi l'arte; e solo / perch'io nol feci Dedalo, mi fece / ardere" [That man, who had little intelligence and yet desired that I showed him my craft, had me burned because I did not make him Daedalus (114–17)]? This may explain his subsequent reference to the "[gente] francesca" (123). The choice of a *fabliau* as intertext would be comprehensible in a canto dedicated to a petty sin which engages in a parody of epic language and anticipates the petty *tenzone* between Sinon and Mastro Adamo.

that is nature, / Whereas your wish to fly through the air / Was against nature]. As Horace puts it in Ode I.3, she wished to fly with "pennis non homini datis" [with wings not given to men]. Her unnatural desire for a metamorphosis is contrasted with the naturalness of procreation, whereby she finally understands not only her own nature but that of the sexual act as well. The conclusion of the *fabliau* goes still further with the proverb "*Qui outrage quiert, il li vient*" [whoever asks for outrage, gets it], which plays on the double meaning of *outrage*: the *pucele*'s original desire is a transgression of nature's laws, whereas her pregnancy is a transgression of the norms of the society she inhabits. She is further described as "trop estoit desmesurée" [too immoderate]: an attempt to go beyond nature is therefore simultaneously an attempt to go beyond measure. The *pucele* is eventually reminded of her nature by her pregnancy, just as she implicitly becomes *mesurée* by setting aside her fantasies and marrying the clerk.

What must be accounted for, however, is the radically different social context into which Boccaccio inserts his reworking of "La damoisele," or in other words what justifies the transformation of a failed avian metamorphosis into a failed equine one. The social lowering of the story seems to occur under the aegis of none other than Apuleius, who in Book Three of his *Golden Ass* narrates precisely such a transformation, wherein Lucius, instead of being transformed into a bird as he desired, is instead metamorphosed, by servant-girl Photis's mistake, into an ass.[13] Dioneo's *novella* itself therefore embodies an Apuleian transmutation: the migration of the story to Puglia and into the company not of rich bourgeois and knights but of poor merchants changes its dynamic entirely. Analogously, the mischievous ingeniousness of the clerk is replaced by the initial reticence of Donno Gianni, and Gemmata's desires are not fantastical, like the *pucele*'s, but strictly pragmatic: a horse would allow for a greater income. Perhaps fittingly, therefore, whereas in the *fabliau* the eventual marriage with the clerk constitutes a social downgrade for the *damoisele* who had been courted by rich knights, Donno Gianni, being a member of the clergy, is of higher status than *compar* Pietro. The sexual act allows for a certain social flexibility, and Boccaccio reverses its potential with respect to the original. The Apuleian parallel also, however, aligns with the central theme of the *fabliau*: the two *novelle* borrowed explicitly from the *Metamorphosis*, that of Pietro di Vinciolo (V.10), also told by Dioneo, and that of Peronella

13 The text is cited from Apuleius, *Metamorphoses*, ed. and trans. Hanson; the translation is from Apuleius, *The Golden Ass*, trans. Kenney, 52.

(VII. 2), both deal with what in the fourteenth century would have been considered sexual deviancy or, as it was more commonly called, acts against nature. At the end of the tenth *novella* of Day Five, after Pietro discovers that in his absence his wife has invited a young man over, he compels the *giovane* to stay the night.[14] In describing what follows, Dioneo is somewhat elliptical: "Dopo la cena quello che Pietro si divisasse a sodisfacimento di tutti e tre m'è uscito di mente; so io ben cotanto, che la mattina vegnente infino in su la Piazza fu il giovane, non assai certo qual piú stato si fosse la notte o moglie o marito, accompagnato" [How exactly Pietro arranged matters, after supper, to the mutual satisfaction of all three parties, I no longer remember. But I do know that the young man was found next morning wandering about the piazza, not exactly certain with which of the pair he had spent the greater part of the night, the wife or the husband (V.10.63)]. This is the only time the *Decameron* refers to homosexual intercourse or sodomy,[15] as it would have been called in the wake of Peter Damian's eleventh-century *Liber Gomorrhianus* (though Cepparello, as "il piggiore uomo forse che mai nascesse" [perhaps the worst man ever born (I.1.14)], is described as being as fond of women as dogs are of cudgels, and Fra' Cipolla, in his nonsense sermon, alludes to sodomitic acts as well).[16]

Intercourse between members of the same sex, however, is only a part of the medieval definition of sins against nature.[17] Thomas Aquinas, in his *Summa Theologica*, lists four different types of "vitium contra naturam" [vice against nature], the fourth of which occurs "si non servetur naturalis modus concumbendi" [if the natural way of lying together is not observed (II.ii 154, 11)]. More specifically, as Vern Bullough has phrased it, "To be safe, almost everything from failure to use the 'normal' position in intercourse (female on her back), to any

14 By acting like the miller in Book IX of Apuleius's *Golden Ass*, Pietro is in fact reactivating the ancient Roman law according to which an adulterer could be subjected to humiliating punishment by the husband (which could include beatings, rape, or even castration). See Walters, "Invading the Roman Body," esp. 39. These punishments are also evoked by Horace in *Satire* I.2.40–4.

15 On the topic of sodomy in V.10, see Conoscenti, "Fra *mala ventura* e *fuoco dal cielo*."

16 Specifically when Fra' Cipolla recounts how "io liberamente gli feci copia delle piagge di Monte Morello in volgare e d'alquanti capitoli del Caprezio" [I was able to place freely at his disposal certain portions of the *Rumpiad* in the vernacular, together with several extracts from Capretius (VI.10.46)]. As Branca explains in his note *ad locum*, this is an instance of metaphoric, homoerotic slang.

17 On the medieval understanding of sodomy and sins against nature, see Jordan, *The Invention of Sodomy in Christian Theology*; Noonan, *Contraception*; Bullough, "The Sin against Nature"; Burgwinkle, *Sodomy*; and Lochrie, *Covert Operations*.

attempt to avoid conception … came to be looked upon as a sin against nature" ("The Sin against Nature," 62). This is particularly relevant to *novella* VII.2, where Peronella makes her husband clean the large jar that her lover, Giannello, has just supposedly bought. As is true for Gemmata later (and in contrast with the *fabliau*), Peronella's substitution of her lover (who is "un giovane de' leggiadri" (VII.2.8)) for her poor husband constitutes a social advancement. This upgrade is not only social but sexual, as the story amply demonstrates, and while she is leaning into the jar, observing her husband's work,

> Giannello, il quale appieno non aveva quella mattina il suo disidero ancor fornito quando il marito venne, veggendo che come volea non potea, s'argomentò di fornirlo come potesse; e a lei accostatosi, che tutta chiusa teneva la bocca del doglio, e in quella guisa che negli ampi campi gli sfrenati cavalli e d'amor caldi le cavalle di Partia assaliscono, a effetto recò il giovinil desiderio. (VII.2.33–4)
>
> [Giannello, who had not fully gratified his desires that morning before the husband arrived, seeing that he couldn't do it in the way he wished, contrived to bring it off as best he could. So he went up to Peronella, who was completely blocking up the mouth of the tub, and in the manner of a wild and hot-blooded stallion mounting a Parthian mare in the open fields, he satisfied his young man's passion.]

Giannello's "unnatural" form of copulation is ironically commented on via the simile of the Parthian mares and stallions; something that is considered perfectly ordinary in the animal world becomes one of the illicit "bestiales … modos" [bestial … ways (*ST*, II.ii 154, 11)] evoked by Aquinas. The paradox is further amplified by the fact that in an attempt to normalize certain sexual behaviours, one of the main theological arguments was that "what the animals do is 'natural'" (Noonan, *Contraception*, 75). A rift therefore appears between natural and theological law, which the *novella* underscores, but only to pass it over as the story reaches its felicitous conclusion.

Having examined the sources of IX.10, we still need to understand how this notion of acts against nature manifests itself in Dioneo's *novella*. A first indication can be evinced from the desire that Gemmata expresses to her husband: "ché non ti fai tu insegnare quello incantesimo, ché tu possa far cavalla di me e fare i fatti tuoi con l'asino e con la cavalla, e guadagneremo due cotanti? E quando a casa fossimo tornati, mi potresti rifar femina come io sono" [Why don't you get him to teach you the spell, so that you can turn me into a mare and run your business with the mare as well as the donkey? We should earn twice as much money, and when we got home you could turn me back into a woman, as I am now (IX.10.12)]. The priest's sexual joke is transformed into a literal desire for material gain, and indeed Pietro's wife seems to be deaf to the sexual *double entendre* implicit in her own use of the verb "far cavalla." Unlike the *pucele* of the *fabliau*, Gemmata does not have any Daedalian fantasies, but simply wants her husband to earn twice as much as he does now. This literalization of Donno Gianni's joke is problematic, however: as Saint Paul would have it, "littera enim occidit, Spiritus autem vivificat" (2 Corinthians 3:6). In this case, Pietro's wife wishes for a metamorphosis, which Augustine in the *De civitate Dei* calls "ars daemonum" [devils' arts] and which is ever associated with the pagan world, instead of trying a more common way of procuring an extra helping hand, such as having children (XVIII.18).

Augustine's remarks on the topic of metamorphoses are of particular relevance to the context of the *novella*, since he recounts a story of travellers being transformed into mares "sicut Apuleius in libris, quos Asini aurei titulo inscripsit, sibi ipsi accidisse, ut accepto veneno humano animo permanente asinus fieret" [just as Apuleius wrote had happened to him, in a book entitled the Golden Ass, when having taken a drug he became an ass with a human mind (*Met.* XVIII.18, 1)]. Nevertheless, he denies the truth of such transmutations, arguing that devils can only change the outer appearance of creatures created by God. Metamorphosis is therefore converted from being an aetiology of nature, as it is in Ovid, into a form of illusion, which is precisely the process played out in IX.10, where Gemmata's Apuleian wish, which constitutes a form of regression toward a pre-Christian world, is frustrated by none other than a priest.

Gemmata's desire can further be understood via Alain de Lille, who in his *De planctu naturae* imagines the activity of nature precisely as a minting of coins: as Nature tells the narrator, she works "Imperantis igitur imperio ego obtemperans operando, quasi varia rerum sigillans numismata ad exemplaris rei ymaginem" [Obeying therefore the demands of authority, stamping the various coins of things in the likeness of the example (*De planctu*, VIII, 30)]. By interpreting the priest's words literally, and by substituting metamorphosis for reproduction, Gemmata effectively perverts the course of nature, thus literalizing Alain's allegory: she wishes to produce not offspring but coins. Furthermore, in the *De planctu*, Alain de Lille establishes a direct relation between language (specifically, grammar) and copulation: the various reproductive organs are associated with nouns and adjectives, just as the roles of the male and female partners are understood as corresponding to the active and the passive voice, respectively. Pietro's wife becomes like the homosexual man, who "Dionaeae artis analogiam devitans, in anastrophen vitiosam degenerat" [Avoiding the analogy of the Dionean arts, he degenerates into sinful anastrophe] (ibid., VIII, 8). Given Boccaccio's intimate acquaintance with Martial's *Epigrammata*, which he would later go on to copy in the manuscript known nowadays as Ambrosiano C.67 sup.,[18] the possibility is not to be excluded that via Gemmata's anastrophe he may be evoking Epigram 19 of Book XI, "Quaeris cur nolim te ducere, Galla? diserta es. / Saepe soloecismum mentula nostra facit" [You ask why I do not wish to marry you, Galla? You are eloquent. Our member often makes grammatical mistakes] (Martial, *Epigrams*). Martial's phrase later goes on to be borrowed and reworked by Juvenal in Satire 6, where he argues that "soloecismum liceat fecisse marito" [it should be allowed for the husband to make grammatical mistakes (l. 456)] (*Juvenal and Persius*). Boccaccio flips the paradigm and in his story attributes a procreational *soloecismum* to the wife. The reference furthermore establishes a connection between the classical world and that of Alain de Lille, uniting the two literary and cultural contexts that serve as the *novella*'s background: both portray sexual behaviour via the paradigm of language. Gemmata misunderstands the grammar of nature just as she misunderstands the irony of Donno Gianni, and by further taking on the active voice and convincing her husband to persuade the priest, she acts contrary to the role that Alain's Nature ascribes to women.[19]

All of this raises the question – why does the couple not have children, given that for a poor merchant they might lend an invaluable hand? Donno Pietro and Gemmata are in fact one of the few married couples in the *Decameron* to be childless (alongside Peronella and Calandrino).[20]

---

18 See Petoletti, "La scoperta del Marziale autografo di Giovanni Boccaccio," as well as "Il Marziale autografo di Giovanni Boccaccio."

19 See Psaki, "Voicing Gender in the *Decameron*." Psaki notes how "In textual precedents that Boccaccio not merely knew but carefully copied into his *Zibaldone Laurenziano* (Florence, Biblioteca Medicea Laurenziana, MS 29. 8), the litany of accusations against women rests stably on simultaneous crimes of sexual and linguistic impropriety" (111). Here, the impropriety concerns both the linguistic and the sexual, if one is to use Alain de Lille's metaphor, though rather than being conscious, it springs in great part from ignorance, as discussed below.

20 On the topic of Calandrino's false pregnancy and the relation between VIII.3 and IX.3, see Marchesi, *Stratigrafie decameroniane* (105–36) and "Sex, Floods, and a Learned Gloss." Calandrino's gathering of stones in VIII.3 becomes a sterile (and parodic) re-enactment of the myth of Deucalion and Pyrrha from Ovid's *Metamorphoses*; indeed, the contrast between the *novella* and its source frames Calandrino's actions as transgressive, as opposed to the piousness of Ovid's elderly

After all, it is this state, rather than some sort of *démesure*, that leads the young woman to desire the transformation that Donno Gianni jokingly recounts. Before turning to the *novella* itself, we may find a pointer in one of the medieval Latin sources for the story, which is a religious exemplum by Jacques de Vitry, which he himself adapts from the *Vitae Patrum*.[21] In the story, a man goes to Saint Acarius to seek his help because his wife has seemingly been transformed into a "jumenta"; the saint utters a prayer and the "dyabolica illusione" ceases, making the man once again recognize his wife. In accordance with Augustine's theory in *De civitate Dei* that devils cannot actually transform beings created by God but can only create an illusion of such a transformation, the exemplum explains that "malefici vel divinatores ... peccatoribus autem illudere solent" [enchanters and diviners ... have a habit of deceiving sinners]. In particular, by means of this "arte diabolica," they can transform wives: "ut vir uxorem suam non valeat cognoscere, vel ut in formas bestiales quidam transformari videantur" [so that a man should not recognize his wife, or that she seems to have been transformed into a bestial shape]. From Boccaccio's point of view, what matters here is the potential double signification of the verb "cognoscere": it is both to recognize and to know someone biblically. In a sense, not recognizing one's wife *as* one's wife becomes synonymous with the preclusion of procreation. The choice of animal is significant: *jumenta* can mean any beast of burden, but most often denotes a mule, which is the sterile offspring of a donkey and a mare.[22] Behind the diabolical illusion there is therefore the threat of childlessness. De Vitry differs here in two ways from the original in the *Vitae Patrum*: in the *Historia Lausiaca*, the wife takes on the appearance of a horse, hence without the

couple. As in IX.10, an excessively literal interpretation is one that does not produce life, or, in the terms given by IX.3, misinterpretation becomes a vehicle for false generation. Nor is it to be excluded that Dioneo is weighing in on the dialogue between Elissa and Filostrato that takes place in the two Calandrino *novelle*: if, as Marchesi argues, VIII.3 proposes a reinterpretation of Ecclesiastes 3:5 and its commentaries by Jerome and Augustine, whereby in view of the ongoing plague, procreation should take precedence over continence, while IX.3 demonstrates how such a reversal of priorities runs the risk of purely promoting hedonistic pleasure, then Dioneo can be said to side with Elissa. Much more than in the case of Calandrino and his wife Tessa, in IX.10 procreation is demanded by necessity, while continence is paradoxically associated with an act that is both "against nature" and against the law.

21 de Vitry, *The exempla or illustrative stories*, 110. The original story is from the *Vitae Patrum* Liber VIII, cap. XIX–XX, cited from Migne, *Patrologia Latina* (*PL*), 73.1109–11.

22 The sterility of mules was well known in the Middle Ages and is mentioned both in Varro's *De re rustica* (Liber II, 1.27) and in Aristotle's *Historia animalium* (VI.xxix).

connotation of sterility, as is the case in the *Decameron*, where on the contrary the name "Gemmata" evokes the budding of a plant. Here too, however, the transformation is primarily in the eyes of the beholders: as the saint tells the monks who bring him the woman, "Equi vos estis, qui habetis equorum oculos; illa enim est femina ita ut est creata, non transformata, sed sic solum apparens oculis eorum qui sunt decepti" [You are the horses, because you have horses' eyes; she, however, is a woman, just as she was created; not transformed, but only appearing thus to the eyes of those who are deceived (*PL* 73:1110–11)]. The illusion is, in a sense, reflexive, just as in IX.10, where Donno Gianni's magical formula is only rendered possible in the first place by Pietro and Gemmata's delusion. After having undone the charm, the saint tells the wife: "Haec enim tibi acciderunt, quod jam quinque hebdomadis non accessisti ad intemerata nostri Servatoris sacramenta" [For this happened to you because for five weeks you did not come to the pure sacraments of our Saviour (*PL* 73:1111)]. In the original, the woman therefore bears part of the responsibility, which is not the case in Jacques de Vitry, who places more emphasis on the husband's non-recognition of his own wife. Lastly, an important element is the *oratione* of the saint, which is parodied in Boccaccio's *novella* by Donno Gianni's incantation; it is therefore possible that the "vision 'prétendue'" described by Todorov, which is created by the priest's magic formula, also has an unveiling quality to it, much like Saint Acarius's.

To return to the *novella*, the link between the exemplary tradition and the story, as well as an answer regarding Gemmata's childlessness, can potentially be found in the words of *compar* Pietro. When he sees the priest having intercourse with his wife, he exclaims that he no longer wants a tail and tells Donno Gianni, "Bene sta, io non vi voleva quella coda io: perché non diciavate voi a me 'Falla tu'? E anche l'appiccavate troppo bassa" ["That suits me," said Neighbour Pietro. "I didn't want the tail. Why didn't you ask me to do it? Besides, you stuck it on too low" (IX.10.21)]. While the first objection is comprehensible within the marital economy of the tale, the second remonstrance is a peculiar one: certainly, one may argue that horses normally have tails above their rump, but given that Pietro has just witnessed the manner in which the tail is attached, the anatomically "higher" alternative evoked by his words would seemingly have been via anal intercourse. Might this be the type of intercourse that the husband is more accustomed to? A confirmation seems to come from none other than Gemmata, who, after all of this, "levatasi in piè di buona fé" (IX.10.23), goes on to call her husband a "bestia" for interrupting the enchantment. Her good faith and innocence seem to suggest that she does not realize what the priest has just done (she is, in this sense, much closer to Alibech than to

Peronella). A possible explanation would be that with Pietro she does indeed engage in a different form of intercourse, which in turn would explain the lack of children. To return to Martial, it can be hypothesized of Pietro that "saepe soloecismum mentula [sua] facit," and perhaps, in a reversal of the epigram's argument, Boccaccio seems to be suggesting that a more educated wife might have corrected his mistake.

Needless to say, *coitus in ano,* as it was usually called in medieval treatises such as the *Liber Gomorrhianus,* also constituted a form of sodomy, and indeed one of the most commonly mentioned. Peter Damian, because his treatise deals primarily with priests, focuses on homosexual relations, citing Leviticus 20:13, "Qui dormierit cum masculo coitu femineo, uterque operatus est nefas" [A man who sleeps with another man, joining him sexually as a woman commits, in either role, a crime] (*LG* III)]. Other authors before and after Damian, however, have often given more importance to heterosexual anal intercourse. Thus, Augustine himself, in the *De bono coniugalis,* in speaking of *concubitus contra naturam* explicitly mentions the situation "Cum vero vir membro mulieris non ad hoc concesso uti voluerit" [When a man wishes to use a body part of his wife not made for that purpose (*De bono coniugali,* 11–12)]. For Gratian, "The worst sin of all, however, was that which was done contrary to nature, defined in the Augustinian sense as a man using a member of his wife not conceded for that purpose."[23] Peter Lombard, similarly, citing Augustine, declares in his *Sentences* that "omnium pessimum est quod contra naturam fit, ut si vir membro mulieris, non ad hoc concesso, utatur" [The worst of all is that which is against nature, as when a man uses a body part of his wife not meant for that purpose (*Libri IV Sententiarum,* Liber IV, Dist. XXXVIII, Cap. III)]. As these examples demonstrate, and as Karma Lochrie has recently underlined, this notion of a sodomitic sin against nature did not necessarily apply primarily, let alone exclusively, to homosexual relations.[24] Indeed, insofar as any acts of anal intercourse involved the misuse of sexual members

23 Bullough, "The Sin against Nature," 62. See Gratian, *Decretum, Pars secunda,* Causa XXXII, Questio vii.

24 See Lochrie, *Covert Operations.* Lochrie questions the existence of a heterosexual-homosexual divide in the Middle Ages, noting "the medieval habit of including sodomy among the marital unnatural acts, rather than making a heterosex-act/same-sex-act distinction" (182). See also Burgwinkle, *Sodomy,* where he too notes that "Mid-twelfth-century compilations of canon law (Gratian) and theology (Peter Lombard's Sentences) made virtually no mention of sodomy or 'unnatural' sex, except as it pertained to the use of women in heterosexual sex" (31). Indeed by the reign of Henry I, "Though still associated principally with the four same-sex acts outlined by Peter Damian in his *Liber Gomorrhianus,* it had moved, as a concept, beyond the all-male environments which provided the context for much of these

and impeded procreation (and was therefore doubly against nature), they would have been classified similarly.

The story therefore seems to be presenting two (or even three) different forms of sins against nature, or sodomy. The first is committed by the priest, who engages in a form of sexual intercourse that, in addition to being adulterous and contrary to his vows, would also be considered against nature due to the *a tergo* position he adopts (which, however, would be perfectly natural for horses, as the story of Peronella reminds us). But as in VII.2, there is a marked contrast between this theoretical unnaturalness and the way Boccaccio describes the act: "levata la camiscia e preso il piuolo col quale egli piantava gli uomini e prestamente nel solco per ciò fatto messolo, disse: 'E questa sia bella coda di cavalla'" [he lifted his shirt, took hold of the dibber that he did his planting with, and stuck it straight and true in the place made for it, saying: "And this be a fine mare's tail" (IX.10.17)]. The male member is here described as a rod for the planting of men, or, in other words, as an instrument of procreation, and in medieval Christian theology, "procreation was the chief criterion for judging whether sexual activity was natural or unnatural, and anything that did not lead to procreation was regarded as unnatural" (Bullough, "The Sin against Nature," 57). And lest there be any doubts, Dioneo specifies that it is inserted into the furrow expressly made for it. As John Noonan has written, the metaphor of ploughing and sowing was one of the three main natural images used to describe sexual intercourse, and was employed by early Christian theologians as diverse as Athenagoras, Origen, Clement, and Ambrose.[25] The analogy is in fact already evoked in another *novella* of Dioneo's, the tenth of Day Two, by Bartolomea, the wife of Ricciardo di Chinzica.[26] Alain de Lille makes use of the same

accounts. By 1130 it seems to have become applicable to a larger pool of individuals and to cover a much wider range of behaviors and excesses" (51–2).

25 Noonan, *Contraception*, 74. These are the same three metaphors for procreation later used by the figure of Genius in the second part of the *Roman de la Rose* written by Jean de Meun (ll. 19547–86).

26 Bartolomea uses the metaphor to justify her escape with Paganino: "E dicovi che se voi aveste tante feste fatte fare a' lavoratori che le vostre possessioni lavorano, quante faciavate fare a colui che il mio piccol campicello aveva a lavorare, voi non avreste mai ricolto granello di grano" [And I can tell you this, that if you had given as many holidays to the workers on your estates as you gave to the one whose job it was to tend my little field, you would never have harvested a single ear of corn (II.10.32)]. Once again, there is an important element of non-recognition: Bartolomea tells her husband that although she recognizes him, "mentre che io fu' con voi, mostraste assai male di conoscer me" [you showed very little sign of knowing *me*, when I was living with you (II.10.31)]. Ricciardo does not recognize the natural

metaphor to describe what he deems to be the corruption of natural procreation: "in sterili litore vomer arat" [the plow makes furrows in sterile ground (*De planctu*, I, 30)]. Dioneo does not stop there, however, going on to describe how "Era già l'umido radicale per lo quale tutte le piante s'appiccano venuto, quando donno Gianni tiratolo indietro ..." [The vital sap which all plants need to make them grow had already arrived, when Father Gianni, standing back ... (IX.10.20)]. To describe the moment of climax, Boccaccio uses a scientific term (employed, for example, by Dante in *Convivio* IV.xxiii.7) but keeps the metaphor of the plants, resulting in a comic incongruity which reflects contemporary anatomical and embryological discussions among theologians.[27] Both images firmly place the act of Donno Gianni within the realm of natural procreation and therefore not only in contrast with the definition of sodomy but also seemingly in opposition to the childlessness of Gemmata and Pietro.

The priest's positional sodomy therefore comes to correct the husband's (seemingly unintentional) orificial sodomy, which has in turn provoked the desire to pervert the grammar of nature in his wife. But why must a priest be the one to, firstly, disclose these acts against nature, and secondly, offer a demonstration of what is natural? If one sets aside the anti-clericalism of the *Decameron* and the association of priests with lechery, which are not as applicable here as in other *novelle*,[28] the place

---

demands of youth and hence his marriage is invalid, according to Bartolomea, since he treated her as his "bagascia" (II.10.37) rather than his wife.

27 On the medieval concept of the *umido radicale*, see Cresciani, "Aspetti del dibattito." Boccaccio's usage of the scientific term is significant here, given that it connects the story to the medical debates of theologians during the twelfth and thirteenth centuries. As Cresciani has observed in her study, there was a tendency among theologians during these centuries to explain human nature no longer along Augustinian lines but in scientific and medical terms. Thus, Albertus Magnus in his *Liber de morte et vita* explains that the cause of a long or short life is not to be found in the *spiritus* but rather in the heat and humidity that pervade the body (*De morte et vita*, tr. 2, c. 7). Dante takes up this same argument in the *Convivio*, where in his discussion of generation he argues that the arc of human life is dependent on the quantity and quality of the aforementioned *umido radicale*. Within the context of IX.10, the evocation of this scientific language serves as a counterpoint to the implicitly evoked theological debate concerning acts against nature: in this case, the physiological element (the semen, which is associated with impregnation) can be said to override the unnaturalness of the sexual position.

28 The lack of premeditated intent on Donno Gianni's part sets him apart from other figures such as Frate Alberto (IV.2), Donno Felice (III.4), Frate Rinaldo (VII.3), and the monk and abbot of I.4.

On the subject of clergy in the *Decameron*, see Ó Cuilleanáin, *Religion and the Clergy in Boccaccio's Decameron*; Smarr, "Clergy in the *Decameron*."

of Donno Gianni could theoretically be taken up by any other figure. But if there is one thing that scholars who study the history of sodomy in the medieval period agree on, it is that the vice is only ever defined in the most abstract of terms. Mark Jordan has noted that the "essential thing to notice in the processes by which 'Sodomy' was produced is that they first abolish details, qualifications, restrictions in order to enable an excessive simplification in thought" (*The Invention of Sodomy*, 29). Indeed, he goes on to note that he has "so much emphasized the silences [surrounding sodomy] because they are so troubling. They are typically justified by appeal to pastoral need. Confessors are not to mention any of the forms of Sodomy for fear of encouraging them in those who might not know about them" (ibid., 113). Bullough analogously notes that the term "sin against nature" often remained unspecified, such as in the *Decretals* issued by Pope Gregory IX in 1234 ("The Sin against Nature," 64), and indeed Lochrie remarks more generally that "writings on the sins against nature from the thirteenth century onward are notoriously inexplicit when it comes to defining what sins against nature, including sodomy, are" (*Covert Operations*, 182). Such was the taboo surrounding sodomy and such was the fear of instilling impure thoughts in one's congregation that priests and preachers must have ironically been almost incapable of preventing it. Hence the importance of the *novella*'s setting: sodomy was primarily associated by theologians and preachers with the upper social classes (Bullough, "The Sin against Nature," 64–5), and even more typically with urban and especially university centres, such as Paris (Burgwinkle, *Sodomy*, 47). Rural Puglia can therefore be imagined as being at the very antipodes of sodomy, and yet here it is, not a product of excessive learning but, on the contrary, of ignorance. As a way of re-establishing the Dionean arts, as Alain de Lille calls them, Dioneo therefore ironically proposes a demonstration, producing that unique form of vision noted by Todorov. And who better, then, to show how it's done than the priest himself, and perhaps, given that Pietro never asked Donno Gianni to offer his services again, he did indeed learn something.

Bibliography

Primary Sources

Alain de Lille. *Literary Works*. Edited and translated by W. Wetherbee. Cambridge, MA: Harvard University Press, 2013.
Alfonsi, Pietro. *Disciplina Clericalis*. Edited by Cristiano Leone. Rome: Salerno, 2010.
Andreas Cappellanus. *De amore*. Edited by G. Ruffini. Milan: Guanda, 1980.
Angiolieri, Cecco. *Le rime*. Edited by A. Lanza. Rome: Archivio Guido Izzi, 1990.
– *Sonnets*. Translated by C.H. Scott and A. Mortimer. London: Oneworld, 2008.
Antologia della poesia italiana. Vol. I. Duecento-Trecento. Edited by C. Segre and C. Ossola. Turin: Einaudi-Gallimard, 1997.
Apuleius. *The Golden Ass*. Translated by E.J. Kenney. New York: Penguin Books, 1998.
– *Metamorphoses*. Edited and translated by J. Arthur Hanson. Cambridge, MA: Harvard University Press, 2014.
Aquinas, Thomas. *Summa theologica*. New York: Benziger Bros., 1947.
Aristotle. *Ethicorum libri*. In *S. Thomae de Aquino Sententia libri Ethicorum*, edited by Ordo Fratrum Praedicatorum. In *Opera Omnia iussu Leonis XIII edita*, t. XLVII. Rome: ad Sanctae Sabinae, 1969.
Augustine. *De bono coniugali*. Edited and translated by P.G. Walsh. Oxford: Clarendon, 2001.
– *De civitate Dei*. Edited and translated by P.G. Walsh. Oxford: Oxbow Books, 2005.
Benvenuto da Imola. *Comentum super Dantis Aldigherij Comoediam*. 5 vols. Edited by G.W. Vernon and J.P. Lacaita. Florence: G. Barbèra, 1887.
Boccaccio, Giovanni. *Boccaccio's Expositions on Dante's Comedy*. Translated by M. Papio. Toronto: University of Toronto Press, 2009.

– *Comedia delle ninfe fiorentine*. Critical edition by Antonio Enzo Quaglio. Florence: Sansoni, 1963.
– *Corbaccio*. Edited by G. Natali. Milan: Mursia, 1992.
– *"Il Decameron* di G. Boccacci, con alcuni disegni a penna." Bibliothèque Nationale de France, Paris, MS Italien 482, fols. 1r–215r.
– *Il Decameron di Giovanni Boccacci[o]*. Edited by P. Fanfani. Florence: Le Monnier, 1857.
– *The Decameron*. Translated by J.M. Rigg. London: Bullan, 1903.
– *Il Decameròn. Quarantacinque novelle col disegno di tutta l'opera*. Edited by G. Lipparini. Bologna: Zanichelli, 1929.
– *Decameron*. Edited by V. Branca. Vol. 4 in *Tutte le opere di Giovanni Boccaccio*, edited by V. Branca. Milan: Mondadori, 1967.
– *The Decameron*. Translated by G.H. McWilliam. London: Penguin, 1972, 1995.
– *Il Decameron. 49 novelle commentate da Attilio Momigliano*. Edited by E. Sanguineti. Turin: Petrini, 1972.
– *Decameron*. Edizione critica secondo l'autografo hamiltoniano. Edited by V. Branca. Florence: Accademia della Crusca, 1976.
– *Decameron*. Edited by V. Branca. Turin: Einaudi, 1980.
– *Decameron*. Edited by M. Bevilacqua. Vol. 3. Rome: Editori Riuniti, 1983.
– *Decameron*. Edited by V. Branca. Milan: Mondadori, 1985.
– *Decameron*. Edited by V. Branca. Turin: Einaudi, 1992.
– *Decameron*. Edited by A. Quondam, M. Fiorilla, and G. Alfano. Milan: Rizzoli, 2013.
– *The Decameron*. Translated and introduced by W.A. Rebhorn. New York and London: W.W. Norton & Company, 2013.
– *Esposizioni sopra la Comedia di Dante*. Edited by G. Padoan. In *Tutte le opere di Giovanni Boccaccio*, vol. 6, edited by V. Branca. Milan: Mondadori, 1965.
– *Famous Women*. Edited and translated by V. Brown. Cambridge, MA: Harvard University Press, 2001.
– *Genealogia Deorum Gentilium*. Translated by C.G. Osgood. In *Boccaccio on Poetry, Being the Preface and the Fourteenth and Fifteenth Books of Boccaccio's "Genealogia Deorum Gentilium."* Princeton: Princeton University Press, 1930.
– *Genealogia Deorum Gentilium*. Edited by V. Zaccaria. In *Tutte le opere di Giovanni Boccaccio*, edited by V. Branca, vols. 7–8. Milan: Mondadori, 1998.
– *Novelle scelte dal Decamerone di G. Boccaccio*. Edited by R. Fornaciari. Florence: Sansoni, 1888.
– *Le opere di G. Boccaccio*. Edited by N. Zingarelli. Naples: Perrella, 1913.
– *Opere di Giovanni Boccaccio*. Edited by C. Segre. Milan: Mursia, 1963–78.
– *Teseida delle nozze d'Emilia*. In *Tutte le opere di Giovanni Boccaccio*, edited by A. Limentani. Milan: Mondadori Oscar, 1992.

– *Tutte le opere di Giovanni Boccaccio*. Edited by V. Branca. 10 vols. Milan: Mondadori, 1964–98.

Cavalcanti, Guido. *Rime*. Edited by M. Ciccuto. Milan: Rizzoli, 1978.

Cicero. *De oratore*. Edited by K. Kumaniecki. Leipzig: Teubner, 1969.

Damian, Peter. *Book of Gomorrah: An Eleventh-Century Treatise against Clerical Homosexual Practices*. Edited and translated by P.J. Payer. Waterloo, ON: Wilfrid Laurier University Press, 1982.

Dante Alighieri. *Divina Commedia*. Edited by G. Petrocchi. Milan: Mondadori, 1966–7; 2nd edition, revised, Florence: Le Lettere, 1994.

– *The Divine Comedy of Dante Alighieri*. Edited and translated by R.M. Durling; notes by R.M. Durling and R.L. Martinez. 3 vols. Oxford: Oxford University Press, 1996–2011.

– *The Divine Comedy of Dante Alighieri. Inferno*. Translated by A. Mandelbaum. Toronto: Bantam, 1982.

– *Purgatorio*. Translated by J. Hollander; edited by R. Hollander. New York: Anchor Books, 2004.

de Vitry, Jacques. *The exempla or illustrative stories from the Sermones vulgares of Jacques de Vitry*. Edited by T.F. Crane. London: Folklore Society, 1890.

"Le Dit de la Nonnete." In *Recueil général et complet des fabliaux des XIIIe et XIVe siècles*, edited by A. de Montaiglon and G. Raynaud, vol. 5. Geneva: Slatkine Reprints, 1973.

Horace. *Horace, Odes and Epodes*. Edited and translated by P. Shorey and G.J. Laing. Chicago: Benj. H. Sanborn & Co., 1919.

Jacob of Voragine. *Legenda aurea*. Edited by G.P. Maggioni. Florence: SISMEL-Edizioni del Galluzzo, 1998.

Juvenal and Persius. Edited and translated by S.M. Braund. Cambridge, MA: Harvard University Press, 2004.

Latini, Brunetto. *Il Favolello*. In *Poeti del Duecento*, edited by G. Contini. Milan-Naples: Ricciardi, 1960.

– *Tresor*. Edited by P. Beltrami et al. Turin: Einaudi, 2007.

Lombard, Peter. *Libri IV Sententiarum*. Florence: Ex Typographia Collegii S. Bonaventurae, 1916.

Lorris, Guillaume de, and Jean de Meun. *Le Roman de la Rose*. Edited by A. Strubel. Paris: Librairie Générale Française, 1992.

Martial. *Epigrams. Volume I: Spectacles, Books 1–5*. Edited and translated by D.R. Shackleton Bailey. Cambridge, MA: Harvard University Press, 1993.

Migne, Jacques-Paul. *Patrologia Latina*. Paris: Garnier & J.-P. Migne, 1844–65.

Montaiglon, Anatole de, and Gaston Raynaud. *Recueil général et complet des fabliaux des XIIIe et XIVe siècles imprimés ou inédits*. Paris: Librairie des bibliophiles, 1872.

Nova Vulgata. In Bibliorum Sacrorum Editio. Editio Typica Altera. Rome: Libreria Editrice Vaticana, 1986. Available online at https://www.vatican.va/archive/bible/nova_vulgata/documents/nova-vulgata_index_lt.html.

L'Ottimo commento della Divina Commedia. Edited by A. Torri. 3 vols. Pisa: N. Capurro, 1827–9.

Petrarch, Francesco. *Petrarch's Lyric Poems: The Rime Sparse and Other Lyrics*. Edited and translated by R.M. Durling. Cambridge, MA: Harvard University Press, 1976.

Quintilian. *Institutio oratoria*. Edited by A. Pennacini. Turin: Einaudi, 2001.

Le Roman de Renart le Contrefait. Edited by G. Raynaud and H. Lemaître. Geneva: Slatkine Reprints, 1975.

Sacchetti, Franco. *Il Trecentonovelle*. Edited by A. Lanza. Florence: Sansoni, 1984.

Seneca. *Minor Dialogs Together with the Dialog "On Clemency"*. Translated by A. Stewart. London. George Bell and Sons, 1900.

– *Moral Essays*, vol. 1. Translated by John W. Basore. Cambridge, MA: Harvard University Press, 1928.

Solomon and Marcolf. Edited by J. Ziolkowski. Cambridge, MA: Harvard University Press, 2008.

Stefani, Marchionne di Coppo. *Cronaca Fiorentina*. Edited by N. Rodolico. In *Rerum Italicarum Scriptores*, 30:1. Città di Castello: S. Lapi, 1903.

Thibaut de Champagne. *Les chansons de Thibaut de Champagne, Roi de Navarre*. Edited by A. Wallensköld. Paris: Champion, 1925.

Vasari, Giorgio. *Le Vite de' più eccellenti pittori, scultori e architetti italiani, da Cimabue, insino a' tempi nostri*. 1550. Turin: Einaudi, 1986.

Villani, Giovanni. *Nuova Cronica*. Edited by G. Porta. 3 vols. Parma: Guanda, 1990.

Secondary Sources

Accademia della Crusca. *Vocabolario degli Accademici della Crusca*, 2001. http://vocabolario.sns.it/html/index.html.

Ahern, John. "Dioneo's Repertory: Performance and Writing in Boccaccio's Decameron." In *Performing Medieval Narrative*, edited by E. Birge Vitz, N. Freeman Regalado, and M. Lawrence, 41–58. Rochester, NY: D.S. Brewer, 2005.

Alfano, Giancarlo. "Scheda introduttiva a *Decameron*, IX.2." In G. Boccaccio, *Decameron*, edited by A. Quondam, M. Fiorilla, and G. Alfano. Milan: Rizzoli, 2013.

Alfie, Fabian. "Cecco vs. Cecco: A Newly Identified Source for Angiolieri's Adversary, Fortarrigo." *Medium Ævum* 83.1 (2014): 121–30.

– *Comedy and Culture: Cecco Angiolieri's Poetry and Late Medieval Society*. Leeds: Northern University Press, 2001.

– "Poetics Enacted: A Comparison of the Novellas of Cecco Angiulieri and Guido Cavalcanti in Boccaccio's *Decameron*." *Studi di Boccaccio* 23 (1995): 171–96.
– "Yes … but Was It Funny? Cecco Angiolieri, Rustico Filippi, and Giovanni Boccaccio." In *Laughter in the Middle Ages and Early Modern Times: Epistemology of a Fundamental Human Behavior, Its Meaning, and Consequences*, edited by A. Classen, 365–82. New York: Walter de Gruyter, 2010.
Allen, Judson Boyce. *The Ethical Poetic of the Later Middle Ages: A Decorum of Convenient Distinction*. Toronto: University of Toronto Press, 1982.
Allen, Shirley S. "The Griselda Tale and the Treatment of Women in the *Decameron*." *Philological Quarterly* 56 (1977): 1–13.
Almansi, Guido. "Lettura della quarta novella del *Decameron*." *Strumenti Critici* 13 (1970): 308–17.
Andrei, Filippo. *Boccaccio the Philosopher: An Epistemology of the "Decameron"*. London and New York: Palgrave Macmillan, 2017.
Andreini, Alessandro, Cristina Cerrato, and Giuliano Feola. "Dalla chiesa alto-medievale di S. Maria al prato alla fondazione del complesso conventuale di S. Francesco. Origine e trasformazioni urbane del prato di Piunte." In *S. Francesco. La chiesa e il convento in Pistoia*, edited by L. Gai, 27–46. Pisa: Pacini Editore, 1993.
– "I cicli costruttivi della chiesa e del convento di S. Francesco dal XIII al XV secolo: Analisi storico-architettonica." In *S. Francesco. La chiesa e il convento in Pistoia*, 47–80.
Ascoli, Albert Russell. "Auerbach fra gli Epicurei: Da *Inferno* X a *Decameron*, giornata VI." *Moderna* 11.1–2 (2009): 135–52.
– "Blinding the Cyclops: Petrarch after Dante." In *Petrarch and Dante*, edited by T. Cachey and Z. Baranski, 114–73. Notre Dame: University of Notre Dame Press, 2009.
– "Boccaccio's Auerbach: Holding the Mirror Up to *Mimesis*." In Ascoli, *A Local Habitation and a Name: Imagining Histories in the Italian Renaissance*, ch. 2. New York: Fordham University Press, 2011.
– *Dante and the Making of a Modern Author*. Cambridge: Cambridge University Press, 2008.
– "Pyrrhus' Rules: Playing with Power from Boccaccio to Machiavelli." In Ascoli, *A Local Habitation and a Name: Imagining Histories in the Italian Renaissance*, ch. 3. New York: Fordham University Press, 2011.
Asor Rosa, Alberto. *"Decameron" di Giovanni Boccaccio*. In Asor Rosa, *Letteratura italiana. Le Opere*, vol. 1: *Dalle Origini al Cinquecento*. Turin: Einaudi, 1992.
Balestrero, Monica. *L'immaginario del sogno nel* Decameron. Rome: Aracne, 2009.
Baratto, Mario. *Realtà e stile nel "Decameron."* Vicenza: Neri Pozza, 1970, 1984, 1993, 1996.
Bàrberi Squarotti, Giorgio. "Le antifrasi di Dioneo." In *Studi filologici letterari e storici in memoria di Guido Favati*, edited by G. Varanini and P. Pinagli, 1:69–90. Padua: Antenore, 1977.

– *"Decameron:* Lidia, Francesca, Dianora e le prove d'amore." *Italianistica* 42.2 (2013): 39–53.

Barolini, Teodolinda. "Dante and Cavalcanti (On Making Distinctions in Matters of Love): *Inferno* V in Its Lyric Context." *Dante Studies* 116 (1998): 31–63.

– "Dante and Francesca da Rimini: Realpolitik, Romance, Gender." *Speculum* 75 (2000): 1–28.

– *Dante and the Origins of Italian Literary Culture*. New York: Fordham University Press, 2006.

– "The Marquis of Saluzzo, or the Griselda Story Before It Was Hijacked: Calculating Matrimonial Odds in *Decameron* 10.10." *Mediaevalia* 34.1 (2013): 23–55.

– "'Le parole son femmine e i fatti sono maschi': Toward a Sexual Poetics of the *Decameron* (*Decameron* II.9, II.10, V.10)." *Studi sul Boccaccio* 21 (1993): 175–97; reissued in *Dante and the Origins of Italian Literary Culture*, 281–303. New York: Fordham University Press, 2006.

– "A Philosophy of Consolation: The Place of the Other in Life's Transactions." In *Boccaccio 1313–2103*, edited by F. Ciabattoni, E. Filosa, and K. Olson, 89–105. Ravenna: Longo, 2015.

– "The Scholar and the Widow (*Decameron* VIII.7): Corrupt Appetite and Moral Failure in Society's Intellectual Elite." In *The Decameron Eighth Day in Perspective*, edited by William Robins, 148–89. Toronto: University of Toronto Press, 2020.

– "Sociology of the *Brigata*: Gendered Groups in Dante, Forese, Folgore, Boccaccio – From 'Guido, i' vorrei' to Griselda." *Italian Studies* 67.1 (2012): 4–22.

– "The Wheel of the Decameron." *Romance Philology* 36.4 (1983): 521–38; reissued in *Dante and the Origins of the Italian Literary Culture*, 224–44. New York: Fordham University Press, 2006.

Barsella, Susanna. "Boccaccio e Cino da Pistoia: Critica alla poetica dell'amore nella parodia di *Filostrato* V e *Decameron* III 5, X 7." *Italianistica* 29.1 (2000): 55–73.

– "Boccaccio, i tiranni e la ragione naturale." *Heliotropia* 12–13 (2015–16): 131–63. http://www.heliotropia.org.

– "I 'marginalia' di Boccaccio all'Etica Nicomachea di Aristotele (Milano, Biblioteca Ambrosiana A 204 Inf.)." In *Boccaccio in America*, edited by E. Filosa and M. Papio, 143–55. Ravenna: Longo, 2012.

– "The Merchant and the Sacred: Artifice and Realism in the *Decameron* I.1." *Quaderni d'Italianistica* 38.2 (2017 [2018]): 11–40 (special issue, *Categories for the "Decameron,"* edited by K. Brown).

– "The Tale of Tedaldo degli Elisei (III.7)." In *The Decameron Third Day in Perspective*, edited by F. Ciabattoni and P.M. Forni, 131–49. Toronto: University of Toronto Press, 2014.

– "Travestimento autorale e autorità narrativa nella cornice del *Decameron*." In *Vested Voices II. Creating with Transvestitism: from Bertolucci to Boccaccio*, edited by F.G. Pedriali and R. Riccobono, 131–44. Ravenna: Longo Editore, 2007.

Battaglia Ricci, Lucia. "La Bibbia nelle opere di Giovanni Boccaccio: un contributo agli studi." In *Gli antichi e i moderni: Studi in onore di Roberto Cardini*, edited by L. Bertolini and D. Coppini, 1:51–61. Florence: Polistampa, 2010.

Bausi, F. "Le *forme del comico* nel *Decameron*." In Le *forme del comico*, edited by S. Magherini, A. Nozzoli, and G. Tellini, 47–59. Florence: Società Editrice Fiorentina, 2019.

Baxter, Catherine E. "*Turpiloquium* in Boccaccio's Tale of the Goslings ('Decameron', Day IV, Introduction)." *Modern Language Review* 108.3 (2013): 812–38.

Beidler, Peter. "Chaucer's *Reeve's Tale*, Boccaccio's *Decameron*, IX, 6, and Two 'Soft' German Analogues." *Chaucer Review* 28.3 (1994): 237–51.

– "The Reeve's Tale." In *Sources and Analogues of the Canterbury Tale*, edited by R.M. Correale, 23–73. Cambridge and Rochester, NY: D.S. Brewer, 2002.

Bentivogli, Bruno. "Sospetti di falsificazione per un sonetto attribuito a Cecco Angiolieri." *Studi e problemi di critica testuale* 77 (2008): 9–37.

Bergin, Thomas G. *Boccaccio*. New York: Viking Press, 1981.

Berisso, Marco, ed. *Poesia comica del Medioevo italiano*. Milan: Rizzoli, 2001.

Bettarini Bruni, Anna. "Cecco Angiolieri, la lirica comica e la nozione di scuola." In *Cecco Angiolieri e la poesia satirica medievale. Atti del Convegno Internazionale. Siena, 26–27 ottobre 2002*, edited by S. Carrai and G. Marrani, 77–99. Florence: Edizioni del Galluzzo, 2005.

Billanovich, Giuseppe. *Restauri Boccacceschi*. Rome: Edizioni di Storia e Letteratura, 1947.

Bloch, R. Howard. *Medieval Misogyny and the Invention of Western Romantic Love*. Chicago: University of Chicago Press, 1991.

Boitani, Piero. *Chaucer and Boccaccio*. Oxford: Society for the Study of Mediaeval Languages and Literature, 1977.

Bose, Mishtooni. "From Exegesis to Appropriation: The Medieval Solomon." *Medium Aevum* 65 (1996): 187–210.

Botti, Francesco Paolo. "A proposito del sogno di Talano ('Decameron', IX 7)." *Intersezioni* 32.2 (2012): 173–87.

Bragantini, Renzo "Premesse sull'ascolto decameroniano. Con primi appunti sul codice biblico nel 'Decameron.'" [2003] In *Ingressi laterali al Trecento maggiore: Dante, Petrarca, Boccaccio*, 69–87. Naples: Liguori, 2012.

Branca, Vittore. *Boccaccio medievale*. Florence: Sansoni, 1956.

– *Boccaccio medievale e nuovi studi sul Decameron*. Florence: Sansoni, 1990, 1995.

– "Coerenza ideale e funzione unitaria dell'Introduzione." In *Boccaccio medievale e nuovi studi sul Decameron*, 31–44. Florence: Sansoni, 1992.

Brown, Katherine A. *Boccaccio's Fabliaux: Medieval Short Stories and the Function of Reversal*. Gainesville: University of Florida Press, 2014.

Brundage, James A. *Law, Sex, and Christian Society in Medieval Europe*. Chicago and London: University of Chicago Press, 1987.

– "Let Me Count the Ways: Canonists and Theologians Contemplate Coital Positions." *Journal of Medieval History* 10 (1984): 81–93.

– "Sex and Canon Law." In *Handbook of Medieval Sexuality*, edited by Vern L. Bullough and James A. Brundage, 33–50. New York: Garland, 1996.

Bruni, Francesco. *Boccaccio. L'invenzione della letteratura mezzana*. Bologna: Il Mulino, 1990.

Buettner, Brigitte. "Past Presents: New Year's Gifts at the Valois Courts, ca. 1400." *Art Bulletin* 83.4 (2001): 598–625.

Bullough, Vern L. "The Sin against Nature and Homosexuality." In *Sexual Practices and the Medieval Church*, edited by V.L. Bullough and J.A. Brundage, 55–71. Buffalo: Prometheus Books, 1982.

Burgwinkle, William. *Sodomy, Masculinity, and Law in Medieval Literature*. Cambridge: Cambridge University Press, 2004.

Cammarota, Maria Grazia. "La storia di Donna Francesca che umilia i suoi spasimanti (*Dec.* IX.1) nelle versioni tedesche di Arigo e Hans Sachs." In *I novellieri italiani e la loro presenza nella cultura europea: rizomi e palinsesti rinascimentali*, edited by G. Carrascón and C. Simbolotti. Turin: Accademia University Press, 2015.

Canovas, Frédéric. "Forme et fonction de l'énoncé onirique dans le texte médiéval: l'example du 'Décaméron.'" *Neophilologus* 80.4 (1996): 555–68.

Cappelletti, Irene. "La brigata in Purgatorio. Qualche ipotesi sulla struttura del *Decameron*." *Heliotropia* 15 (2018): 57–92.

– "Una proposta per la struttura del Decameron: primi appunti." In *Intorno a Boccaccio. Boccaccio e dintorni, 2015*. Atti del seminario internazionale di studi, edited by S. Zamponi, 65–76. Florence: FUP, 2016.

Cappozzo, Valerio. "Il *Decameron* e il *Libro dei sogni di Daniele* nel cod. Vaticano Rossiano 947." *Studi sul Boccaccio* 42 (2014): 163–78.

– "'Delle verità dimostrate da' sogni': Boccaccio e l'oniromanzia medievale." In *Boccaccio 1313–2013*, edited by F. Ciabattoni, E. Filosa, and K. Olson, 203–11. Ravenna: Longo Editore, 2015.

Cardini, Franco. "Sognare a Firenze fra Trecento e Quattrocento." *Quaderni Medievali* 9 (1980): 86–120.

Cazalé Bérard, Claude. "Filoginia/Misoginia." In *Lessico critico decameroniano*, edited by R. Bragantini and P.M. Forni, 116–41. Turin: Bollati Boringhieri, 1995.

Cervigni, Dino S. *Dante's Poetry of Dreams*. Florence: Olschki, 1986.

– "The *Decameron*'s Ballads and Emilia's Happy Song." *Annali d'Italianistica* 31 (2013): 131–71.
– "Fiammetta's Song of Jealousy: Are the Young People Still at Play?" *Annali d'Italianistica* 31 (2013): 469–508.
– "Making Amends and Behaving Magnificently: *Decameron* 10's Secular Redemption." *Annali d'Italianistica* 31 (2013): 416–58.
Cesari, Anna Maria. "L'*Etica* di Aristotele del codice Ambrosiano A 204 inf.: Un autografo del Boccaccio." *Archivio Storico Lombardo* 93–4 (1968): 69–100.
Chiappelli, Fredi. "L'episodio di Travale e il 'dire onestamente villania' nella narrativa toscana dei primi secoli." In *Il legame musaico*, edited by P.M. Forni, 21–40. Rome: Edizioni di Storia e Letteratura, 1984.
Chiecchi, Giuseppe. "Sentenze e proverbi nel Decameron." *Studi sul Boccaccio* 9 (1975–6): 119–68.
Ciccuto, Marcello. "All'ombra della Garisenda: preistoria del visibile nella cultura poetica di Dante." In *Figure d'artista. La nascita delle immagini alle origini della letteratura*, 13–56. Fiesole: Cadmo, 2002.
– "Un'antica canzone di Giotto e i pittori del Boccaccio. Nascita dell'identità artistica." *Intersezioni* 16.3 (1996): 403–16.
– "Gli anticlassici di Vasari." In *Autorità, modelli e antimodelli nella cultura artistica e letteraria tra Riforma e Controriforma, Atti del Seminario internazionale di studi*, Urbino-Sassocorvaro, November 9–11 2006, edited by A. Corsaro, H. Hendrix, and P. Procaccioli, 389–94. Manziana: Vecchiarelli, 2007.
– "Il novelliere en artiste: strategie della dissimiglianza fra Boccaccio e Bandello." In *L'immagine del testo. Episodi di cultura figurativa nella letteratura italiana*, 113–56. Rome: Bonacci, 1990.
– "Petrarca e le arti: l'occhio della mente fra i segni del mondo." *Quaderns d'Italià* 11 (2006): 203–21.
– "'Trattando l'ombre come cosa salda'. Forme visive della 'dolcezza' di Stazio nel Purgatorio dantesco." *Studi sul canone letterario del Trecento: per Michelangelo Picone*, edited by J. Bartuschat and L. Rossi, 57–66. Ravenna: Longo, 2003.
Ciccuto, M., and F. Furlan, eds. "Dossier: Comicità e stile nel Boccaccio." *Humanistica* 4 (2009): 11–80.
Clarke, Kenneth P. "The Poetics of the Paratext: Rubricating the Vernacular." *Le tre corone* 6 (2019): 69–106.
Cleaver, Natalie A. "Authorizing the Reader: Dante and the Ends of the *Decameron*." Dissertation, University of California, Berkeley, 2012, available at http://digitalassets.lib. Berkeley.edu/ etd/ucb/text/Cleaver _berkeley_0028E_12283.pdf (open access).
Coccetti, Fabio. "*Decameron* IX.4: Considerazioni sulla struttura della novella." *La Rassegna della letteratura italiana* 92.2–3 (1988): 304–6.

Conoscenti, Domenico. "Fra *mala ventura* e *fuoco dal cielo*: La sodomia in *Decameron* V 10 e nelle *Esposizioni sopra la Comedia*." *Heliotropia* 5.1–2 (2008): 39–56.

Contini, Gianfranco. *Poeti del Duecento*. Edited by G. Contini. Vol. 2, part I. Naples: Ricciardi, 1995.

Cottino-Jones, Marga. *Order from Chaos: Social and Aesthetic Harmonies in Boccaccio's "Decameron."* Washington, DC: University Press of America, 1982.

Coulter, Cornelia C. "Boccaccio's Knowledge of Quintilian." *Speculum* 33 (1958): 490–6.

Cresciani, Chiara. "Aspetti del dibattito sull'Umido radicale nella cultura del tardo medioevo (secoli XIII–XV)." In *Actes de la II Trobada internacional d'estudis sobre Arnau de Vilanova*, edited by J. Perarnau, 333–80. Barcelona: Institut d'Estudis Catalans, 2005.

Cuomo, Luisa. "Sillogizzare motteggiando e motteggiare sillogizzando: dal 'Novellino' alla VI giornata del *Decameron*." *Studi sul Boccaccio* 13 (1981–2): 217–65.

Cursi, Marco. "Giovanni Boccaccio – Autografi." In *Autografi dei letterati italiani. Le origini e il Trecento*, edited by G. Brunetti, M. Fiorilla, and M. Petoletti, 47–63. Rome: Salerno editrice, 2013.

D'Ancona, Alessandro. *Cecco Angiolieri da Siena, poeta umorista del secolo XII*. In *Studi di critica e storia letteraria*. Bologna: Zanichelli, 1912.

D'Andrea, Antonio. "Le rubriche del *Decameron*." In *Il nome della storia. Studi e ricerche di storia e letteratura*, 98–125. Naples: Liguori, 1982.

Davidsohn, Robert. *Storia di Firenze*. 8 vols. Florence: Sansoni, 1956–68.

Decameron Web, 2015. https://www.brown.edu/Departments/Italian_Studies/dweb.

Delcorno, Carlo. "Ironia/Parodia." In *Lessico critico decameroniano*, edited by R. Bragantini and P.M. Forni, 162–91. Turin: Bollati Boringhieri, 1995.

Digital Dante. Columbia University Libraries, 2015. http://digitaldante.columbia.edu.

Divizia, Paolo. "Una doppia forzatura logica nella novella di Pinuccio e Adriano (*Decameron* IX, VI)." In *Forme del tempo e del cronotopo nelle letterature romanze e orientali. X Convegno Società italiana di filologia romanza, VIII Colloquio internazionale Medioevo romanzo e orientale (Roma, 25–29 settembre 2012)*, edited by G. Lalomia, A. Pioletti, A. Punzi, and F. Rizzo Nervo, 399–413. Soveria Mannelli: Rubbettino, 2014.

Duyos Vacca, Diane. "Converting Alibech: 'Nunc spiritu copuleris.'" *Journal of Medieval and Renaissance Studies* 25.2 (1995): 207–27.

Eisner, Martin. *Boccaccio and the Invention of Italian Literature: Dante, Petrarch, Cavalcanti, and the Authority of the Vernacular*. Cambridge: Cambridge University Press, 2013.

Enciclopedia Dantesca. Online edition. Rome: Treccani, 1970. http://www.treccani.it/enciclopedia/.
Fenzi, Enrico. *La canzone d'amore di Guido Cavalcanti e i suoi antichi commenti*. Genoa: Il melangolo, 1999.
– "Petrarca e la scrittura dell'amicizia." In *Motivi e forme delle "Familiari" di Francesco Petrarca*, edited by C. Berra, 549–90. Milan: Cisalpino, 2003.
– "Ridere e lietamente morire. Un'interpretazione del Decameron." *Per leggere* 7.12 (2007): 121–50.
Ferrante, Joan. "The Frame Characters of the *Decameron*." *Romance Philology* 19 (1965): 212–26.
Ferreri, Rosario. "Ciacco, Biondello e Martellino." *Studi sul Boccaccio* 24 (1996): 231–49.
Fido, Franco. "Architettura." In *Lessico critico decameroniano*, edited by R. Bragantini and P.M. Forni, 13–33. Turin: Bollati Boringhieri, 1995.
– "Dante personaggio mancato del libro galeotto." [1977] In *Il regime delle simmetrie imperfette. Studi sul "Decameron,"* 111–23. Milan: Franco Angeli, 1988.
– *Il regime delle simmetrie imperfette: Studi sul "Decameron."* Milan: Franco Angeli, 1988.
– "Retorica e semantica nel 'Decameron': tropi e segni in funzione narrativa." [1977] In *Il regime delle simmetrie imperfette. Studi sul "Decameron,"* 91–102. Milan: Franco Angeli, 1988.
– "Silenzi e cavalli nell'eros del Decameron." *Belfagor* 38.1 (1983): 79–84.
– "The Tale of Ser Ciappelletto (I.1)." In *The Decameron First Day in Perspective*, edited by E.B. Weaver, 59–76. Toronto: University of Toronto Press, 2004.
Filosa, Elsa. "Motivi anti-tirannide e repubblicani nel *De mulieribus claris*." *Heliotropia* 12–13 (2015): 165–87.
Fontes-Baratto, Anna. "Le thème de la 'beffa' dans le 'Décameron.'" In *Formes et significations de la "beffa" dans la littérature italienne de la Renaissance: Boccaccio, Machiavelli, Grazzini, Bandello, Straparola, Parabosco, Giraldi Cinzio*, 11–44. Paris: Université de la Sorbonne Nouvelle, 1972.
Forni, Pier Massimo. *Adventures in Speech*. Philadelphia: University of Pennsylvania Press, 1996.
– "Boccaccio tra Dante e Cino." *Quaderni d'italianistica* 16.2 (1995): 179–95.
– *Forme complesse del "Decameron"*. Florence: Leo Olschki, 1992.
Parole come fatti. Naples: Liguori, 2008.
– "Realtà/verità." *Studi sul Boccaccio* 22 (1994): 235–55.
– "Retorica del reale." *Studi sul Boccaccio* 17 (1988): 183–202.
Francesconi, Giampaolo. "11 aprile 1306: Pistoia apre le porte a Firenze, dopo un anno di assedio. Cronaca, costruzione e trasmissione di un evento." *Reti Medievali Rivista* 8 (2007): 1–26. http://www.retimedievali.it.

– "Firenze e Pistoia in età comunale. I diversi destini di due città della Toscana interna." In *La Pistoia comunale nel contesto toscano ed europeo (secoli XII–XIV)*, edited by P. Gualtieri, 73–100. Pistoia: Società pistoiese di storia patria, 2008.

Frye, Northrop. *The Great Code: The Bible and Literature*. Toronto: Academic Press Canada, 1982.

Getto, Giovanni. *Vita di forme e forme di vita nel "Decameron."* Turin: Petrini, 1966, 1972, 1986.

Giaccherini, Enrico. "*The Reeve's Tale* e *Decameron* IX, 6." *Rivista di letterature moderne e comparate* 29 (1976): 99–121.

Gittes, Tobias Foster. "'Dal giogo alleviati': Free Servitude and Fixed Stars in *Decameron* 9." *Annali d'Italianistica* (2013): 381–415.

Giunta, Claudio. *Versi per un destinatario*. Bologna: Il Mulino, 2002.

Goldberg, Lea. "'La vita serena' (Saggio sulla narrativa del Boccaccio)." In *Romanica et Occidentalia. Etudes dédiées à la mémoire de Hiram Peri (Pflaum)*, edited by Moshé Lazar, 43–55. Jerusalem: Magnes Press-Université Hébraïque, 1963.

Grudin, Michaela Paasche, and Robert Grudin. *Boccaccio's "Decameron" and the Ciceronian Renaissance*. New York: Palgrave Macmillan, 2012.

Heffernan, Carol Falvo. "Chaucer's 'Miller's Tale' and 'Reeve's Tale,' Boccaccio's 'Decameron,' and the French Fabliaux." *Italica* 81.3 (2004): 311–24.

Hollander, Robert. *Boccaccio's Dante and the Shaping Force of Satire*, 109–68. Ann Arbor: University of Michigan Press, 1997.

– *Boccaccio's Last Fiction: "Il Corbaccio"*. Philadelphia: University of Pennsylvania Press, 1988.

– "The Struggle for Control among the *novellatori* of the *Decameron* and the Reason for Their Return to Florence." *Studi sul Boccaccio* 39 (2011): 243–314.

– "Utilità." In *Boccaccio's Dante and the Shaping Force of Satire*, 69–88. Ann Arbor: University of Michigan Press, 1997.

Hollander, Robert, with Courtney Cahill. "Day Ten of the *Decameron*: The Myth of Order." In *Boccaccio's Dante and the Shaping Force of Satire*, 109–68. Ann Arbor: University of Michigan Press, 1997.

Holmes, Olivia. "Doing unto Others, or Sienese Polyamory (VIII.8)." In *The Decameron Eighth Day in Perspective*, edited by W. Robins, 190–204. Toronto: University of Toronto Press, 2020.

Istituto Opera del Vocabolario Italiano. *Corpus OVI dell'italiano antico*, 2005. http://gattoweb.ovi.cnr.it.

– *Tesoro della lingua italiana delle origini*, 1997–2017. http://tlio.ovi.cnr.it/TLIO/

Jones, Ann R., and Peter Stallybrass. *Renaissance Clothing and the Materials of Memory*. Cambridge: Cambridge University Press, 2000.

Jordan, Mark D. *The Invention of Sodomy in Christian Theology*. Chicago: University of Chicago Press, 1997.

Kircher, Timothy. "Boccaccio and the Appearance of Reality (*Decameron* 8.3/9.3)." *Heliotropia* 16–17 (2019–20): 83–105.

– *The Poet's Wisdom: The Humanists, the Church and the Formation of Philosophy in the Early Renaissance*. Leiden and London: Brill, 2006.

Kirkham, Victoria. "An Allegorically Tempered *Decameron*." *Italica* 62.1 (1985): 1–23.

– "Morale." In *Lessico critico decameroniano*, edited by R. Bragantini and P.M. Forni, 249–68. Turin: Bollati Boringhieri, 1995.

– *The Sign of Reason in Boccaccio's Fiction*. Florence: Olschki, 1993.

Koff, Leonard M., and Brenda Deen Schildgen, eds. *The Decameron and the Canterbury Tales: New Essays on an Old Question*. Madison, NJ, and London: Fairleigh Dickinson University Press and Associated University Presses, 2000.

Kriesel, James. *Boccaccio's Corpus: Allegory, Ethics, and Vernacularity*. Notre Dame: University of Notre Dame Press, 2018.

Langer, Ullrich. "The Renaissance Novella as Justice." *Renaissance Quarterly* 52.2 (1999): 311–41.

Lee, A. Collingwood. *The Decameron, Its Sources and Analogues*. New York: Haskell House, 1972.

Letao, David D. *The Pregnant Man as Myth and Metaphor in Classical Greek Literature*. Cambridge and New York: Cambridge University Press, 2012.

Levalois, Christophe. *Le symbolisme du loup*. Milan: Archè, 1986.

Lochrie, Karma. *Covert Operations: The Medieval Uses of Secrecy*. Philadelphia: University of Pennsylvania Press, 1999.

Lummus, David. "Boccaccio's Three Venuses: On the Convergence of Celestial and Transgressive Love in the *Genealogie Deorum Gentilium Libri*." *Medievalia et Humanistica* n.s. 37 (2011): 65–88.

– "The *Decameron* and Boccaccio's Poetics." In *The Cambridge Companion to Boccaccio*, edited by G. Armstrong, R. Daniels, and S.J. Milner, 65–82. Cambridge: Cambridge University Press, 2015.

Maglio, G. *La coscienza giuridica medievale. Diritto naturale e giustizia nel medioevo*. Padua: Cedam, 2014.

Manni, Domenico Maria. *Istoria del Decamerone di Giovanni Boccaccio*. Florence, 1742.

Manni, Paola. *La lingua di Boccaccio*. Bologna: Il Mulino, 2016.

Marchesi, Simone. "Dire la verità dei sogni: la teoria di Panfilo in *Decameron* IV, 6." *Italica* 81.2 (2004): 170–83.

– "Intenzionalità tragica e intendimento comico in *Decameron*, V 8." *Humanistica* 2 (2009): 31–41.

– "Sex, Floods, and a Learned Gloss: Reading Dante's Commentators within the Decameron." In *Dante Notes* (online, January 2019).

– *Stratigrafie decameroniane*. Florence: Olschki, 2004.

Marcus, Millicent J. *An Allegory of Forms: Literary Self-Consciousness in the "Decameron,"* 79–92. Saratoga: Anma Libri, 1979.

– "Misogyny as Mis-reading: A Gloss on *Decameron* VIII, 7." *Stanford Italian Review* 4.1 (1984): 23–40.

Mariani Zini, Fosca. "Du plaisir d'être indifferent et de la vertu du désintérêt." In *Ut Philosophia Poesis. Questions Philosophiques dans L'Œuvre de Dante, Pétrarque et Boccace*, edited by J. Biard and F. Mariani Zini, 223–57. Paris: Vrin, 2008.

Marino, Lucia. *The Decameron "Cornice": Allusion, Allegory, and Iconology*. Ravenna: Longo, 1979.

Markulin, Joseph. "Emilia and the Case for Openness in the *Decameron*." *Stanford Italian Review* 3 (1983): 183–99.

Marrani, Giuseppe. "La poesia comica tra'200 e'300. Aspetti della fortuna di Cecco Angiolieri fuori Toscana." In *Cecco Angiolieri e la poesia satirica medievale. Atti del Convegno Internazionale. Siena, 26–27 ottobre 2002*, edited by S. Carrai and G. Marrani, 101–22. Florence: Edizioni del Galluzzo, 2005.

Marti, Mario. *Cultura e stile nei poeti giocosi*. Pisa: Nistri-Lischi, 1953.

Martinez, Ronald L. "Calandrino and the Powers of the Stone: Rhetoric, Belief and the Progress of *Ingegno* in *Decameron* VIII.3." *Heliotropia* 1.1 (2003): 1–26.

Massèra, Aldo F., ed. *I Sonetti di Cecco Angiolieri editi criticamente ed illustrati*. Bologna: Zanichelli, 1906.

Mazzetti, Martina. "Boccaccio e Cino. La costruzione di una poetica tra riscritture, echi e (false) parodie. In *Cino da Pistoia nella storia della poesia italiana*, edited by R. Arqués Corominas and S. Tranfaglia, 209–32. Florence: Cesati, 2016.

Mazzoni, Francesco. "Il canto V dell'*Inferno*." In *Inferno: letture degli anni 1973–76*, edited by S. Zennaro, 97–143. Rome: Bonacci, 1977.

Mazzotta, Giuseppe. *The World at Play in Boccaccio's "Decameron"*. Princeton: Princeton University Press, 1986.

Merriam-Webster Dictionary, 2017. http://www.merriam-webster.com.

Migiel, Marilyn. *The Ethical Dimension of the Decameron*. Toronto: University of Toronto Press, 2015.

– *A Rhetoric of the Decameron*. Toronto: University of Toronto Press, 2003.

Milanese, A. "Affinità e contraddizioni tra rubriche e novelle del *Decameron*." *Studi sul Boccaccio* 33 (1995): 89–110.

Mineo, Nicolò "La sesta giornata del 'Decameron', o del potere delle donne." In *La novella e il comico. Da Boccaccio a Brancati*, edited by N. Merola and N. Ordine, 73–95. Naples: Liguori, 1996.

Morosini, Roberta. "'La Bele Conjunture' o 'Il Gioco degli Incontri' in *Decameron* IX.6." *Romance Languages Annual* 9 (1998): 260–5.
Mortimer, Anthony. "Extra Material on Cecco Angiolieri's *Sonnets*." In *Sonnets*, translated by C.H. Scott and A. Mortimer, 271–9. London: Oneworld Classics 2008.
Muscetta, Carlo. "Giovanni Boccaccio e i novellieri." In *Storia della letteratura italiana*, vol. 2, *Il Trecento*, edited by E. Cecchi and N. Sapegno. Milan: Garzanti, 1965.
Nasti, Paola. *Favole d'amore e "saver profondo": La tradizione salomonica in Dante*. Ravenna: Longo, 2007.
Neumeister, Sebastian "Die Praxis des Lachens im Decameron." In *Semiotik, Rhetorik und Soziologie des Lachens*, edited by L. Fietz, J.O. Fichte, and H.W. Ludwig, 65–81. Tübingen: Max Niemeyer Verlag, 1996.
Neuschäfer, Hans-Jörg. *Boccaccio und der Beginn der Novelle*. Munich: Wilhelm Fink Verlag, 1969.
Noonan, John T. *Contraception: A History of Its Treatment by the Catholic Theologians and Canonists*. Cambridge, MA: Belknap Press of Harvard University Press, 1986.
Ó Cuilleanáin, Cormac. "Man and Beast in the *Decameron*." *Modern Language Review* 75 (1980): 86–93.
– *Religion and the Clergy in Boccaccio's Decameron*. Rome: Edizioni di Storia e Letteratura, 1984.
Olson, Kristina. *Courtesy Lost: Dante, Boccaccio, and the Literature of History*. Toronto: University of Toronto Press, 2014.
Ortalli, Gherardo. *Lupi genti culture: Uomo e ambiente nel medioevo*. Turin: Einaudi, 1997.
– "Natura, storia e mitografia del lupo nel Medioevo." *La cultura* 11.3–4 (1973): 257–311.
Oxford English Dictionary, 2017. http://www.oed.com.
Pascale, Miriam. "La 'camera oscura molto'. Note su una 'metafora realizzata' (*Decameron* III 6 e VII 8)." *Italianistica* 48 (2019): 75–83.
Peirone, Claudia. "Per aver festa e buon tempo e non per altro … IX giornata." In *Prospettive sul Decameron*, edited by G. Bàrberi Squarotti, 149–63. Turin: Tirrenia Stampatori, 1989.
Perfetti, Lisa. *Women and Laughter in Medieval Comic Literature*. Ann Arbor: University of Michigan Press, 2003.
Peruzzi, Simone L. *Storia del commercio e dei banchieri di Firenze in tutto il mondo conosciuto dal 1290 al 1345*. Florence: Cellini, 1868.
Petoletti, Marco. "Il Marziale autografo di Giovanni Boccaccio." *Italia medioevale e umanistica* 46 (2005): 35–55.
– "La scoperta del Marziale autografo di Giovanni Boccaccio." *Aevum* 80 (January–April 2006): 185–7.

Picone, Michelangelo. "L'arte della beffa: l'ottava giornata." In *Introduzione al Decameron*, edited by M. Picone and M. Mesirca, 203–25. Florence: Franco Cesati, 2004.

– "Autore/narratori." In *Lessico critico decameroniano*, edited by R. Bragantini and P.M. Forni, 34–59. Turin: Bollati Boringhieri, 1995.

– "Leggiadri motti e pronte risposte. La sesta giornata." In *Introduzione al Decameron*, edited by M. Picone and M. Mesirca, 163–86. Florence: Franco Cesati Editore, 2004.

– "Il principio del novellare: la prima giornata." In *Introduzione al Decameron*, edited by M. Picone and M. Mesirca, 57–78. Florence: Franco Cesati Editore, 2004.

Pirandello, Luigi. "Un preteso poeta umorista del XIII secolo." In *Saggi, poesie, scritti varii*, edited by M. Lo Vecchio-Musti, 247–62. Milan: Mondadori, 1965.

Piras, Antonella. *La Toscana di Boccaccio. Itinerari culturali nel paesaggio toscano attraverso il "Decameron."* Milan: Ledizioni, 2013.

Pluskowski, Aleksander. *Wolves and the Wilderness in the Middle Ages.* Woodbridge, Suffolk: Boydell Press, 2006.

Psaki, Regina. "Voicing Gender in the Decameron." In *The Cambridge Companion to Boccaccio*, edited by G. Armstrong, R. Daniels, and S.J. Milner, 101–17. New York: Cambridge University Press, 2015.

– "'Women Make All Things Lose Their Power': Women's Knowledge, Men's Fear in the *Decameron* and the *Corbaccio*." *Heliotropia* 1.1 (2003): 1–13.

Richards, I.A. "Metaphor." In Richards, *The Philosophy of Rhetoric* [1936], 87–138. New York: Oxford University Press, 1965.

Richardson, Brian. "The 'Ghibelline' Narrator in the *Decameron*." *Italian Studies* 33.1 (1978): 20–8.

Rossi, Luciano. "In luogo di sollazzo. I *fabliaux* nel *Decameron*." In *Leggiadre donne … Novella e racconto breve in Italia*, edited by F. Bruni, 13–27. Venice: Marsilio, 2000.

– "Ironia e parodia nel 'Decameron': da Ciappelletto a Griselda." In *La novella italiana. Atti del Convegno di Caprarola (19–24 settembre 1988)*, 365–405. Rome: Salerno Editrice, 1989.

Rowland, Beryl. *Animals with Human Faces: A Guide to Animal Symbolism.* Knoxville: University of Tennessee Press, 1973.

Rumble, Patrick. "Framing Boccaccio: Pasolini's Adaptation of the *Decameron*." In *Allegories of Contamination: Pier Paolo Pasolini's Trilogy of Life*. Toronto: University of Toronto Press, 1996.

Russo, Luigi. *Letture critiche del "Decameron"*. Rome and Bari: Laterza, 1977.

Ruthenberg, Myriam Swennen. "The Tale of Ricciardo and Catella." In *The Decameron Third Day in Perspective*, edited by F. Ciabattoni and P.M. Forni, 108–30. Toronto: University of Toronto Press, 2014.

Salisbury, Joyce E. *The Beast Within: Animals in the Middle Ages.* New York: Routledge, 2011.

Santagata, Marco. "Un tassello per Calandrino pittore." In *Per civile conversazione. Con Amedeo Quondam,* edited by B. Alfonzetti, G. Baldassarri, E. Bellini, S. Costa, and M. Santagata, 1031–7. Rome: Bulzoni, 2015.

Savelli, Giulio. "Riso." In *Lessico critico decameroniano,* edited by R. Bragantini and P.M. Forni, 344–71. Turin: Bollati Boringhieri, 1995.

Scancarelli Seem, Lauren. "Nolite iudicare: Dante and the Dilemma of Judgment." In *Writers Reading Writers: Intertextual Studies in Medieval and Early Modern Literature in Honor of Robert Hollander,* edited by J.L. Smarr, 73–88. Newark: University of Delaware Press, 2007.

Sedgwick, Eve Kosofsky. "Paranoid Reading and Reparative Reading." In *Touching Feeling: Affect, Pedagogy, Performativity,* 123–52. Durham, NC: Duke University Press, 2003.

Segre, Cesare. "La beffa e il comico nella novellistica del Due e Trecento." In *Notizie dalla crisi,* 85–97. Turin: Einaudi, 1993.

Selig, Karl-Ludwig. "Decameron IX/7 and X/4 and the Text Within." *Teaching Language through Literature* 27.2 (1988): 34–9.

Sherberg, Michael. *The Governance of Friendship: Law and Gender in the "Decameron."* Columbus: Ohio State University Press, 2011.

Silber, Gordon. *The Influence of Dante and Petrarch on Certain of Boccaccio's Lyrics.* Menasha, WI: George Banta Publishing, 1940.

Sinicropi, Giovanni. "Il segno linguistico del 'Decameron.'" *Studi sul Boccaccio* 9 (1975–6): 169–224.

Smarr, Janet L. "Altre razze ed altri spazi nel *Decameron.*" In *Boccaccio geografo,* edited by R. Morosini, 133–58. Florence: Edizioni Polistampa, 2010.

– *Boccaccio and Fiammetta: The Narrator as Lover.* Urbana and Chicago: University of Illinois Press, 1986.

– "Clergy in the Decameron: Another Look?" *Heliotropia* 11.1–2 (2014): 55–64.

– "Symmetry and Balance in the *Decameron.*" *Mediaevalia* 2.1 (1976): 159–87.

Spani, Giovanni. "Il vino di Boccaccio: Usi e abusi in alcune novelle del *Decameron.*" *Heliotropia* 8–9 (2011–12): 79–98.

Staples, Max A. *The Ideology of the Decameron.* Lewiston: Edwin Mellen Press, 1994.

Steinberg, Justin. "Mimesis on Trial: Boccaccio's Realism, Legal Verisimilitude, and the Trials of the Decameron." *Representations* 139 (Summer 2017): 118–45.

Stoppino, Eleonora. "Contamination, Contagion and the Animal Function in Boccaccio's *Decameron.*" *Critica del Testo* 17.3 (2014): 93–114.

Surdich, Luigi. "La 'varietà delle cose' e le 'frondi di quercia': la nona giornata." In *Introduzione al "Decameron,"* edited by M. Picone and M. Mesirca, 227–65. Florence: Franco Cesati Editore, 2004.

Tateo, Francesco. *Boccaccio*. Bari: Laterza, 1998.

Tesoro della Lingua Italiana delle Origini (*TLIO*). Online edition. Rome: Consiglio Nazionale delle Ricerche-Opera del Vocabolario Italiano, 1997–present. http://tlio.ovi.cnr.it/.

Todorov, Tzvetan. *Grammaire du Décaméron*. The Hague: Mouton, 1969.

Trin, Antoine. *Les loups dans la légende et dans l'histoire*. Rodez: Éditions Subervie, 1980.

Trokhimenko, Olga V. "Believing That Which Cannot Be: (De)Constructing Medieval Clerical Masculinity in *Des münches not*." *German Quarterly* 85.2 (2012): 121–36.

Tufano, Ilaria. "Il regime comico nelle *Rime* del Boccaccio." *Humanistica* 4.2 (2009 [2010]): 55–9.

Van der Voort, Cok. "Convergenze e divaricazioni tra la prima e la sesta giornata del *Decameron*." *Studi sul Boccaccio* 9 (1979–80): 207–41.

Varvaro, Alberto. *Vocabolario Storico-Etimologico del Siciliano* [*VSES*]. Vol. 2. Palermo and Strasbourg: Centro di Studi filologici e linguistici siciliani-Éditions de linguistique et de philologie, 2014.

Vasari, Giorgio. *Le Vite de' più eccellenti pittori, scultori e architetti italiani, da Cimabue, insino a' tempi nostri*. 1550. Turin: Einaudi, 1986.

Vasvári, Louise. "'Buon cavallo e mal cavallo vuole sprone, e buona femina e mala femina vuol bastone': Medieval Cultural Fictions of Wife Battering." In *Discourses on Love, Marriage, and Transgression in Medieval and Early Modern Literature*, edited by A. Classen, 313–36. Tempe: Arizona Center for Medieval and Renaissance Studies, 2004.

Veglia, Marco. *"La vita lieta." Una lettura del Decameron*. Ravenna: Longo, 2000.

Vocabolario degli Accademici della Crusca (Venezia, 1612). Online edition. Pisa: Accademia della Crusca/Scuola Normale Superiore, s.d. http://vocabolario.sns.it/.

Walters, Jonathan. "Invading the Roman Body: Manliness and Impenetrability in Roman Thought." In *Roman Sexualities*, edited by J.P. Hallett and M.B. Skinner, 29–43. Princeton: Princeton University Press, 1997.

Weaver, Elissa B. "Dietro il vestito: la semiotica del vestire nel *Decameron*." In *La novella italiana. Atti del convegno di Caprarola (19–24 settembre 1988)*, 701–10. Rome: Salerno, 1988.

Zanni, Raffaella. "La 'poesia' del *Decameron*: le ballate e l'intertesto lirico." *Linguistica e letteratura* 1–2 (2005): 59–142.

Contributors

Federica Anichini, PhD in Italian Studies from New York University, published her monograph *Voices of the Body: Liminal Grammar in Guido Cavalcanti "Rime"* in 2009. Her book illustrates the influence of natural philosophy, medicine in particular, on Guido Cavalcanti's poetry. Her current research centres on the relationship between urban environment and creativity in the Florentine medieval vernacular tradition. Her publications include the 2012 article "*Inferno* IX: Passing within City Walls and beneath the 'velame de li versi strani'" (*Mediaevalia* 33) and the essay "In Dialogue with the Imageless Vision: Constructing Language in *Paradiso* III," included in *Dante and Heterodoxy: The Temptation of Radical Thought in the 13th Century* (Cambridge, 2014). Federica Anichini teaches at New York University, Florence.

Albert Russell Ascoli, PhD in Romance Studies (Italian) from Cornell University 1983, is Gladyce Arata Terrill Distinguished Professor Emeritus of the University of California, Berkeley. He is the author of three books: *Ariosto's Bitter Harmony: Crisis and Evasion in the Italian Renaissance* (Princeton, 1987); *Dante and the Making of a Modern Author* (Cambridge, 2008); and *A Local Habitation, and a Name: Imagining Histories in the Italian Renaissance* (Fordham, 2011), as well as of numerous articles and book chapters, in English, Italian, and German. He has collaboratively edited five essay collections, including a double issue of *Renaissance Drama* entitled "Italy and the Drama of Europe" (with William West, 2010), *Italian Futures*, an issue of the electronic journal *California Italian Studies* (with Randolph Starn, 2011), and, most recently, the *Cambridge Companion to Petrarch* (with Unn Falkeid, 2015). He has held a number of fellowships, including the NEH Mellon Rome Prize at the American Academy in Rome (2004–5). He is an elected "socio" of the Academy Letters and Science in the Istituto Lombardo and of the

Accademia dell'Arcadia in Rome. In winter–spring 2017 he was visiting professor at the Villa I Tatti in Florence. He served as President of the Dante Society of America from 2014 to 2020. His current research projects include a monograph on Boccaccio's complex interrogations of representational realism and philosophical naturalism in the *Decameron,* building on a series of essays he has published since 1992.

Susanna Barsella graduated from the Johns Hopkins University and is Professor of Italian for the Modern Languages and Literatures Department and the Center for Medieval Studies at Fordham University. Dr Barsella's main area of research is in Italian medieval literature with a specific interest in the literature of early humanism. Her publications range from Dante to Petrarch, Boccaccio, and Michelangelo, and on the idea of work from antiquity to the Middle Ages. Dr Barsella's interests also embrace twentieth-century literature, with publications on Pirandello, Gadda, and twentieth-century poetry. Her book *In the Light of the Angels: Angelology and Cosmology in Dante's Divina Commedia* was published by Olschki in 2010. She has published *The Humanist Workshop: Essays in Honor of Salvatore Camporeale O.P.,* coedited with Francesco Ciabattoni, in 2012. She has served as treasurer and vice-president of the American Boccaccio Association and she is currently the co-organizer of the ABA Summer School in Paleography.

Johnny L. Bertolio graduated in Classics from the Scuola Normale Superiore and from the University of Pisa, and he holds a PhD in Italian Studies from the University of Toronto. His areas of research extend from early humanism to the late Renaissance, and comprise a particular interest in the reception of Greek and Latin works as well as of the Bible in Italian literature. On these topics he has written articles for various academic journals, including *Giornale storico della letteratura italiana, Lettere italiane,* and *Renaissance Studies*. He published a monograph and edition of Leonardo Bruni's *De interpretatione recta* (Rome, 2020), and a handbook of Italian literature for non-mother-tongue learners, *Le vie dorate* (Turin, 2021).

Patrizio Ceccagnoli is an Associate Professor of Italian at the University of Kansas. Previously, he taught Italian at University of Massachusetts Amherst, Fordham University, and Columbia University, where he received his PhD in 2011. Ceccagnoli authored the first critical edition of an unpublished work by Filippo Tommaso Marinetti, *Il Poema di Fiume* (L'*Ellisse,* V) and, in collaboration with Paolo Valesio, the first edition of Marinetti's posthumous novel *Venezianella e Studentaccio* (Milan, 2013).

Together with Susan Stewart, he translated two books of poetry written by Milo De Angelis, published as a single volume under the title *Theme of Farewell and After-Poems* (Chicago, 2013), which was nominated for a National Award in 2014 by the American Literary Translators Association. In 2020, he translated Anne Carson's *Economy of the Unlost* into Italian. He is a managing editor of *Italian Poetry Review*.

Marcello Ciccuto is Professor of Italian Literature at the University of Pisa. He has been a Visiting Professor at the Universities of Toronto, Baltimore, Fordham, Paris VIII, Berlin, and Barcelona. He is a former Fellow of the Harvard University–Villa I Tatti (1988–9) and the president of the Società Dantesca Italiana in Florence. He has focused much of his research on the relationship between literature and the arts and has published essays on Dante, Petrarch, Boccaccio, humanism, and the Renaissance, and nineteenth- and twentieth-century literature. His critical monographs include *L'immagine del testo. Episodi di cultura figurativa nella letteratura italiana* (Rome, 1990); *Figure di Petrarca: Giotto, Simone Martini, Franco bolognese* (Naples, 1991); *Icone della parola. Immagine e scrittura nella letteratura delle origini* (Modena, 1995); *I segni incrociati. Letteratura italiana del'900 e arte figurativa* (2 vols., Lucca, 1998 and 2002); *Figure d'artista. La nascita delle immagini alle origini della letteratura* (Florence, 2002). He has published several editions of medieval and early Renaissance texts, ranging from Marco Polo's *Milione* to Poggio Bracciolini's *Facetiae*.

Grace Delmolino is Assistant Professor of Italian at the University of California Davis. She holds a PhD from Columbia University in Italian and Comparative Literature and Society. She is associate editor of *Digital Dante* (http://digitaldante.columbia.edu) as well as a former Graduate Fellow at Columbia's Institute for Research on Women, Gender, and Sexuality. Her research deals with Boccaccio, Dante, canon law, gender, and the history of consent. Her first book examines the influence of Gratian's *Decretum* on Boccaccio's *Decameron*, with particular attention to discourses of consent, obligation, and debt.

Maria Pia Ellero is Associate Professor at the University of Basilicata, Department of Humanities, where she teaches Italian Literature. She received her PhD in Italian Literature from the University of Pisa and pursued her post-doctoral training at the Scuola Normale Superiore and at the National Institute for Renaissance Studies, in Florence. She has held teaching positions in several Italian universities. Her research focuses on two main fields: the theory and history of rhetoric (in particular in Renaissance and twentieth-century tradition), and the interplay of classical philosophy and literature in medieval and Renaissance Italy. In this field of studies, she has published a monograph on Giordano Bruno and edited his *Spaccio de la bestia trionfante*, for Les Belles Lettres and Classici UTET, as well as essays on Tommaso Campanella, Giambattista Gelli, and Alessandro Piccolomini. She is currently working on the dialogue with classical and philosophical sources in Boccaccio's *Decameron* and *Elegia di madonna Fiammetta*. The first results of this research are published in various academic journals, such as *Giornale storico della letteratura italiana*, *MLA*, *Lettere italiane*, and *Strumenti critici*.

Simona Lorenzini graduated from the University of Pisa in 2003 *cum laude* with a thesis in modern Italian literature. She received a PhD in Humanist and Renaissance Civilization from the Istituto Nazionale di Studi sul Rinascimento (Florence, 2008), with a dissertation on the Latin bucolic poetry of Dante, Petrarch, and Boccaccio and its connections with the classical and medieval pastoral tradition. After moving to the USA in 2009, Simona completed her PhD in Italian and Renaissance Studies at Yale University with a dissertation – "Questioning the Utopian Myth in Renaissance Pastoral Drama: From Poliziano to Guarini" – written under the direction of Professor Giuseppe Mazzotta (2016). Simona has published on Boccaccio and medieval literature, on Isabella Andreini and her use of pastoral conventions vis-à-vis Tasso and Guarini, and on contemporary Italian experimental writings. Simona is currently a full-time Lector at Yale University.

David Lummus is an Assistant Professor of Italian at the University of Notre Dame. His research focuses on the literary culture of the Italian fourteenth century. He is the author of *The City of Poetry: Imagining the Civic Role of the Poet in Fourteenth-Century Italy* (Cambridge, 2020) and the editor of *The Decameron Sixth Day in Perspective* (Toronto, 2021). He has also co-edited a book with Martin Eisner titled *A Boccaccian Renaissance: Essays on the Early Modern Impact of Giovanni Boccaccio and His Works* (Notre Dame, 2019).

Simone Marchesi is Associate Professor of French and Italian at Princeton University. His main research interest is the dialogue with classical and late antique texts engaged in by medieval Italian writers, especially Dante, Petrarch, and Boccaccio. He has published two monographs on medieval Italian authors: *Stratigrafie decameroniane* (Olschki, 2004), and *Dante and Augustine: Linguistics, Poetics, Hermeneutics* (University of Toronto Press, 2011). He has also edited and translated into Italian

Robert Hollander's commentary on the *Commedia* (Olschki, 2011), of which he has also curated an edition for Italian high-school audiences (Loescher, 2016). In collaboration with the Italian artist Roberto Abbiati, he has produced the book *A proposito di Dante* (Keller Editore, 2020), comprising a hundred glosses and drawings illustrating as many tercets from the *Commedia*. He has served as vice-president and then president of the American Boccaccio Association and is currently editor in chief of the *Electronic Bulletin of the Dante Society of America* (now *Dante Notes*).

Max Matukhin is a PhD candidate in the Department of Comparative Literature at Princeton University. He received his BA from the University of Cambridge and has been a visiting student at the Scuola Normale Superiore of Pisa and the University of Bologna. His work currently focuses on the phenomenon of false confessions and sermons in Old French, Italian, and Middle English literary texts between 1150 and 1400.

Index Locorum

Index of Names

The Index of Names reflects all personal and place names mentioned in the volume. Italics indicate characters in the *Decameron*. Narrators and main characters in each novella are indexed as "passim" in the essay dedicated to them.

Ingram Content Group UK Ltd.
Milton Keynes UK
UKHW040003270523
422446UK00011B/255/J